MW01055628

SOUTHERN BELLY

Also by John T. Edge

A Gracious Plenty: Recipes and Recollections from the American South
Donuts: An American Passion
Hamburgers & Fries: An American Story
Fried Chicken: An American Story
Apple Pie: An American Story

Southern Belly

The **Ultimate** Food Lover's Companion to the South

John T. Edge

pen & ink illustrations by
Blair Hobbs

Algonquin Books of Chapel Hill 2007

Published by
ALGONQUIN BOOKS OF CHAPEL HILL
Post Office Box 2225
Chapel Hill, North Carolina 27515-2225

a division of
WORKMAN PUBLISHING
225 Varick Street
New York, New York 10014

 Revised and expanded edition,
Algonquin Books of Chapel Hill, June 2007.
Published in different form in hardcover by Hill Street Press in 2000.
Printed in the United States of America.
Published simultaneously in Canada by Thomas Allen & Son Limited.
Pen and ink illustrations by Blair Hobbs.
Design by Anne Richmond Boston.

Library of Congress Cataloging-in-Publication Data

Edge, John T.
Southern belly: the ultimate food lover's companion to the South / by John T. Edge;
pen & ink illustrations by Blair Hobbs.—1st paperback ed.
p. cm.
Originally published: Athens, Ga.: Hill Street Press, 2000.
Includes index.
ISBN-13: 978-1-56512-547-6
1. Cookery, American—Southern style. 2. Restaurants—Southern States—
Guidebooks. I. Title.
TX715.2.S68E3285 2007
641.5'975—dc22 2006032603

10 9 8 7 6 5 4 3 2 1
First Paperback Edition

For my father,
John Thomas Edge Sr.,
who taught me how to use
knife, fork, and pen

TODAY'S
MENU
25¢
25¢
MEAT LOAF-PLATE
MAHSED POTATOES
TURNIP GREENS
CORN BREAD
PINTO BEANS
10¢ • CHILI • 10¢
• HOT DOGS, BURGERS •
• DRINKS •
COKES, PEPSI, TEA
COFFEE, BEER, ETC.

contents

Introduction

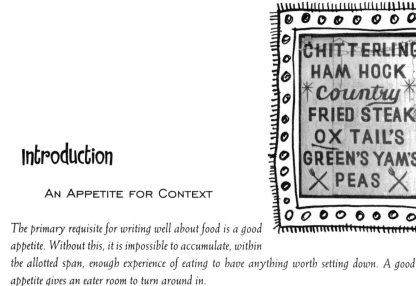

An Appetite for Context

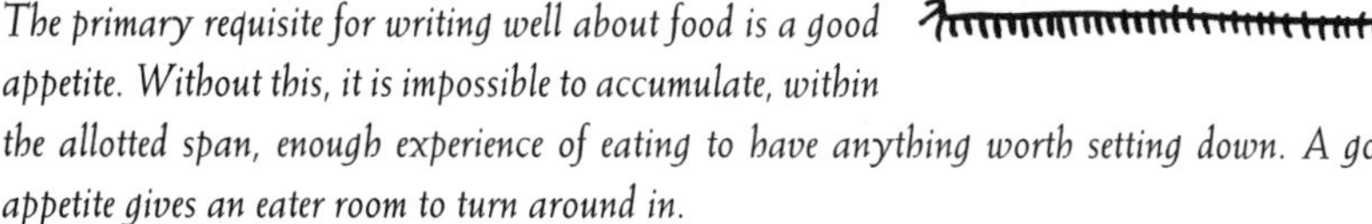

The primary requisite for writing well about food is a good appetite. Without this, it is impossible to accumulate, within the allotted span, enough experience of eating to have anything worth setting down. A good appetite gives an eater room to turn around in.

—*A. J. Liebling*

My appetite is faceted.

I crave honest food: fiddler catfish, rolled in spiced cornmeal and fried in a cast-iron skillet; pimento cheese made with hand-shredded sharp cheddar, chopped pimento peppers, homemade mayonnaise, and precious little else; dusky collard greens swimming in potlikker; whole-hog barbecue, pulled from a hickory-stoked pit, hacked into juicy bits, and doused with a thin sauce of vinegar and pepper; deviled eggs spiked with sweet pickle relish and dusted with paprika; red tomatoes eaten out of hand as their summer-ripe juices trace down my forearm.

What is more, I have an appetite for the lore that defines life in the South. When I sit down at table, I want to commune with cooks past and present. I want to know their life stories. I want to understand their struggles. In other words, I'm as interested in the 1964 fight to integrate Ollie's Barbecue in Birmingham, Alabama, and the life story of Greenville, South Carolina, mayonnaise maven Eugenia Duke, as I am in whether Deacon Burton of Atlanta, Georgia, fried his chicken in lard or shortening.

The third facet is more oblique. In the pages that follow, I seek, for the most part, to showcase restaurants and artisans that matter. Herein you'll visit places where

community is fostered. You will meet people whose time at the stove reinforces the tethers of civic life. Such roles comes with experience and so, by and large, the people you meet and the restaurants you visit will be veterans of the Southern scene. Two decades is the general measure I use for inclusion, but there are, of course, exceptions.

If I did my job well, this book will read like a social history of Southern food. Not a history of the conventional kind mind you, but a mosaic-like portrait of the South as told through its foods, a pastiche of people and places that sates both mind and belly. To my mind, much of what has been written about Southern food is quaint condescension, foisted upon the reading public by interlopers with a taste for good macaroni and cheese but no understanding of the cultural milieu we call the South. I aim to fix that, and point the way to some of the best eats that ever crossed your palate.

In large part, I write of commercial establishments and the people who run them. In an ideal scenario, you would travel the South, stopping off at this farmer's kitchen to sample a wedge of cornbread shot through with crisp pork cracklins, or that fisherman's hut for a stew of oysters and cream gilded with a skein of rich, sweet butter. Yes, Southerners are a hospitable people, but invitations to sup at a stranger's home are few these days, so I have chosen to write of people and places that require no special access or knowledge save a good map. Let me be very clear: I don't rank the restaurants profiled herein, nor do I tell you what hours they are open. In other words, this is not just a guidebook. A guidebook would only tell you where to eat; *Southern Belly* aims to tell you a story and to serve up some great eats alongside.

This is a very subjective work, a proudly personal, admittedly skewed take on life beneath the Mason-Dixon divide. My South includes Alabama, Arkansas, Florida, Georgia, Kentucky, Louisiana, Mississippi, North Carolina, South Carolina, Tennessee, Texas, and Virginia.

In defining what constitutes the South, I ignored matters of Confederate or Union affiliation during the Civil War or mapping based on where kudzu grows, or where soft drinks are known generically as Coke versus pop, looking instead to whether a preponderance of the citizens staked a claim to being Southern. And so, based on recent travels through eastern Texas and northern Florida, I welcome those precincts to the fold. And, once again, the District of Columbia slipped in the back door. Raise a hue and cry if you like, but it's my book. Here's hoping a perusal of these pages makes for good reading—and good eating.

SOUTHERN BELLY

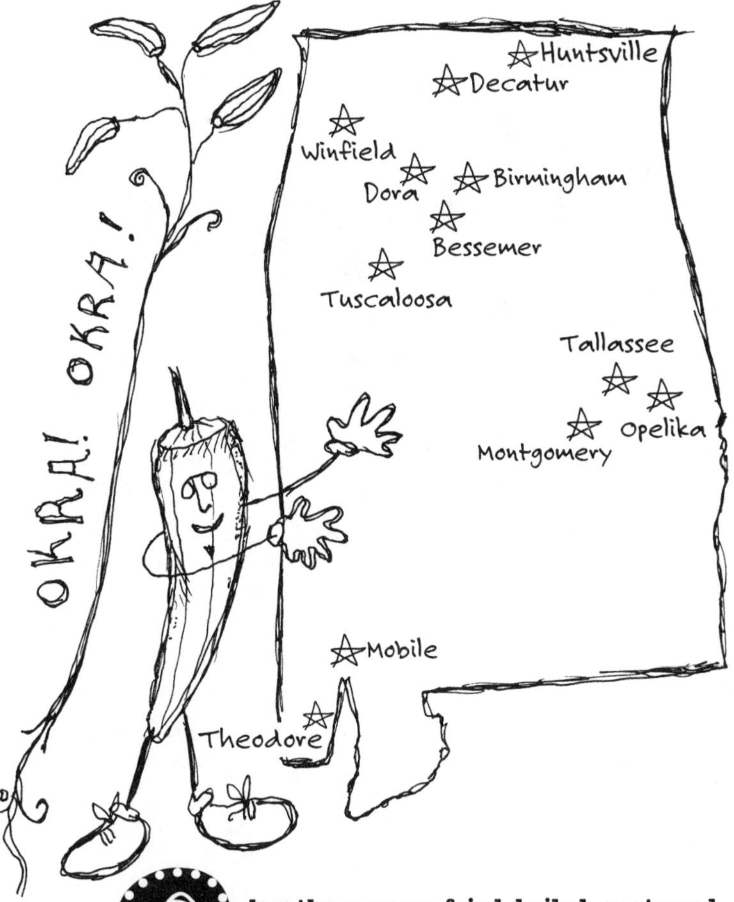

Okra three ways: fried, boiled, or stewed with tomatoes. A casserole of sunny, yellow squash enrobed in a caul of cheese. Red, ripe tomatoes, pearly ears of corn, collard, mustard, and turnip greens sold by the bushel at the Montgomery Curb Market. That's what I like about Alabama. But, Lord, let's not forget oysters from Wintzell's in Mobile or ribs from Tuscaloosa's Dreamland or West Indies salad from Bayley's down in Theodore. Along the way, we meet Eugene Walter, the patron saint of Mobile, and Birmingham's Ollie McClung, who in 1964 fought the Supreme Court to keep his barbecue restaurant segregated.

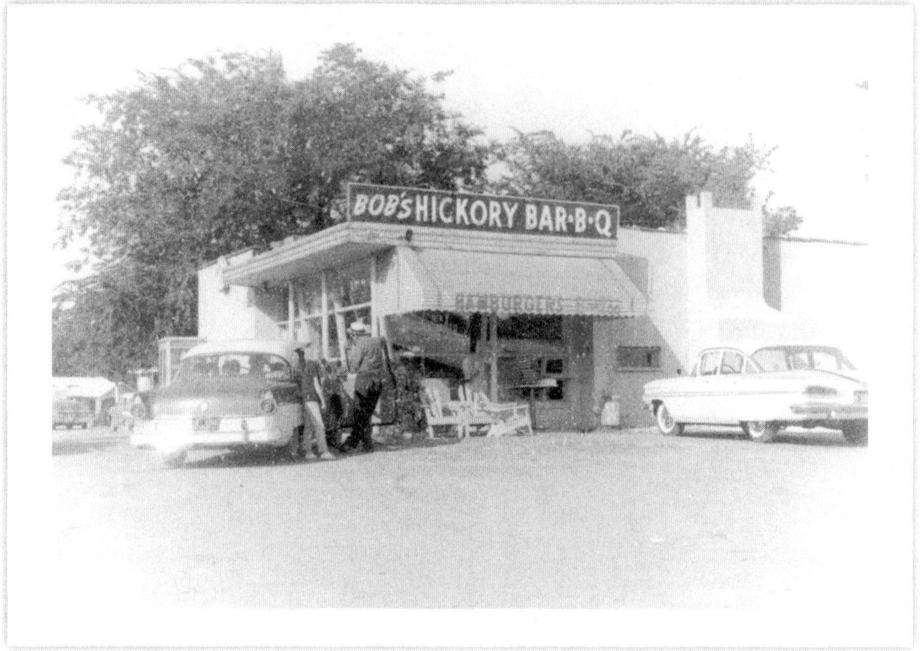

Bob's, the 1950s-era predecessor to Bob Sykes Bar-B-Q of Bessemer.

Bessemer

Bob Sykes Bar-B-Q

In the fall of 1957 Bob Sykes traded in the first new car he had ever bought—a 1954 Ford with low miles and good tires. In exchange, he received a one-year lease on a building in Birmingham's Central Park neighborhood. Sykes named his little drive-in the Ice Spot. "I guess they didn't really need the car," recalls his son, Van, present-day proprietor of the family business. "He and my momma could walk to the place from home."

At first they served burgers and hot dogs, shakes and sodas. But in time, Bob Sykes' yen to serve old-fashioned pit barbecue would displace more mundane fare. "My daddy got to experimenting on the weekends with barbecue," Van tells me. "He wanted to get it right, to serve something he was proud of. He grew up in the little farming community of Cumberland City, Tennessee, near Clarksville, back when they would still hold hog killings on cold winter days, and there was this local black

man that everybody knew by the name of Buck Hampton. Mr. Hampton would travel from farm to farm, building a pit and smoking meat for people. He was kind of a pitmaster for hire. I think my daddy was trying to re-create that taste from his past when he started out. Years later I can remember riding with my daddy back home to look for Mr. Hampton. He was an old silver-haired guy. Daddy told him how he was cooking the meat, what he was doing, and Mr. Hampton told him about a few adjustments he should make."

In the ensuing years Bob and his wife, Maxine Sykes, would move the restaurant from Birmingham to the nearby steel mill town of Bessemer—changing the name to Bob's Hickory Pit and then Bob Sykes Bar-B-Q—eventually growing their business to a fourteen-unit chain and winning a regionwide reputation for tender, smoke-suffused pork shoulder meat and spareribs. In 1963 Dot Brown joined the crew and her recipes for coleslaw, potato salad, beans, and peerless, meringue-crowned lemon pie are still in use today. "She was like a second momma to me," says Van.

Today Bob Sykes Bar-B-Q is set in a vaguely 1970s-era building with a towering fun house sign out front and an open pit just inside the front door. That's just the way Van wants it: "My mother's determination and business sense built this location back in 1977. And I've tried to change it as little as possible. My nephew, Jason Jewell, is working with me now. We still start the fire at 3:30 in the morning, salt down the meat, and smoke it over green hickory wood for eight to ten hours. My pitman, Alonzo Scott, has been with us since 1978. He knows how to build a fire right. He knows that on a cold, misty, overcast day, the fire's going to burn slower, and so he has to prop open the back door of the restaurant to get enough air moving around. My woodman has been bringing me my green hickory since 1995. By now he knows better than to slip some oak in on me. He knows what I want. That's not the kind of knowledge that can be duplicated. That's what barbecue is all about."

1724 NINTH AVENUE / 205-426-1400

BRIGHT STAR

When Bright Star founder Tom Bonduris arrived in Alabama from his native Greece, Bessemer was a boomtown, a steel-making center to rival Pittsburgh. "My great-uncle was not the only Greek to arrive in the early 1900s," co-owner Jimmy Koikos tells me. "Back then, there were Greek immigrants opening all kinds of cafés. Bessemer was a place with a future, a place full of hope, and they called their restaurants names like the Gold Star and the Bright Star."

During the early years, the Bright Star was a simple café with a horseshoe-shaped bar and a few tables scattered about. But as Bessemer prospered, so did the Bright Star. By 1915 an elegant oil mural was hanging in the dining room, rendered by an itinerant painter who was more than willing to trade brushstrokes for beefsteaks. Under the leadership of Bill Koikos, the café was transformed into a grand dining hall. The elder Koikos—born in Telata, Greece, in 1894—moved to Bessemer in 1920 and began working at the Bright Star the day after his arrival. He remained at the restaurant for the next sixty-eight years, until his death in 1988.

Today his sons Jimmy and Nick are in charge, and though the logos are wearing off the monogrammed china, the restaurant still exudes a timeless, if not fussy, beauty. Dark wood panels the walls and heavy linen naps the tables; red leather booths beneath and brass chandeliers glinting above.

The food is Greek to the core: tenderloin of beef marinated in oregano, lemon juice, olive oil, and garlic; broiled chicken livers in the same bright sauce; a salad made of mesclun topped with a tangle of anchovies and a fat slab of feta. Sure, there's catfish on the menu, and they even offer a chicken breast that purports to be Southern fried, though I've never seen a soul order it, especially when presented with a menu chock-full of Greek treasures.

Does that mean that the Bright Star isn't Southern? Hardly. Consider first the family's longevity in the Bessemer community—nearly a century of feeding the sons and daughters of Alabama. And if that doesn't do it for you, take the time to talk with Jimmy about the days when Bear Bryant was the head football coach at the University of Alabama and Shug Jordan was the man at rival Auburn University. For those who weren't able to get a ticket to the game, a table at the Bright Star was the next best thing. Waitresses wore the jersey of their chosen team; the hostess wore a referee's stripes. And Alabama and Auburn fought it out on the floor of the Bright Star over plates of red snapper in brown butter; broiled shrimp in lemon sauce; and

fat, well-marbled porterhouse steaks. It was just like being at the game—only the food was far better.

304 Nineteenth Street / 205-426-1861

Birmingham

Niki's West

Like many of the Birmingham area's storied restaurants—including the Bright Star in Bessemer—Niki's is Greek-owned. "Your hosts, Pete C. Hontzas and Teddy Hontzas," proclaim the place mats that paper the scarred wooden tables. But for the most part, this cafeteria is a study in ethnic assimilation. The favored beverage is sweet tea, rather than retsina; and breadbaskets are filled with popovers instead of pita.

There's a slight nautical theme to this old warhorse of a cafeteria, what with the stuffed marlins and swordfish that arc across the fieldstone walls. Mackerel almondine and deep-fried snapper throats often show up as specials, and the restaurant's logo is a silhouette of a lone fisherman pulling a seine net up out of the sea. Appearances, however, can be deceiving. Thanks to its location—across the street from the Jefferson County Truck Growers' Association terminal—vegetables are the kitchen's true forté.

On my most recent summertime visit the steam table boasted a good three dozen vegetables, including three kinds of okra: whole pods blanched in a bath of boiling water; thick slices, battered and fried to a crusty, dark brown; and ropy fingers, luxuriating in a tomato sauce. What's more, there were vats of buttery creamed corn, fat, pillowy butter beans, earthy black-eyed peas, and bright, squeaky cabbage. One bite of the saccharine-sweet stewed tomatoes is all that it takes to remind me that, botanically, those bright red orbs are indeed fruits.

233 Finley Avenue / 205-252-5751

Barbecue and the Bar

The Civil Rights Act of 1964 was a watershed in the black struggle for equality. It stipulated that any business engaged in interstate commerce could not discriminate on the basis of race. If a Georgia hotel hosted guests from South Carolina, then it was subject to the law. If an Alabama restaurant bought its produce from Mississippi, it, too, was subject to the law.

In protest, many Southern restaurants closed. Others turned private, closing their doors to all but members. Known to some as "key clubs," these private restaurants continued to cater to an exclusively white clientele. Others still dug in their heels and fought for the right to bar blacks as a matter of choice.

Soon after the act was passed, the McClungs, father and son proprietors of Ollie's Barbecue in Birmingham, filed suit in federal court seeking to enjoin the Justice Department from enforcing the public accommodations clause of the new law. At the time, service for black patrons was limited to take-out orders, and the elder McClung claimed that if he served blacks in the dining room, he would lose his white customers.

Early on, a three-judge federal panel ruled in the McClungs' favor, but Supreme Court Justice Hugo Black—an Alabama boy himself—stayed that ruling and the case was soon heard by the full court. The question addressed by the Supreme Court was this: does the U.S. Constitution give Congress the authority to force a privately owned restaurant to cease discriminating on the basis of race?

On Monday, December 14, 1964, the Supreme Court handed down its ruling in support of the Justice Department. By that Thursday, the *Birmingham News* was reporting that blacks had been served at the restaurant. The McClungs accepted the decision in the following statement released to the press: "As law-abiding Americans we feel we must bow to the edict of the Supreme Court. We are deeply concerned that so many of our nation's leaders have accepted the edict which gives the federal government control over the life and behavior of every American. This could well prove to be the most important and disastrous decision handed down by this court. We plan no further legal action, but shall continue to pray that somehow the freedom of all our citizens will one day be restored."

The elder McClung has since passed away, but until September of 2001 his son continued to run the family business from a new outpost in the Birmingham suburb of Hoover. During a recent conversation he reflected on his family's role in the landmark case. "It was about race and then again it wasn't," he tells me. "On the surface it was about who had access to public accommodations and who didn't. On a deeper level it was about whether the federal government could intrude upon the day-to-day operations of small businesses. That was the camel's nose under the tent. Today we have to deal with the Americans with Disabilities Act, and our bathroom is twice as big as it should be. Before '64, if somebody in Washington had told folks down here to do something like that, they would have been run out of town on a rail. Before '64, if I had been conscience-stricken enough to serve blacks in my restaurant, I would have. I wasn't, mind you."

Milo's Sweet Tea

Sure, they stock bottles and cans of sweet tea in the cooler of most every Southern convenience store. If you like tinny-tasting brews spiked with aspartame and artificial lemon flavoring, then go ahead, knock yourself out. As for me, I'll brew my own, or scour the grocery store refrigerator cases for a pint of Milo's brand sweet tea.

Milo Carlton opened his first burger stand in 1946, on Birmingham's Northside. Milo's primary business was hamburgers, thin disks of meat, swabbed with a deep brown slurry that reminds you of both A-1 sauce and the peculiar barbecue sauce that local Greek-owned diners ladle on hot dogs hereabouts. French fries sprinkled with an orange-hued seasoning salt and iced tea stoked with a cane field of sugar formed the core of the menu. During the late 1970s, his little burger stand was so popular that Milo began leaving the closed sign up all day long, secure that he would get all the business he could handle from the regulars who knew to come rap on the window.

Over the course of the past fifty-plus years, Milo's has become a localized chain of more than a dozen locations. Though I have long been a fan of their tea, I did not come to know of its wider availability until very recently when I spied a plastic, orange juice–style pint back behind the counter at Mike's hot dog stand in

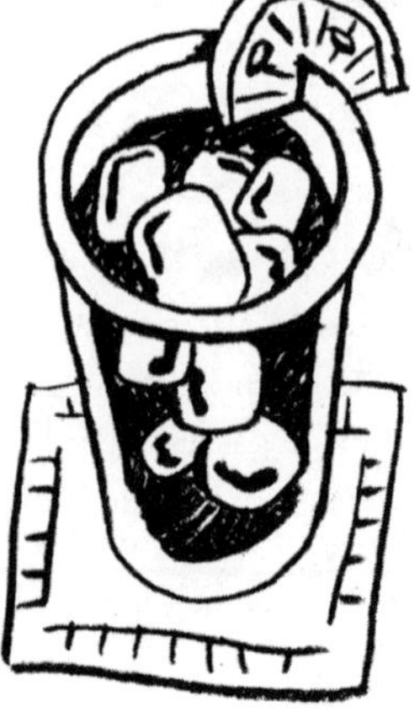

Homewood. It turns out that in 1989 Milo's began packaging its sweet tea in gallon jugs and selling them in local grocery stores. In 1997 they added pint servings and began selling those in local restaurants.

Milo's now brews tens of thousands of gallons of tea each week, and demand is spiraling ever upward. The tea is viscous stuff, deep amber in color, and as sweet as a clump of church lady's divinity. Truth be told, it may be too sweet for you, dear reader, but I can't think of a better belly wash to follow a vinegar-drenched barbecue sandwich or an onion-capped chili dog.

MILO'S SWEET TEA IS AVAILABLE AT WESTERN SUPERMARKETS AND OTHER OUTLETS IN BIRMINGHAM AND ENVIRONS.

Decatur

Big Bob Gibson's Bar-B-Que

Don McLemore, proprietor and grandson of founder Big Bob himself, is a student of barbecue, an aficionado of sauce styles and wood types who collects bottled sauces like some men collect stamps or coins. He makes it a point to stop at every barbecue joint he passes on the roadway. "I'll eat a little bite as I go," he tells me, seated in the cavernous dining room of his family's ranch-style restaurant. "I might stop at four or five places in a day when we're traveling. For me, it's like research. It's good for my business, good for my barbecue."

Over the years, inspired by his travels, Don has introduced a few new twists on the old smoked meat theme, items like barbecue salads and barbecue stuffed baked potatoes. But his real accomplishment has not been so much innovation, as the cultivation of an experienced team of cooks. "Jerry Knighten is still in charge of the pits," Don tells me. "He started working for my grandfather as a dishwasher back in 1945. I think he was sixteen at the time. You won't find anybody better at it." One taste of Big Bob's tender pork shoulder meat, and you'll say a silent prayer for his continued good health.

Big Bob's old place, soon after they installed that famous neon pig with the dancing feet.

But Mr. Knighten isn't the only long-serving employee here. Mattie Johnson is moving a bit more slowly these days, but she still clocks in every morning at 4:00 A.M., just as she has done since she began working for Big Bob back in 1948. Mrs. Johnson makes the pies that make Big Bob Gibson's famous. Not long ago this spry septuagenarian underwent surgery for a rotator cuff injury, sustained no doubt while rolling out crust number 229,337, or something such as that. Chocolate, lemon, or coconut—take your pick. As for me, I dote on the coconut, with its jiggling core of creamy custard and bone-white border of flaky crust.

I'm also a fan of their white sauce, a mayonnaisey concoction, thinned with vinegar and shot through with black pepper. It has the consistency of the runoff that seeps from a mound of coleslaw. I love the stuff, slathered on barbecue chicken, poured on top of French fries; hell, it's a good salad dressing. Rarely found outside of northern Alabama, the sauce is a Big Bob original. But, unlike much of what makes this barbecue joint so great, no one remembers the story behind the sauce. "I'm just about positive it started here, but I can't tell you when we first made it, or who first made it," says Don. "I know it was after 1925 when my grandfather opened up. But even my mother can't remember when it was."

1715 Sixth Avenue SE / 256-350-6969

Dora

Leo and Susie's Green Top Café

Like many of the working-class folk of north-central Alabama, Leo Headrick spent much of his adult life toiling in the local coal mines that fed the iron furnaces of Birmingham, first in the Maylene mine over in Shelby County and later in the Maxine mine in Walker County. When he retired in 1973 with his pension, his wife, Susie, hoped he'd take it easy for a change. "He came home one day and said he was going to buy the Green Top, and I said to him I was against it right off," Susie told me. "Of course, that was a long time back. Now I like to tell people that he made two good decisions in life: marrying me and buying the Green Top."

At the time the Headrick family took over operations in 1973, the Green Top had already been open for more than twenty years, earning a reputation as the destination of choice for fine smoked pork and icy cold beer. "It used to be that this was one of the last places to stop off and get a drink before you hit the Mississippi line," recalls present-day manager Richard Headrick. "When my father took over, well, he was a real promoter, so he started pulling more folks in with all his shenanigans." Richard's mother, Susie, remembers that Leo "liked to get tipsy and sing for anybody who would listen. His favorite song was 'I'm Gonna Be a Wheel Someday,' by Fats Domino." I ask her if he played guitar, too, and a man at a nearby table shouts up at me, "Hell no, son; he couldn't play a guitar, but I saw him play a broom every once in a while."

Ever since Leo passed away back in 1996, regulars say that the Green Top has become a little less raucous, though it retains the feel of a 1950s-era roadhouse. Situated at the crest of a hill, the cinder-block building claims two trucker strip joints as neighbors: the Sugar Shack and the Boobie Trap. George Jones and Tammy Wynette are in heavy rotation on the jukebox. And a long bar still stands at the center of the government-green dining room, where more often than not, you'll find a local boy with a snootful, elbows propped on the counter, scarfing down an oversized barbecue sandwich.

Like his father before him, Richard is a pitmaster of the old school, who cooks pork shoulders fourteen to sixteen hours over hickory wood, and then hacks the meat into little crusty chunks before piling it on a bun and ladling on a catsupy red sauce with a pepper kick. Hand-cut French fries, sweetish coleslaw, and a longneck Budweiser complete the feast. Ask nicely, and Richard might even rustle up a plastic cup and pour you a beer for the road.

7530 HIGHWAY 78 / 205-648-9838

Huntsville

WATERCRESS CAPITAL OF THE WORLD

We Southerners dote on greens. Collard, kale, beet, mustard, turnip, rape, poke, dock, and lamb's quarters are just a few of our favorites. And while most any Southerner worth his salt pork can talk intelligently of collard or turnip greens, watercress—with its peppery bite—is, for many, a cipher among Southern crucifers.

But there are provinces of the South where it was once known well. Drive east from Huntsville on Ryland Pike toward the burg of Gurley. Along Hurricane Creek, within sight of Mary's Barbecue, you'll find a patch or three of watercress. The green is not that hard to spy, if you take the time to look, for it flourishes in lowlands and on creek banks hereabouts.

Not too long ago watercress bogs were easier to spot. During the first half of the twentieth century, Huntsville was the epicenter of American watercress cultivation. The local limestone springs were part of the draw for the Dennis Watercress Company, which at the height of its production, hand-harvested and shipped more

than 2 billion bunches of cress to wholesale and retail customers including Brennan's in New Orleans and the White House in Washington, D.C.

Today, little evidence of that heyday remains. Few Southerners still cook with watercress. Sure, it's often cited as one of the pureed greens in the original oysters Rockefeller from Antoine's in New Orleans. And you see watercress and cream cheese sandwiches at a few tea rooms. But the case of Antoine's is peculiar. And as for those tea rooms, they are usually fey affairs, dolled-up imitations in the English tradition. No, when watercress was favored by Southerners it was likely to play a part in a salad of killed greens.

Some people might call the dish wilted salad. I prefer the more countrified appellation, killed salad, because it more accurately represents the preparation technique: toss various fresh lettuces and greens in a bowl, adding a bit of chopped white onion, maybe some green onion, too. Fry a couple strips of bacon until crisp. Crumble the bacon over the lettuce. Add a bit of vinegar to the hot fat remaining in the skillet. Stir, adding a dash of sugar and pepper. Pour the hot liquid over the salad until, well, it's pretty much dead. And then garnish with slices of boiled egg.

Mobile

Eugene Walter Gastronomic Gadabout

If the title "patron saint of Mobile" does not exist, then I would make a strong argument that one be established and posthumously bestowed upon Eugene Walter. A native of the Azalea City, he worked as a novelist, poet, essayist, artist, lyricist, actor, designer, translator, humorist, botanist, epicurean, philosopher, and imp. He published numerous chapbooks of poetry, acclaimed collections of short stories, prize-winning novels, and treatises on culinary history that will stand the test of time. Though the term is often overused, Walter was a true Renaissance man. His work in the broad field of

“In Rome I live as I lived in Mobile. On my terrace garden I have five kinds of mint, five kinds of onions and chives, as well as four-o'clocks and sweet olive.”

culinary letters was intelligent and playful, worthy of comparison to the best of M. F. K. Fisher.

In the 1953 novel *The Untidy Pilgrim,* Walter introduced the world to a delightfully skewed vision of his native city. "Down in Mobile they're all crazy, because the Gulf Coast is the kingdom of monkeys, the land of clowns, ghosts and musicians, and Mobile is sweet lunacy's county seat," he wrote. Throughout his life Walter espoused the virtues of good food and drink. Of Mobile natives he observed, "It's a toss-up whether they rank the pleasures of the table or the pleasures of the bed first, but it's a concrete certainty that talk follows close after."

While in Rome, Italy, Walter ate and drank with a group of friends that included Federico Fellini. He worked as a translator on several Fellini films and wrote the lyrics for the song "What Is Youth?" in Franco Zefferelli's film of *Romeo and Juliet.* And yet, no matter where he might be, the love of Southern food and frolic remained at the core of his being. "In Rome I live as I lived in Mobile," he wrote. "On my terrace garden I have five kinds of mint, five kinds of onions and chives, as well as four-o'clocks and sweet olive. I take a nap after the midday meal; there is always time for gossip and for writing letters."

Walter's dedication to the Southern culinary arts brought him back home in 1969 to write *American Cooking: Southern Style,* the best of the Time-Life Foods of the World series. In succeeding years, he wrote about the foods of the South for numerous publications, including *Harper's Bazaar* and *Gourmet.* In his later years he wrote an overlooked jewel, *Hints and Pinches: A Concise Compendium of Herbs and Aromatics with Illustrative Recipes and Asides on Relishes, Chutneys, and Other Such Concerns.* Illustrated with Walter's fanciful pen-and-ink drawings, the book is a fun house encyclopedia of the culinary arts. One of his color-saturated drawings from that period is on display at Rousso's Restaurant, a seafood warehouse in downtown Mobile. It depicts a regal lady attired in a purple and gold striped skirt, her hand resting on an oversized fork as if it were a scepter. The caption reads: "The Devil's dear Grandmother pondering what menu to serve when she invites Pat Robertson, Jerry Falwell and Jesse Helms to dine in Hell with Hitler and Mussolini."

Eugene Walter was interred at Mobile's historic Church Street Graveyard on April 2, 1998, after a spirited wake. He was seventy-six years old. A line from one of his Monkey poems might serve well as a panegyric:

We've eaten all the ripened heart of life
And made a luscious pickle of the rind.

Indeed he did. Indeed he did.

Morrison's Cafeteria

Cafeterias were all the rage in New York and Chicago when Mobilians G. C. Outlaw and J. A. Morrison opened the first Morrison's in the fall of 1920 at St. Emanuel and Conti Streets. It wasn't the first cafeteria to open in the South—Britling's in Birmingham purportedly enjoyed that distinction—but it was the first such establishment to introduce a decidedly Southern wrinkle, waiters. Outlaw and Morrison couldn't imagine asking one of their lady customers to select her own fried chicken and mashed potatoes, stewed tomatoes and butter beans from a steam table and then haul the tray back to her seat. It just wasn't proper. Instead, they stationed white-coated waiters at the end of the serving line who, for a small tip, toted trays to the tables.

Morrison's was an immediate hit. By 1921 a second location opened in Mobile and a third in Pensacola, Florida. Others quickly followed. At the height of Morrison's success, the chain claimed more than 150 locations scattered throughout the Southland. Alas, Morrison's is no more, the victim of an aging customer base and a changing Southern palate. The death knell sounded back in the spring of 1998, when the company announced it was selling out to a relative upstart, Baton Rouge, Louisiana–based rival, Piccadilly.

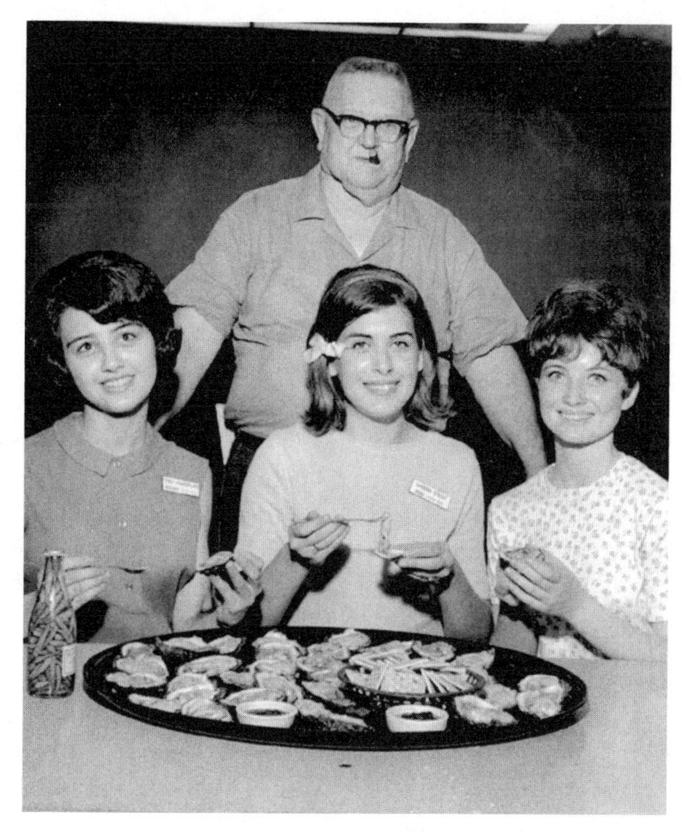

Home of beauty queens and sourpusses alike.

Wintzell's Oyster House

A relic of the days when oysters were trencherman's fare, consumed by the dozen while leaning against an oak bar, Wintzell's is—in the best sense of the word—a rude place. Though founder Oliver Wintzell, his gray hair always trimmed to a buzz, a fat cigar protruding from his pugnacious face, passed away in 1980, his irascible spirit still presides here.

Hand-lettered placards tacked to every conceivable surface announce old man Wintzell's many philosophies. "If you are in a hurry, we will mail your lunch," reads one. "Diplomacy: The art of saying, 'Nice Doggie' until you can find a rock," reads another. Somewhere among the tens of thousands is the very first one Wintzell ever

hung on the wall, not long after he opened in 1938. It reads: "A man can sometimes get a pearl out of an oyster, but it takes a pretty girl to get a diamond out of a crab." By the 1970s Wintzell's witticisms were taking on a more political tone, and soon he was running for local and state office on the oyster ticket. "I will be prepared at all times to shoot from the lip and be quick on the drawl," he promised in a thirteen-point platform released during a campaign for county sheriff.

All wordplay aside, make no mistake about it, Wintzell was serious about oysters. In the restaurant's heyday, he owned his own oyster beds at nearby Portersville Bay and employed several oystermen whose sole job it was to harvest the mollusks for sale in the restaurant. Even the placards owe their origin to Wintzell's devotion to oysters. "Well, customers used to ask me a lot of questions," he explained to a newspaperman some years back. "It was hard to answer them and get the oysters opened, so I started the signs to get across some of the information they wanted. Now they keep so busy reading, they don't ask questions."

Soon after Wintzell's death, the restaurant went into a decline, changing hands a couple of times and then closing for a while. Long-term employees like master oyster shucker Willie Brown, a veteran of more than thirty years behind the bar, were furloughed.

In 1996 Wintzell's reopened after a gentle refurbishment that preserved the patina of old. Soon after, Willie Brown returned to shuck. More recently, Wintzell's has opened lesser branch locations. Locals grumble, but the gumbo is still dark and murky and good. And the West Indies salad—a marinated seafood concoction considered to be a Mobile original—still tastes of sweet white onion and sweeter white crab.

605 DAUPHIN STREET / 251-432-4605

Montgomery

Georgia Gilmore
Girth, Grit, and Sass

A hero at the stove.

On a weeklong ramble about Montgomery, I came upon a historical marker like none other I had seen before. Located just south of the capitol on Dericot Street, in a working-class neighborhood of tidy brick and frame bungalows, it stands in honor of one of the unsung heroines of the Civil Rights Movement, one of those people Martin Luther King Jr. called a "member of the ground crew." It reads:

Georgia Gilmore
February 5, 1920–March 3, 1990

Georgia Gilmore, cited as a "solid, energetic boycott participant and supporter," lived in this house during the days of the Montgomery Bus Boycott. Once arrested on a bus, Gilmore was ardent in her efforts to raise funds for the Movement and organized the "Club From Nowhere" whose members baked pies and cakes for sale to both black and white customers. Opening her home to all, she tirelessly cooked meals for participants including such leaders as Dr. Martin Luther King Jr. and Dr. Ralph David Abernathy. Her culinary skills contributed to the cause of justice as she actively worked to encourage civil rights for the remainder of her life.

"Her culinary skills contributed to the cause of justice as she actively worked to encourage civil rights for the remainder of her life."

As I discovered during conversations with Georgia Gilmore's family, friends, and colleagues, though the erection of the marker was an admirable gesture, it was a meager assessment of her life's work.

Georgia Gilmore was more than just a "solid, energetic boycott participant and supporter." As remembered by almost everyone, she was a mountain of a woman, nearly 250 pounds of girth, grit, and sass. "She was a lady of great physical stature," recalled Reverend Thomas E. Jordan, pastor of Lilly Baptist Church. "She didn't take

any junk from anybody. It didn't matter who you were. Even the white police officers let her be. She wasn't a mean person, but like it was with many black people, there was this perception that she might be dangerous. The word was, 'Don't mess with Georgia Gilmore, she might cut you.' But Lord, that woman could cook. I loved to sit down at her table for some good greasing."

Chris' Hot Dogs

Talk to natives of Memphis, and it seems as though every third person has a good Elvis story. The King ate jelly donuts here, bought his bananas and peanut butter there. That sort of thing. Around these parts the local music hero is Hank Williams, and the stories are just as good.

At Chris', a derelict downtown institution founded by Greek immigrant Chris Katechis in 1917, they say that ole Hank would drop by late in the evening, his band mates in tow, the whole crew drunk as coots and craving chili dogs. Sometimes Hank just sat at the counter and scribbled song lyrics. Other times he and his compatriots tore up the place. And many a former counterman claims that he threw Hank out on his ear.

These days Chris' isn't much to look at, just a narrow storefront divided into a rabbit warren of rooms, some of which sport improbable porthole-like showcases filled with ceramic clowns playing the accordion, others, fancy deviled egg plates.

On the day I visit, a couple of Alabama highway patrolmen are the sole customers. I plop onto one of the dozen chrome and vinyl stools in the front room, and soon I'm munching a weenie topped with a few strands of kraut, a smear of mustard, and a thin skein of chili sauce. It's not bad really, but only a local, weaned on Chris' dogs, would claim to love it. On my way out the door, I spy another little showcase by the front window. The contents on display—a plastic model weenie and bun, a vintage china bowl emblazoned with Chris' logo, and a retired box grater, presumably used for onions—make for a curious still life.

138 Dexter Avenue / 334-265-6850

MARTIN'S

Exhibit A, for those who would argue that integration failed completely, is this old-line Montgomery restaurant, once the favorite of race-baiting politico George Wallace and legions of avowed segregationists. Now it's home to an integrated noonday crowd who come to munch down on country fried steak blanketed in a thick, scratch gravy; fat pole beans; and crisp corn muffins.

The façade, a faux Colonial storefront in the Country Club Centre strip mall, is a couple of notches above the norm for a meat 'n' three restaurant, but there's nothing fancy about Martin's, which has been in business since 1949. Glass-topped tables, bentwood chairs, gum ball machines by the door: it's a country café come to town. The menu, sheathed in plastic, is covered with ads for local businesses, one of which promises, "Mickey Griffin is to real estate as Martin's is to fried chicken." And the fried chicken is indeed good: fat white breasts in a crisp mantle of crust; tender dark-meat drumsticks, savory and just a tad spicy.

Over the course of lunch I fall into conversation with a thirty-something-year-old man at the next table. We talk of barbecue and football before getting around to more serious matters. "Didn't this restaurant used to be whites only a few years back?" I ask, lobbing the question like a softball.

Rather than being taken aback, he replies readily, thoughtfully. "I've been eating here for a good while," he says. "Of course, I never tried to eat here when blacks weren't allowed. Now you didn't ask this but I'm going to tell you anyway. You see those two black waitresses? Well, that's a new thing, real new. There were always black women in the kitchen, but it's only been since around 1996 or 1997 that they let black women start waiting tables. They started out real gradual, letting them do waitressy things, moving them up slowly. Nowadays, no one pays much attention to it. Well, I guess I still do. I'm black; I notice things like that. When you're black, you develop an ability to notice things like that, same as a dog in the wild develops teeth to protect itself."

1796 CARTER HILL ROAD / 334-265-1767

Montgomery Curb Market

Established in 1927 by the local Jaycees in cooperation with the Auburn University Agricultural Extension Service, this is a democratic institution of the highest order, owned and operated as a farmers' cooperative since opening day. Though there was a time when you could find dressed fryers and live lambs for sale, today fruits and vegetables reign.

The scene is a vignette from yesteryear. Bare lightbulbs dangle above, casting harsh shadows over early morning shoppers wending their way through the old tin-roofed open-air building. The floor is poured concrete. The ceiling insulation is held in place by a net of chicken wire. And the smell of black dirt—that fecund soil so favored by farmers—perfumes the air.

I wander down one aisle and then another, past the stall where Sherell Smitherman sells cheese biscuits and fried pies, past Morris Taylor's display of double-yolk eggs. I stop and admire Jim Causey's peach pound cakes and jelly rolls, and dawdle for a while at Vivian Tatum's booth, the one with the burned wood sign that proclaims it to be Pea Heaven. I talk for a while with Donna Mims and beg a taste of one of the delicate local figs she's selling for just a couple dollars a basket.

It's late summer when I visit, and there are tubs of shelled butter beans, wood slat baskets of prickly okra, cardboard flats of red, ripe tomatoes, and Chilton County peaches. Golden lobes streaked with crimson, sweet and ridiculously juicy, those peaches are the true bounty of the dog days. But let us not neglect the watermelons, specifically those black and green striped beauties known as rattlesnake melons, one of which is split open along its belly with a couple of forks poked into the red meat, just daring me not to take a taste. Without a moment's hesitation, I sink a fork in, pull out a big meaty chunk, and spit out a few seeds. Soon I'm hefting a fat round one into the trunk of my car, bound for home, trying to remember where I put that big ole washtub.

1004 Madison Avenue / 334-263-6445

Opelika

Chuck's Bar-B-Que

Just off the main drag in Opelika, salvation and sin coexist in a cinder-block building. Sin is served up in the guise of succulently smoked barbecue pork, napped with a mustardy sauce, and served alongside thick, meaty Brunswick stew. For the best this pit has to offer, order a plate, "chipped on the block," with stew and slaw. Though the barbecue is good—sinfully good—it is the sacred, not the profane, that makes this place special.

In the South evangelical Christianity is rarely subtle. Bible thumping and pulpit pounding are the norm. And yet there is something to be said for proprietor Chuck Ferrell's sneaky attempt at securing his fellow man's salvation.

As I walk to the rear of the restaurant with an empty plate and a full stomach, I notice alongside the trash can a stack of bright blue pamphlets that proclaim: "Something Better than Barbecue." I open the tract.

"If you will take a few minutes to read this testimony, you will see how my family and I discovered that there is something better than barbecue or any amount of money or anything else this world has to offer, You cannot buy it, and you cannot earn it. It is a gift for every born again believer in Jesus Christ."

Need I even tell you? They're closed on Sundays.

905 Short Avenue / 334-749-4043

Tallassee

Hotel Talisi

There was a time not too long past when any Southern town of even minor note could claim a hotel of grandeur, a place where birthdays were celebrated, balls given, honored guests housed. Sadly, most of the old dowagers have been converted into office buildings or, worse yet, torn down to make way for one more parking lot. Not so for the redbrick Hotel Talisi, open since 1928. Under the stewardship of

current owners Bob Brown and Roger Gaithier, the hotel has been transformed into a peculiar place to stay—and eat.

The lobby is a riot of color and whimsy: concrete statuary, papier-mâché angels, and airbrushed wedding portraits fight for the eye's attention, so much so that you almost miss the lovely old antique secretaries and sideboards that line the walls. Upstairs, velour-covered armchairs rest on Persian rugs. Harlot-red, plush carpeting stretches on, yard after yard after yard. Crystal chandeliers hang in the formal dining room. There's a shaggy little faux Lhasa apso dog with synthetic fur on the side table by the front desk. The overall effect is one of overwrought, faded beauty that verges upon vamp.

Things take a decided turn toward normal in the informal dining room, where weekday buffet lunches are held. On the day I visit, the steam table is chock-full of Southern casserole cookery: Halloween-orange sweet potato casserole dotted with puffy mini-marshmallows, creamy broccoli casserole studded with ham, vats of crowder peas and green beans, and a barnyard of fried chicken. I miss two of the restaurant's specialties: a turnip green casserole larded with cheese and horseradish, and a squash casserole made with ranch dressing. Yeasty cloverleaf rolls, little tubs of tomato conserve, and vinegary cucumbers round out the feast.

On my way out, I stop to talk with Bob. "You've got to come back on a Sunday," he tells me. "My sister plays melody on the piano and accompanies herself on the organ. Plus that's when we serve that famous squash casserole. We do it the old-fashioned way; we don't use any of that Campbell's soup mix in it, just ranch dressing."

14 Sistrunk Street / 334-283-2769

Theodore

Bayley's

Bill Bayley was a big man. Big size. Big ideas. Said he was the inventor of West Indies salad, a layered assemblage of onions and crabmeat, cooled in an ice-water bath, beloved by coastal folk. Said he was the first man to batter and fry crab claws, too. During Bayley's lifetime, few people took issue with his claims to fame. I'm not inclined to argue, either, for if you go looking for good eats near the Alabama shore, you will find yourself on his trail.

Before he became a restaurateur, Bayley worked first as a steward, later as a chef for a shipping company. In 1947, along with his wife, Ethyl, he opened a restaurant south of Mobile on what is now Dauphin Island Parkway. They started out small. He worked the kitchen; she worked the front. But talent bears fruit. What began as a one-room grocery was soon a grand dining hall.

Bayley was Falstaffian, a cigar-chomping man of great appetites. He was a showman who, in a bid to lure families with children, rented projectors from the local library and showed Westerns and cartoon shorts. At his core, however, he was a cook, expert at frying chicken and all manner of fish.

Family and friends tell a number of stories about how he came to assemble West Indies salad, his trademark dish. Bayley often told reporters that he dreamed it up when he bought a tow sack of lobsters, while sailing the West Indies. But his son, Bill Jr., opts for a more direct, less romantic explanation. "He loved cucumbers and onions in vinegar and oil and he always put ice water in it," Bill Jr. told a newspaper reporter. "I guess that's how he came up with it."

Fried crab claws came later, say the early 1960s. After years of busting open crabs, pulling the sweet meat from the shell and claws for West Indies salads, the elder Bayley devised a better way to crack a claw. The result was a drumstick-shaped edible, with a thin crab pincer (the handle) at one end and a fat ball of crab (the treat) at the other. Rolled in meal or cracker crumbs and fried, the meaty end of the drumstick proved the ideal appetizer, especially when dipped in a lemony cocktail sauce.

Bill Bayley died a while back. In succeeding years, fried crab claws, like West Indies salad, have spread far and wide. But south of Mobile, at what locals still call Bayley's Corner, it's possible to taste these dishes—along with stuffed shrimp and crab omelets and homemade onion rings—in situ, in what was once a catering kitchen for the elder Bayley's restaurant and is now a porcelain block–bedecked roadhouse, under the direction of his son.

10805 Dauphin Island Parkway / 251-973-1572

See Bill Bayley's coveted **West Indies Salad** recipe on page 30.

Tuscaloosa

Dreamland

They moved John Bishop's throne inside after he passed away back in 1997 at the age of seventy-six. Put it right in the middle of the place, hard by the entrance to the bathrooms. For years, maybe even as far back as 1958 when Dreamland opened, the oversized redwood chair sat out back underneath the carport near the pit, and it was there that Big Daddy, as he was called, received guests. With a Sherlock Holmes–style pipe protruding from his lips, and a Dreamland gimme-cap perched atop his bald head, he presided over a barbecue empire, selling ribs, white bread, chips, and drinks. Nothing more.

These days, his daughter, Jeannette, is in charge, and the Dreamland empire is expanding rapidly with locations throughout Alabama and beyond. Word has it that at these branches, you can get fries and slaw to go with that slab of ribs, but here, in deference to Big Daddy, you need not peruse a menu to make your decision. The only decisions to ponder are: How many bones do you want? Barbecue or regular chips? Beer or Pepsi?

From the street Dreamland looks like a country juke joint, nestled in the midst of a neighborhood of asbestos-shingled homes and swaybacked trailers. A soot-covered chimney rises from the back corner of the building. Through the trees you can spy the towering Taco Bell sign out on the highway. Inside there are just four booths, eight tables, and a good dozen or so stools at the counter. Did I mention that it's dark inside? Very dark. So much so that you might deem Dreamland the perfect spot for an afternoon assignation or, better yet, a date with a couple of racks of ribs.

On my most recent visit, it's lunchtime and the place is at full tilt. Every table is full, so I snag a seat at the bar. I order a rib sandwich, and the counterman gives me one of those *Does this silly white boy know that a rib sandwich is just three ribs on loaf bread?* looks, thinks better of it, and goes off to fetch my order.

By this time my eyes have adjusted to the light, and I turn to take in my surroundings. License plates and beer posters, knickknacks and gewgaws blanket the low ceiling. Fraternity boy doggerel is scrawled on the walls. Behind the register, a bumper sticker proclaims, "And on the eighth day, well, you know . . . Dreamland."

But what really catches my eye and gets me to thinking is that while this is a black-owned, black-run business, the clientele—at least on this spring day—is exclusively white. Now that could be interpreted in any number of ways. You could chalk it up to what my friend Lolis Elie, author of *Smokestack Lightning,* calls the "natural rhythm school of Southern cooking," an allowance on the part of whites that blacks have an innate ability to cook, same as they can sing and dance and play basketball. Or you could conclude that, at least at Dreamland, integration is a fait accompli, that the Southern palate now knows no color. I'm still thinking when my ribs arrive. Crusty on the outside, tender on the inside, swaddled in a piquant sauce tasting of vinegar and tomato and maybe a hint of curry, they're a Southern sacrament. I swab at a puddle of sauce with a slice of white bread and say my thanks.

5535 Fifteenth Avenue East / 205-758-8135

Now that's a smokestack.

Archibald's Bar B Que

Many informed eaters believe that Dreamland has gone 'round the bend. Gone Hollywood. Gone, quite frankly, to hell. I think they're wrong. Sure, what began as a joint has morphed into a chain. But that sauce—even the grocery store version—remains among my favorites. And it's still a pleasure to gnaw a bone in that low-ceilinged room.

All that said, if you pine for an experience that recalls what Dreamland *may* have been like before the crowds descended and the Bishops took their show on the road, detour west a few miles to Archibald's, where you're likely to find Paulette Washington, daughter of founder George Archibald, hacking ribs and slicing shoulders, serving sandwiches of charred pig parts to those who are lucky enough to claim one of the five stools that face her hickory-stoked pit. In business since 1962, Archibald's is a smoke shack archetype, the sort of place that haunts every chowhound's dreams. And it's waiting, just down the road.

1211 Martin Luther King Jr. Boulevard / Northport / 205-345-6861

Waysider

I fell in love with the Waysider soon after I reached for a pat of butter to slather on one of those thin tiles of coarse cornbread they serve hereabouts. Miracle of miracles, it was just that: a pat of butter, a lemony yellow square of salted, churned cream, sandwiched between a white cardboard base and a thin slip of wax paper. These days most restaurants stock little plastic tubs of margarine emblazoned with names that read like false promises: Country Crock, Farm Churn, and I Can't Believe It's Not Butter. But not the Waysider, a Tuscaloosa institution since 1951.

It was a good start to a great first meal at the Waysider. Soon after sampling that butter-drenched cornbread, a waitress appeared with my order: salmon croquettes, fried squash, and field peas with snaps. All good, all served with a smile. I polished off my plate and dove into a bowl of meringue-crowned banana pudding, having decided early in the meal that I would take advantage of the dietary loophole printed right there on the menu for all to see: "You may substitute dessert for one of the three vegetables that come with every lunch."

But it was not until recently that I had the opportunity to sample my first Waysider breakfast. Approaching the red and white shingled house, I could smell the frying ham at twenty paces. By the time I was on the front porch, I swear I could already taste the buttermilk biscuits. Owner Linda Smalley led me to one of the fifteen-odd tables scattered about the dining room, and I strapped on the feedbag. I ate pluperfect buttermilk biscuits dunked in redeye gravy, those same biscuits crumbled in brown gravy, a good rasher of streak-o-lean, a couple of eggs scrambled soft, a few slices of red-ripe homegrown tomato, and an ocean of salty, firm grits. I didn't learn until it was too late that if you ask nicely, the cooks will whip up a batch of elephant-shaped pancakes—no doubt a nod to the University of Alabama mascot. The toddler two tables over looked happy with his, dissecting the great animal's trunk with a fork and smearing pats of butter over all.

1512 Greensboro Avenue / 205-345-8239

Marie Rudisill

You may have known Marie Rudisill as the Fruitcake Lady from the *Tonight Show*. She first appeared onstage with Jay Leno in December of 2000, teaching Mel Gibson to cook. Marie, who had just written a book, *Fruitcake: Memories of Truman Capote and Sook,* was sassy. She was bawdy. She did and said things that only a nonagenarian can get away with. In 2001 she returned to Burbank to stuff a turkey with Hugh Grant. While the cameras rolled, she cupped Grant's rear and, judging its curvature, called it—if my memory serves—"a nice little biscuit."

In 2002 the native of Monroeville, Alabama, began serving as the show's advice columnist. In a recurring segment, "Ask the Fruitcake Lady," Marie—dressed in a severe black suit, her gray hair pinned in a bun, her talon-like fingernails lacquered red—addressed matters of fidelity, grooming, and bathroom etiquette. She was combative. She did not suffer fools. She used decidedly unladylike words like "pecker" and "lazy son-of-a-bitch."

Her performance was camp. But her outré Southern pedigree came honestly. Marie was the sister of Truman Capote's late mother, Lillie Mae Faulk Persons Capote, who committed suicide in 1954. Capote called Marie "Aunt Tiny." She helped raise him. And like her nephew, who was a Johnny Carson–era *Tonight Show* favorite, she employed cathode rays to her advantage. But, as was the case with Capote, Marie will not be remembered by the demimonde for the flame and spittle and slur captured in television appearances. Nor will she be remembered for the fruitcake book.

Marie Rudisill will be remembered as the author of a slim 1989 volume, *Sook's Cookbook: Memories and Traditional Recipes from the Deep South.* Using plantation daybooks from the early 1800s as her primary sources, weaving in character studies of friends

and neighbors and relatives from Monroeville, she wrote one of the best cookbooks to hit Southern shelves. It's a portrait of place. It's a portrait of people. It's full of recipes for green olive jambalaya and watermelon-rind preserves and poinsettia cake. And, sadly, it's now out of print.

I love that book, but my recollections of Marie are more personal. After I helped with a book-deal negotiation, Marie phoned. She was, at the time, eighty-nine. And she was effusive in her thanks. "I'll do anything for you," Marie said, her tone raspy, her timbre bright. After a three-beat pause, she added, "Except sex." A hail of cackles followed. And soon after, a dial tone.

Winfield

Car Lot Bar-B-Que

Tacked to the back wall of this unlikely restaurant is a framed newspaper ad from the 1976 grand opening of Roger Guin's Oldsmobile dealership. Ask Roger about those days and he'll tell you he made a good run of it, sold more than a few cars, treated his customers with respect, paid his people fairly. But somewhere along the way, the car industry changed: "I got out when the getting was good."

But he couldn't stay away for long. Back in the mid-1990s he opened a little used-car lot. "I wasn't aiming to get rich," he'll tell you. "I just wanted to keep my hand in the business." Late-model pickups, four-door sedans with low miles and good tires, and, every once in a while, a souped-up Camaro or Firebird: he sold what the folks of western Alabama told him they wanted. Business was steady. Not great, mind you, just steady.

And then one day back in 1998 Roger had a flash of inspiration. What did politicians do when they wanted to draw a crowd? Why, they'd hold a barbecue. Throw up a tent, smoke some meat, stir up a kettle of sauce, and soon the world would beat a path to your door. In short order, Roger built himself a pit, right in the side of the car showroom.

Best place in the South
to get a Chevy and a sandwich.

Despite an early sales spike, the car-buying public never came calling. Today, though he still sells a vehicle every once in a while—recent offerings include a cherry Ford F150 pickup, a Chevy Blazer with monster truck tires, and a Pontiac Bonneville with a new pearly white paint job—the old showroom has given way to a dining room where locals feast on pulled pork that spent fifteen-plus hours cooking over hardwood coals. Last time I went through town, I fantasized about stopping off at Roger's place to do a little business—figured I'd trade my old junker for a lifetime supply of his barbecue sandwiches.

235 Bankhead Highway / 205-487-2281

West Indies Salad

an homage to Bayley's

Serves 4 to 6

Some restaurants guard their trademark recipes. Not Bayley's, down near the shore, where West Indies salad was born. Bill Bayley appeared on the local morning shows, telling everyone how to do it. He gave the recipe away to charity cookbook publishers, too. Soon it was popping up everywhere, from the Sahara in Montgomery to Wintzell's, just down the road in Mobile. Many ditched the ice water step, thinking that would dilute the brackish whang of the crab. Yep, that's where they probably went wrong.

1 medium onion, finely chopped
1 pound fresh claw crabmeat, picked through for shells and cartilage
½ cup vegetable oil
¼ cup apple cider vinegar
½ cup ice water
Salt and freshly ground black pepper

Spread half the onion over the bottom of a large bowl. Cover with separated crab lumps and then remaining onion. Season with salt and pepper. Add the oil and vinegar. Strain the ice water through a sieve to remove the ice cubes; add the well-chilled water to the salad. Cover and refrigerate to marinate for at least 2 and up to 12 hours. Toss lightly and taste and adjust for seasoning with salt and pepper before serving.

Arkansas

Pies, pies, my goodness the pies. Coconut cream, chocolate meringue, pineapple cream, egg custard, lemon, pecan, chess, and apple. Arkansans are a pie-mad people. They also dote on stone-ground grits from the War Eagle Mill, battered deep-fried pickles from the town of Atkins, and sloppy barbecue sandwiches slathered with sauce from old man Shadden over in Marvell. Speaking of barbecue, make sure you pay homage to Lawrence Craig of De Valls Bluff, a veteran riverboat cook who took to the pits more than fifty years ago. His story is one for the ages.

Pie in the sky

Atkins

Stalking the Fried Dill Pickle

Southerners have had a long love affair with all things fried. We eat fried chicken by the tub, savor fried oysters drenched in hot sauce, munch fried okra like popcorn, and still relish a mess of fried chitlins now and again. But dill pickles? Fried? Despite the empirical truth of their vinegary and greasy goodness, there are some things that give even a Southerner reason to pause.

And so it was when I first encountered fried dill pickles. I paused—long enough to ask three questions: Why would anyone do such a thing to a perfectly good pickle? Who was the first brave soul to drop a mess of pickles in hot oil? And, when did this great event first take place? Simple enough questions—or so I thought.

Two restaurants claim to have been the originators of this gastronomic oddity. According to the owners of the Hollywood Café in Robinsonville, Mississippi, fried dill pickles made their debut in 1969 when a desperate cook, confronted by a dining room full of patrons, a vat of bubbling oil, and a scarcity of catfish, reached for an industrial-sized jar of dill pickle chips. The story goes that he rolled them in the batter intended for the catfish, served them to a crowd of incredulous but famished diners, and then sat back to savor the praise.

It's a good story, parroted by many. But, according to Bob Austin of Atkins, Arkansas, "It's a damn lie." Bob claims to have invented the fried dill pickle in 1960 while operating the Duchess Drive In, directly across the street from the pickle plant in Atkins. "I had an inspiration one day and just started working on the batter," he says. "Staring out the window at that pickle plant all day, your mind gets to wandering. So I sliced some pickles and fixed up a batter. My batter beats all. And I'm not telling anybody what's in it. I'll sell it to the right person, but nobody's getting it for free. The rest, they're all imposters. Nobody has been able to duplicate it since."

A few years back the Duchess closed. Bob retired. These days, those "original" pickles are available only during Picklefest, Atkins' annual spring celebration, when the local VFW hall sets up a booth and sells them on the street. "Yep, they're the only ones that I let use my recipe," says Bob. "That's your one chance if you want to try the real thing."

Benton

Ed and Kay's

Arkansas is a pie lover's paradise, a land where soft, white mounds of meringue soar heavenward from pie shells ringed with oh-so-flaky crusts, where tart lemon custards jiggle luxuriantly with just the slightest prod from a fork.

Profiles of the best, including Mary's Family Pie Shop, follow. But there's no doubt in my mind that, when it comes to meringue, there's no pie house in the state that piles it higher than Ed and Kay's, operated by Kay Diemar in this little plank-sided rectangle of a building since 1982.

Plate lunches and dinners are tasty: the stewed cabbage is chock-full-o-pork, the chicken is pan-fried to order, and the soupy squash and cornbread dressing is laced with a good measure of fragrant sage. The Parker House rolls are yeasty and light. They even serve deviled eggs come summertime.

But seated at one of the Naugahyde booths with a laminated place mat advertising the Razorback Car Wash and Quick Lube laid out before you, the pies are what command your attention. There they are, over on the back wall, displayed in a retrofitted, three-shelf, brass greenhouse with a mirrored backing: pineapple cream, coconut cream, chocolate cream, egg custard, lemon, pecan, and apple.

Dead center is the winner, baker Nita Nash's pride and joy, known around these parts as a PCP or pineapple, coconut, and pecan pie, crowned by a bell-shaped bouffant of meringue that must rise a full foot and a half. The filling is a creamy wonder, the meringue an architectural tribute to the excesses of the baker's art, done Arkansas style.

15228 Interstate 30 (Sevier Street Exit) / 501-315-3663

De Valls Bluff

Lawrence Craig
He Chose Cooking

Lawrence Craig was a national treasure, a gentleman of the old school who started slow smoking barbecue in the early 1940s when he was a cook on the snag and dredge boats that plied the Mississippi River, keeping the channels clear for navigation.

I first met him in 1997 in our nation's capital. He was there at the invitation of the Smithsonian Institution, to cook barbecue on the Mall, to let the nation know how they did it back in his hometown of De Valls Bluff, Arkansas.

As much as I liked his food, his life story was what really interested me. We sat and talked for hours beneath the boughs of a stately oak. I can still see his face beaming with pride at what the years had wrought.

> "We kept chickens up on the roof of the boat and when it was time to eat one, well somebody had to kill it and dress it, and I'd cook it up."

"Folks always talk about how black folks are good cooks. There's a reason for that. Back when I was growing up there were two kinds of jobs black folks could get without being challenged by white folks: cooking and heavy lifting.

"For instance, back before I started cooking, I worked for the U.S. Corps of Engineers on the Mississippi River . . . Now when I first started out, coal and wood fueled the boat. And it was a black man's job to do the heavy, dirty work of feeding the fire. But when they started using oil, when all you had to do was turn a knob, well, they got a white man to sit down and turn that knob, and that became a white man's job.

"So I chose cooking. I figured that no one else wanted to stay in that hot kitchen all day. I figured I had the green light. My mother had been a cook in white folks' homes and gotten along just fine. So

I chose cooking. Back then that was acceptable. Folks thought black folks could cook—same as they thought black folks could sing and dance, that we had rhythm and could play musical instruments . . .

"When I was working on the dredge boat, we kept chickens up on the roof of the boat and when it was time to eat one, well somebody had to kill it and dress it, and I'd cook it up. We butchered our own cows and pigs, too. When we were on the boat, we cooked 'em on the oil burning stove.

> "We did all right. More than fifty years it's been open now, serving white folks and black folks the same barbecue. I'm right proud of that."

"During the off-season, when I was back home in De Valls Bluff, I started doing a little bit of barbecuing. We'd dig a pit in the ground and lay an old bedspring across it, fill the pit with coals, slap the meat on the springs and lay a piece of tin across the top to conserve heat and concentrate the smoke. You had to stay by the fire all night and all day . . . When the buses would come rolling into town, we'd meet 'em at the door and sell sandwiches to everybody.

"By 1947 my brother Lesley and I opened our own barbecue place right down the road . . . We did all right. More than fifty years it's been open now, serving white folks and black folks the same barbecue. I'm right proud of that."

Craig's Barbecue

While we were together in Washington, I pledged to visit Mr. Craig often. I imagined monthly visits. But time was not on our side. When I did manage to make the trek, we sat in his front yard, talking and laughing, reminiscing about our time on the Mall. Lunchtime came and went and I grew hungry, my stomach rumbling in protest. In time I bid Mr. Craig good-bye, and made my way three doors down to his café, a tidy concrete rectangle with a separate pit house out back. Inside, it looked just as I imagined it would: paneled walls, a few tables scattered about, a bathroom reachable only through the kitchen.

Mr. Craig assured me that the current operators still use his recipes for slaw and sauce, and the pork hams are still slow smoked on the pit he built long ago. I was anxious to taste that sauce of his again. I remembered how he told me they made it: vinegar, mustard, catsup, a lot of black pepper, and a healthy slug of what Mr. Craig

called "the meat drippings"—in essence the grease that dripped from the hams while they cooked. And I wanted some of that apple, green pepper, and cabbage slaw piled on my sandwich.

In a short time a waitress came barreling out of the kitchen, my sandwich in her grasp. I took a bite. Perfection. The meat was tender, suffused with smoke, and napped with that fiery sauce I remembered; the slaw snapped with crispness. I said a silent prayer of thanks that Mr. Craig chose cooking.

HIGHWAY 70 WEST / 870-998-2616

MARY'S FAMILY PIE SHOP

Mary Thomas gilding the lilies.

A trip to Craig's Barbecue is not complete unless you step across the street to Mary Thomas' Family Pie Shop, a squat masonry rectangle set directly across the street in the backyard of a ranch-style home. Since the early 1980s, Mary Thomas has been baking pies in what was once a bicycle repair shop, winning praise throughout the South for her coconut, lemon, sweet potato, pecan, and egg custard pies. The only sign posted is a jerky "Pie Shop" spray-painted on the front of the building.

Late in 1999 Mary Thomas told me that she was hanging up her apron. "I'm tired," she said. "I'm thinking somebody will take over this place. But I'm not counting on it." Her flirt with retirement served as proof of the fragile condition of Southern cookery. But hope springs eternal. As of this printing she's still open, still baking what many believe to be the best pies in the South. "I'll be here as long as I can," she told me. "I was sick for a year or so, but with the help of the good Lord, I'll be here a long, long time."

HIGHWAY 70 WEST / 870-998-2279

Fayetteville

Herman's Rib House

Herman's is a wreck, a woebegone white plaster and brick Tudor relic set in the midst of a gravel parking lot, hard by a four-lane highway. The windows are patched with duct tape and the red-shingled roof looks suspect. There's not even a sign out front, just "Herman's" painted on the south wall in a faded, florid script. Arrive at an off hour and you'll swear the place is condemned, closed by a building inspector looking out for the best interests of the good citizens of Fayetteville.

But step past the unruly privet hedge that guards the entranceway, let the screen door slap behind you, and soon you're transported into another world, where cordovan-colored wood paneling glows with an inner warmth, and red wines are poured with a heavy, sure hand. Founded in 1964 by Herman Tuck, this restaurant, like Lusco's over in Greenwood, Mississippi, belongs to that rarefied coterie of Southern establishments where the tawdriness of the surrounding area and the ramshackle exterior of the building itself serve as insulation against time's steady progression.

Seated in a captain's chair at one of the stolid wood tables, a red and white checked tablecloth spread out before me, the modern world seems far away. Up front Nick Wright, the owner, is working the flattop griddle where house-cut T-bones and tenderloins sizzle away. Shelby Rogers trundles back and forth across the dark dining room, taking complimentary baskets of saltines and salsa to newcomers. White men and women, plump and prosperous looking, smoke and drink and laugh with what can only be described as a joy bordering upon abandon.

I order a ten-ounce fillet, rare, with hash browns, salad, and Texas toast, and turn to watch Bruce pull my fillet from the little roll-top cooler and scoop a handful of cubed potatoes onto the griddle alongside. Steam blossoms high in the air above the splatter of grease from the steak, and I sip from my wineglass and say a prayer that the bright promise of progress never darkens Herman's doorway.

2901 College Avenue / 479-442-9671

Helena

King Biscuit Time

King Biscuit Time, first broadcast on Helena's KFFA radio in 1941, at a time when few, if any, black voices could be heard on the radio, made bluesman Sonny Boy Williamson one of the first black media stars of the modern South. The fifteen-minute broadcast, sponsored by the Interstate Grocer Company, distributor of King Biscuit Flour, was an instant hit with the denizens of the Delta. Despite the fact that the station's signal could not be heard much farther than seventy-five miles away, Williamson's fame skyrocketed.

What's more, sales of King Biscuit Flour soared. By 1943 Interstate was selling bags of Sonny Boy Corn Meal, emblazoned with a caricature of Williamson sitting on a gunnysack of meal, a harmonica in his hand. In time the show took on a life of its own, in the same way that the Martha White Self-Rising Flour jingle, recorded by bluegrass pioneers Lester Flatt and Earl Scruggs, came to be an audience favorite, even among those Southerners born and raised on biscuits made with White Lily flour.

The meal that launched a bluesman's career.

Though Sonny Boy has passed on, Sonny "Sunshine" Payne continues to air the program at 12:15 each weekday afternoon, opening each show since 1965 with a hearty, "Pass the biscuits 'cause it's *King Biscuit Time* on KFFA radio!"

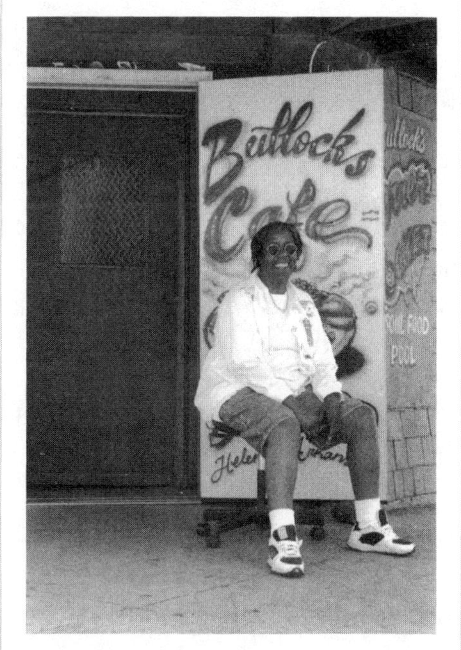

A bright beacon on a blighted street.

Bullock's Café

Helena was once a rowdy river port where roustabouts prowled the docks by day, and bluesman worked the jukes by night. These days, like many Mississippi Delta towns, it's a good bit quieter. Indeed, it's downright desolate.

Don't tell that to Cora Bullock, who runs a café down on Missouri Street. "Child, we run out of food most days," she told me. "Ever since I started cooking down here back in 1986—same year my baby child was born—folks been wolfing this stuff down."

The front room of the café is decorated with beer posters, and a pool table takes up a good bit of the floor space. Christmas lights blink no matter the season. Seated at one of the three creaky bar stools—when the sun goes down, Bullock's is transformed into a juke—you can catch a glimpse of Cora in the back room, her sweet face framed by a pair of glasses, hunkered down over a battered old electric stove, sweat beading on her brow. Talk to her, she's got a story to tell.

Cora admits the neighborhood is in a bit of a decline—"Coke Lies, Crack Kills" warns the poster by the bar—but she's doing just fine, thank you. "If I wasn't cooking,

I just don't know what I would do," she says. "I started out cooking when I was nine, cooking for my family. It was either cook or chop cotton, and I'd rather cook any day. Now I just cook out of my head. I go to the store every day and see what looks good."

One taste and you'll be glad she took to cooking. On the day you visit, you're likely to be handed a scrap sheet of paper, maybe an old manila envelope, on which she has scrawled that day's menu. Dense meatloaf in a sweetish tomato gravy, chicken wings or turkey necks swimming in broth, pigs' tails, pigs' feet, good old fried chicken, mashed potatoes thick with milk and larded with butter, fat butter beans bursting at the seams: she serves it all and seasons each dish assertively, almost violently, with salt and peppers both black and red.

On your way out the door, pick up one of the airbrushed aprons Cora sells. The one I bought features a kaleidoscopic still life of a plate lunch in repose.

201 Missouri Street / 870-338-1183

Pasquale's Tamales

Used to be when you walked in the front door of Pasquale's, the first thing you noticed, mounted on a far wall, was a sepia-toned photo in a severe Victorian frame. "That's my daddy," Pasquale's proprietor, Joe St. Columbia, would say, gesturing to the little boy flanked by the Victorian-garbed man and woman. "He used to tell me that his daddy—my grandfather—came over to America in 1892 from Cephalu, Sicily, and this is as far as his money took him."

Helena was good to the St. Columbias. As the town grew, the family prospered. Joe's father ran a taxi service and a grocery business, selling meat and meal to the sharecroppers who tended the cotton fields. When Mexican laborers began making their way up from Texas to work the cotton harvests in the early teens, they traded with the St. Columbias. After all, strangers in a strange land have to stick together. In turn, the St. Columbias learned how to make tamales, the food that has sustained the family ever since.

"Back during the depression my father was approached by a young black couple—Maggie and Eugene Brown—who wanted to open up a little café," recalled Joe, who's inclined toward chef's whites and sporting a floppy red and green hat. "Tamales

were starting to catch on all around the Delta. So my daddy said, 'Okay, we'll open as long as you make 'em like I tell you to.' Well, it took off from there. That was over on Elm Street when the Browns ran it. Called it Elm Street Tamales. Today, we're still using the same recipe. Tamales are the Delta in a nutshell, an Italian man's recipe, learned from Mexicans, perfected by African Americans."

Though Joe has since closed the restaurant, his family still peddles tamales from a fleet of trucks that work the roadways of Arkansas. And the tamales that Pasquale's turns out are just as good: bundles of cornmeal, piquant spices, and ground beef, wrapped in corn shucks and steamed to perfection. Joe may have retired, but don't think for a moment that he has quit cooking. "In the spring we'll make spaghetti with fennel," he says. "And in the fall I'll make Italian sausage with the seeds."

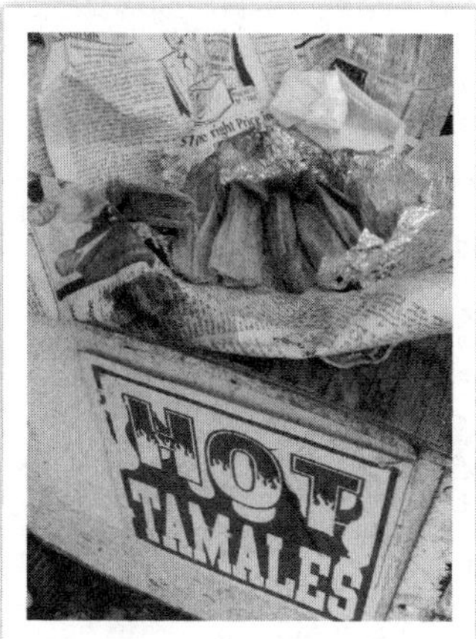

On-the-run eats, served from carts throughout the region.

877-572-0500

Hot Springs

McClard's

Hot Springs is a rough-and-tumble old resort town, a onetime haunt of the gamblers and gangsters who came to soak in the waters and bet on the ponies. During Prohibition, Al Capone was a regular visitor, as was his archenemy Bugs Moran.

J. D. McClard, patriarch of the McClard family barbecue dynasty, remembers those days well. "Alvin Karpis—he was Public Enemy Number One for a good while—used to love our barbecue goat," he recalls. "I was just a young boy then, and I'd deliver an order to his room. He'd open the door and you could see girls running all around with next to nothing on. Ol' Alvin would give me a fifty-cent tip, and I'd be on my way. Boy, I would've voted for him for governor!"

The goat and gangsters are now gone, but little else has changed at this 1928 vintage shrine to smoked meat and small-town charm. They still cook barbecue the old fashioned way. Take a peek out back, behind the whitewashed stucco dining room, and you'll

McClard's Sauce

McClard's barbecue sauce is among the best in the land, a heady concoction of tomato puree, vinegar, red and black peppers, onions, sugar, and Lord knows what else. It's a world-class sauce, a worthy complement to smoked beef or pork. And, as luck would have it, the ruddy stuff comes complete with a great story.

"My parents had a little tourist court out on the highway, nine little cabins set around a restaurant," J. D. McClard tells me. "Well, this fellow stayed with us a month or so, and when it came time to leave, he couldn't come up with the ten dollars he owed us. He told my parents he'd give them his barbecue sauce recipe instead, said it was 'the world's greatest barbecue sauce.' That was back during the Depression, and they figured they didn't have much of a chance of getting any money out of him, so they said okay. Turns out, he was an honest man. The tourist court's been gone, but that's the same sauce we use today. Ain't nothing better. We keep the recipe downtown in a safe deposit box, locked away, safe and sound."

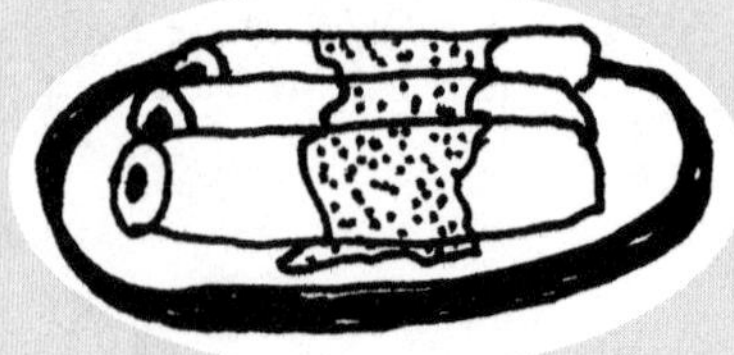

spy the pits: two pagoda-shaped, double-decker monstrosities, loaded down with pork hams on top, sirloin butts on bottom. "That way, the juices from the pork baste the beef," confides J. D. And, no matter the time of day, there always seems to be an ancient, primer-splotched pickup pulling into the parking lot, its bed sagging with a couple of cords of green hickory wood.

Inside, the dining room is simplicity incarnate: twelve red swivel stools facing a low counter, eighteen booths spread out across a gleaming black and white tile floor, and white walls covered with pictures of famous folks and politicos. In the background, you can hear the throaty hiss of deep fryers at work.

Order a spread, one of the restaurant's signature dishes, and you'll get a meal of gargantuan proportions: a clunky oval platter covered with corn chips topped with two house-made tamales strewn with barbecue beef and chili beans, spritzed with barbecue sauce, and showered with shredded cheese and chopped onion. It's a nap-inducing, texturally complex, train wreck of a meal, one of the most glorious dishes in Dixie. But don't stop there. The ribs will bring tears to your eyes, and the chopped pork is a smoky revelation. The fries are hand-cut, greaseless, golden brown, and damn near perfect. Forgo the catsup, and ask for a monkey bowl full of McClard's justly famous barbecue sauce for dipping.

505 Albert Pike Road / 501-624-9586

Little Rock

Sims' Bar-B-Que

Morning, noon, and night, there's a plume of smoke spiraling from the chimney of this brown brick bunker, home to Sims' Barbecue since 1947. Inside, a jukebox over in the corner is playing lazy R&B. Budweiser posters celebrating the "Great Kings of Africa" plaster the walls. Slices of sweet potato pie and luminescent red velvet cake sit by the cash register.

Step to the counter and order a rib sandwich, and you'll get a good half-dozen bones piled willy-nilly atop a couple of slices of white bread, the whole affair drenched in a torrent of dirty-yellow sauce with a vinegary nose and an apple cider–sweet base. Though this sauce style is more common to central South Carolina and pockets of eastern Alabama, it's been swabbed on Sims' meats since day one, says Vinita Settlers, whose mother and father, Estella and George Sims, first began cooking whole hogs over hand-dug earthen pits back in 1937.

"They were living out in the Hardscrabble Community on the southwestern edge of Little Rock and they got to cooking hogs for the holidays, for Labor Day and the second weekend of June," Ms. Settlers tells me. "Hardscrabble wasn't a very big place, maybe one hundred folks if you count chickens and dogs and everything. Long about ten years later my Uncle Allen Sims started his own business; he moved it to the city."

Today, in addition to the original Thirty-third Street location, Sims' operates two branches in Little Rock. The business was controlled for a brief time by another family, but Allen Sims' great-nephew, Ronnie Settlers, is now at the helm. "Yes, it's a real family business," says Ms. Settlers. "We're right proud of our family. We're especially proud of our barbecue."

716 West Thirty-third Street / 501-372-6868

LINDSEY'S

Founded in 1956 by Church of God in Christ bishop D. L. Lindsey, this Little Rock institution has, in more recent years, taken to cooking its meat on a newfangled, commercially manufactured smoker. Accordingly the ribs and pork shoulder lack the distinctive bite of hickory that makes for a clearly superior smoke shack meal. But all is not lost. The fried peach and apple pies are still heaven sent—flaky envelopes bursting at the seams with sweet fruit.

And though D. L. Lindsey has since passed on, his family continues to operate a business in which a bishop could take pride. A case in point: among the offerings on the menu is a bereavement platter, piled high with ribs, sausage links, pork shoulder, chicken, coleslaw, potato salad, and a loaf of bread—the perfect item for the harried Southerner who has too little time to cook, but cares too much for the family of the bereaved not to appear at their front door soon after he hears of a tragedy, bearing a platter of country cooking on high.

After I polished off my pie, I asked the woman behind the counter whether they sold many of the platters. "Oh yes," she replied. "But we put so much on them that I'm sure we lose money. We try to help out the families in our community in our own way. It's the Christian thing to do."

203 EAST FOURTEENTH STREET / 501-374-5901

Marvell

SHADDEN'S GROCERY

Country stores like Shadden's were once the rule rather than the exception—weary wooden buildings with wide front porches and, inside, shelves stocked with cans of baked beans, tins of tuna, barrels full of pickles and crackers. Pigs' feet and pickled eggs floating in murky jars, that sort of thing.

Shadden's, built in the 1890s, is a relic of that past, a dinosaur limping off alone toward an uncertain fate.

Mr. Shadden usually sits just inside the front door, smoking cigarettes and swapping gossip. "U Kill It, We Grill It," says the sign behind the counter. The shelves are filled with yesterday's stock overruns: butterfly-shaped hair barrettes, cans of

potted meat, and pouches of Days Work chewing tobacco. By the register is a Plexiglas display case piled high with eight-track tapes. "Groovin' with Stan Getz" was hot the last time stock was replenished. The floor, a crazy quilt patchwork of splintered wood and faded yellow linoleum, creaks with each step. And yes, jars of pickled eggs and pigs' feet sit atop the bar, rising and falling like ectoplasm in some sort of low-rent lava lamp.

Barbecue sandwiches are cheap as dirt, hot as hell, and may well be one of the best bargains in the whole of the Southland. Cold beers are yours for the taking; just reach into the rolltop cooler next to the counter.

Moments after you place your order, you'll hear a steady thwack, thwack, thwack coming from the kitchen, and soon your sandwich arrives: irregular chunks of tender, smoky pork—cooked for at least twelve hours, says Shadden—heavy on the outside meat, napped with a fiery red sauce, and crowned with sweet coleslaw, all tucked within a toasted bun.

I ordered a second sandwich for the road, and left pondering whether I should install an eight-track player.

19771 Highway 49, four miles west of Marvell / 870-829-2255

Tontitown Italian Eats

Settlers of Tontitown—many hailing from the Veneto and Marche regions of Italy—came to the hills of Arkansas in roundabout fashion. Recruited by cotton lords to work the alluvial soil on the western bank of the Mississippi River, the Italians proved ill matched to both task and place. They were subsistence farmers, averse to the dictates of monoculture; they were highland and seaside dwellers, and were smothered in the miasmic heat of the delta lowlands; they were *foreigners* in a land that did not brook intrusion. (Their 1895 arrival warranted a front page headline in the *Springdale News*, "Dagoes Coming.")

Two years passed. Malaria took its toll. Austin Corbin, sponsor of the colony, died, and the colony foundered. Then, in January of 1898, Father Pietro Bandini of Rome, arrived to lead his kith, Moses-like, to a 700-acre plot of forlorn Ozark timberland. The Italians worked quickly to transform their new home. They tended apple seedlings and grapevine cuttings. They kept sheep and made cheese, according to an early visitor, "in the approved Lombard and Tuscan manner, sunned on green fern leaves." They preserved fruit in "the Southern Italian style, cut open, filled with almonds and wild fennel . . . and flattened out to dry in the sun on wicker trays."

Loosed from their homeland, community feeds proved important for the settlers of Tontitown. Tradition holds that Virginia Morsani, along with Mary Bastianelli, cooked a fifty-egg batch of spaghetti in 1898 for the Tontitown harvest festival. En route from her home to the church, Morsani balanced a dishpan full of sauce on her head. Soon the cooks added roast chicken. And in a nod to the palates of their neighbors (and potential customers) fried chicken debuted by 1910. The typical Tontitown meal has remained the same ever since: homemade spaghetti, swamped in a ragù of chicken livers and beef; drumsticks and breasts and thighs, salted and peppered, battered and fried—the two cultures conjoined: Italian and Southern.

One hundred years hence, Arkansas Smokehouse, up the road in Farmington, now crafts Tontitown salamis, cured not with salt in the prevailing Italian tradition but smoked the Arkansan way, and War Eagle Mill in Rogers has been known to ratchet their stones down on occasion, switching from a coarse grits grind to a Tontitown-fine polenta one. And in Tontitown proper, one, maybe two, restaurants cleave to the old ways.

Mary Maestri's

Irishwoman Mary Quinn married Italian Aldo Maestri in 1906. Mary learned Italian cookery from Aldo's mother. It took a while. Of early efforts, her mother-in-law once said, "When Mary gets through rolling the spaghetti, it looks like a possum hide—a leg here and a tail there." By the early 1920s, Mary got the hang of it, and she and Aldo opened a restaurant in the family home. Today, her grandson, Danny Maestri, is at the helm, and though the restaurant is in its dotage, the spaghetti sauce still packs the punch of gizzards pulled from local birds.

956 Highway 412 East / 479-361-2536

See a riff on Mary Maestri's recipe for **Tontitown Salad** on page 48.

VENESIAN INN

Opened in 1947 by Germano Gasparoto, a native of the Veneto, this forthright restaurant—terrazzo floors, beaded board ceiling, oak wainscoted walls—serves lacy fried chicken and house-made spaghetti noodles in a red sauce. What's more, the onion rings are gossamer, and beer is served in a frosted pony glass. By the register, proprietor Linda Mhoon sells wheat rolls and angel hair pasta.

582 HIGHWAY 412 WEST / 479-361-2562

War Eagle

WAR EAGLE MILL

For much of the past century grist mills were small-town fixtures, humble buildings set hard by the town creek or river, where folks from the surrounding countryside brought their wheat and corn, rye and oats to be ground into meal. Most everyone lived within a morning's wagon ride of their local mill.

Since the first mill was built at War Eagle in the 1830s (and washed away in 1848) this bucolic little valley village in the Ozarks has been the home of three successive mills, the latest of which was constructed in 1973 by Zoe Caywood and family. As it now stands, War Eagle Mill is a three-story, red clapboard building sidled up next to a dammed river, the current from which turns an eighteen-foot, undershot cypress waterwheel morning, noon, and night. Spanning the War Eagle River—and framing the scene—is an elegant, steel-buttressed bridge with plank flooring.

Inside, toward the back of the building, powered by the wheel, is a Rube Goldberg assemblage of pulleys and gears linked to a shimmying red metal box, inside which turn two buhr stones incised with deep furrows. Keep the stones close together, and when hard corn passes through, it comes out the other end as grits. Ratchet the stones down just a bit for a finer grind and you get cornmeal; tighter still, and the product is corn flour.

Upstairs Zoe puts these products and many more to good use at the Bean Palace Restaurant, where each morning you can pull up a stool to a trestle table flocked with a red and white checkered tablecloth, and feast on dark, sweet buckwheat pancakes served with a metal goose-handled pitcher of syrup, and thick, yellow grits capped with a dollop of pale gold butter. For lunch, mugs of beans and ham are served on graniteware plates alongside wedges of soft cornbread made from meal ground just hours before. Above, tacked to the eaves, are old flour sacks advertising Southern Daisy and Dixie Darling cornmeal, Navajo Maid and Sleepy Eye spring wheat flour—peculiar, sad reminders of days long past.

Off Highway 12, thirteen miles east of Rogers / 479-789-5343

Tontitown Salad

an homage to Mary Maestri's

Serves 4 to 6

Back in the old country, in Italy, the vinegar was likely balsamic and the oil was crushed from olives, but in America, new adaptations were made, new tastes forged. This vinaigrette-dressed salad, adapted from the house salad at Mary Maestri's, will remind you of other Southern-Italian salads, say the one at Lusco's in Greenwood, Mississippi, but the garlic whomp is stronger here.

Dressing

1 cup apple cider vinegar
2 tablespoons very finely chopped garlic
2 tablespoons freshly grated Parmesan cheese
1 tablespoon salt
1 teaspoon freshly ground black pepper
2 cups canola oil

1 head of iceberg or romaine lettuce
Salt and freshly ground black pepper
Garlic powder

To make the dressing, combine the vinegar, garlic, Parmesan cheese, salt, and pepper in a large glass jar or jug, preferably one with a narrow opening. Shake well to combine. Add the canola oil a little at a time in four batches, shaking well between each addition.

To core the iceberg lettuce, hold the head core end down and rap it firmly against a counter or tabletop. (The pressure forces the core into the head, making it easy to lift or twist out with your fingers. Or, simply cut out the core using a stainless-steel, plastic, or ceramic knife, as carbon steel will cause discoloration.) If using romaine lettuce, cut the tough end off and tear the lettuce into bite-sized bits.

Rinse the lettuce under cool running water. Tear apart and place in a salad spinner or kitchen towel to dry. Place dry lettuce in an oversized bowl with salt, pepper, and garlic powder, to taste. Add a little dressing, tossing to coat. Taste and adjust seasoning for salt and pepper. Serve immediately. The remaining dressing may be kept covered in the refrigerator for up to one week.

North Florida

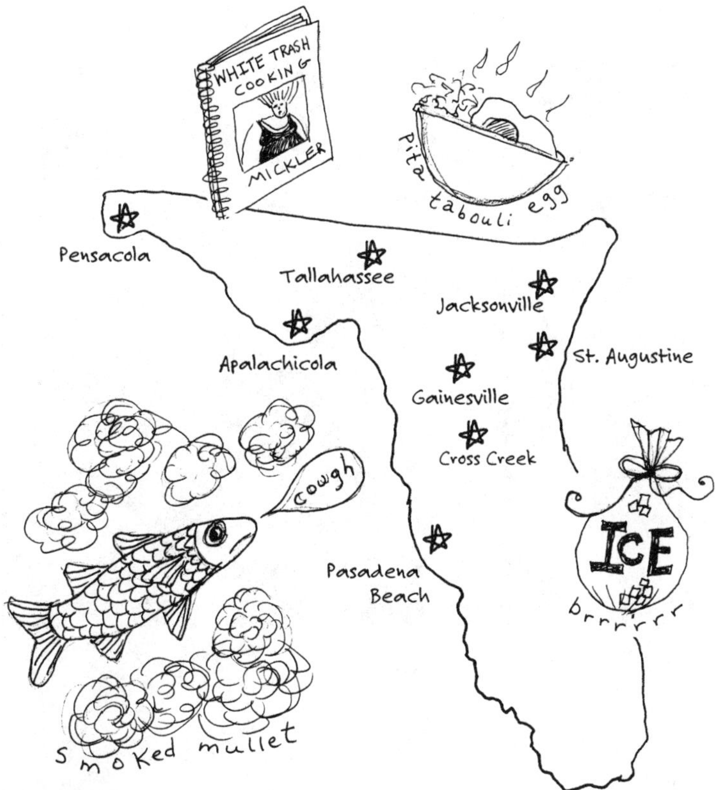

Mullet and oysters and shrimp. Travel through northern Florida offers untold opportunities to feast on all three. Milk-marinated fillets of mullet at Chet's in Pensacola; oysters on the half shell, served on a lunchroom tray from the raw bar at Indian Pass; locally caught shrimp, reverse-butterflied, rolled in cracker meal, and not so much fried as poached in oil, from O'Steen's in St. Augustine—a world of trencherman feeds awaits, far from the land of air-conditioned nightmares perpetrated by condo commandos.

N.B.: This book covers northern Florida, with a dip down to accommodate the inclusion of Ted Peters Famous Smoked Fish near St. Petersburg.

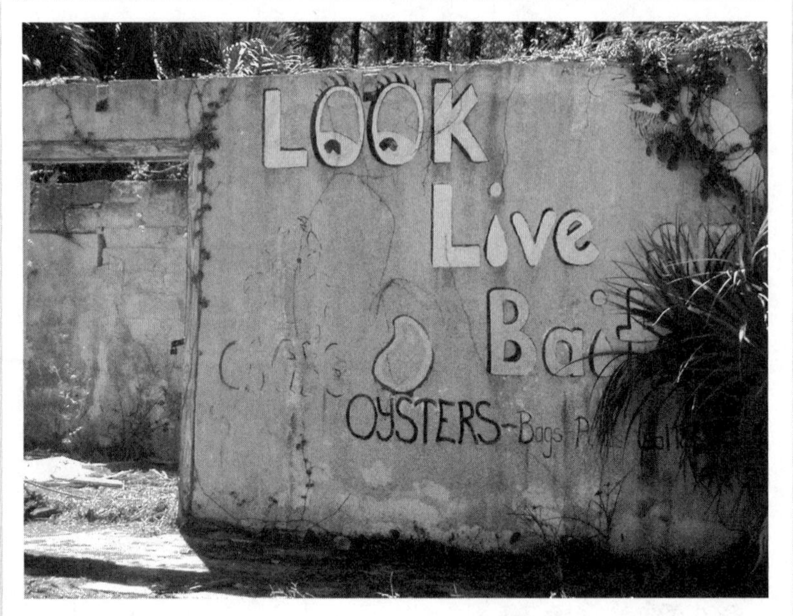

Roadside relic from 13 Mile.

Apalachicola

FRESH OYSTERS

Tommy Ward, steward of Buddy Ward and Sons, a family enterprise in business since 1930, is a curator of local maritime history, an unapologetic booster for Apalachicola oysters. Look into his eyes, listen to his raspy voice, and you'll know he speaks a truth when he tells you: "I've been out to Oregon, to Washington State and California. I'll put my bay, my water, my oyster up against anybody's. No contest."

Tommy manages a ragtag coterie of oyster catchers. Some, like the fellow who works a green skiff painted with the slogan "Old Goat," tong for bivalves in public waters. But others like Joey, Tommy's brother, work the family's leased oyster beds, piloting a cultivator machine that while spinning round and round like a marine take on Mr. Toad's Wild Ride scoops oysters from the bottom without need for tong plunges.

No matter the manner in which the oysters make it from the depths to the dock, Tommy ensures that they make it from the dock to the tables of Apalachicola. Oysters from Apalach end up in some of the country's best seafood houses. But even a *grand plateau de fruits de mer* devoured in a temple of culinary pursuit like the Oyster Bar in New York's Grand Central Station can't match eating a dozen at a cinder-block joint on Florida's Forgotten Coast, where the commute from water to table is just a few miles on a lonesome bayside blacktop, flush with palmetto, shaded by pines.

Before you slurp, you should know that the oysters of Apalach are ephemeral products of maritime geography. Put another way, Apalachicola Bay is cordoned from the salt water of the Gulf of Mexico by the necklace strand of St. Vincent, St. George, and Dog Islands. And the bay is bisected by the fresh water–bearing Apalachicola River. So depending on the way the wind is blowing, the bay is either taking on salt water through the passes that cut the islands or it's taking on fresh water by way of the river.

And since oysters are efficient filterers of water, their character is always in flux. A salt-bearing west wind means salty oysters will likely arrive on the docks at 13 Mile. East-wind oysters will probably arrive fresh, which, in local parlance, has nothing to do with time elapsed from water to the bar and everything to do with oysters that lack a briny punch.

To get a bead on such as this, snag a stool at Papa Joe's, a workingman's bar and restaurant at Scipio Marina, and James Hicks will shuck you a dozen or three. He was born out near Tommy Ward's dock and shuck house, a place some, owing to the distance from town, know as 13 Mile, and others, in homage to Tommy's mother, Martha Pearl, and her cousin Fannie Pearl, know as—you guessed it—Pearl City.

James is a garrulous man, pushing seventy. He's worked the water most of his life. (It's a family tradition. Oddys, his wife, arrives at 13 Mile at 3 A.M. each weekday to shuck gallons for Tommy.) Trust James. He'll give you the scoop on saline. His blade work is clean, his oysters always free of effluvium and well matched to a sauce of catsup, horseradish, and lemon juice. And the longnecks he slides your way are frostbitten.

Indian Pass Raw Bar, the other great oyster emporium hereabouts, is a few miles west of the Ward docks, in the opposite direction from Apalach. This means that, condo encroachment aside, it's in the boonies.

Opened in the early 1900s as a commissary for a turpentine camp, the clapboard building has, since the 1980s, been the oyster bar of choice for the countrypolitan set. In the wake of Hurricane Kate in 1955, owner Jimmy McNeil devised a plan to transition the family wholesale oyster business from harvesting for others to selling on the half shell.

Today, Jimmy and company pull oysters from his family beds as well as a few leased beds, pop them open by the dozen, and serve them on plastic trays. In addition to raw oysters, Jimmy also serves broiled ones, topped with butter and Parmesan cheese, but truth be told, these bivalves taste best with no embellishment save a spritz of lemon, maybe a dash of horseradish.

PAPA JOE'S OYSTER BAR / 301-B MARKET STREET / 850-653-1189
INDIAN PASS RAW BAR
INTERSECTION HIGHWAY 30-A AND INDIAN PASS ROAD / 850-227-1670

John Gorrie
The Iceman Cometh

With its Rube Goldberg assemblage of tubing and condensers, it looks like a marriage of a sewing machine and a locomotive, retrofitted for use as a still.

Along one wall is a faux aquarium, flush with taxidermied hermit crabs and horse conchs, lightning welks and hog chokers. I'm not quite sure what purpose such a display serves in a museum dedicated to local luminary John Gorrie, the man who pioneered mechanical refrigeration and the manufacture of ice, but those queer names do make me smile.

Front and center is the true focal point of this grandma's attic–style museum, opened in 1957 by the state of Florida: a model of Gorrie's ice machine, built to three-quarter scale. With its Rube Goldberg assemblage of tubing and condensers, it looks like a marriage of a sewing machine and a locomotive, retrofitted for use as a still. By way of the original, Gorrie laid claim in 1851 to U.S. Patent 8080.

A doctor by training, Gorrie arrived in the port city of Apalachicola in 1833. He wasted no time. By 1837 he was mayor. By 1841, flummoxed by a yellow fever epidemic that claimed as many as 70 percent of its victims, he began eradication experiments. Gorrie was convinced the fever was caused by decaying plant matter, moisture, and heat. In response, he oversaw the draining of wetlands and began toying with the concept of artificial cooling.

His machine was built on the principle that the evaporation of liquids and the resultant expansion of gases would lower the temperature of brine to below freezing. After submerging metal boxes of unadulterated water into the brine, the water froze into blocks of ice.

Although Gorrie foresaw his invention as a response to the ravages of malaria, food and drink applications arose quickly. The story told most often is of a Bastille Day stunt, staged in the miasmic heat of a Florida summer, wherein Gorrie and compatriots served champagne, chilled by blocks of artificial ice, to a coterie of dubious European visitors.

More plebeian, but perhaps prophetic in a region of the South that would, in coming years, build an economy based on the shipment of shellfish and oranges, was Gorrie's baroquely phrased prediction that "animals or fruit, when divested of life, may be preserved entire with all their juices in low temperature; this principle of producing and maintaining cold might be made instrumental in preserving organic matter an indefinite amount of time, and thus become an accessory to the extension of commerce."

JOHN GORRIE MUSEUM AND STATE PARK
46 SIXTH STREET / 850-653-9347

Cross Creek

Marjorie Kinnan Rawlings Historic State Park

Dragonflies swoop through the yard, darting among the orange trees. Roosters strut and peck for feed in the crabgrass. Clothes dry on the line in the summer sun. Planters, crafted from eviscerated truck tires, erupt with riots of daisies. A dog scratches at the screen door of a clapboard Cracker-style farmhouse.

Cross Creek, the community that writer Marjorie Kinnan Rawlings claimed as home in 1928, has, in the years since her 1953 death, awakened from its slumber. But Rawlings' house appears, in large part, as she left it. In the company of a docent who talks of Rawlings like she were a kindly aunt, I wander the grounds and ramble the house.

We pause on the screened front porch, where Rawlings wrote the works that garnered her a Pulitzer Prize. In the living room we admire the pendant chandelier she made from a white mixing bowl. And in the kitchen we ponder the cook stove where Rawlings and Idella Parker, the woman she called "the perfect maid," stirred pots of oxtail pilau and baked skillets of cornbread and pans of biscuits. (Rawlings once wrote that her literary ability "may safely be questioned as harshly as one will, but indifference to my table puts me in a rage.")

CROSS CREEK
by
Marjorie Kinnan Rawlings
Author of "The Yearling"

The book that begat the cookbook.

Marjorie Kinnan Rawlings came south in search of a muse. She found what she sought at Cross Creek, the place she called "half-wild backwoods country," the place where she wrote *The Yearling* and *Cross Creek*.

Rawlings aspired to write big-picture fiction by way of a tight-focus look at her new surroundiings. And she succeeded. What she didn't intend was to become a cookery writer. Yet her descriptions of time at the stove and at table proved so compelling that her publisher commissioned *Cross Creek Cookery*, a 1942 compendium of recipes and lore wherein she offers recipes for soft-shell cooter soup and Crisco-cut biscuits.

Of the latter Rawlings opines, "It's an old tale that the South is known as the land of the hot biscuit and the cold check. Yet a part of the placidity of the South comes from the sense of well-being that follows the heart-and-body-warming consumption of breads fresh from the oven. We serve cold baker's bread to our enemies, trusting that they will never impose on our hospitality again."

In her neighbors, Rawlings found inspiration for her fiction—and her table. When you drive through the Big Scrub to her home, you, too, will have the chance to commune with her Cracker muse.

The Yearling

Chances are good that Marjorie Rawlings, a devotee of Cracker home cooking known to present fried catfish on Wedgwood china, did not serve her guests duck confit. But that's what the screened porch–fronted Yearling, in business since 1952, aims to do. And, oh yes, they have fried gator, too.

Gone are the days when the core menu was cooter, catfish, and frog legs. Now, the Yearling, a cozy restaurant with wood-paneled walls and galvanized tin ceilings, festooned with all manner of Rawlings memorabilia, is best appreciated as a place for a snack, maybe a cup of tomatoey seafood chowder and frosty mug of beer. Or you might opt for a slab of prime rib. J. R. Jenkins, grandson of Rawlings employees Will and Martha Mickens, still works the grill, cooking sixteen-ounce buck cuts and twelve-ounce yearlings.

14531 Country Road 325 / 352-466-3999

Gainesville

Louis' Lunch

Born in Sicily in 1896, Louis Pennisi landed at Ellis Island in 1914. After settling in Gainesville, he shoveled coal into boxcars before working the streets as a peddler. Ice cream was the good of choice. Soon he was churning his own, and Louis' Pure Ice Cream was born.

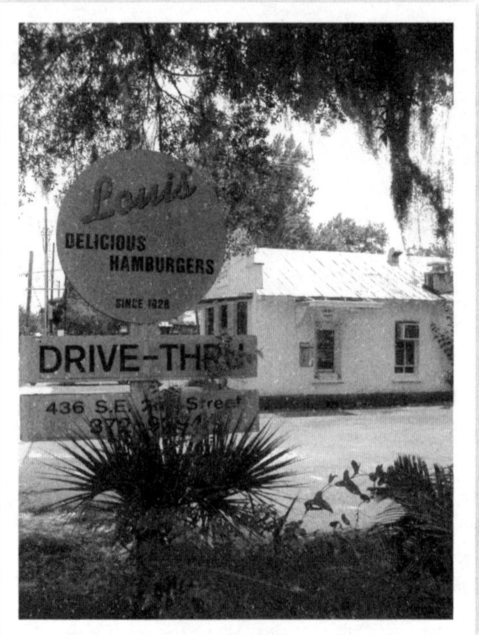

Inside, a haze of burger grease hangs in the air.

In 1928 Pennisi opened a café. He sold ham sandwiches and hamburgers. The latter, a combination of beef, turkey, breadcrumbs, and spices, was an homage to his mother's meatballs. Pennisi just squashed them flat and stuffed his burgers inside slices of white bread.

By 1935, he built a block and stucco building with an L-shaped counter front and center. Not much changed in ensuing decades. Pennisi added egg sandwiches in, say, the thirties. Then cheeseburgers. Fries, later still.

When the lunch rush hit, Pennisi was ever at the stove, although somewhere around his ninetieth year he curtailed his hours. By the time the elder Pennisi died at the age of 106, his son Tommy, born in 1937, was at the helm.

Today, Tommy is still there, frying his grandmother's meatball burgers in a cast-iron skillet puddled with vegetable oil. (They emerge crusty at the edges and sort of creamy at their core and are comparable to the dough burgers of Booneville, Mississippi.) Working alongside is Joyce Philman, the woman he married in 1973 and divorced in 1974, as well as their daughter, Emily Cheves.

Seated at a counter stool, beneath the beaded board ceiling, I imagine Tommy—charmingly old-school in his black shorts, black socks, and black shoes, wearing a

paper skiff—marking his ninetieth birthday within the spartan confines of this working-class café, dishing burgers to the great-great-grandchildren of the men his father first served.

I try to relate as much, but it seems that Tommy's hearing is shot. (When I compliment the pleasant crunch of his burger, he responds with directions to the bathroom.) Tommy's legs, however, appear strong. And that's what a great grill man requires, firm calves and an unshakable resolve to stand tall by the stove each day. I figure Tommy inherited that—along with the business—from his father.

436 SE Second Street / 352-372-9294

Jacksonville

Beach Road Chicken Dinners

Ken and Tena Ferger, owners of this circa 1939 institution, set on the old beach road, think enough of their chicken to sell the dregs—brittle crumbs of salty batter that tend to flake off the deep-fried birds and settle at the bottom of holding vessels—for about a buck a bowl. And judging by my experience, the Fergers are not inclined toward hubris.

In the red and yellow main dining room, at a table set family-style with a platter of thinly crusted drumsticks and thighs, a bowl of cream-sauced green peas, and a basket of homemade biscuits, I spoon tawny dregs that taste of schmaltz into a bowl of gravy-capped mashed potatoes in need of oomph. And the dregs do the trick, adding texture and nuance and salt. The bird parts, on the other hand, need no help. Fried to a greaseless crisp they are models of the thin-crusted and lightly seasoned form.

That greaseless chicken and those downy biscuits are testaments to a host of cooks who have called Beach Road home. Josephine Barberry, known as Mama Jo, was queen of the kitchen for more than thirty years, working the bread board, cutting dough into biscuits with an empty Carnation milk can. Although Barberry still stops off for an occasional after-church visit, her niece, Gloria Bartley, is now at the center of the kitchen maelstrom.

An engaged owner is also important, acknowledges Gloria, who's been on the job since age fifteen. She can remember the days soon after founder Earl Majors retired. He was still living across the street from the restaurant, Gloria tells me, as I butter

another buttermilk-scented biscuit: "He would watch the place through his bathroom window, watch the line of people waiting to get in. He would time the wait and if we weren't getting them in fast enough—remember now, he had already sold the place—he would pick up the phone and call the hostess and bless her out. That's the kind of man he was, the kind of place this is."

4132 ATLANTIC BOULEVARD / 904-398-7980

WHITEWAY DELI

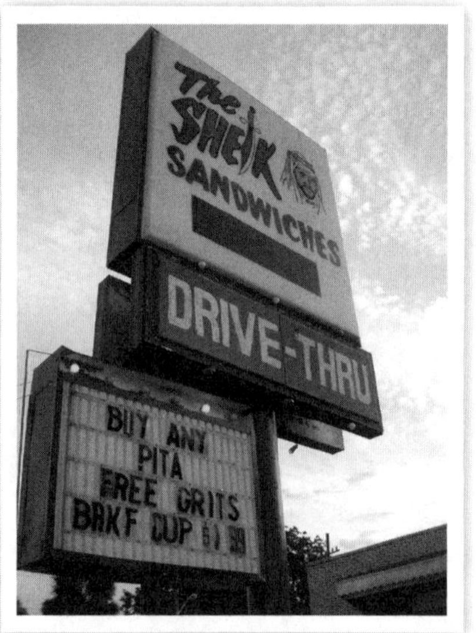

Pita and grits, a peculiar Jacksonville tradition.

The Sheik on North Main Street, in business since the 1970s, is one of six fast-food shops in a Jacksonville chain. Like the unaffiliated Desert Rider downtown and Desert Sand on Beach Boulevard, they serve sandwiches—club, ham and cheese, bacon and egg, that sort of thing—tucked into pita bread. By my count, a couple dozen or more sandwich shops around town share a similar bill of fare. Come breakfast, pita cheese toast is a favorite. So is the link, egg, and cheese sack. Not to mention the breakfast in a cup, a sundae-like stack of grits, patty sausage, and eggs. At lunch, the steak-in-a-sack and the cold cut–stuffed camel rider are the main events.

The term *camel rider* might play as a pejorative in most cities, but here in Jacksonville—which has among the largest Arab Middle Eastern communities on the East Coast—it's a marker of influence among immigrants and the descendants of immigrants who, fleeing the economic decline and religious persecution of the Ottoman Empire, began settling in the area in the 1890s.

Many Arab immigrants made their way as peddlers. Some opened groceries, which in time evolved into sandwich shops. Assimilation was the watchword. Mohammed became Mo. Saliba became Sal. Men with surnames like Hazouri built houses of worship like Mount Olive Syrian Presbyterian Church. By 1915 the Syrian American Club was thriving. The Ramallah American Club followed in the 1950s.

For reasons that are unclear, pita bread—and sandwiches stuffed into pita bread—function as totems of both assimilation and enduring ethnic identity among Arabs of Jacksonville. Even sandwiches like the Anne Beard (turkey, tabouli, feta, peppers, and Italian dressing), served by Sam Salem, owner of the Whiteway Delicatessen in the Riverside neighborhood, broadcast Middle Eastern origins by means of the customary envelope.

Sam, who took over the 1927 vintage café from his father, Paul, a native of Ramallah, probably serves the best pita sandwiches in town. Though he's proud of his desert rider, I dote on Whiteway's tabouli omelet. Served in a cardboard boat, it's a puff of egg layered with slabs of feta and a cool scoop of parsley, bulgur, and tomato, the whole affair stuffed inside a warm pita pouch.

When I ask Sam whether he considers the term *camel rider* a pejorative, he changes the subject and directs my attention toward the archive of candid customer photos he has taken over the past thirty-odd years. Sam's chronicle of life at Whiteway is exhaustive, filling dozens of scrapbooks, scores of boxes. By way of an answer, he picks a box up at random and begins sifting through what he calls his "collage of people," calling every second subject by name, reciting their life stories, telling me who they are, who they were, and where they are now.

1510 King Street / 904-389-0355

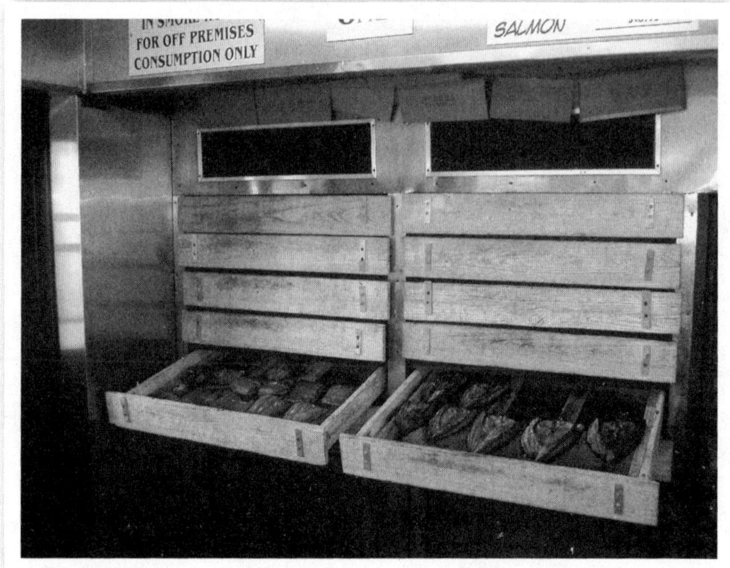

That famous chifforobe smoker.

Pasadena Beach

TED PETERS FAMOUS SMOKED FISH

This roadside haunt, in business since 1951, comes by its shabby-chic look and old Florida credentials honestly. The namesake was a New York native, a plumber by trade, who, like many a snowbird, came south in search of warmer climes. "They called him 'the Bear,'" Mike Lathrop, current proprietor and nephew of the late Peters, tells me when I belly to the bar one morning. "He was bigger than life, a man of immense physical strength and presence. His first place was the Blue Anchor out on St. Pete Beach. He would set up out front, smoking fish to sell to people driving by. That's how it all started."

As Lathrop and I talk, traffic swishes by, and the cement-floored restaurant begins to fill. At a trestle table, two policemen dig forks deep into bowls of bacon-flecked potato salad. Nearby, a father, clad in a surf-print shirt and flip-flops, shows his young son how to twist a backbone free from the sweet flesh of a smoke-blackened mullet that's splayed open like a cheap paperback. At the end of the bar, a woman in tennis whites slathers relish-spiked smoked-mullet spread on a saltine, spritzing each swab of fish pâté with lemon and hot sauce.

"He was a great salesman," says Mike. "Bear would fan the smoke up when he saw people coming. Of course, he wasn't the first guy to smoke a mullet—that goes back to the Indians—but we're pretty sure he was the first guy to move the smoking of mullet from the backyard to the front, the first guy around here to put it on a restaurant menu."

Peters made his reputation on mullet. He did not single-handedly rescue the fish from ignominy, but he did, over the course of a forty-odd-year career, convince a goodly number of locals and tourists that mullet was worthy of a taste. Three bites into a tub of Peters' smoked mullet dip and they were converts.

And so it goes. Sitting at the bar, I dig into my tawny-hued fish. (Like bluefish and mackerel, mullet is an oily fish that stands up well to the heat of a wood-fueled fire.) Between pulls on my beer, I swivel and spy the adjacent cookhouse where Lathrop and his team smoke mullet—as well as mackerel, mahimahi, and salmon—in what appears to be an oversized chifforobe, outfitted with wire-lined drawers and fueled by smoldering oak logs.

My mullet is a bit drier than I recall from previous pilgrimages. Maybe the broiler cook, the fellow who reheats the smoked fish before serving it on a platter with coleslaw and potato salad, was distracted while running my mullet under the flame. More likely, the mullet is as good as ever and the culprit is my own outsized expectation. No matter, I take solace in a bowl of moist and creamy mullet dip, which I smear on saltines and eat until my belly aches.

1350 South Pasadena Avenue / 727-381-7931

Pensacola

The Coffee Cup

Cleora Rutledge stands facing the grill. Her back is to the tile-floored restaurant. She has a spatula in one hand, a trowel for cleaning the flattop in the other. A dozen or so spin stools line the counter behind her. "A lot of them come in to harass me," she tells me, with a gold-toothed smile and a head toss in the direction of my fellow diners. "And I give it right back."

Wayne Cage opened the Coffee Cup in 1945. His vision was a "place where you can bring your friends and be proud of your coffee cup." It worked. By the 1950s the

Coffee Cup had taken its place alongside Jerry's Drive-In as a fulcrum of Pensacola life. And so it remains, a de facto clubhouse, the place where cops and attorneys, drywall hangers and artists, dilettantes and debutantes gather to eat grits and eggs in the morning, smothered liver and onions at lunch.

Much of the Coffee Cup's success is testament to the service of longtime employees. Willie Ladd worked here forty years, honing a reputation for the best chicken and dumplings on the Gulf Coast. As for Rutledge, she came on board as a dishwasher in 1968. "Back then I could work here but I couldn't eat here," she tells me, her smile still bright, her manner matter of fact. "Now everybody belongs."

Although I love Rutledge's puffy sausage and cheese omelets, and I admire the wrist flick she employs when turning out two over-easy, it's her way with grits—and her way with quips—that keep me coming back. When I ask her the secret, when I tell her that I believe her regular buttered grits are so rich they must be laced with lard, she responds "Whole milk and real butter." And she moves on. Nassau grits, a local specialty thick with tomatoes and various cured pork products, merit little more. "Gotta have both," she says, which I translate into meaning both ham and bacon.

Although I'm not that big on T-shirts, I buy my son a Coffee Cup edition on my way out the door. The breast is stamped with their logo, a cup swirling with coffee steam. It's the back, however, that captivates by way of a bold slogan, "No Grits, No Glory." "Cleora was wearing a shirt just like this when she served me," I tell my son, when I present his shirt with a flourish and a promise to stir a pot of grits soon.

520 East Cervantes Street / 850-432-7060

For a riff on the Coffee Cup's **Nassau Grits** recipe, see page 73.

Mullet Holiday

I thought I knew mullet. I had put in my time at Ted Peters. I was familiar with the lexicon. Along the Mississippi coast, they call smoked mullet Biloxi Bacon. Down in Louisiana, it's Grand Isle ham. I believed that I was fluent in the physiognomy and gastronomy of mullet, by which I mean that I had gnawed my share of cornmeal-battered, deep-fried mullet backbones and had enjoyed picking the sweet white flesh from the ribs with my teeth. But only recently have I come to truly appreciate the many splendors of mullet.

A few days in Pensacola do the trick. At Jerry's Drive-In, a relic of the 1940s outfitted with molded plywood booths and tabletops plastered in ads for personal-injury attorneys, I order two fried oysters and a brace of fried mullet as my friend Jim Shirley, a local chef, tells me of the days when Jerry's served draft beer in sixty-four-ounce jars that looked like propane tanks and fishermen caught mullet by the ton in oversized gill nets.

No matter how you cook mullet, it's got to be fresh.

Popularity begets problems. It seems that, not too long back, mullet were overfished and in danger of depletion. As a corrective, voters passed a state constitutional amendment in 1995 banning nets larger than 500 square feet. That's what I learn at the Marina Oyster Barn, a clapboard rectangle framed by cast-iron filigree, perched on Bayou Texar. Seated at the back bar, I talk with Dale Rooks, who took over operations when his father, Thomas, died in 1979.

Dale tells me that the mullet he sources feed on grass. "Makes for a clean taste," he says of the fish that are sometimes dismissed as trashy bottom feeders. "And Pensacola always has clean-tasting mullet." When I press Dale for the secret of his sweet fish he tells me that he gets his catch delivered twice a day. And then he introduces me to sisters Eva Young and Mary Connor, who have been frying fish here since 1971 and 1975, respectively. "Ninety percent cornmeal and ten percent flour," says Dale, by way of further explanation. "And don't use salted meal or the fish will turn too brown."

My mullet holiday doesn't turn epiphanic, however, until I settle in at Chet's Seafood out on Navy Boulevard, where, on a good day, you can squeeze into one of the dozen or so dinette tables and eat fried mullet seven ways. By my count, that adds up to whole fish, fillets, milk-marinated fillets, backbones, red roe, so-called white roe (actually sperm), and gizzards.

That's right, gizzards. Like chickens, mullet have those little grinder boxes in

their gullets. (In the case of mullet, their diet is heavy in hard shell algae, which they churn to get at the oil within.) Fried mullet gizzards, if you're wondering, taste like firm calamari. And while I'm not that fond of the white roe, I like the red stuff—rolled in meal, fried gently, and set atop a pool of grits. But even red roe can't compare to Chet's milk- and garlic-marinated fried mullet fillets. They are among the more platonic tastes to cross my palate. At least that's what I'm thinking when course six, fried mullet backbones, hits the table.

CHET'S SEAFOOD / 3708 NAVY BOULEVARD / 850-456-0165
JERRY'S DRIVE-IN / 2815 EAST CERVANTES STREET / 850-433-9910
MARINA OYSTER BARN / 505 BAYOU BOULEVARD / 850-433-0511

St. Augustine

O'STEEN'S RESTAURANT

St. Augustine, Florida, is lousy with history. Hop one of those faux-trolley buses that trundle about, navigating narrow streets that recall back-of-town New Orleans, and you'll learn that in 1565 Pedro Menendez de Aviles staked his claim with a Spanish flag. That date, as any booster will tell you, makes this Atlantic Coast city the oldest continually occupied European settlement in the United States.

Stay on the trolley and you'll glide by the so-called Fountain of Youth, site of a natural spring near the spot where Don Juan Ponce de Léon first stepped ashore in what he dubbed La Florida. You'll also pass attractions billed as the Oldest House, the Oldest Drugstore, and the Oldest Wooden Schoolhouse.

What you won't gain on the putt-putt train is a sense of where to eat. You see, St. Augustine boasts a tourist façade that, come dinnertime, can be difficult to penetrate.

Granted, you might not want to follow in my footsteps, chatting up locals of long tenure, tracking down dishes like grundiga (a tomato-thickened mull of beef liver, hearts, and lungs), mondonga (tripe and chitlins, seasoned with rignum leaves), and gopher stew (mostly tortoise and onions). So here's a tip: rather than succumb to the lesser charms of the straight-out-of-the-box seafood houses that hug the waterfront, you should seek dishes born of Minorca, the island off the coast of Spain which, in addition to the delight known as mondonga, has bequeathed to St. Augustine a roster of peculiar and piquant shellfish chowders and pilaus.

The first and last stop for all things edible and Minorcan is O'Steen's Restaurant, a twenty-table concrete shoe box, in business since 1965, set across the Bridge of Lions, opposite the historic city core. Although founder Bob O'Steen was not a member of the tribe, Minorcan Lonnie Pomar, the current proprietor, has worked the fryers here for more than forty years. And his lineage shows.

Come in on Friday and you have a good chance of snagging an order of shrimp pilau, a jambalaya-like mélange of rice and onions and such, enlivened by ground datil peppers. Thursday oftentimes means sausage pilau. Tuesday it's chicken pilau. Every day, Lonnie dishes Minorcan clam chowder, which, were it not for the healthy dose of datil peppers that floats in the stew pot, would be comparable to Manhattan clam chowder.

Although no one seems to be clear about why, the presence of datil peppers has come to be considered a signature of Minorcan cookery. Check that. A better phrasing might be: Datil peppers have become integral to Minorcan cookery as practiced in and around St. Augustine. You see, back in the old country, datils were unknown.

Unraveling how Minorcans came to St. Augustine is easier than explaining datils. So I'll start there. In 1768, 1,200 settlers departed Minorca for Florida, bound for a speculative indigo plantation south of St. Augustine at what is now known as New Smyrna. Political strife and privation followed. In 1777 the colonists fled the wrath of their overseers, seeking refuge in St. Augustine where, over the course of the next couple centuries, they distinguished themselves in, among other fields, fisheries.

No one knows if the colonists brought datil peppers with them. Some argue that the Minorcans acquired the peppers from enslaved Africans encountered at New Smyrna. Others believe that the Minorcans, who had long cooked with peppers back home, adopted the datil as their own when the Caribbean-born pepper made a beachhead by way of Cuba. More than likely, the Minorcans did give the incendiary peppers their name, for the green to gold pods somewhat resemble dates, a linkage cemented by the knowledge that *datil* is the word for the fruit of the date palm in both the Catalan and Spanish languages.

Speaking of which, O'Steen's does not flinch when it comes to datils. Lonnie stirs the stuff into nearly everything he makes. Even his fried shrimp, lightly battered in cracker meal and cooked to an ethereal blond crisp, get their kick when you dip them in "pink sauce," a trademark blend of catsup, mayonnaise, horseradish, house-made datil pepper sauce, and house-made datil pepper vinegar.

And we're just getting started. Cruets of that same pepper vinegar, bobbing with stubby green datils, are front and center on each table. (Locals pour a glug or two on their collard greens.) And there's the house datil pepper sauce, the sweet-hot table sauce that Lonnie and company pour into decommissioned Grolsch beer bottles.

Of course, there's Datil Squeezins, made by Timmy Colee, a veteran of thirty-odd years in the O'Steen's kitchen. Like Lonnie's uncooked table sauce, Timmy's cooked version gets its color from catsup, and can, after a bit of finagling, be purchased when you step to the register to pay your bill.

Dear reader, you should know that your appearance at the register will be fraught, not because of the bill—which will be paltry—but because, when you push back from your table at O'Steen's, full of history and hot sauce, you will be surrendering both situational citizenship in Minorca and claim to one of America's premier trencherman restaurants.

205 Anastasia Boulevard / 904-829-6974

Tallahassee

Bradley's Country Store

The porch of this vintage 1927 institution is a hive of activity. A clutch of three county employees, each wearing blue work shirts with their names sewn above the pockets, munch foot-long sausage dogs as catsup and relish drips a Rorschach on the concrete. The screen door slaps closed behind a man who, between hitches of his pants, crab-walks down the stairs, lugging a galvanized washtub to his truck. From the top step, a grouping of picnic tables is visible, set in the sand beneath the boughs of a moss-necklaced oak.

Inside, Janet Bradley Parker, great-granddaughter of founder Mary Bradley, works the register. Over by the flip-top Coke cooler, she stocks bags of circus peanuts and candy orange slices. The plank-floored aisle her grandparents devoted to underwear and dog food now displays what Janet calls, apologetically, "Cracker Barrel stuff." CDs of "Uncle Handsome's Redneck Poetry." The Jeff Foxworthy oeuvre, that sort of thing.

Along the rear wall is a meat case. A man named Rabbit is in charge. He sells liver pudding, which the family makes from pig liver, feet, and skins, the mix sweetened with onions, spiced with sage and salt and pepper. And hog's headcheese, too, made from, well, you know.

But country sausage—coarsely ground, stuffed into links, and house-smoked over oak and hickory—is the keeper, the draw that pulls people twelve miles down the road from Tallahassee, onto the front porch, through the screen door. After the workers depart, I snag a rocker and eat a grill-blistered link, tucked within a hot dog bun and smeared with mustard. And I savor each bite, reveling in the play of smoke and pork and sage.

10655 CENTERVILLE ROAD / 850-893-1647

SHINGLES CHICKEN SHACK

A stone's throw from the wastewater treatment plant, over near Coal Chute Park, at what might best be described as the intersection of Mill Street and Miles Street, is this joint posing as a restaurant, opened in 1968 by Henry Shingles.

A neon beer sign blares through the front window. Inside, an oversized shop fan stirs the air. Banners for the Florida A&M Rattlers football team hang at eye level. Tufted Naugahyde booths line one wall. The other is dominated by a Ms. Pac-Man game and a jukebox, stocked with Bobby Blue Bland and Little Milton.

The menu board advertises bream and mullet, as well as chicken livers and gizzards. Like the other folks in line I order chicken, a leg and a thigh. In response, I get the same sweet guff they did.

Of course, you'll want to use your hands.

"You see these arms?" asks Irma, daughter of Henry. "You see these scars? I was raised up in this place, in the middle of all this grease," she says, gesturing to the rear of the kitchen where a deep fryer spits and hisses. "If you want chicken, you'll wait for my brother. He'll cook it for you, but I'm not getting in that mess."

When I assent, Irma slides a longneck beer my way. "Next one's on the house," she says. "Might be a while." But the wait is shorter than she predicted and the chicken Darryl eventually dishes is well salted and brittle-crusted, the perfect accompaniment for a third beer. I thank Irma, defer another gander at the scars that

blotch her forearms, and exit as the jukebox rattles and shakes and Little Milton sings, "If grits ain't groceries . . ."

905 MILES STREET / 850-681-2626

Ernie Mickler
White Trash Culinary Chronicler

White Trash Cooking was among the most unlikely best sellers to ever climb the charts. It was published with a spiral binding, in the manner of the South's beloved community cookbooks. The background for the cover image of a fleshy-armed woman in a flower-print halter was a patchwork of Tabasco sauce, Ritz crackers, and Velveeta cheese, bricolaged with those everyday icons Uncle Ben, Aunt Jemima, and Martha White, all of which was overlaid on a photostat of mulched turnip tops and precisely rectangular turnip roots—the sort of vegetable matter that does not come fresh from the farm but straight from the can.

" Listen here, buddy, this be's the victuals of white, Southern rural peasants . . . Hit'll eat! "

On the inside cover, Jonathan Williams, the original publisher, declared, "If you were trying to explain these recipes and snapshots and all to some grand maître like Paul Bocuse, you'd say: 'Listen here, buddy, this be's the victuals of white, Southern rural peasants . . . Hit'll eat!'" Williams suggested that the reader imagine Bocuse and his ilk "swooning over such delicacies as 'Big Reba's Rainbow Icebox Cake,' 'Tutti's Fruited Porkettes,' and the 'Cold Collard Sandwich,' as the Durkee's dressing drips onto their cravats."

For those who did not dog-ear a copy, mixing up Goldie's Yo Yo Pudding and Mona Lisa Sapp's Macaroni Salad, baking Resurrection Cake, Grand Canyon Cake, and Vickie's Stickies, for those who have never had the pleasure of pondering recipes for Canned Corn Beef Sandwiches, Potato Chip Sandwiches, and Girl Scout One-Eyed Egg

Sandwiches—and for those who once knew but have since forgotten their glories—a Mickler primer is appropriate.

> "I like my sloppy joes on cornbread, which is real lowdown."

Ernest Matthew Mickler, baby-faced with the unstudied good looks of a country boy come to town, was born in 1940, in Palm Valley, Florida, near St. Augustine. His father was a shrimper. His mother worked as a cook and a filling-station attendant. Mickler was fond of telling interviewers that his family lived without electricity until he was seventeen or eighteen, in "the middle of the swamp," at "an old fish camp." He described the buildings as "crude-cut cypress," the family privy as "out of doors."

Mickler's father died when the boy was six. Mickler called him a "mean SOB." He once called his mother, Edna Ray Mickler, "the low-downdest White Trash that ever walked the face of the earth." But he aimed to flatter. "Mama was a great fisherman," Mickler said. "Redfish, bass, trout, drum on the hook and line. Mullet in the net. And she shrimped, too. Caught tubs of fish."

By way of the book, Mickler became a media celebrity, cooking chicken feet and rice with David Letterman—and starting an on-stage trash-can fire in the process. And he became an arbiter of pop culture. When Tammy Faye Bakker, wife of the fallen PTL founder Jim Bakker, offered her sloppy joe recipe to the PTL's 900-line callers, Mickler defended Tammy Faye's inclusion of canned chicken gumbo soup and her instructions that a cook will "know if you have enough catsup when it gets the right degree of redness." Mickler told a reporter, "I bet it's delicious. But I like my sloppy joes on cornbread, which is real lowdown."

Soon more than 200,000 copies of the book were in print. But trouble followed money. In December of 1986, in the wake of a *People* magazine article that referenced a $45,000 royalty payday, an attorney representing the Ledbetter family of Alexander City, Alabama, threatened suit over Mickler's unauthorized use of their daughter's photograph on the book cover.

The Ledbetters joined an unlikely cadre of people who, taking note of the book's success, threatened suit against Mickler. The most curious complainant was the Junior League of Charleston, publishers of *Charleston Receipts*, the ultimate white-glove Southern cookbook.

The good ladies of Charleston claimed that twenty-three recipes in *White Trash Cooking,* including roast possum and broiled squirrel, were lifted almost verbatim.

Meanwhile, Mickler went to work on his second book, *Sinkin Spells, Hot Flashes, Fits and Cravins.* The back cover shows Mickler, in his prime, tending a cast-iron skillet roiling with grease. In the background, at the sink, is a man in briefs and a white T-shirt—his partner, Gary Jolley. By way of *White Trash Cooking,* Mickler outed the South's White Trash. With book two, he outed himself.

"I casseroled them to death," Mickler said of *Sinkin Spells,* the book he had written and collected in fits and starts, much of it while on book tour for *White Trash Cooking.* No matter what Mickler might suggest, *Sinkin Spells* was a more mature effort, one that utilized the recipes and folio form but shifted the focus to food ceremonies, like dinner after a cemetery cleaning, the casserole luncheon of a quilting circle, and the wake of Mickler's own mother.

Sadly, "One Side of a Conversation between Gracie Dwiggers and Rosetta Bunch about Edna Rae's Wake and Funeral, Told over the Phone" was one of Mickler's last efforts. *Sinkin Spells, Hot Flashes, Fits and Cravins* was published in November of 1988. Mickler died of AIDS soon after. But today, his books stand as testaments to the working-class cooks of Florida—and beyond.

Nassau Grits

an homage to the Coffee Cup

Serves 4 to 6

We all know cheese grits. The best use hand-grated cheddar, the worst processed dairy goo. Nassau grits are, however, little traveled beyond Pensacola, the epicenter of their enjoyment. In *The Florida Cookbook: From Gulf Coast Gumbo to Key Lime Pie,* Jeanne Voltz traced the recipe to a gentleman named Henry Richardson, whom she said discovered a similar dish while on a fishing expedition to the Bahamas. Voltz snagged the original recipe, from his niece Molly Biggs. In the ensuing years, the Coffee Cup has adapted that recipe to suit their needs—and so have I.

½ pound bacon
1 medium onion, finely chopped
1 bell pepper, seeded and finely chopped
¾ cup ground or finely chopped ham (about 6 ounces)
1 14-ounce can chopped tomatoes
1 teaspoon finely chopped garlic
¾ cup uncooked white grits
Salt and freshly ground black pepper

Heat a large skillet over medium heat. Add the bacon and cook, turning once, until crisp, 5 to 7 minutes. Remove to a plate lined with paper towels. Once cooled, crumble into bits and set aside.

Pour off all the bacon drippings except for 2 to 3 tablespoons. Add the onion and bell pepper and sauté until the onion is translucent, 3 to 5 minutes. Add the ham, stirring to mix well. Cook, stirring occasionally, for 10 minutes. Add the tomatoes and garlic and reduce the heat to low. Simmer, stirring occasionally, for 30 minutes.

Meanwhile, cook the grits as directed on the package instructions. When they reach a creamy state, stir in the ham and tomato mixture. Taste and adjust for seasoning with salt and pepper. Transfer to a large serving bowl and crumble the bacon over the top. Serve immediately.

GEORGIA

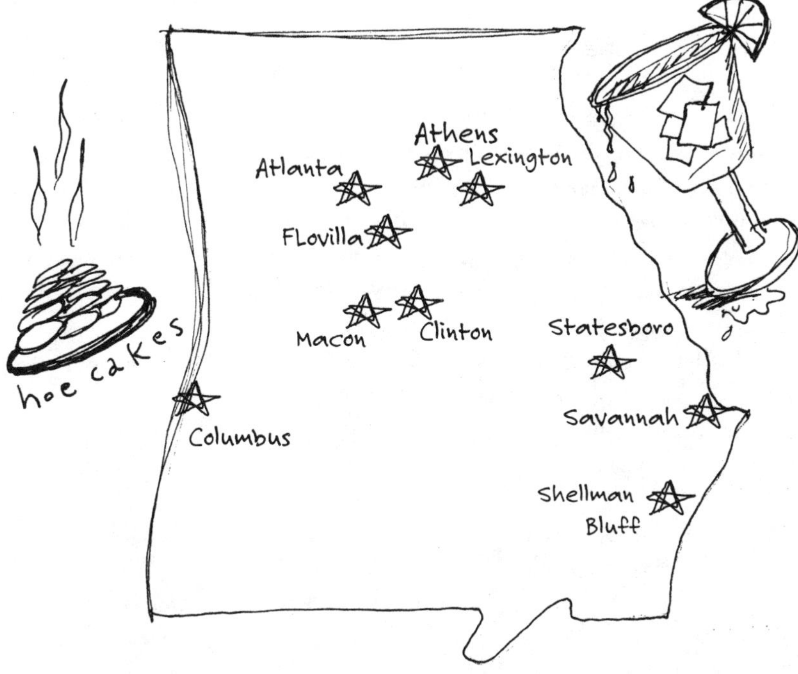

I'm a Georgian by birth. I mark my years by my eats. I was weaned on a steady diet of barbecue sandwiches, Brunswick stew, and sweet tea from Old Clinton Bar-B-Q. During my teens, I wolfed down chili dogs and slaw-capped dogs from the Nu-Way in Macon. While in my early twenties, I developed a taste for Atlanta icon Deacon Burton's fried chicken. What is more, along the way, I came to respect the Deacon as much more than a talented fry cook. His grease was the grease that bound Atlanta, black and white, young and old, rich and poor. To sup at his table was a blessing.

Athens

Meat 'n' Three Cafés

Athens has two great meat 'n' three cafés. At Weaver D's, a cinder-block diner on the edge of downtown, Dexter Weaver has, since 1986, served the signature foods of the African American experience: crisp chicken drumsticks, straight from the fryer basket. Nutmeg-spiked sweet potato soufflé, too. Collard greens in a fatback-enriched potlikker. And cheddary squash casserole. Across town at Wilson's Soul Food, a storefront café in business since 1981, Angelish Wilson dishes fried pork chops, white rice sopped in pan gravy, collard greens, and butter beans.

Weaver D's is the more famous spot. The rock band R.E.M. named an album "Automatic for the People" in homage to Weaver's slogan, his response to almost any communication from a request for cornbread to a comment on local politics. "It's automatic," Weaver will tell you. And then an explanation: "I'm for the people, I work for them."

I've long been a fan of Weaver's. And I remain a fool for any vegetable casserole he serves. But, of late, I've been as likely to duck into Wilson's. The location, near the Hot Corner, the traditional epicenter of African American commerce in Athens, is part of the draw. So is the honest interior: walnut paneling on the steam table side, faded bamboo-patterned wallpaper in the dining room.

Slide your brown plastic tray along the track that fronts the steam table, perusing the choices. On Tuesday, chicken and dressing is front and center. On Wednesday, salmon croquettes. Greens every day, either collards or turnips, depending upon what the Wilsons can get fresh. On the side there's homemade chowchow, which, despite a namby-pamby appearance, packs a fiery wallop. For dessert there's sweet potato pie, with an umber custard and a crisp crust.

If you're lucky, Angelish Wilson will be working the line. Introduce yourself and she'll steer you toward what's best. (Return the next day and she'll remember your order, and should you choose a fried pork chop again, she'll suggest a vegetable plate.) Ask about her family history and you'll hear about her father M. C. Wilson. "Rich or poor or living under a bridge, he would treat everybody the same," Angelish will tell you, sketching the philosophy that animates her café. "And that's how we aim to act, too."

Weaver D's / 1016 Broad Street / 706-353-7797

Wilson's Soul Food / 351 North Hull Street / 706-353-7289

Atlanta

CARVER'S COUNTRY KITCHEN

Casseroles are maligned by righteous eaters, and I've done my share of bad-mouthing. In a magazine article I referred to cream of mushroom soup as the "ubiquitous duct tape of culinary creation." I was being snide. I believed my palate was somehow superior. Those were the dark days, before I had the chance to eat at Carver's Grocery, a white brick hutch with wire-caged windows, set on the eighteen-wheeler-thrummed western fringes of downtown.

Sharon and Robert Carver are the proprietors. Robert ran it as a true grocery from 1975 until 1990, when Sharon quit her real estate job to cook. She began serving fried chicken, fried catfish, and hot dogs in the cement-floored store. She added meat loaf and chicken-and-dumplings. But Sharon, who favors shamrock-green aprons and swoops her gray hair up, found her métier in the cooking of casseroles, dishes that claim a lineage back to ancient admixtures like Moroccan tagines and French cassoulets.

The word *casserole* entered the English language in 1708. But the American iteration did not come to the fore until 1934, when Campbell's introduced a tinned concentrate of cream of mushroom soup. Tuna noodle casserole followed. And in that wake came Sharon Carver's broccoli soufflé, inspired by a 1960s-era cookbook from the Rocky Mount, North Carolina, Junior Women's Club.

"It's got mayonnaise, mushroom soup, cheddar, and eggs in it," says Sharon of the wedges of green velvet she dishes from a hotbox at the back counter, alongside a trompe l'oeil window box framed by flower-print curtains. "My sweet potato casserole has eggs, sugar, evaporated milk, butter, pumpkin spice mix, and brandy flavoring. It came from the same book. People love our hash brown casserole, too. That came from a little spiral-bound book done by the wives of real estate agents in Donaldsonville, Georgia. I got rutabagas; no one does them anymore. Robert got that recipe from a fellow he met in the grocery store, an old A&P now run by a bunch of Koreans. I mash them up with salt and pepper and sugar and butter."

Ask Sharon the key to her success and she doesn't flinch. "My secret ingredients are cream of mushroom soup, sugar, and salt," she says. "You got to have that flavor. That's what gets you hooked. That's what gets everyone addicted to my food."

1118 WEST MARIETTA STREET / 404-794-4410

Sweet Auburn Curb Market

The urban renewal programs of the 1960s were either (1) well-intentioned, misguided, and ultimately unsuccessful attempts to replace substandard housing with high-rise apartments outfitted with the latest comforts or (2) insidious and covert attempts to displace our nation's poorer citizens, cordoning them off as an attempt to make the city safe for an increasingly frightened white citizenry while simultaneously setting the groundwork for real estate profiteering by city fathers and their cronies.

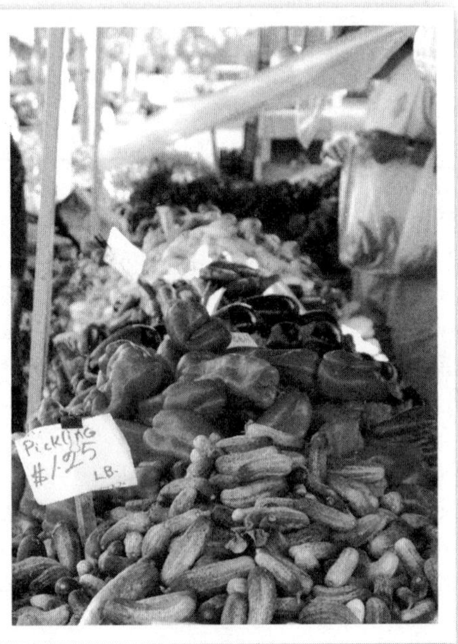

Farmers' markets are where country comes to town.

Urban renewal and the construction of the interstate highway system almost killed what had come to be called the Municipal Market. When erected in 1924, the graceful brick building was at the epicenter of commercial life in the fast-growing city. The highbrow Atlanta Women's Club raised funds for construction efforts. Night and day, the market teemed with poultry growers from up around Gainesville and sweet potato farmers from down around Jackson. But as Georgia's economy evolved, and agriculture took a backseat to manufacturing and service industries, the market fell into a long decline. Auburn Avenue, the heart of the nearby black business district, never recovered from the loss of its longtime core of captive buyers engendered by Jim Crow. Urban renewal programs and interstate construction were the coup de grâce.

By the late 1970s, Atlanta was debating whether to tear the building down. But cooler heads prevailed. Today, the market—rechristened the Sweet Auburn Curb Market—still struggles. (On a recent visit, I watched as a man dropped a watermelon in the parking lot and, when he realized what he had done, began eating sticky bits of fruit while challenging all comers to a seed-spitting contest.)

That is not to say that the market is without merit. Indeed, the real story here is that Sweet Auburn has survived all these years. Of late, things are looking more hopeful. On a recent visit I spied, among the vendors of honeycomb tripe, hog's headcheese, rank meat, and collard greens, the baked goods of Sonya Jones, proprietor of the Sweet Auburn Bread Company. Though Jones—a graduate of the prestigious Culinary Institute of America—has since moved from a stall in the market to a freestanding shop down the street, her sweet potato muffins, pies, and cheesecakes still evoke the market sensibility, the possibilities of urban Atlanta.

SWEET AUBURN CURB MARKET / 209 EDGEWOOD AVENUE / 404-659-1665
SWEET AUBURN BREAD COMPANY / 234 AUBURN AVENUE NE / 404-221-1157

HAROLD'S BARBECUE

Aleck's Barbecue Heaven was Atlanta's premiere black-owned barbecue spot. The white flip side of that same coin is surely Harold's, a low-slung red cinder-block bunker of a joint which has been in business since 1947 and is located just down the road from the Atlanta Federal Penitentiary. It goes without saying that the neighborhood is kind of sketchy. Like the Pen, Harold's boasts bars on its windows.

Inside, you'll find knotty pine paneling plastered with religious bumper stickers—"My Boss Is a Jewish Carpenter"—and a row of stools facing a long linoleum-topped bar. Order a sliced pork sandwich and lean back to watch as they toast two slices of white bread over an open pit tucked into a side wall, then layer on thin slices of pork. The sauce, a thin tomato concoction with a pronounced vinegar whang, perfectly complements the pork, which, truth be told, lacks the smoky punch of years gone by.

Unlike many of the South's best 'cue joints, the side dishes at Harold's are not afterthoughts. Their Brunswick stew is one of the best in the state, thick with tomatoes and corn. And the coarse cornbread is studded with sweet, rich cracklins, the solids left from rendering lard.

Founder Harold Hembree passed away a few years ago, but his widow and children vow to carry on. The bars stay on the windows, the cracklins stay in the corn bread, and Harold's name stays on the door.

171 MCDONOUGH BOULEVARD SE / 404-627-9268

Deacon Burton

Fried Chicken and the Legacy of the Late Deacon Burton

He was a king among cooks.

There are as many schools of thought about the proper preparation of Southern fried chicken as there are Southern cooks standing at the stove on a Sunday afternoon, tongs at the ready, chasing a crusty thigh around a cast-iron skillet.

Some would have you soak that bird overnight in an ice-water bath; others would have you do the same in a rich vat of buttermilk spiked with hot sauce. There are those who call for a quick dip in wheat flour, others who swear by cornmeal. Some add a little egg along the way. A proud few look to the Colonel for inspiration and go heavy on the herbs and spices. And we're just getting started. We haven't even dealt with the issue of fat. I'm of the lard school (for reasons both sentimental and savory), but there are many fine cooks who wouldn't dare set their skillet on the stovetop unless it's brimming with Crisco. And then there's the question of whether the chicken should be cooked in a covered or uncovered skillet. It's enough to make you call up Popeye's for takeout.

"Wash 'em, put 'em in some flour, season 'em with salt and pepper and some grease. That's all.

There was, however, a quiet season in this seemingly eternal debate. At least among Atlantans. From 1961 until 1993—the years that Deacon Lyndell Burton ran his little white brick grill over in Inman Park—most folks were willing to cede that whatever way the Deacon did it, well, that was the best.

Deacon was a minimalist. Ask him how he fried his chicken and he'd reply, "Wash 'em, put 'em in some flour, season 'em with salt and pepper and some grease. That's all." It was *just that* simple. And yet, the chicken that emerged from the Deacon's iron skillets was perfect:

tender legs coated in a thin, brittle blanket of crust, and snow white breasts, juicy beneath a peppery mantle of brown.

What Deacon wasn't telling was that he had spent a lifetime perfecting his technique. At the age of six he began his schooling at the stove of his mother, Ida, in Watkinsville, Georgia. On Christmas Eve, 1924, at the age of fourteen, he ran away from home and found work by Christmas Day, washing dishes at a downtown Atlanta restaurant. By the time Deacon was in his early twenties, he had cooked in some of Atlanta's finest dining rooms, including the venerable Capital City Club, and had opened his own café on the city's outskirts.

> "See this boy with the old knock-knees, we're gonna feed him some black-eyed peas."

But it was not until he took up residence at the corner of Edgewood Avenue and Hurt Street that he came into his own. There—his thin black face creased by a mischievous grin, his white pleated chef's hat poking high above the greasy haze of the kitchen—Deacon dished out rice napped with a true brown gravy, hoecakes as light and ethereal as any madeleine ever imagined by Proust, black-eyed peas heady with the taste of cured pork and dank earth, and, yes, skillet after cast-iron skillet of peerless fried chicken. In his spare time he ran a radio repair shop and served as a deacon in the Free For All Baptist Church. Unlike the Colonel, Lyndell Burton's title was not merely honorific.

It seems as though all of Atlanta passed through his cafeteria line at least once before the Deacon passed away in 1993 at the age of eighty-three. And if it was your first time, the Deacon wouldn't let you get away without taking time out to say hello. I can still remember my first pass through the line, my celadon-colored lunchroom tray billowing clouds of pork and pepper scented promise. "See this boy with the old knock-knees," he called out over the clang of the little Liberty Bell he kept at the ready for such occasions. "We're gonna feed him some black-eyed peas."

Son's Place

When the Deacon passed away in 1993, Burton's Grill chugged along for another year under the watchful eye of Lenn Storey, the Deacon's illegitimate son and heir apparent to the legacy of Atlanta's fabled fry cook. But there was trouble boiling in

the pot. A passel of Deacon's heirs claimed the restaurant was theirs to inherit and managed to convince the Georgia Supreme Court of the same. By March of 1995 Storey was out.

Three weeks later, Burton's Grill reopened under new management. Unfazed, Storey set up shop two doors down in a battered yellow frame building, calling his café Son's Place. Much bad blood was spilled, much good chicken was served. Along the way the original Burton's Grill was sold to a group of New Yorkers intent on making a killing during Atlanta's Olympic summer of 1996. They stowed away the cast-iron skillets, pulled out the deep fryers, added a terrace, and failed. Miserably. Soon a froufrou Italian restaurant stood at the corner of DeKalb and Edgewood.

All the while Son's Place was turning out fine fried chicken, cooked, rumor has it, in the same ebony skillets once tended by the Deacon. To assuage the fears of the faithful, Storey set up the same cafeteria-style line, stocked it with a stack of those familiar Melamine lunchroom trays, and planted himself front and center, just like the Deacon, ready to meet his public.

Some say Storey's fried chicken is almost as good as his father's. If that's so, it's surely the best in town. What's more, his collards sing with the taste of pork and a hint of sugar. And his hoecakes are the perfect sponge for sopping a puddle of pot-likker. For breakfast, nothing could be finer than a salmon croquette; a fried drumstick; a mound of creamy, white grits; and a cat-head biscuit.

100 Hurt Street / 404-581-0530

The Varsity

Places like the Varsity give lie to the old saw that Southerners—and by extension Southern restaurants—move like turtles rather than rabbits. Before you step to the counter at this Atlanta institution, you had best heed the signs posted near many of the cash registers, "Have your order in mind and your money in hand," or the counterman is likely to fix you with a scowl and call out over your shoulder, "Who's ready to order? C'mon step up! What'll ya have? What'll ya have? Talk to me!"

Founded in 1928 by Frank Gordy, the Varsity is revered the world over. Ask a dedicated grease-hound—especially a Southern one—about America's top hot dogs and he is as likely to mention the Varsity as Nathan's of Coney Island fame.

Clowning at the counter.

Each year, thousands of the newly converted belly up to the gleaming stainless steel counter at the 800-seat North Avenue location, set across a yawning twelve-lane interstate gully from the campus of Georgia Tech, bark out an order, and then retreat to their table with a couple of chili-slaw dogs, maybe a cheesesteak, a bag of rags (French fries), and an F.O. (frosted orange) in their clutch. Orders snake their way from the kitchen along a custom-made conveyor belt, picking up trademark toppings along the way—meaty chili and mayonnaise-laced coleslaw for those dogs, a swab of oily pimento cheese on that hamburger steak. Fresh-cut French fries and onion rings emerge from their baptism in hot grease, crisp and sweet.

In Atlanta, where, William Faulkner's opinions aside, the past may well be dead, few things endure, save this vaguely Deco silver and red restaurant with the curt service. Generations of Atlanta children have spent a restive morning squirming in a church pew, quieted by the promise of an afternoon trip to the Varsity. Junior executives and Junior Leaguers, sweat-soaked mechanics and white-stockinged attorneys alike stand in line for what everyone seems to call a "grease job." One bite of a chili dog and you'll know why—sweet oil bursts forth on the palate like a geyser. It's a gourmand's delight, a cardiologist's nightmare. And still they come: 5,000 feet of hot dogs, 2,000 pounds of onions, 300 gallons of chili served. Each day. Every day. "Who's ready to order? C'mon step up! What'll ya have? What'll ya have? Talk to me!"

61 North Avenue / 404-881-1706

Flossie Mae
That Crazy Curbhop

The wunderkinds of haute couture could have learned from Flossie Mae.

During the days of America's love affair with the drive-in, the Varsity employed nearly 100 curbhops, young black men for the most part, famed for their hustle, their temerity, and quick wit. In the early years, some would jump on a car's running board as it wheeled into the parking lot and might well be bolting for the kitchen to retrieve an order of rings and a bag of rags before the car came to a rest. Others sang a song, told a joke, or shuffled a dance. The quest was to impress—and to garner fat tips. Comedian Nipsey Russell got his start on the Varsity blacktop in the 1940s, trading quips and dishing dogs, as did a legion of doctors and lawyers, dentists and mortgage bankers.

But the grand old man of the Varsity carhops will always be the late John Raiford, known to generations of Atlantans as Flossie Mae. You could always spot Flossie, the "Wild Hat Man," across a crowded lot, a loopy riot of color and whimsy, trash and treasure perched atop his head. One week he'd sport a circle of plastic forks and toy army men with a feather boa for a plume, the next a vegetable colander ringed with prescription bottles and heart-shaped lollipops.

"To earn big money, you got to give a big show."

Flossie Mae began working at the Varsity in 1937 at the age of twenty. Already a veteran curbhop—he began his career at the Pig and Whistle barbecue joint a few years earlier—he soon learned the lesson that would prove to be his watchword. "To earn big money, you got to give a big show," he once told me as I munched down on a dog and parted with a tip twice the size of my bill.

And he gave a show—clowning, chiding, singing, dancing, and winning an army of admirers. When Flossie jumped up on your running board, his crazy headgear tilted at a precarious angle, and called out the menu in a singsong rap, you ordered twice as much food and left three times the normal tip. In 1993 Flossie Mae retired after fifty-six years of service at the Varsity. In 1997 he passed away.

Lester Maddox

Restaurateur and Unlikely Governor

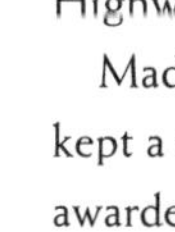

Cover art from a recording of a defiant press conference staged in 1964.

"You pick it out, we'll rick it up."

Gawky and jug-eared, with oversized horn-rim glasses, a wisp of a body, and a voice pitched at a frequency only yellow-dog Democrats could hear, Lester Maddox was an unlikely terror. I remember the first time I laid eyes on him. It was the summer of 1974, and Lester was on the campaign trail once again, preaching the gospel of states' rights and peddling a bicycle backward around the Jones County courthouse. It was the closest thing to a circus I had seen come through the little town of Gray, Georgia, and I was enthralled. I couldn't understand why my parents despised this little man. He wasn't a threat; he was a clown, a flop-shoed circus sideshow performer. I begged my father to let me buy one of the little wooden souvenir axe handles he was selling.

What I didn't know at that young age was that Maddox had a deserved reputation as one of the South's most unrepentant segregationists, and his election as governor in 1966 was considered by many to be one of the state's darkest hours. "I am ashamed to be a Georgian," said Martin Luther King Jr. upon learning Maddox was to be his state's governor.

But it was not merely political bluster and blunder that won Maddox notoriety. Since 1947 he had run a restaurant, the Pickrick, on Hemphill Street just north of downtown. The name, said Maddox, was an invitation: "You pick it out, we'll rick it up." And pile it up he did. For nearly twenty years Maddox sold skillet-fried chicken and buttermilk biscuits, turnips, and homegrown tomatoes to travelers on Highway 41, then the primary north-south route through the city.

Maddox was a born showman, a promoter of the old school, who kept a nesting bantam hen by the front door of the restaurant and awarded a prize to whomever guessed when she would lay her eggs. His ads in the Saturday edition of the *Atlanta Constitution* were pop-culture icons of the late 1950s, equal parts reactionary political

commentary on everything from the Communist Menace to the Warren Court and testaments to the virtues of the Pickrick's home cooking. Maddox prided himself as a friend of the common man, who kept prices low and quality high. All were welcome. All ate well—so long as you were white.

It was his God-given constitutional right to refuse service to anyone he darn well pleased.

The Civil Rights Movement came late to Maddox's corner of the world. It was not until the spring of 1964 that black citizens began showing up at the Pickrick front door, intent on sitting down for a meal. For most of that spring and summer, Maddox repelled any advances, waving a pistol in the air and declaring that it was his God-given constitutional right to refuse service to anyone he darn well pleased.

And so it went until July 2 when President Johnson signed the Civil Rights Act of 1964, outlawing discrimination in any business engaged in interstate commerce. That evening, three black ministers came to the Pickrick. Maddox met them at the door, an axe handle at his side. Maddox swung the axe handle that night, bashing the roof of one of the ministers' cars. They left, but many more followed in their wake, and soon Maddox was embroiled in a federal court case that sought to test the constitutionality of the newly enacted law. On August 10, Maddox lost his last appeal and soon thereafter he closed his beloved Pickrick, taking to the road on a quixotic campaign for governor, selling axe handles to supporters, tokens of their shared will to resist. A little more than two years later, he took the oath of office.

Mary Mac's Tea Room

Tearooms—dolled-up dining rooms where the tables were set with china and silver and the curtains dripped with lace—were once the exclusive province of the "Ladies Who Lunch" set. A few of the old Southern rooms remain, though for the most part they are now in their dotage, victims of a shrinking leisure class and a dearth of white gloves.

Atlanta once claimed numerous such luncheon spots, among them the Frances Virginia Tea Room, a grand palace on Peachtree Street, and Mary Mac's Tea Room on Ponce de Leon. Frances Virginia put away her doilies in 1962, but Mary Mac's is as vital as ever.

Founded, like many Southern restaurants, just after World War II, Mary Mac's was

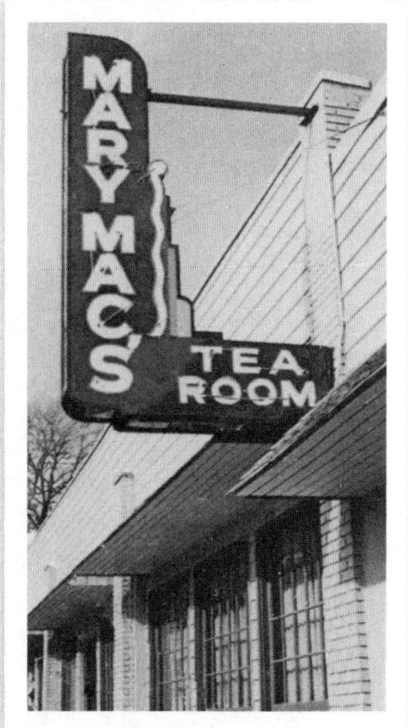

A cultural constant on Ponce de Leon.

run—on and off—from 1956 until 1998 by the late Mary Margaret Lupo. In the hands of Mrs. Lupo what was once a delicate enterprise was transformed into a trencherman's heaven, a sprawling four-room complex seating over 200, where you filled out your own order with a nub of a pencil and dabbed at the corners of your mouth with a coarse dishtowel instead of a linen napkin. And the menu, rather than offering chicken salad–stuffed tomatoes and Melba toast, is a veritable encyclopedia of Southern cooking: chicken pan pie and country fried steak, country ham and calf's liver, stewed corn and pole beans, squash soufflé and candied yams, to name but a few of the more than ten entrees and twenty vegetables offered on a typical day.

The most curious dish on the menu may well be the cup of potlikker offered as a starter, perhaps a vestige of the days when the whole of the nation seemed embroiled in discussion over the proper consumption of the soupy leavings from the bottom of a pot of greens.

That was back in 1931, during the height of the Depression, when Huey Long, U.S. senator-elect from Louisiana, and Julian Harris, editor of the *Atlanta Constitution,* were debating the relative merits of dunking or crumbling cornpone in potlikker. It all began rather innocently when Harris appended an editor's note to a wire story about Long and his devotion to potlikker. Harris claimed it was a dish best enjoyed by crumbling pone into potlikker. Long took offense, he was an avowed dunker.

Soon, presidential candidate Franklin D. Roosevelt was weighing in as an adopted Georgian. The *New York Times* published weekly reports. Poems were penned, songs sung. The debate raged for nearly three and one-half weeks, and each day the *Atlanta Constitution* kept readers abreast of the developments with articles that, more often than not, landed on the front page. And, yes, even those grand ladies' tearooms got into the spirit of the day, serving potlikker in china teacups with a corn stick on the side.

224 Ponce de Leon Avenue / 404-876-1800

See Mary Mac's recipe for **Potlikker Soup** on page 102.

Waffle Doo-Wop

I like these songs. They have a good beat and you can eat to them.

For many Southerners, Waffle House is the high altar of hash houses, and the bright yellow Scrabble-board signs that loom high above what seems like every interstate exit in the land are beacons of consistency and comfort, promising soft, scrambled eggs; crusty hash browns (scattered, smothered, and covered); and golden waffles, drenched in butter and syrup.

Open since 1955, this Georgia-based chain of 1,200-plus restaurants has won a loyal, almost fanatical following of fans. Rather than rely on television advertising, the company has long exploited the loyalty of its customer base, most famously in its inclusion of a dozen or more Waffle House songs on each of the restaurant's jukeboxes.

It all began in 1984 when Mary Welch Rogers, wife of Waffle House CEO Joe Rogers Jr., cut the first single, "Waffle House Family." Since then a couple of new songs have been introduced each year, among them a falsetto tale of discovery, "There Are Raisins in My Toast," sung by Danny Jones to the tune of "Big Girls Don't Cry," not to mention "Waffle House Hashbrowns (I Love You)," by Billy Dee Cox. "You know I long for you," Cox croons. "You melt in my mouth. I'm crazy about you, pretty golden hashbrowns."

Until recently, these little ditties were not to be heard outside the yellow, orange, and faux wood confines of a Waffle House, but with the release of *Waffle House Jukebox Favorites Volume 1*, ten of the tastiest cuts are now available on compact disc.

Clinton

Old Clinton Bar-B-Q

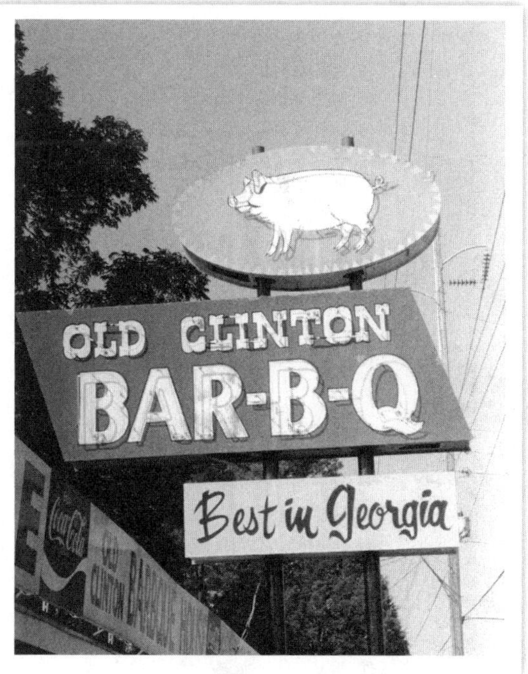

You'll find sawdust on the porch, gravel in the parking lot.

I spent what seems like the better part of my childhood on a Schwinn five-speed bike, burning up the blacktop road that ran between my home and this low-slung roadhouse with the sawdust-covered front porch. From the pits of Old Clinton emerged the first plate of barbecue I ever tasted: sweet, smoky meat hacked to shreds, perfumed with a sauce tasting of vinegar and pepper, maybe a hint of tomato; Brunswick stew, thick with chicken, fresh pork, and corn; milky coleslaw, rich with mayonnaise. To this day, I don't think I've tasted a meal that satisfies me so.

Until her death in 1996 at the age of eighty-six, Mittie Coulter—everyone called her Lady—was the keeper of the flame. I can see Mrs. Lady now, her smiling face framed by a wreath of gray curls and blue smoke, chopping the smoked meat with two butcher knives, pouring on sauce as she goes.

On a recent trip back home I sat down to talk with her son Wayne, who now runs Old Clinton: "My daddy—his name was Roy—he had an old country store that he started up around 1938. He used to have a pit in a log cabin over on the side where he cooked whole hogs, but they never did much to speak of. It wasn't until the new highway came through back around '58 that we built this place and started cooking barbecue regular. We started out with hams. Now we do hams and shoulders. My father built the pits and all, but we used my mother's recipes for the barbecue and sauce and stew. She learned how from her mother, Nora Crutchfield, from up around Round Oak."

My taste for history sated, I sat down to eat a sandwich. I would like to say that it was as platonic as ever, but the pork seemed to lack a bit of the smoke I recall. Empirical truths aside, after all these years, Old Clinton sauce still runs in my veins; smoke from their pits still clouds my eyes.

HIGHWAY 129 / 478-986-3225

Columbus

SCRAMBLED MEMORIES

Once in a while on summer afternoons when I was growing up—say between the ages of twelve and fifteen—my father would escort me down to the pool hall on Cherry Street in Macon. It seemed to me the darkest, manliest place on the planet, echoing with the clink of bottles and the soft clatter of pool balls.

We would hop up on a couple of stools, wave down the counterman, and place our order: two scrambled dogs, all the way. Before I had a chance to take a good pull from my Coke, two clunky white platters were slung on the counter before us. On each, buried beneath a molten mountain of chili, was a bright red weenie, cradled in a bun, smothered with chili, sprinkled with onions, and – this part was crucial—topped with a good handful or two of Oysterette crackers.

When that old pool hall closed in the late 1970s, I assumed, erroneously, that the scrambled dog died with it. Turns out, they're served all over Georgia these days—at Macon's Nu-Way Weiners, at Monroe's Pool Hall in Americus, at the Cordele Recreation Parlor, and at Dinglewood Pharmacy in Columbus, to name but a few.

DINGLEWOOD PHARMACY

Truth be told, Dinglewood gets my vote for top dog. Folks around Columbus will even go so far as to argue that their city is the origin point of the dish. And they may well be right. Lieutenant Stevens, who has been the counterman at Dinglewood since 1945, traces the lineage this way: "I learned from a fellow by the name of Sport Brown, who had it taught to him by a man named Firm Roberts, who used to run a restaurant here back in the '20s."

As to how the dish spread beyond Columbus, Stevens is at a loss. But Blanford Gandy, whose brother-in-law, Roy Gandy, opened my favorite old Macon pool hall back in 1937, has an idea: "Roy went over to collect a debt from a man in Columbus back in '42—they were betting on politics or horses, I don't know what all. They say he brought back the recipe for scrambled dogs with him."

The rest, as they say, is just grease down the gullet.

1939 WYNNTON ROAD / 706-322-0616

Flovilla

FRESH AIR

For many barbecue pilgrims, this is the high holy house of Georgia smoke shacks. Founded in 1929 and run since the 1940s by G. W. Caston and his heirs, Fresh Air can claim any number of Georgia's best barbecue spots as its progeny including Bob Newton's Old Brick Pit in Atlanta and my favorite, Old Clinton Barbecue. Old Clinton proprietor, Wayne Coulter, recalls traveling with his father Roy to eat Fresh Air barbecue and take a look around. "He may have gone up there one day with a tape measurer to figure out how they did things," Wayne once told me. "Everybody knew Fresh Air back then. We even fixed up the front of our place to look a little like theirs."

Indeed, the façades of Old Clinton and Fresh Air bear a striking resemblance to one another, but what Roy Coulter and hundreds of other restaurant owners came to inspect were the unique pits that Fresh Air has employed for as long as anyone can remember. Constructed with a firebox at one end and linked to the meat grill by an L-shaped tunnel, the pits are fashioned in such a way that they both conduct and

cool the smoke as it travels along the tunnel toward the meat—a perfect solution for long, slow smoking.

In the past few years Fresh Air has expanded, adding branch locations in Macon, Athens, and elsewhere, but for a taste of the real stuff you had best seek out the mother church, hard by the roadside in the piney woods south of Jackson. Be sure and knock the sawdust off your shoes before you step inside.

1164 HIGHWAY 42 / 770-775-3182

Lexington

PAUL'S BARBECUE

Pitmasters of the highest caliber are rarely the first generation in their family to marry smoke to meat, for barbecue cookery is not so much a learned art as an inherited one. How to kill and gut a pig, how to build a flue that draws, how to stoke a fire so that it doesn't flare, or, worse yet, die out—that is the stuff of familial dowry.

George Paul learned at his uncle's knee. "He had him a barbecue place for near about sixty years," George tells me as he mops sweat from his freckled face with the sleeve of a work shirt. "Used to be that people would come to town for court days and he started cooking out in the yard, selling barbecue to folks for dinner. I was always helping out around the pit, but it was his deal you know. Then one day he stopped; he left it with me and that was that. That next weekend, I cooked some barbecue and took it by my mama's house to see what she thought. Had to see if it was about right. She told me what she thought and I made a few changes and I've been doing it this way since, oh, sometime around 1983."

George's little store is a simple affair: white batten-board walls rising up from a concrete floor. Up front is his uncle's old chopping block, a massive square of maple, now concave from years of cleaver work. There's a space heater in the center of the room, but since the eaves of the building are open to the air, it's more often used as a place to balance a flimsy plastic plate of barbecue and stew. Everyone sits in metal folding chairs around rickety tables draped with flowered tablecloths.

George cooks the hams—twelve hours on an open pit over hickory and red oak—out at his farm and then brings them into town every Saturday morning, where the meat is pulled from the bone and sauced lightly with a vinegary concoction. The doors open around 9:00 in the morning, and by 1:30, maybe 2:00, they're out of the ruddy Brunswick stew, thick with corn, tomatoes, beef, pork, and turkey. The sweet, smoky pork may last a little longer, say, 2:30 at the latest. By the time they close up at three, all that is left are the bags of Bunny-brand white bread that sit on each tabletop.

HIGHWAY 78, DOWNTOWN LEXINGTON / 706-743-8254

Macon

H&H CAFÉ

During the Southern rock heyday of the late 1960s and early 1970s, Mama Louise Hudson's H&H restaurant was the Schwab's Drug Store of the Macon music scene, the place where bands came, hoping to be discovered. You never knew who you might find at one of the oilcloth-clad tables: Jaimoe Johnson of the Allman Brothers, Jimmy Hall of Wet Willie, maybe even Phil Walden himself, the Capricorn Records president and rock-and-roll star maker of the moment.

"At the H&H, they didn't care if we were white or black or purple," former Allman Brothers roadie Red Dog Campbell once told me. "Mama didn't say anything if we were tripping our asses off. Now she might tell me to come in the back door instead of the front when I was messed up, but really she just fed us fried chicken and loved us."

Along with her first cousin Inez Hill, Hudson opened the H&H in 1968. It was (and remains) a humble café, comparable to many others in the South, serving baked ham and fried chicken, ropy okra and collard greens, candied yams and sweet potato pie. Though the food was rib-sticking, the cook was the real draw. At a time when bands like the Allman Brothers were short on funds, Hudson was a de facto mother to many. She fed them, gratis. No questions asked, no IOUs signed.

"Those boys were hungry," Hudson told me, recalling the first time the Allmans came in, hoping to eat on credit. "Wasn't nothing bad about them. But all I did was come out with those two plates they were asking for. I felt like I was doing something wrong, but that's what I did. A couple of weeks later, they come back in, asking could they have something to eat. I told them yes, but it won't be no two plates and six forks this time. All y'all is eating."

The Allman Brothers struggled through the late 1960s. But in time the band

repaid its debt. By late 1971 their new album was climbing the charts, and their shows were selling out larger and larger halls. Mama Louise soon became a Sunday night fixture at the band's flophouse-cum-headquarters. On the cover of their second album, *Idlewild South*, the band included her in the credits. "Vittles: Louise," reads the inscription.

Today, Hudson's brick-fronted restaurant is hallowed ground for the Allman faithful. The walls are covered with photos of the band: Duane Allman on a lake bank, fishing pole in hand; Gregg Allman and Duane, asleep on a tour bus; Dickey Betts and Mama Louise, arm in arm. There's even a stained-glass mushroom—a nod to the band's drug of choice—hanging in the front window. In the pantheon of Allman Brothers Band belief, Mama Louise is now revered as a sort of saint, a kind-hearted caretaker of wayward hippie souls.

807 FORSYTH STREET / 912-742-9810

NU-WAY WEINERS

The original Nu-Way looks much the same as it did in this 1950s-era photograph.

Before the Varsity was even a twinkle in founder Frank Gordy's eye, Nu-Way Weiners was doing a booming business. Famous since 1916 for the sweet heat of the chili sauce on the dogs; the flaky ice in the cups of Coke; and the dark, rich chocolate milk, served icy-cold to generations of Macon children, this local chain may well have been the model for its more famous rival in Atlanta.

One look at the uncanny similarity of the restaurant menus and you can't help wondering if the Varsity stole its schtick from the folks at Nu-Way.

Nu-Way president Spyros Dermatas is more than diplomatic: "The way my uncle tells the story, Mr. Gordy traveled all around the South, all the way down to Orlando, Florida, exploring different restaurants and concepts. He stopped in Macon and talked with Uncle George and Uncle Gus because he had heard of Nu-Way. He saw what

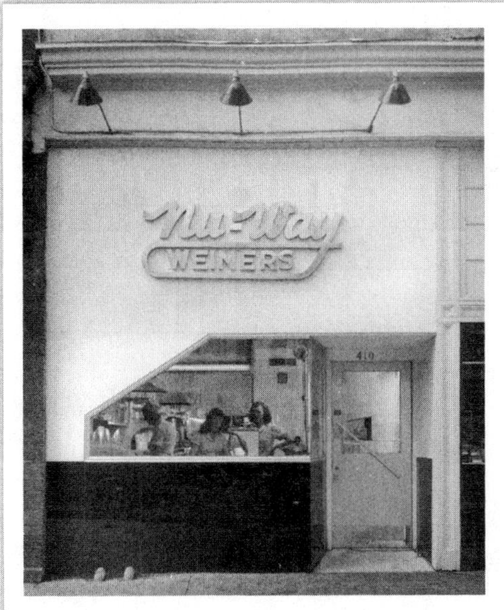

Macon's citadel of greasy goodness.

they were selling. Mr. Gordy was very impressed. He went back and introduced the hot dog on his menu and the rest is history. You gotta give him credit; they've done a good job with it."

On your first pilgrimage to Spyros' weenie stand, seek out the original Nu-Way location on Cotton Avenue. Complex directions aren't necessary. Just head downtown and look for the 1930s vintage neon sign with its blinking promise, "Best Weiner in Town."

Upon arrival, snag a seat at the counter and order a chili-slaw dog. Lying in neon-hued repose on a steamed bun that threatens collapse, your hot dog will be slathered with chili and mustard, topped with finely diced onions and, if you get the slaw, crowned with a heaping helping of creamy sweet cabbage.

Midway into your first bite, a latent culinary curiosity comes alive. Compelled to know the secret of the sauce that smothers the bright red dog, you ask: "Is that cinnamon I taste? Maybe a hint of chocolate?" Bear down hard in your questioning and you are likely to learn that, though the chili sauce is a closely guarded family secret, rich with eleven spices, the real power behind the throne is as Southern as sweet tea.

"Since the late '20s we've been spooning a little barbecue sauce on each dog," confesses Spyros. "It's a sweet sauce; we make it ourselves. It kinda smooths out the chili taste. We roast pork shoulders and hams, then cut them up real fine and toss them in with the barbecue sauce. First-generation Greeks started this place and Greeks still own it, but we're Southern now."

430 Cotton Avenue / 478-743-1368

Savannah

Desposito's

Back in 1965 when Carlo Desposito took over the operation of this little tin-roofed fish camp at the base of the Thunderbolt Bridge, he featured three items and three items only: steamed shrimp, steamed crabs, and cold beer. If his wife, Walton, had her say, that would still be the extent of the menu. But these days their son David runs the place, and, well, he's got some newfangled ideas. "I remember when I told Mom I wanted to start selling bottled beer instead of cans," David says. "We really went back and forth on that one. She just didn't want to change. And you can imagine what she said when I added shrimp salad."

These days you will still find the menu to be rather limited. In addition to the original three items, there are low-country baskets filled with shrimp, sausage, corn, and potatoes, not to mention beautiful but tiny steamed oysters, deviled crabs, David's curry-spiked shrimp salad, and, bowls of chili, an aberrant addition likely to send Walton to an early grave. And yet, her protestations to the contrary, on many nights you can still find the woman with the curly gray hair behind the bar, attired in a T-shirt that proclaims, "I Got Crabs at Desposito's."

On the night I visit, the place is packed. In the back room a victorious football team is gathered around a wooden table papered with yesterday's *Savannah Morning News*. At the center of the table is stacked a collection of tin beer trays strewn with spent crab carcasses. Everyone's drinking Bud in the bottle. On the side porch a tennis matron in whites picks daintily at a tray of steamed oysters. At the bar, members of the house dart team sit on thrones of a sort, high-back vinyl barstools with seats that David rescued from an old outboard boat. David is in the kitchen, working the steamer, slinging trays of crabs across the bar, dishing up cups of Desposito's special cocktail sauce, a peculiar but tasty concoction spiked with yellow mustard and A-1 sauce. There's a young kid over by the door trying to feed a quarter into the Gayety Beer Frame Regulation Bowling Game. It could be 1965. The jukebox rattles to life, and Dean Martin begins to sing "Born to Lose."

187 Macceo Drive / 912-897-9963

Ever the gracious hostess, Mrs. Wilkes passes a bowl of peas to America's favorite newsman, Walter Cronkite.

Mrs. Wilkes'

There was a time not too long past when any Southern town of import boasted a boardinghouse, where a drummer with a trunk full of patent medicines or an insurance salesman in town to renew a policy could expect to find a spartan room furnished with a clean bed and a dining room that offered three square meals a day.

Typically these were rambling, clapboard homes, lorded over by a proud Southern lady of the old school, unaccustomed to earning a living by dint of the sweat from her own brow. In some cases her husband had passed away, and rather than sell the family homeplace she began taking in boarders. Others, like the mother of Craig Claiborne, the Mississippi-born former editor of the *New York Times* food page, stepped in when their husbands were down on their luck, unable to earn a living to support the family. In his memoir, *A Feast Made for Laughter,* Claiborne recalls how his mother came to take in boarders:

"When my father found himself totally without funds, without borrowing capacities, and almost without hope, the decision was made for my mother to take in

boarders. This was a logical move because a rooming and boardinghouse was one of the few paths a properly brought up and aristocratic young Southern woman could follow while holding her chin and prestige up."

The late Sema Wilkes came to run a boardinghouse by a less conventional route. "My husband and I were living up in Toombs county, at Vidalia, when the government wanted our farm for an air base," she once told an inquisitive eater. "So my husband came to Savannah to work on the railroad, and when I came we stayed at this boardinghouse. Old Mrs. Dennis Dixon owned it then and was short of help, and asked would I help? I said I'd try and one thing led to another and I bought her out."

That was back in 1943. In the intervening years, precious little has changed at this gray brick reliquary of Southern cookery, save the banishment of roomers in the 1960s. Each morning at 11:00 sharp the dinner bell rings and a horde of hungry eaters jockeys for position at one of the round oak tables spread with a cornucopia of country cooking: soft whorls of mashed sweet potatoes brightened with a bit of lemon; black-eyed peas swimming in a porcine potlikker; creamed Irish potatoes spiked with mustard; collard greens, squash casserole, creamed corn, stewed okra; and platter after platter of crusty fried chicken, gooey chicken and dumplings, and rosy, country-cured ham. But don't reach for that fork before a member of the Wilkes family says the blessing. All heads bow, all kitchen clatter ceases when he or she steps to the center of the low-ceilinged dining room and pronounces, "Good Lord, bless this food to us. And to us thy service. Amen."

107 West Jones Street / 912-232-5997

Savannah Soul

Nita Dixon has long been heralded as the queen of Savannah soul cookery. She started out in the 1980s, peddling lunches to dock workers. Over time, she parlayed her success into Nita's Place, a shoe-box restaurant with a steam table full of back-of-the-stove favorites like smothered shrimp and stewed okra. Nita enjoyed a good run in the 1990s. Locals and tourists alike flocked to get a taste of her food. It helped that Nita was the kind of cook who, apropos of nothing but her mood, would belt out an a capella gospel number.

But the tourism boom catalyzed by John Berendt's *Midnight in the Garden of Evil,* and later Paula Deen's omnipresence on Food TV, left Nita in the lurch. By the early oughts her restaurant was closed and Nita was working again as a peripatetic cook and caterer.

On a recent trip to Savannah, I failed to track Nita down. Word had it that she was cooking at Shabazz, a fried fish take-away. After a platonic breakfast of Nita-worthy smothered shrimp and eggs at the relatively new Mom & Nikki's, I traveled the length of Martin Luther King Jr. Drive, stopping here and there in search of her.

When I arrived at Shabazz, she was not at the stove. Seated at one of the four picnic tables, arrayed on a concrete apron, beneath the boughs of a moss-draped live oak, I consoled myself with a brow-beading sandwich of cayenne-spiked deviled crab on toasted wheat. For dessert, I ate bean pie, a Muslim riff on the sweet potato standard.

After a quick detour to the Rib Castle, a hutch of a place in business since the 1950s, with a hickory- and pecan-stoked pit embedded in the side wall and a deserved reputation for the best ribs in the city, I regained focus and reacquainted myself with an old haunt, Walls Bar-B-Que.

Set on a narrow dirt lane at the heart of the historic district, Walls dates to 1943. That's the year Dick Walls asked his wife, Janie, whether she would prefer he build her a beauty salon or a restaurant. When she chose the latter, he threw up this clapboard two-story.

It's as forthright a barbecue joint as you're ever likely to see: The creosote-framed pit is back left. Seating comes by way of three orange plywood booths, liberated from a fast food restaurant. There's no air-conditioning, and on a recent summer day the wall-mounted thermometer was pegged somewhere north of 95° F.

Contrary to the name, barbecue is not the Walls family's forte. Deviled crabs are. Studded with celery and mounded on tinfoil-crafted faux shells, they taste like the kind of dressing you always hope to find in a stuffed flounder dish. In other words, they're great. And so are the collard greens, pleasantly leathery and punched with cured pork. As for the tomato-strafed red rice, a signature dish of Savannah, while the Walls family take on that dish may not match my memories of Nita's, the pleasant reality dished hereabouts satisfies.

Mom & Nikki's / 714 Martin Luther King Jr. Boulevard / 912-233-7636
Walls Bar-B-Que / 515 East York Lane / 912-232-9754

The Fish Camp of Your Dreams

Fish camps and fry houses are fast vanishing: victims of customers who prefer to eat their fill in modern air-conditioned warehouses, rather than tumbledown, tar-paper and cinder-block shacks; and restaurant owners who care more about country-cute interiors and nightly cash register receipts than creamy coleslaw and onion-flecked hushpuppies.

Some have closed—Edisto Motel Café in Jacksonboro, South Carolina, and Pritchett's in Columbus, Georgia. Others coast along, sustained by reputations won years before. And yet there are survivors, places where the sweet, white fish shatters beneath your teeth and the beer is so cold it makes your molars ache, where battered plywood walls are covered with graffiti, and fish are fried in cast-iron skillets the way God intended them to be.

Problem is, such places keep a low profile. They rarely advertise. There's no need; the gravel parking lot is packed every weekend. Locals guard their secret haunts with a fervor. When I told a friend I was planning to write about one of his favorites, he said, "Go ahead write about it all you want. Just don't give out the address and phone. If you do, I'll string you up. It's hard enough to get a table in there now."

One of the best such fish camps is down along the Atlantic shore, an hour or so south of Savannah.

Shellman Bluff

Speed's Kitchen

Speed's is—how should I say this?—rustic. Set in a trio of trailers—two double-wides and one single—it's a dive, pure and simple. Country music on the jukebox; lusty seafood on the menu. Flounder stuffed with fresh, local crabmeat; milky oyster stew chock-full of fat, sweet mollusks; and crab au gratin, rich with cheddar cheese and buttered bread crumbs: you won't find better versions of these coastal staples. Service is sassy. On my last visit I was talking with the fellow at the next table when our waitress plopped his platter of fried chicken down with a flourish. "Here you go—one half of a dead bird," she said with a wink and a sneer. Maybe she was disgusted with him for ordering chicken in a seafood joint; I didn't ask. Speed's can be a bit difficult to find, so you had best call ahead for directions.

912-832-4763

Statesboro

Vandy's

One taste of the orange-tinged, mustard-kissed sauce that they slather on sandwiches at this Statesboro institution, and you'll take to wondering if there isn't a South Carolinian tending the pits, for it is there that mustard sauces are most often savored. Turns out that founder Vandy Boyd was indeed a South Carolina native, born and raised near the town of Aiken, says his son Doy Boyd.

"Daddy made that sauce up himself," Doy tells me. "But he only lived in South Carolina when he was young. By the late 1920s he was running a little barbecue stand over in the town of Portal, here in Georgia. After a while, the family went to sharecropping, but when I went off to World War II, well, he couldn't get the crop in like he used to so he started barbecuing full time. He opened up here in Statesboro back in 1946, in a back corner of the Bargain Corner Grocery. He and my momma were cooking open pit, over oak."

By 1953 Boyd had moved his stand to new digs, a peach-colored concrete-block building with a separate pit house set on a Statesboro side street. In the intervening years, the restaurant weathered a few storms including a desegregation suit brought by the U.S. Justice Department in the late 1960s and a family squabble in the early 1970s that resulted in Doy opening a separate location known as Boyd's.

Today, the Boyd family operates neither Boyd's nor Vandy's, but the good open pit–cooked pork 'cue endures, thanks in part to the long service of dedicated

employees, such as Charlie Pierce, who's been smoking shoulders and butts to a turn since 1973. And what of that South Carolina-style sauce? Same as it ever was. Vandy's son Carl still stirs it up by the gallon for the current owners.

22 West Vine Street / 912-764-2444

Potlikker Soup

an homage to Mary Mac's Tea Room

Serves 4 to 6

Think of this soup as a ham hock and collard consommé. That's what it looks like, what it tastes like. And keep in mind: despite what you may think, this is a delicate potage, appropriate for a ladies-who-lunch habitat like Mary Mac's. Pepper vinegar, drizzled upon serving, sharpens the flavors, bringing collard to the fore.

Greens

5 cups water
1 ham hock
2 pounds collard greens
2 teaspoons salt
1 teaspoon freshly ground black pepper
Pinch of sugar

Soup

1 ounce fatback, diced (about 3 tablespoons)
4 cups homemade chicken stock or low-sodium chicken broth
1 cup cooked collard greens with juice
Salt and freshly ground black pepper
Pepper vinegar, for serving
Cornbread, for serving

To make the greens, heat the water in a large pot over high heat. Add the ham hock and reduce the heat to simmer. Cook, stirring and turning the hock occasionally, until the water is well-flavored, about 45 minutes.

Meanwhile, fill the sink with water. Add the greens and agitate in the water so the grit will fall to the bottom of the sink. Remove the greens and drain the sink. Clean the sink and repeat the process until no grit remains. Cut away heavy ribs and discolored spots from leaves. Chop the greens into bite-sized ribbons. Add the prepared chopped greens to the ham hock broth. Season with salt, pepper, and sugar. Cook until very tender, 45 minutes. Set aside.

To make the soup, heat a large pot over medium heat. Add the cubed fatback and cook until brown, about 5 to 7 minutes. Drain the rendered fat. Add the chicken stock and greens with juice. Season with salt and pepper. Bring to a boil and reduce the heat to simmer. Cook for about 5 minutes for the flavors to combine. Taste and adjust for seasoning with salt and pepper. Serve in small bowls. Pass the pepper vinegar and cornbread for crumbling or dunking.

KENTUCKY

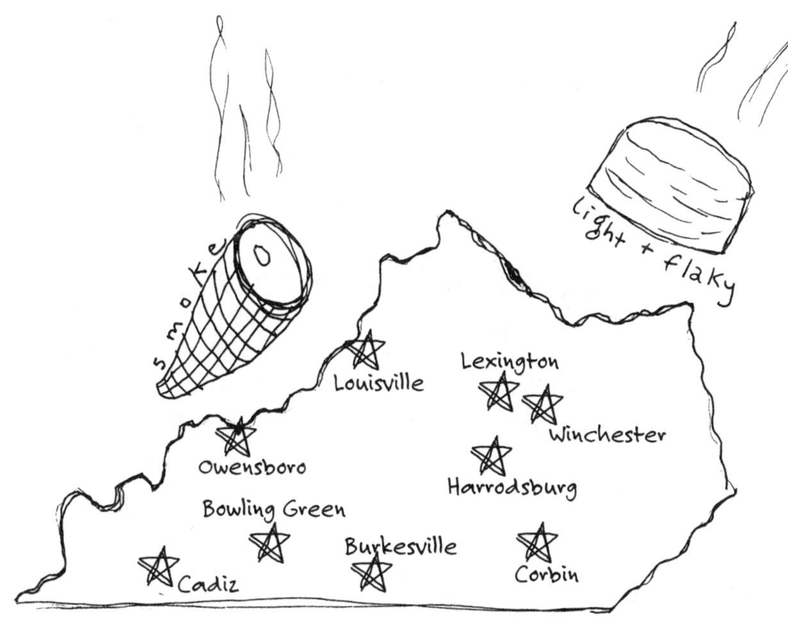

Here in the Bluegrass state, they cure and smoke pork hams until they are rosy and salty, sweet and smoky. Doug Freeman from up around Cadiz may well be the best ham man in Kentucky. An audience with him is the chance of a lifetime. Across the state on the banks of the Kentucky River, tavern cooks fry up messes of banana peppers and pack crocks full of pungent, garlicky beer cheese. I can't get enough of either.

Bowling Green

Duncan Hines
Flying the American Roadways

More than just a name emblazoned on a box of cake mix, Duncan Hines was America's pioneer restaurant critic. Long before the Zagat folks were on the scene, before Jane and Michael Stern penned their first sentence of polysyllabic praise for a highway hash house, this silver-haired printing salesman was plying the American roadways in search of good food and clean lodging, making note of which North Carolina restaurant broiled the best T-bone steak and who baked the best pecan pie in Alabama.

> "The finest lemon pie I ever had was in a town of fifty people. It cost ten cents."

At first he just shared his finds with friends and colleagues. But in 1935 Hines compiled a list of his favorites and mailed out 1,000 or so copies as a Christmas card. The next year, he published an enlarged version titled *Adventures in Good Eating*. And by 1939 he was selling more than 100,000 copies of the guide a year, more than enough to quit his sales position in Chicago and return home to Bowling Green, Kentucky.

Not long ago, no well-stocked glove box was without a copy of Duncan Hines' guidebook.

At a time when auto-owning Southerners were first taking to the highways en masse, Hines' no-nonsense reviews were a balm to the anxious traveler worrying where he might find a good hot meal so far from home. Like his readers, Hines was not a man easily seduced by linen napkins and silver cutlery. "The finest lemon pie I ever had was in a town of fifty people,"

An admirer presents a love offering of cornbread muffins.

he once said. "It cost ten cents. One of the poorest was in a large New York hotel. That cost forty cents."

Travelers trusted Hines, could identify with his simple appraisals, his blunt writing style. "The food is plain but wholesome," he wrote of the Mimosa Tea Room in Baxley, Georgia. Of New Orleans' famed Arnaud's, he noted only, "This restaurant is a favorite with native New Orleans people. Superb shrimp dressing is in demand."

Though Hines prided himself on his integrity—arriving unannounced at restaurants and paying for all his own meals—late in his career he did agree to an endorsement deal, lending his name to a line of cookware and foodstuffs. In 1956, three years prior to his death, Procter & Gamble purchased Hines' cookware and foodstuff lines as well as the right to market his guides and plaster his visage on their pasteboard boxes of cake mix.

Judy's Castle

I spent the better part of one winter morning seeking out a Bowling Green restaurant which I imagined would earn Duncan Hines' approval. He was a particular cuss, and the search was not an easy one, for Bowling Green now boasts one of the largest ratios of chain restaurants to people in America. But by lunchtime I found my spot, Judy's Castle. Their motto: "No hassle at the castle."

Locals recall the days when Herb and Maxine Lowe ran the little diner back in the 1960s. "Herb used to call everybody Dingler," a fellow in a corner booth told me. "And his wife, Maxine, well, she ruled the place with an iron fist. The Castle was the place we skipped first period class to eat biscuits and hang out. They were yeast biscuits, and in good weather, they rose up to two or three inches high. In bad weather, they were flat as they could be. It didn't matter."

Today, the Durbins, a husband and wife team, are in charge, with Paul at the stove and Felicia working the dining room floor. Salmon patties on Monday, chicken and dumplings on Tuesday, stuffed green peppers on Wednesday, and white beans cooked to a porridge, sweet potatoes in a citrusy syrup, and dressing full of sage and celery most every day: the menu reads like a hit parade of honest country cooking. And though the setting is far from grand, the Durbins keep a clean Castle, likely to win Hines' seal of approval.

Biscuits made every morning from scratch rarely last until lunch, but I was lucky enough to snag the last one, a slight disk of bone-white bread with a high crown and a cottony interior. "I learned from this ole bowlegged good ole country girl by the name of Tina Potter, who used to work with the Lowes," Paul told me. "That was the first thing I did when we bought this place, was ask her to teach me how to make the biscuits. My customers would have run me out of town if I hadn't learned how to make them. We respect the reputation this place has built up over the years. When we bought it back in '94, all we changed were the locks."

1302 Highway 31 West Bypass / 270-842-8736

Burkesville

Corner Pool & Lunch

I am willing to hazard a guess that chocolate gravy is a dish most often enjoyed in the upland South. Though I have heard of it being served in the Arkansas Delta and also in the piney woods of southern Georgia, in my travels I have seen it on but two restaurant menus: the Kountry Kitchen in Moulton, a town in the foothills of Alabama, and the Corner Pool & Lunch, in the southern Kentucky town of Burkesville.

Of those two spots, only the Corner Pool & Lunch, a onetime bus stop–cum–recreation parlor and now a tidy café, raises chocolate gravy–drenched biscuits to a high art. Owner Azure Grider starts from scratch, laying a foundation of homemade biscuits on the front counter for all to see. On the stove, a cast-iron skillet of creamy sausage gravy burbles; beside that rests a battered tin pan half-filled with water, in which floats a second pan, brimming with chocolate gravy, rich as sin, dark as Satan's black heart.

I order a chocolate gravy biscuit and watch Azure spring into action, retrieving a warm biscuit from a soup kettle where he keeps his stash. A twist of the wrist and the biscuit cleaves in two. Azure places the biscuit halves on the plate, interior sides down, "so that they don't turn to mush from soaking up the gravy, and so you can cut into them easy with your fork." Azure reaches for a ladle of molten chocolate, enrobes the biscuit halves, and slides it onto the counter. I sink my fork into the goo, noticing only now that there is a freckle-faced kid sitting three stools down with a wide-mouth vessel of chocolate gravy before him, a spoon in hand. Somewhere beneath the brown lagoon that fills his bowl, I assume there must be a biscuit.

500 Court House Square / 270-864-2735

Cadiz

Doug Freeman
Ham Man

The Italians wouldn't put up with this. Imagine some governmental agency coming between the good citizens of Rome and their supply of *prosciutto di Parma*. And you can be sure that the French would raise a ruckus if Parisians were cut off from their artisanal sources for *saucisson sec*.

But for the most part, we Southerners just knuckled under when the U.S. Department of Agriculture declared that unless a ham is cured in a USDA-inspected facility, it cannot be commercially transported across state lines or served in a restaurant. In other words, Trigg County ham producers like Doug Freeman and Charlie Bell Wadlington, Tennie Vanzant and Kerry Fowler, who like their fathers and grandfathers before them put up hams the old-fashioned way, could no longer ship their product to customers in the Carolinas, much less California, nor could they sell their hams to the local café.

> "My wife and I used to sell our hams to pay our fertilizer bill. Those days are gone."

Never mind that nary a soul has ever fallen ill from ingesting a true country ham, while outbreaks of botulism seem to be rife in our nation's baloney and hot dog processing plants. "That's as poor a law as I've ever heard of," Doug Freeman tells me when I stopped by his farm to pick up one of those teardrop-shaped beauties hanging in the back of his smokehouse. "I remember when I was a boy everybody up and down the road killed their own hogs. My father used to buy his groceries on credit and settled up with the store when he brought in those hams. Some years they even owed him money. My wife and I used to sell our hams to pay our fertilizer bill. Those days are gone."

Traditionally the cycle starts sometime around November, soon after cold weather sits in for good. After the hogs are butchered and the lard rendered, hams are trimmed of excess fat and submerged in a vat of salt with perhaps a little sugar added to the mix. There the hams rest for a period of two to five weeks before being wiped down and hung to cure.

Ask twenty folks what is best done next and you're likely to get

"A butcher with one of those saws will spray the ham with dust. But if you do it yourself and you're real careful, you can slice it up nice and clean."

twenty different answers. Some smoke their hams for a few days over smoldering hickory while others like Freeman add a bit of sassafras wood to the mix. Most agree that hams must go through what are called the summer sweats, wherein excess moisture not coaxed out by time spent in the salt trickles away during the infernal heat of summer.

Nearly a year passes before Freeman pulls his hams down from the rafters of the family smokehouse. Curing a country ham takes patience, but with the first bite you will soon resolve that it is worth any amount of money, any length of wait, for the meat is as sublime a treat as you are likely to ever sample: smoky, sweet, and bracingly salty if sliced and fried, salt-kissed and mellow if boiled.

And though you may curse the government regulations that are to blame for a decided drop in ham production by some of the old masters, there is an ancillary benefit to this unwarranted governmental intrusion: if you travel to Trigg County, you get to meet kind folks like Doug Freeman. Ask nicely, and he'll give you a lesson in carving that lovely hunk of hog flesh, so that you can avoid flecks of what Doug calls sawdust and you might recognize as bone dust. "A butcher with one of those saws will spray the ham with dust," says Doug. "But if you do it yourself and you're real careful, you can slice it up nice and clean."

605 New Hope Road / 270-522-8900

N.B.: Doug Freeman is angling to retire any day now. If he can't take care of you, Colonel Bill at Newsom's Country Hams will.

Newsom's Country Hams
208 East Main Street / Princeton / 270-365-2482

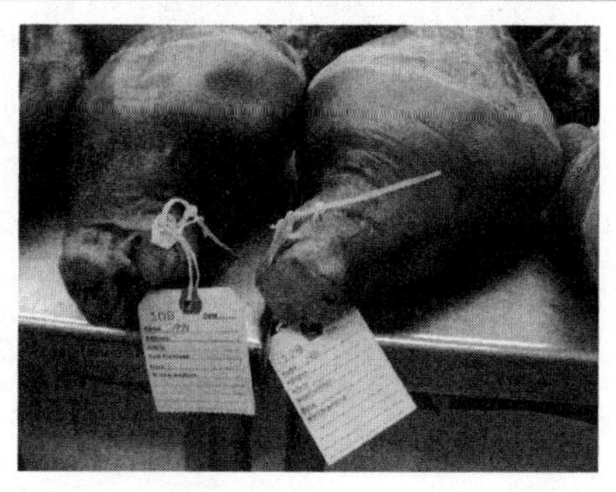

Still life with cured pork haunch.

Corbin

Birthplace of Kentucky Fried Chicken

Tolstoy came late to the bicycle, learning how to ride at the age of sixty-seven. Harland Sanders, of Kentucky Fried Chicken fame, did not begin actively franchising his fried chicken business until the age of sixty-five. Before then Sanders had worked as a farmhand, studied law by correspondence course, sold insurance, manned a steamboat ferry, and operated filling stations, most famously at a little spot on Highway 25, one-half mile north of Corbin.

What began as a modest service station grew quickly and Sanders added a small café and later motel rooms. "I had a little room in the corner of the service station about fifteen-foot square that was used for storage," Sanders wrote in *Life as I Have Known It Has Been Finger Lickin' Good*. "About a month after I had been there I went and got me a piece of linoleum for sixteen dollars on credit . . . I put that down on the floor and wheeled the family dinin' room table into the room. We had six chairs, so that was our restaurant seating capacity."

Thanks to the quality of his cooking, and a flare for showmanship that would give P. T. Barnum pause, Sanders' fame grew exponentially. Governor Ruby Laffoon made him a Kentucky colonel in 1935, and by 1939 fellow Kentuckian Duncan Hines was touting the Colonel's fried chicken and country ham in his *Adventures in Good Eating* guides. But there was trouble ahead. In the 1950s a new interstate highway was planned, bypassing the now-thriving Harlan Sanders Court and Café.

Rather than move, the Colonel—by that time sixty-five years of age—auctioned off his business and soon was on the road, selling franchise rights to restaurateurs interested in replicating his pressure-cooked fried chicken, seasoned with those famous eleven herbs and spices. For more than ten years he traveled across the country by car, cooking batches of chicken for restaurant owners and their employees. If the restaurant owner liked what he tasted, Sanders struck a handshake deal that required a nickel payment for each chicken dish sold.

By 1964 the white-suited dandy had more than 600 franchise outlets in the U.S. and Canada. That same year, he sold his interest in the U.S. company for $2 million to a group of investors. Though the Colonel remained a public spokesman for the company, in his later years he would complain that, as interpreted by corporate

America, his beloved Kentucky Fried Chicken now tasted like "nothing more than a fried doughball wrapped around some chicken."

Harrodsburg

Beaumont Inn

At the Beaumont Inn, situated in a former finishing school for young ladies built in 1845, the columned main house is staid, the floral-wallpaper-flocked dining room almost dowdy. But the ham that emerges from this kitchen is the best that you're likely to taste in a restaurant. The secret, according to the kitchen staff at the Beaumont, is that they purchase one-year-old hams from a local producer and then promptly hang them for one more year before serving.

The resulting two-year beauty is a paragon of pork—salty, sweet, savory, and just a tad bit earthy. Served with matchbook-sized biscuits made with lard, an exemplary corn pudding that threatens collapse under its own caloric heft, and a bevy of other Southern vegetables, this is a swoon-inducing meal.

After dinner, drunk on ham and hospitality (the folks at the Beaumont are exceedingly nice), I need a place to collapse, so I make my way to the front porch and snag one of the rocking chairs. As the cicadas sing and my food settles, I make inquiries as to how one might purchase a two-year-old ham like the Beaumont serves. I am rebuffed, politely but firmly. "You can't get this kind of cooking anywhere else but at home," says the fellow in the next rocker. "Two-year-old hams never leave the farm where they were cured. Count yourself lucky, son."

638 Beaumont Inn Drive / 859-734-3381

Lexington

Spalding's Bakery

Too many storied institutions renovate or expand with an eye toward reinvention. Often, a funky roadside joint with a hard-earned patina begets a soulless aircraft hangar with aluminum siding.

I'm not advocating poverty as style. Many Southern food institutions start in private homes, at backyard pits, on side porches. Others evolve from convenience stores or corner groceries. Those locations are not born of romantic instinct. They are necessary compromises. Once a certain degree of success is achieved, the building of a true storefront is not an exercise in hubris; it's the realization of a dream delayed.

But food, as a literary theorist might argue, is as much about context as text. Too much gussying wipes clean the memories cultivated over decades of operation. The vibe suffers. And so do the pleasures of eating.

Spalding's Bakery, a Lexington fixture since 1929, recently moved from a downtown Victorian storefront to new quarters, on a ragtag stretch of roadway, across from Jif peanut butter plant. The new place isn't nouveau. It's a faithful replication of the old, with a bigger and better kitchen tacked on the rear.

Martha Edwards, granddaughter of founder B. J. Spalding, is the one who, in consultation with her uncle, James Spalding, curated the vibe. She's also the baker most devoted to their caramel-icing-draped cinnamon buns. The exterior recalls the old location. Same redbrick. Similar white-framed picture windows. Inside, stark white walls, wooden showcases polished to a sheen, and a scroll-embossed National cash register.

Alongside the register is a feeder roll of tissue paper, a stack of white pasteboard boxes, and a ball of twine for securing those boxes once Martha and her fellow family members stack them with, among other lovelies, cinnamon buns, carrot cupcakes, and honey-glazed donuts.

Speaking of donuts, I can say without equivocation that Spalding's yeast-raised and honey-glazed trademarks did not suffer in the relocation. They are among the best available in the South. Unlike machine-made antiseptic products cranked out perfectly round and unerringly glazed by the gross, Spalding's serves craggy circles of dough that are crunchy on the outside, cottony on the inside, and slicked with a honey icing that is gobsmackingly good.

780 Winchester Drive / 859-252-3737

Louisville

Brown Hotel

Thanks in part to the season of parties that culminates in the annual run for the roses at Churchill Downs, Louisville has enjoyed a long and well-deserved reputation as the citadel of high society in the Bluegrass state. And for much of the city's history, the Brown Hotel has been the epicenter of the social whirl. Debutante parties, Christmas balls, weddings by the score: the Brown has been the address of import since the doors opened in 1923.

Brian Logsdon and Joe Castro, deep in the bowels of the Brown Hotel kitchen.

And it was here, just a few short years after the hotel opened, that the Hot Brown sandwich was created by chef Fred K. Schmidt. Though guests of the day dined in grand style on caviar and lobster, sweetbread croquettes, and strawberries Romanoff, by the wee small hours of the morning when the band ceased playing, most were clamoring for a late-night breakfast. Schmidt, bored with cooking platter after platter of ham and eggs, did what cooks have been doing from time immemorial; he tried something new. In an oral-history interview collected by the hotel, a former employee recalled the very night: "[Schmidt] said, 'I have an idea for an open-faced turkey sandwich with mornay sauce over it.' At that time turkeys were used only for Thanksgiving and Christmas, and they had just started selling them year-around. I said, 'That sounds a little flat'; and the chef said, 'I'm going to put it under the broiler.' The maitre d' said, 'It should have a little color, too.' So Schmidt said, 'We'll put two strips of bacon on it.' I said, 'How about some pimento,' and that's how the Hot Brown came to be."

Though the sandwich has long since been adopted by seemingly every restaurant in Kentucky, with each adding its own little fillip, from replacing the mornay with low-rent sausage gravy to substituting highfalutin smoked salmon for the turkey, the Brown Hotel still serves the city's definitive Hot Brown. On a recent Saturday morning I took a seat in the hotel's J. Graham's Restaurant and sank into an overstuffed chair to await my prize. In short order it arrived in a brown faux skillet made of crockery, trailing scents of toasted cheese and fried bacon. The mornay sauce was still burbling when my waiter presented the dish with a flourish. One forkful and I knew I was in the presence of something special, a dish unparalleled in its richness, its reckless disregard for dietary restraint. Within moments I was wiping the last bits of mornay from the skillet with a toast point. Two cups of hot coffee later I was able to clamber to my feet, sated but woozy.

335 WEST BROADWAY STREET / 502-583-1234

For the Brown Hotel's legendary **Hot Brown Sandwich** recipe, see page 125.

BENEDICTINE SPREAD

Mayonnaise-rich sandwich spreads are a constant of Southern life. In Smithfield, Virginia, they grind yesterday's country ham trimmings, mix in a bit of mustard and mayonnaise, maybe a taste of relish, and slather it on store-bought white bread. In Oxford, Mississippi, my friend Mary Hartwell Howorth concocts a devilish tub of pimento cheese about once a week, adding yard onions and sage to a mix of shredded cheese, chopped pimentos, and mayonnaise. She likes it spread on rye or rough wheat. And from Charlotte, North Carolina, to Conway, Arkansas, you can bet that when the local garden club gathers for a white-glove ladies luncheon, chicken salad–stuffed finger sandwiches, served sans crust, will be front and center.

But only in Kentucky are you likely to taste that singular spread known as Benedictine, for it was here in the city of Louisville that Miss Jennie Benedict first stirred up a batch, and it is here—and perhaps only here—that the sight of a tub of green, cucumber-spiked spread of mostly mayonnaise and cream cheese elicits not shock but salivation.

Born at Harrods Creek, Kentucky, in 1830, Miss Jennie founded her Louisville catering company in 1893, working from a small kitchen behind her house. To announce the opening of her business she printed 500 fliers offering "to take orders, from a cup of chocolate to a large reception, sandwiches on short order, cakes large or small, trays and dainty dishes for the invalid."

Though Benedictine spread was not among her original offerings, Miss Jennie began serving it while operating a tearoom in later years. After catering a St. Louis wedding reception just before World War I, Benedictine spread won her such acclaim that the Missouri city is reputed to have offered Miss Jennie a guaranty of $1 million in business should she choose to relocate. Louisvillians raised such a hue and cry at the thought of losing dear Miss Jennie that she resolved to stay put, observing, "So great was the pressure brought to bear, that I promptly abandoned the thought of even considering such a move."

Miss Jennie died in 1928. In the ensuing years it seems that all of Louisville has attempted to replicate her recipe. None have quite succeeded, but I favor the restaurants and caterers who amp up the brightness of the mix by adding a healthy slug of green food coloring.

Flabby's Schnitzelburg

Settled in the 1850s by German Catholics in search of religious refuge, Germantown has, over the decades, expanded to include Paris Town, a French Huguenot enclave, and Schnitzelburg, a triangle-shaped German neighborhood within a neighborhood. In redbrick Louisville, it's a place apart, where clapboard shotguns and camelbacks are the primary housing stock.

Corner taverns, working-class dens of equity, serve as de facto living rooms for the neighborhood. Huelsman's 19th Hole, Steve and Judy's, Check's Café, the Old Hickory Inn—all serve beer. Most serve food, which prompts local wags to refer to the assemblage of a dozen or so bars as the Germantown Food Court.

The menus reveal. Fried fish platters and sandwiches are holdovers from the days when Catholics didn't eat meat on Fridays. The prevalence of bean soup speaks to the prominence of Appalachian expatriates. Fried chicken is, depending upon your prejudices, a totem of Louisville's Midwestern or Deep Southern populations.

Flabby's, which began as a grocery store in the 1890s and morphed into a tavern in the 1950s under the ownership of Jim "Flabby" Devine, serves the traditional Germantown bill of fare. But they tend a little more retro than most. Bratwurst and

A workingman's palace.

kraut, limburger on rye with hot beer mustard, and senfschnitzel (pounded and breaded pork with egg and dill sauce) are all a part of the daily rotation.

No matter, I go simple when I grab a stool at this warhorse of a restaurant and bar, ordering a pork schnitzel sandwich on a seeded white bun. The name may be German but the taste is Southern. Fried hard and dressed with gobs of mayonnaise, it's the perfect ballast for beer drinking, which is, after all, the customary activity of tavern-goers.

On my way out the door, I notice that the catercorner Old Hickory Inn has installed one of those scrolling, electronic banner signs to advertise its adherence to working-class values. Hereabouts, that translates into disdain for nonsmoking ordinances, love of weekend karaoke, and support for American troops stationed overseas.

1101 Lydia Street / 502-637-9136

Mazzoni's

In 1884, at a time when oysters were so plentiful that barkeeps tossed in a couple with each drink sold, two brothers—Angelo and Phillippe—immigrated to Louisville from Pietranera, Italy, and opened a downtown saloon. Beer by the keg, whiskey by the barrel, and oysters by the croaker sack: the brothers Mazzoni worked to slake the thirst and sate the hunger of the working-class men of Louisville.

During those early years Phillippe journeyed back to Italy each summer, almost invariably returning with a nephew in tow, putting him to work in the family saloon. After numerous transatlantic crossings, he decided to remain in his homeland, and by 1909 Angelo was the Mazzoni in charge. Today, his great-grand-nephew Greg Haner is keeper of the family history, protector of the Mazzoni legacy, trustee of the fabled rolled oyster, a dish that my friend Ronni Lundy once described as "steamy and sexy, ocean-tanged, barroom sullied, low-rent, and high art."

Rolled oysters are nothing more than fist-shaped croquettes of three to five mollusks, dusted with cracker meal, dipped in a murky flour and water mixture called pastigna, rolled in seasoned cracker crumbs, and fried hard. Served in a small monkey bowl filled with oyster crackers, it's as localized a specialty as you are likely to ever come across, unless you take into account the dishes called oyster knuckles once popular in some Nashville saloons.

Though the original downtown location closed some years back, Greg has managed to preserve the feel of an old saloon at this suburban outpost. Above, a pressed tin ceiling looms. Behind the bar a wide mirror captures the manic pace of the countermen as they work to open beers and sling bowls of oyster rolls, platters of tamales, and sandwiches of fried codfish on rye to waiting customers.

Greg moves the fastest, keeping up a friendly banter with waiting customers who have stopped in for a roll, a beer, and a bit of barroom gossip. It's a role that he was born to play, indeed was reared to play. In a day when veteran restaurateurs can claim two decades in the restaurant business, Greg's family has served Louisville in three different centuries.

2804 Taylorsville Road / 502-451-4136

Suburban Social Club

Louisville is a city of clubs. Perhaps it is attributable to the city's long status as an industrial center, where unions held sway and men banded together for the common good. Maybe it's a vestige of the day when newly arrived immigrants gathered on weekends to sing songs of their homeland and savor the foods of their youth. No matter, Louisville is a city of joiners.

In addition to the inevitable Jaycee and Civitan, Kiwanis and Optimist, Elk and Moose clubs, many men of the Germantown neighborhood claim membership in the All Wool and a Yard Wide Democratic Club, a fraternity united by an unwavering allegiance to the party of FDR and a tradition of Friday afternoon fish fries held throughout the spring and summer. Though their tradition is strong, their fish flaky and fine, the good Democrats can't hold a candle to the men of the Suburban Masonic Lodge, who since the early 1920s have been holding a Saturday afternoon fish fry that draws devotees from throughout the city.

Situated on Louisville's South End in a neighborhood once popular with the families of railroad men who worked on the L&N, or Louisville and Nashville line, the Suburban Lodge has been part and parcel of the fabric of working-class Louisville since its founding in 1902. What began as a way to raise funds for lodge expenses has become a one-day feast that has generated hundreds of thousands of dollars for local children's charities.

I arrive midafternoon, during the slight lull between lunch and dinner. No matter, there is still a line stretching back from the counter along the concrete-block wall. Thirty-odd tables are scattered about the meeting hall, but there's hardly a seat to be had. Up front, a man with a floppy fish hat on his head and a smile on his face is making change and handing out brown paper bags stuffed full of fish sandwiches. By the time customers make the door, a grease stain blooms from the bottom of the bags.

I watch the men skeining the fish from monstrous deep fryers with nets that look like they were made for oversized goldfish. The choices are simple: fish by the pound, fish by the plate, fish by the sandwich. And, though bream and spot, channel cats and pan flounder, may be more often thought of as favorite Southern fishes, here things are different. "It's all cod, it's all fried, it's all good," says a fellow in line beside me.

In short order I retrieve my prize and rather than beat a path to the car, I settle at a table, rip open the bag, peel back the rye bread that has begun to melt into the surface of the sandwich, and sprinkle on a bit of the chopped, marinated onions that come with each order. Taking the lead of everyone around me, I forgo a spritz of cocktail or tartar sauce. The fish is as toothsome and sweet as I have ever tasted, a convincing argument that what makes for good fried fish is hot oil and an experienced hand, not fancy batter mixes or proximity to the sea.

A few days later I talk with John Rupley, a retired railroad switchman who has been a member of the lodge since the 1950s. He sets me straight on why their fish is so good, their weekly gathering so popular: "We've been doing this for a long time. We buy only the best, premium grade Icelandic cod from the coldest waters. And we fry it hard in hot oil. It's that simple. I don't like to talk figures but we go through about a ton of it each Saturday. It takes thirty men to run the operation but we're happy to do it. In many ways it's a social activity for us; it's part of being a Mason."

3901 South Third Street / 502-368-3161

Owensboro

Moonlite Bar-B-Que Inn

Throughout much of the South, the preferred barbecue meat is pork. Sure there may be a few closeted beef lovers in Arkansas, perhaps there's a scattering of possum aficionados in southern Alabama, but for the most part the pig reigns supreme—except along the Ohio River in northwestern Kentucky, where in cities like Owensboro and Henderson, mutton—mature lamb—is the meat of choice.

In the late summer and early fall, parish picnics sponsored by local Catholic churches have been a draw since the early 1800s when Welsh and Dutch settlers made their way into the region, sheep in tow. One of the first written references to barbecue mutton is an 1806 account of the wedding feast of Thomas Lincoln and Nancy Hanks, the parents of Abraham Lincoln.

Today, taste for the gamy meat remains localized and unimpeachable. Some businesses have taken to printing wallet-sized cards embossed with the summer season's roster of church barbecues, which in any other Kentucky community would boast the local high school basketball team's schedule. And though locals might argue that the best barbecue mutton and burgoo—a huntsman's concoction somewhat similar to Brunswick stew—are to be found only at these picnics, quite a few Owensboro

restaurants do a fine job with the stuff, including George's, Old Hickory, Shady Rest, and the Moonlite Bar-B-Que Inn.

As a rule, I like underdogs, unsung heroes, and unlikely champions. I prefer restaurants more likely to be touted by a tubby cop on the beat than a glitzy billboard towering above an interstate exit ramp. Yet, despite its status as the biggest barbecue joint in town, despite the omnipresent advertising and rampant commodification—everything from sponsorship of a stock car to production of canned burgoo offered for sale in local supermarkets—I can't help but like the Moonlite.

The family that cooks together stays together. Just ask the Bosleys, pictured here in the pits at Moonlite.

It's a sprawling behemoth of a restaurant, surrounded by a good acre of black asphalt. Forklifts loaded down with hickory ricks scoot from one building to the other. Sheep carcasses arrive by the trailer load. A monstrous pagoda-style pit sits at the center of the kitchen, fueled by a subterranean firebox stoked with hickory coals.

The mutton itself is surprisingly subtle, kissed by a touch of smoke, a hint of lamb-like whang. Doused with a glug of Worcestershire-spiked black-dip barbecue sauce, the ribs (really chops) are my favorites, for they benefit from a thin vein of fat that runs along the bone, keeping the meat comparatively juicy. The burgoo is a textbook version thick with corn and potatoes, onions, chicken, and yes, mutton.

And despite the restaurant's size and fame—Calvin Trillin once sang the praises of their mutton in a *New Yorker* article—it's still a family-focused company, not too far removed from the day in 1963 when Hugh Bosley Sr., furloughed from his distillery job, raised the capital to purchase a little barbecue stand by selling the family home. Today, more than a dozen Bosley kith and kin run the place. Chances are, most days, you'll spot Ken Bosley by the register and Janet Bosley Howard walking the dining-room floor. Oh, and if you happen to take note of a table tent promoting the sale of white zinfandel by the glass, look the other way. Even the best in the business get some things wrong.

2840 West Parish Avenue / 270-684-8143

Starnes' Barbecue

"You can go thirty or forty miles from here just across the river and the barbecue will be different," says pitman Tim Starnes, grandson of restaurant founder Floyd Starnes. "They might do their meat different, their sauce different. It's all different out there. But we do it the way we've always done it, cooking over hickory for ten to twelve hours. And all our sandwiches get toasted, always have. We're scared of change. We get a lot of ribbing about the color of the paint on this place," he says, his arms sweeping wide to take in a lime-green cinder-block building that would seem more at home in Miami Beach. "I know in my heart that if we painted it a different color, our business would fall off."

Tim's family business has been a part of Paducah since 1958. Though the surrounding neighborhood has changed—across the way the Dragon House Chinese restaurant looms with an eighty-item buffet—Starnes' remains reassuringly hidebound. The spare interior is a throwback to the 1950s: nineteen stools and two booths set around a horseshoe-shaped counter with an island at the center. Bottles of sauce line the counter; a vinegary smell lingers in the air. On the day I visit, I am one of two customers, the other an older gentleman—a hunter—who stopped in for a sandwich and a quote on getting a shoulder of venison smoked. "Fifty cents a pound," comes the reply from Tim.

The gentleman wolfs down his sandwich in four quick bites and is gone. Moments later my own sandwich arrives. Wrapped tight in a blanket of waxed paper, it is as tidy a barbecue sandwich as I have ever seen. No hunks of meat spilling out of a bun, no sauce smearing the wax paper, just finely chopped pork—crunchy with outside meat—doused with a lively vinegar and pepper sauce, served between two slices of wasp's nest white bread, the whole affair smashed flat and toasted brown by one of those mysterious machines that resembles a clothes press. I offer my compliments to Tim but he shrugs them off: "It's what we've been doing since day one. Like I told you, we're scared of change."

1008 Joe Clifton Drive / 270-444-9555

Winchester

Hall's on the River

Gone are the days when bar food meant a pickled egg, swimming in a brine tinted pink by beet juice, or a pig's foot put up by the barkeep at a neighbor's hog killing. Today, Buffalo chicken wings are as much a barroom menu fixture in Bardstown, Kentucky, as they are in Buffalo, New York, the city of their birth. But a few peculiar bar food favorites endure, rarely seen elsewhere. In Kentucky fried banana peppers and beer cheese top the list.

Though the historical record is scant (bars tend to leave few records save old debt ledgers), general consensus holds that both were born on the Kentucky River, in the wilds south of Lexington. Over at Hall's, a riverfront restaurant and tavern of Colonial vintage near Winchester, they claim a lineage that goes back to the 1930s when Johnny Allman, a onetime captain of the Kentucky Highway Patrol, ran a riverside tavern widely credited with introducing the two items. (That said, I have an inkling that at least the beer cheese may have preceded Allman, dating back at least to the days when saloons were inclined to ply drinkers with free eats. Beer cheese represented a novel use for stale beer.)

A description: fried banana peppers are the simplest of the two, butterflied or halved mild pickled peppers, sheathed in batter, fried until brown, and oftentimes served with a spicy cocktail sauce spiked with horseradish. Some versions have a pronounced vinegar nose that seems to rise like a noxious cloud off the plate; others fail because the batter slips off with the first bite. Like the fried dill pickles of Arkansas and Mississippi, though they sound simple enough, fried banana peppers require a deft hand, a good batter, and hot grease.

Beer cheese, also known as snappy cheese, may look like Cheez Whiz, but it's actually pungent, yeasty, garlicky stuff that packs a wallop. Along the river, any number of bars serve up their own take on it, but Hall's wins my vote for the best, if only because they employ Mrs. Jean Bell, who worked under the watchful eyes of Johnny Allman and has been stirring up her version since 1965. Served in pleated, paper specimen cups alongside a selection of crudités, the taste of the neon-orange spread varies from day to day, depending upon the whims of the cook. Don't even think about asking Mrs. Bell for her recipe unless you can take a good tongue lashing. I left the kitchen at Hall's, propelled solely by the withering gaze she cast my way when I was so audacious as to ask whether she preferred to use fresh beer or stale beer when making a batch.

1225 Boonesboro Road / 859-527-6620

Hot Brown Sandwich

from Brown Hotel
Serves 4 to 6

Might as well admit it: this is ideal hangover food, just the kind of thing you crave, say, around 11:00 in the morning, when the bottle is still too much with you. The bland comfort of turkey breast. The salty bite of bacon. The creamy consolation of mornay. And I believe that such an application may well be what Fred K. Schmidt, the Brown Hotel chef, imagined when he first concocted this dish as a late-night feed.

8 to 12 strips bacon
2 tablespoons heavy cream (optional)
1/2 cup (1 stick) unsalted butter
6 tablespoons all-purpose flour
3 to 3 1/2 cups whole milk, room temperature
6 tablespoons freshly grated Parmesan cheese, plus more for garnish
1 large egg, beaten
1 to 1 1/2 pounds roast turkey, thinly sliced

Salt and freshly ground black pepper
8 to 12 slices toasted white bread, (crusts removed, optional)

Heat a large skillet over medium heat. Add the bacon without crowding, and cook, turning once, until crisp, 5 to 7 minutes. Remove to a plate lined with paper towels and keep warm. Repeat with remaining bacon, if needed.

Place the heavy cream, if desired, in a small bowl. Using a whisk, beat until light and fluffy, about 45 seconds. Set aside.

Heat the butter in a medium saucepan over low heat. Blend in the flour, and cook slowly, stirring until the butter and flour foam without coloring. Add the warm milk all at once. Immediately beat vigorously with a whisk to blend the liquid and roux. Bring to a boil and then reduce heat to simmer. Remove from the heat and add the Parmesan cheese and egg. Fold in the whipped cream, if using. Taste and adjust for seasoning with salt and pepper.

For each Hot Brown, place 2 slices of toast on a metal (or flameproof) dish. Cover the toast with a liberal amount of turkey to make an open-faced sandwich. Pour a generous amount of sauce over the turkey and toast. Sprinkle with additional Parmesan cheese. Place the entire dish under a broiler until the sauce is speckled brown and bubbly. Remove from broiler, cross 2 pieces of bacon on top, and serve immediately.

LOUISIANA

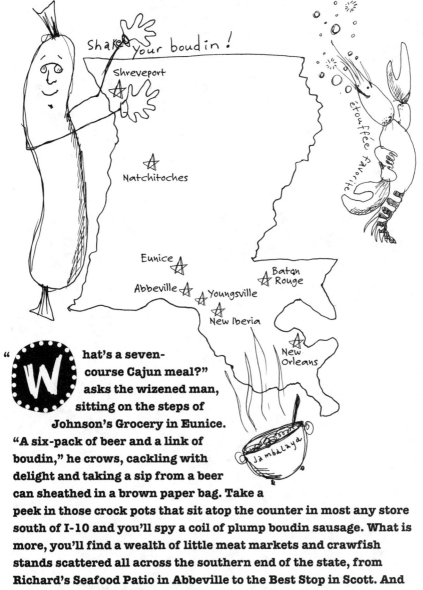

"What's a seven-course Cajun meal?" asks the wizened man, sitting on the steps of Johnson's Grocery in Eunice. "A six-pack of beer and a link of boudin," he crows, cackling with delight and taking a sip from a beer can sheathed in a brown paper bag. Take a peek in those crock pots that sit atop the counter in most any store south of I-10 and you'll spy a coil of plump boudin sausage. What is more, you'll find a wealth of little meat markets and crawfish stands scattered all across the southern end of the state, from Richard's Seafood Patio in Abbeville to the Best Stop in Scott. And then there's New Orleans, where you can't swing a dead cat without hitting a great poor boy shop or oyster house. Meet Tee Eva, who sings, dances, and dishes up a mean pecan pie at her Magazine Street snowball stand. Or lend an ear to the story of Creole chef Eddie Baquet, famous for his gumbo, red beans and rice, and pork chops with oyster dressing.

Abbeville and New Iberia

Oyster Houses

Still life with bivalves and root beer.

Locals like to tell of the days when Joseph Dupuy would pole his skiff down the Vermilion River some twenty miles, harvest bushel after bushel of giant bivalves with a pair of oversized oyster tongs, and then turn around and pole his way back upriver to the little town of Abbeville, where he would sell his prize for a pittance. By 1869 he built a little bar of sorts by the river, catty-corner from the St. Mary Magdalen Catholic Church. In a short while, the cold, salty elegance of the mollusks he pulled from the local waters won Abbeville a reputation as the Cajun Country's premier oyster town.

When Joseph died in 1928, his son Tee-Tut and his wife Loretta took over operations. Their son Roland followed, picking up his first oyster knife at the tender age of ten. The restaurant has seen a few changes in ownership since, including a long stint in the 1980s and 1990s when it was operated by Jack Faris, who now owns a glitzy nearby spot known as Shucks. Today Dupuy's is but one of three oyster bars in this 11,000-person town. Black's joined the fray in 1967 when the Borque family bought out Musemeche's Restaurant around the corner. Shucks followed in 1995.

In the intervening years, all of the Abbeville oyster bars have made moves up market, adding pasta and crab cakes and other folderol. Of the three, Dupuy's retains the most integrity. It has never been a fancy place: terrazzo tile floors, a horseshoe-shaped bar, a few oilcloth-covered tables scattered about the dining room, and a parking lot paved with spent shells. On a recent visit, the oysters, presented on a tray of crushed ice, smacked of salt like they should. Across the street at Black's, now housed in an elegant former dry goods store, I sampled one of the best oyster stews that has ever graced my palate. Thick with chopped celery, onions, and plump oysters with a skein of butter floating on top of the milky

morass, it was pluperfect. Either bar seems a fitting culinary tribute to the old oysterman Joseph Dupuy.

DUPUY'S OYSTER HOUSE / 108 SOUTH MAIN STREET / 337-893-2336
BLACK'S OYSTER BAR / 319 PERE MEGRET STREET / 337-893-4266

CRAWFISH BOILING POINTS

Locals call them boiling points or seafood patios, and they are so prevalent in modern-day Louisiana that it is difficult to imagine they are recent arrivals on the scene. Most are housed in prefabricated metal buildings—oversized garages really—with poured concrete floors and neon beer signs shining from narrow window slits. A few older boiling points are set in concrete-block roadhouses or barn-like structures covered in tar paper or galvanized metal siding.

No matter the setting, the trappings—and menu offerings —are similar. Out back you'll find gargantuan boiling pots perched atop propane-fired flames. Inside, tables often covered in yesterday's newspaper are set with rolls of paper towels and scattered about a bare-bones dining room. There's a sink over in the corner for washing up. The menu is usually pretty simple: crawfish is the primary draw, though shrimp and crab are also offered, depending upon seasonal availability. All are boiled in a fiery slurry of cayenne pepper, salt, and any number of other spices from bay leaf to nutmeg. Boiled potatoes, boiled onions, and boiled corn are the side dishes of choice, though of late, some boiling points have taken to offering everything from gumbo to French fries.

Richard's Seafood Patio

Opened in 1957 by Ovey "Red" Richard, this corrugated-tin-sheathed building is the oldest known boiling point in Cajun Country. "There was another place over in Lafayette that had crawfish on the menu, but they never sold much of it," seventy-something-year-old Red tells me. "Hell, even the filling stations sell boiled crawfish now, but it just wasn't that way when I was coming up. Ask the old-timers around here, they'll tell you I was the first one. I come from a family of meat men. My brother runs Richard's meat market, and I'm the only one in the family that strayed, but I haven't regretted it, no. We got our crawfish out of the rice fields back before they knew to call them crawfish farms. Rice-field crawfish is still the best. They don't have that iodine taste that deep water crawfish get from eating the water lilies in the basin."

When Red retired back in 1983, his son Calvin took over the day-to-day operations, introducing a few innovations of his own, including a custom-crafted, and now patented, crawfish tray with a sliding, partitioned insert to keep the empty shells separate from the mound of crawfish, corn, potatoes, and onions yet to be eaten. But he still cooks crawfish the way his father taught him to, plunging the little critters in a saltwater bath to wash the mud off and induce the crawfish to "spit up," before tossing them in cast-iron kettles burbling with rock salt and red-pepper-spiked water. Though they will sprinkle a bit of extra red pepper on the outside of the crawfish for those who like a lot of heat, Calvin, like his father before him, believes that too much cayenne—especially when sprinkled on the outside—ruins a good tray.

1516 South Henry Street / Abbeville / 337-893-1693

Guiding Star

Like Richard's, the Guiding Star is a simple place, a joint really, with three pool tables on the side and a dining room filled with wood tables papered with old copies of the *Daily Iberian*. There are some who argue that Hawk's over near Rayne serves bigger, better crawfish. Others swear by Crawfish Town USA, a tourist spot just off the interstate in Henderson. Others still dote on D. I.'s in Basile, long popular with locals on Mardi Gras runs.

But for my money, if the Guiding Star is not the best, then it's surely among the best boiling points in the state. It's a simple formula, really: cold, cold long-neck beers, and fat, sweet, fiery crawfish, seasoned with Tabasco mash, the sludge left after the vinegary liquid has been drained from an aged cask of Tabasco. Owner Ralph Shaubert buys his mash by the cask, but should you be in the area, you can stop by the Tabasco plant on Avery Island and pick up a two-quart plastic bag of the fiery stuff for a couple of dollars.

4404 Highway 90 West / New Iberia / 337-365-9113

Baton Rouge

Silver Moon Café

Most everything that issues forth from the kitchen of proprietor Seabell Thomas leaves in a bowl: delicious white beans, soupy, salty, and chock-full of pork; jambalaya, larded with strands of dark-meat chicken and spicy sausage; and even, on occasion, fried chicken, crisp as can be. "That's so nothing gets away from you," says Mrs. Thomas, a white kerchief fixed on her head and a bean-splattered apron tied around her waist. "We serve that way so everything stays right where we put it. If it was on a plate, you might lose some of that good gravy over the side."

The Silver Moon is instantly recognizable to me. Like Mama Dip's in Chapel Hill, North Carolina, and late and lamented Mama Lo's in Gainesville, Florida, it's a black-owned, black-run restaurant, dispensing home cooking to an integrated crowd.

On the day I visit, the parking lot is packed with late-model Volkswagens, Toyotas, and a couple of BMWs to boot. "I Love Tri-Delt," boasts one bumper sticker. Inside, twelve-odd tables topped with green and white oilcloth are scattered about the concrete-floored dining room. There's not a spare seat to be had. The patrons are almost exclusively white, fresh-faced sorority and fraternity types for the most part. My companion, a newly arrived Northerner, looks confused.

I try to explain that many white Southerners were raised on food cooked by black women. Even if your parents were of meager means, a black cook was oftentimes hired to cook the evening meals, I tell her. And many white Southerners were wet-nursed by black women. So doesn't it stand to reason that when these kids leave home for the first time, many of them end up here, craving the food they grew up eating?

206 West Chimes Street / 225-387-3345

Lionel Key

A Touch of the Green: Uncle Bill's Creole Filé

Filé maker Lionel Key is a proud man. Not boastful, mind you, but proud. Proud of his product, proud to be the inheritor of a family tradition of filé making that began back in the early years of the twentieth century with his late great uncle, Bill Ricard, born blind to a family of farmers in Rougon, Louisiana.

> "You got to hit the maul dead center to get the grind right, to pulverize the leaves fine. . . . It's a real solid sound, like a home-run ball coming off a bat."

As a youth, Ricard cut sugarcane on Alma Plantation near Lakeland, Louisiana. In later years he turned to making filé, grinding sassafras leaves to a fine, dusky-green powder and selling it to neighbors when they came calling for a bit of the green to thicken their gumbo.

In 1982, Lionel began a two-year apprenticeship at the knee of his uncle Bill, learning the art and science of filé making: when to harvest the sassafras leaves, how to cure them, where to store them, and, most important, how to get the grind right, how to properly plunge a pecan-wood maul into the cavity of a cypress stump brimming with dried sassafras leaves until the leaves have been reduced to a powder, fine as silt, fragrant as a spring flower.

"He used to tell me to listen for the sound to tell if I was hitting it right," Lionel recalls. "You got to hit the maul dead center to get the grind right, to pulverize the leaves fine like he taught me. It's a real solid sound, like a home-run ball coming off a bat. The filé ends up much finer. You put some of that machine-ground, commercial stuff in a pot of gumbo and it'll sink to the bottom quick, but my filé is light as a feather; it'll just float on top 'til you stir it in. And the flavor; there's just no comparison. Mine has a bright lemony punch to it."

In 1984 Uncle Bill passed away at the age of ninety, but thanks to Lionel, his legacy lives on. Among the fans of Lionel's filé are some of Louisiana's top chefs. "John Folse, he uses my filé over at Lafitte's Landing in Donaldsonville," says Lionel. "And Leah Chase over in New Orleans, she says mine is the only kind she'll use at her restaurant."

But Lionel is quick to add that most of his customers are just plain folks, intent upon stirring up the best pot of gumbo possible. Some Saturday mornings, you can find him selling recycled baby-food jars full of Uncle Bill's Creole Filé at the Red Stick Farmers' Market in downtown Baton Rouge.

For those unable to make it to Baton Rouge, contact Uncle Bill's Creole Filé at 225-267-9220.

Eunice

Boudin for Breakfast

Despite what the folks at Popeye's Fried Chicken would have you believe, boudin—rice and seasoned ground pork parts stuffed in a sausage casing—is about the closest thing to Cajun fast food. Take a look on the counter of most every convenience store south of I-10 and you'll spy a crock pot by the cash register, full of taut links flecked with green onion and red pepper. Though there was a day when boudin was a by-product of a wintertime boucherie or hog killing, these days it's a year-round treat munched on the go with a cold beer in the afternoon or a hot cup of coffee in the morning.

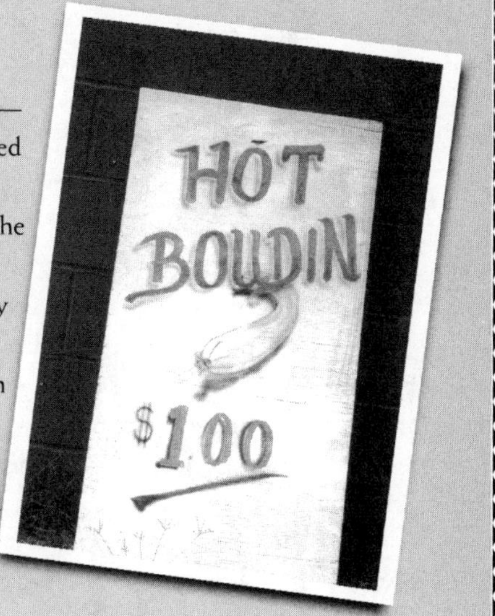

The sign you want to see come breakfast time.

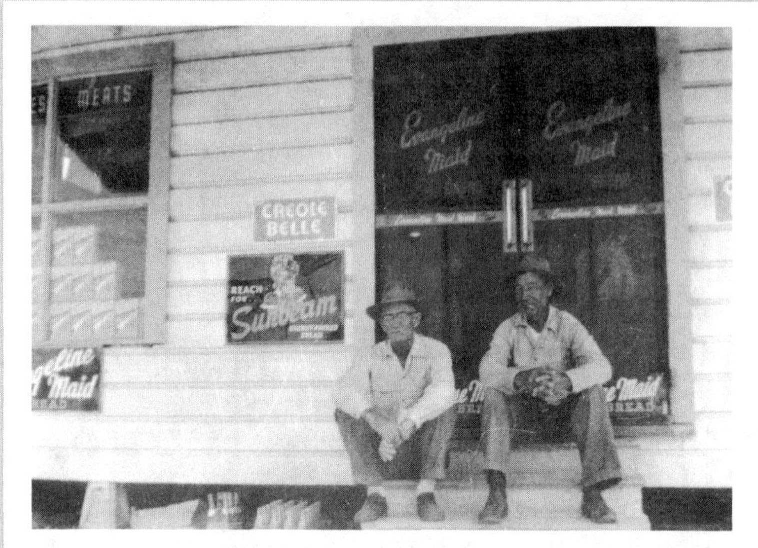

Arneastor Johnson and friend on the porch of the family grocery.

Johnson's Grocery and Best Stop

In Eunice, the Johnson brothers—Wallace, Stephen, and Matthew—have long reigned as the grand old men of the commercial boudin business. When their father, Arneastor Johnson, first opened a little grocery in Eunice back in 1937, boudin was rarely sold retail. Sure, a farmer might bring in a few links he had left over from a boucherie and trade them for a sack of meal, but for the most part, the pork that filled a link of boudin never left the farm on which that pig was slaughtered. That all changed sometime around 1948 when Arneastor took to selling boudin on Saturday mornings.

"Saturday was the traditional day for hog killings," Wallace Johnson told me on an earlier visit. "My mother fixed big batches of rice, and they would cook up the meat, chop the onions and celery and bell peppers, and stuff the sausages with an old cow horn. We went on like that for a while until we added Wednesdays. Then when the oil boom hit bottom a while back, we started making it every day because we do a lot of credit business and selling boudin brought us walk-up business, cash business."

Until recently, the grocery looked little changed from founder Arneastor Johnson's day. The well-oiled wood floors shone; the shelves were stocked with local staples like Community Coffee and Evangeline Maid–brand bread; the smoke-

house out back still clouded most mornings with smoke from a smoldering oak fire. Indeed the only thing Arneastor might not recognize was the little arrow-shaped placard they hung from the ceiling a few years back, pointing the way to the meat counter. It read Rue Boudin, and on many a Saturday morning a line full of tourists and locals alike stretches back from the meat counter, beneath the cardboard arrow, and nearly out the door. At press time, Johnson's was in transition, serving boudin on Thursday through Saturday only, and my allegiance was drifting toward the Best Stop in Scott, where in addition to great boudin, you can snag a bag of cracklins or a stuffed beef tongue .

JOHNSON'S GROCERY / 700 EAST MAPLE AVENUE / EUNICE / 337-457-9314
BEST STOP / 511 HIGHWAY 93 NORTH / SCOTT / 337-233-5805

RUBY'S CAFÉ

Scholar Sidney Mintz argues that for a region to claim a cuisine of its own, it must have an educated, opinionated class of eater, familiar with the nuances of local food and drink. Based on a recent meal at this humble four-stool, eight-table, back-street café, I would argue that no region of the South can claim a greater concentration of such educated eaters than Acadiana. I met five or six of them firsthand while pondering my lunchtime menu choices.

On a battered orange stool to my right sat a man of maybe sixty, extolling the virtues of making coffee "the old fashioned way, like Ms. Ruby does it." When I asked the waitress what he meant, she chimed in with a lengthy exposition on the fine art of brewing café noir. "Ms. Ruby makes a coffee sack out of unbleached cotton cloth," she told me. "And she drapes the ends over the sides of a pot with the sack hanging down and pours the water over that real slow like. When she finishes we pour it in smaller coffeepots and put them in skillets filled with water. They stay over a low flame to keep warm, and the water keeps the coffee from burning."

My next question was directed at a second waitress, embroiled in debate with a clutch of farmers about the prospects for the local crawfish crop. The crawfish were coming in late that year, and, worse yet, they were small. When I asked her whether I should get the pork roast or the stewed and fried shrimp over rice, she fixed me with a look that said, *You ain't from around here, are you, sport?* and asked, "So you don't want the ponce? Why didn't you ask about the ponce?" After assuring her—and the gathering onlookers—that I bore no prejudice against eating pork stomach stuffed with sausage, she steered me toward the shrimp.

What emerged from the little cubbyhole of a kitchen some minutes later is one of the best meals I've ever had the pleasure to eat: a spicy étoufée of shrimp, topped with five or six lacy shrimp, fried in an egg wash and flour batter, the whole affair piled high atop a mound of fluffy white rice. On the side was a lesser puddle of mashed potatoes and a scattering of peas separated by a crescent of cantaloupe. I polished off my plate in no time and asked if it was okay to pop my head in the kitchen to pay my respects to the cook.

I was able to get little information out of Ruby Watts, save that she was born in 1929 and came to work here in 1954 as a waitress when Mae Simmons owned the place. "It's been mine since 1957, honey, now shoo, this is my dinner hour," she said. "And if you come back, you try that pork roast."

N.B.: In the years since my first visit, Ruby Watts passed away. Melinda Aguillard is now the owner, and Theresa Labrano is the cook. They uphold the standards that Miss Ruby set.

221 West Walnut Avenue / Eunice / 337-550-7665

Natchitoches

Cane River Meat Pies

Along the Cane River in the central Louisiana city of Natchitoches, street vendors once peddled meat pies, little crescent-shaped brown bundles stuffed with spiced ground pork, beef, onions, green peppers, and garlic. Inspired by that tradition, James Laysone began making them in the 1960s, first at the Loan Oak Grocery and later at his restaurant, Laysone's Meat Pie Kitchen, still in business down on Second Street.

But locals will tell you that to taste the best that Cane River country has to offer, you've got to have a connection, you've got to know one of the older Creole ladies who still fries up a couple dozen every few days to sell to friends and neighbors. Failing that they will direct you to St. Augustine Church in the nearby community of Isle Brevelle, where on the second weekend of October the church celebrates its anniversary with a fair, selling meat pies by the hundreds to raise funds. In-the-know locals fill their freezers full.

New Orleans

If New Orleans is not the South's premier restaurant city (only Mason, Tennessee, and De Valls Bluff, Arkansas, can mount a challenge based on good eats per capita), then I'll eat my hat, wash it down with castor oil, and follow that with a relevé of nutria tartare. In fact, New Orleans is such a great restaurant city that writing about its food presents me with a problem. In short: Which restaurants do I choose; which dishes do I sample and report back to you, the reader? Which stories do I tell? Do I take you on a tour of the grand old dining rooms like Antoine's, in business since 1840 and famed as the origin point of oysters Rockefeller, or Commander's Palace, the elegant Garden District restaurant run by the Brennan family and once the home kitchen of superstar chefs Emeril Lagasse and Paul Prudhomme?

And what of Prudhomme's restaurant, K-Paul's, a Cajun outpost in a Creole city? Shouldn't any attempt to write about the foods of Louisiana include an homage to this Opelousas native—the man who single-handedly invented blackened redfish and lays claim to having introduced the turducken when he stuffed a trio of deboned fowl filled with aromatic dressings, one inside the other—chicken inside duck inside turkey?

And let's not forget that frumpy French Quarter favorite Galatoire's, where generations of New Orleans swells have cooled their heels out front on the Bourbon Street sidewalk, waiting for a table inside the mirror-flanked dining room famous for crabmeat ravigote, trout Marguery, and café brulôt, among many other seminal Creole dishes prepared with French flair.

A peek inside the kitchen at Antoine's, one of New Orleans' temples of gastronomy.

The restaurant known as Dooky Chase's must be a part of this culinary conversation, too, for it has long been the city's premier destination for Creoles of Color. It opened in 1941 as a sandwich shop, supported in part by the profits that founder Edgar "Dooky" Chase made from an old New Orleans tradition: gambling.

Dooky's did not ascend to the upper echelon of Creole cookery until Leah Chase, the wife of Dooky's son, came to the fore, introducing dishes like shrimp Clemenceau, veal grillades, and chicken breasts stuffed with oyster dressing swaddled in a marchand du vin sauce. Mrs. Chase also expanded the restaurant and outfitted the dining rooms in grand style, hanging a fine art collection including woodcuts

by Elizabeth Catlett and vibrant oil paintings of Mardi Gras Zulu parades by Bruce Brice.

Little known to all but the neighborhood regulars, Dooky's has long run a corner sandwich shop, selling fried oyster poor boys on pan bread, stuffed crabs, and a peppery Creole gumbo. By the time you read this, Leah Chase will be, following a post-Katrina rebuild, back at her store. That gumbo, served in a Styrofoam go-cup, was one of the best I have ever tasted—thick with sausage, crab, and fat sweet shrimp, swimming in a smoky, chocolate-brown liquid spiked with cayenne and thickened with filé.

One taste and my problem was solved: the burden of writing about the long roster of great restaurants in New Orleans lifted. I would write of the gutsy, simple fare of New Orleans rather than the temples of haute cuisine, keeping in mind that Dooky's began as a sandwich shop; Paul Prudhomme was once a skinny kid in knee pants, born in the cross-roads Cajun town of Opelousas; and sixteen-year-old Antoine Alciatore first flung the doors open to a humble "pension" on St. Louis Street back in 1840, serving simple foods to the butchers, bakers, and fish-mongers of the French Market.

Poor Boys

Sandwiches may well be America's most contentious comestible. In Philadelphia, Pennsylvania, they squabble over who was the first to squirt Cheez Whiz on sliced beef and slip it inside a roll. In Miami, Florida, folks debate the relative merits of the mojo-drenched pork-stuffed treats known generically as Cuban sandwiches. But only in New Orleans are you likely to witness a fistfight over who proffers the city's best poor boy and how the storied sandwich got its name.

First the name: The more effete will tell you that *poor boy* is an Americanized elision of the slang term *pour boire*, translated from the French as "for drinks," a reference to the tips left on tables that would presumably buy a beverage for a waiter. That explanation may satisfy some linguists, but most native New Orleanians turn up their noses at such rarefied conjecture.

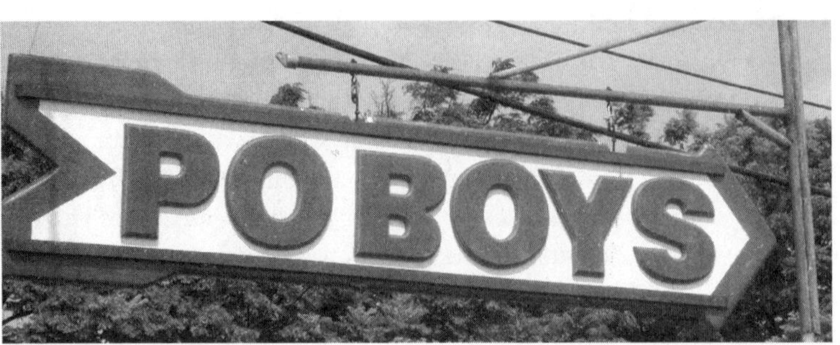

Poor boys are omnipresent.

Ask men of a certain age and they're likely to tell you that the poor boy as we know it was born when the local Streetcar Workers Union, Division 194, went on strike in 1929. Brothers Bennie and Clovis Martin, who ran a sandwich shop first in the French Quarter and later on St. Claude Avenue, were former streetcar conductors, resolved to support their comrades in arms. From July through October the Martin brothers fed the striking men for free, hailing each one, "Here comes another poor boy." Granted, they were not the first to serve a slab of ham or roast beef stuffed inside a loaf of French bread, but they were the most likely men to coin the name. Along with baker John Gendusa, who at their request modified the traditional tapered loaf so that three sandwiches of equal width could be sliced from each, the Martins are the true progenitors of the poor boy.

As for who serves the city's best poor boys, there are as many answers as there are corner sandwich shops. Mother's down on Poydras has its advocates, who swear by their Ferdi Special, a ham and roast beef concoction smothered in gravy, thick with bits of roast beef. Others swear at Mother's and say the lines are too full of tourists, the prices too high. R and O's out by the Lakefront has its fans. So does Domilise's, set on an Uptown side street where the fried shrimp poor boys are fabled. There is no such thing as the definitive poor boy, no way of codifying the sandwich genre and pronouncing one version the best, for even as you read this, another purveyor is opening his doors for the first time, angling to make the best poor boy in the city.

The Croatian Oyster Dynasty

Over the past fifty or sixty years, the New Orleans oyster industry has—forgive the pun—undergone a sea change. The shuckers who work the wholesale trade have shifted from men of Cajun French or Creole ancestry to Vietnamese women.

As for the openers who work the raw bars, they were once owner-operators, Italians and Croatians for the most part. Today, the owners rarely walk the duckboards and the openers are far more likely to be African American or, post-Katrina, Latino.

The Croatian presence, however, remains strong, a vestige of the waves of immigrants from the Dalmation coast who disembarked (or jumped ship) here beginning in the 1840s. In years past there was Gentilich's across from City Hall and Ziblich's on Claiborne. Today, the Cvitanovich family operates Drago's in Metairie, famous for char-grilled oysters on the half shell. Nearby, the Vodanoviches run Bozo's, another suburban outpost with a decidedly suburban feel, equally famous for poor boys overstuffed with corn flour–crusted oysters. "Iches, Viches, and Son-of-a Bitches, we're all Croatian," says Tommy Cvitanovich. "And almost all of us are related."

Bozo's / 3117 Twenty-first Street / Metairie / 504-831-8666
Drago's / 3232 North Arnoult Road / Metairie / 504-888-9254

Hansen's Sno Bliz

According to the Roman calendar, summer begins in June. Try and tell that to a native of subtropical New Orleans. When it comes to marking the seasons down here, calendars don't count for much. Instead, locals with a sweet tooth will tell you that summer arrives on the Saturday after Easter, when Hansen's Sno Bliz throws open their screen door and serves the first customer on a five-month annual run.

New Orleans is chockablock with snowball stands, jerry-rigged roadside huts that dispense cones of shaved ice drenched in a saccharine torrent of syrup. But Hansen's—set in a cinder-block rectangle on Tchoupitoulas Street in the city's Uptown neighborhood—is different. The late Ernest and Mary Hansen were the couple who defined that difference, the husband and wife team responsible for making good on the placard behind the counter, the one that reads, "Air-Condition Your Tummy With a Hansen's Sno Bliz."

In 1934 Ernest decided to build a better snowball. At the time, untold vendors

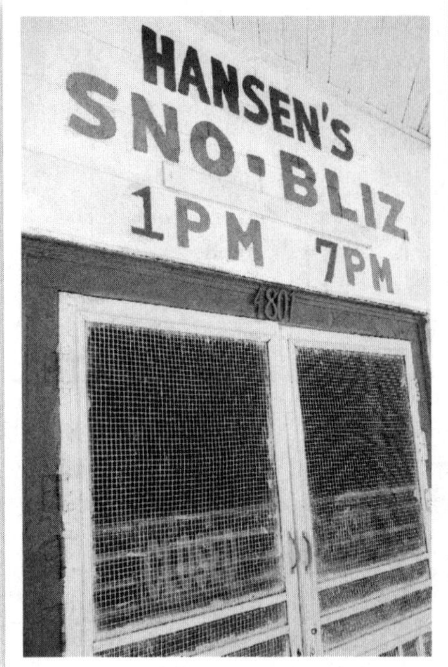

Home of peerless frigid sweets.

worked the streets of the city, rasping ice from oversized Eskimo blocks with the same sort of wood plane your dad might have used to shave down the kitchen door when it stuck. "That never seemed clean to me," he told me. "They always seemed like they got a little dirt in there. I though I could do it better. Figured I could build a machine to shave the ice. " He succeeded. And he earned U.S. Patent 2525923.

Mary developed her own syrups and sold snowballs from a rickety stand in her mother's front yard. She set her price at two cents, when the going rate was a penny. "But we always gave good value," she said. "We always gave three squirts of syrup, one for the Father one for the Son, and one for the Holy Ghost."

Over the years, Hansen's acquired a mystique, an ethic worthy of its status as beloved neighborhood institution. Time and flights of fancy begat a lexicon of confections. What will it be? A baby duper, a duper, or a super-duper size? And then there are the variants on the snowball theme—like the hot dog, a spumoni-like snowball and fruit combo, and the oversized tubs of shaved ice sold to the local frat houses, just ready to be doused with a jolt of Golden Grain.

For the most part, though, the Hansen's have kept it simple. Miss Mary and Mr. Ernest have since passed, but their granddaughter, the beatific Ashley Hansen, still peddles shaved, syrup-stoked ice by the cup and bucket to any and all for five precious months. You might want to mark Hansen's opening date on your calendar for next year. Think of it as the Sno Bliz Solstice.

4801 Tchoupitoulas Street / 504-891-9788

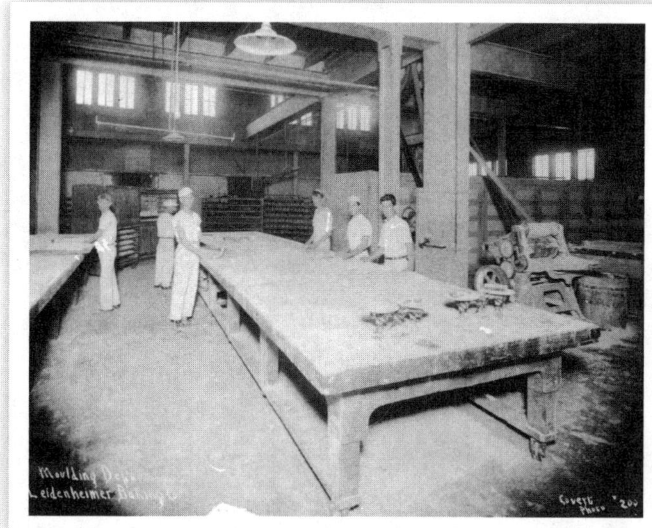

Over the years, little has changed at Leidenheimer's.

Leidenheimer Baking Company

Central Grocery buys their seeded muffuletta rounds here. When constructing hot-sausage poor boys, Parkway Tavern reaches for Leidenheimer-baked flutes. Galatoire's gets its table bread here, the tapered loaves that waiters butter and broil for their best customers. When Antoine's calls to order pistolletes, thinner and crustier cousins to the traditional poor boys loaves, they ask for *bread sticks*, referencing a possible antecedent in *pistou*, the French word for soup.

Founder George Leidenheimer was of German extraction. More than likely, he landed here with a talent for baking hearty ryes. (Back in Deidesheim, Germany, the Leidenheimers still operate the town bakery.) But he adapted quickly to the new-world norm. "There were hundreds of small bakeries then," says his great-grandson Sandy Whann, current-day proprietor. "And they did untold variations on what we know now as French bread."

Some of these are lost to the ages. An early and undated catalog of Leidenheimer offerings includes Rex and Comus breads (named, no doubt, for Mardi Gras krewes), as well as Frog bread, a likely pejorative allusion to the French origins of a particular loaf. The poor boy loaf itself is a bit easier to track. Although Sandy is quick to give credit to the Gendusa Bakery for crafting the first poor boy loaf, he says that Leidenheimer's has introduced its own wrinkles.

"I suspect that back when poor boys were more likely to be stuffed with meat and potatoes, our loaves were heavier, more substantial," says Sandy, reaching for a thirty-two-inch Zip loaf which his restaurant customers will cut into three portions for their poor boys. "As Gulf seafood became more readily available, we lightened the loaf."

Leidenheimer's loaf is now the city's loaf, the perfect foil for fried oysters or fried shrimp. (Judging by the way most roast-beef poor boys fall apart in my hands, it may no longer be the perfect conveyance for beef and gravy.) No matter. Fresh from the ovens of this Central City bakery, it's light as a cloud with a downy crumb and a parchment crust. It's the daily bread of rich and poor, black and white, the French bread sacrament that all of New Orleans claims as its own. And you can find braces of it in better poor boy shops throughout town.

Available in better poor boy shops throughout the city.

Parasol's

You expect the food to be good when your bar mates are off-duty chefs from two of New Orleans' most esteemed and expensive restaurants: Commander's Palace and Brigtsen's. They, like you, have come to sample one of the city's best roast beef poor boys.

Dressed with shredded lettuce, pickles, tomatoes, mustard, mayonnaise, and gobs of fresh brown, garlickly gravy, this two-fisted sandwich looks like a train wreck. The flimsy paper plate quakes beneath the weight. Delivered with a tall stack of napkins, this poor boy demands your respect.

All the beef is roasted on the premises. Eighty pounds of Irish pride leave the kitchen every day. One neighborhood regular orders one-half for him and one-half for his dog, explaining, "If I didn't, he'd snatch the damn thing out of my mouth."

Opened in 1952 by Louis Passauer, ramshackle Parasol's has remained true to its roots in the Irish Channel. It is here that the city's most raucous St. Patrick's Day party takes place. More important, it is here that the mythical Irish marriage of beef and potatoes reaches new heights when you order a half roast beef poor boy and a half French fry poor boy.

2533 Constance Street / 504-899-2054

N.B.: Of late, I've been just as likely to grab a poor boy at Parkway Tavern, where proprietor Jay Nix has breathed life back into a 1920s vintage barroom. In its prime Parkway served as a canteen for workers at the nearby American Can Company. Nowadays American Can has gone condo but Parkway endures, serving what I believe to be the best hot-sausage poor boy in town, stuffed with griddle-fried patties of incendiary local pork.

Parkway Tavern /
538 Hagan Drive / 504-482-3047

Among the contenders for best poor boy men in New Orleans.

The Muffuletta

Located across Decatur Street from the French Market, Central Grocery is the mother church of the muffuletta. Created around 1906 by a recently arrived Sicilian immigrant, the muffuletta gets its name from a round, seeded loaf of bread, indigenous to Sicily. Central Grocery founder Salvatore Lupo is thought to have first made the sandwich for some fellow countrymen who stopped in his shop each afternoon to get the ingredients for a four-course meal: meat, cheese, olive salad, and bread.

Sitting in the cramped shop amid a jumble of crates and barrels, the men balanced their plates on their knees and attempted to eat their meals. According to family lore, Lupo grew tired of cleaning the detritus of their meals from the floor of his shop, so in a feat of cultural assimilation and culinary invention, he sliced open a loaf of muffuletta bread and stuffed the remaining ingredients inside. His countrymen came to clamor for Salvatore's sandwich. Soon thereafter all of New Orleans came calling for the distinctive round loaf stuffed with ham, salami, mortadella, provolone, and garlicky olive salad.

Since those early years, muffulettas have spread far beyond the bounds of the Crescent City. If my personal experience is any indication they may have spread a bit too far—both in terms of geography and content—for I've eaten faux muffs in Atlanta trapped

within the confines of a hamburger bun, and vile, oily assemblages of lunch meat in Baton Rouge; I've wolfed down seafood muffulettas in San Antonio and vegetarian versions in Santa Fe. But the best and the most genuine muffulettas are still found in New Orleans.

LIUZZA'S

This neighborhood relic is a bit off the beaten path in Mid-City. And, to tell the truth, they don't even serve a muffuletta. What they do serve is a Frenchuletta. Combine this French bread–encased version of the classic with an order of fried eggplant and an icy chalice of draft beer for an exceptional meal, far from the maddening mass of tourists. One last word: beware the Pizzauletta. It's a recent menu addition and not up to the same standards as the sandwich.

3636 BIENVILLE STREET / 504-482-9120

THE NAPOLEON HOUSE

Home to the best sit-down muffuletta in the French Quarter. Though the olive relish is diced a bit too fine for my taste, the meats are of good quality, and the bread is warm and forgiving—all the better to soak up the fragrant, garlic-infused olive oil that seems to ooze out with every bite. Built in 1797 for the mayor of New Orleans, the home was offered to Napoleon as refuge in 1821. Alas, Napoleon never made it. Today this cool, dark, dank bar provides a welcome respite from the hectic pace of life in the Quarter: opera on the loudspeakers, crumbling beauty all around.

500 CHARTRES STREET / 504-524-9752

CENTRAL GROCERY

This is the mother church of the muffaletta, the greasy grail. It looks right: a classic old-world grocery jammed with foodstuffs. It smells right: the sweet scent of olive oil and the salty tan of cured meat envelope you at the threshold. Though some locals carp that the sandwiches have slipped a notch, and others embrace the heated version served by The Napoleon House, you will be hard-pressed to find a better rendition of the classic sandwich.

923 Decatur Street / 504-523-1620

Pascal's Manale

Like many of New Orleans' best neighborhood restaurants, Pascal's, in business since 1913, serves Creole-Italian foods in a clubby warren of small dining rooms attended by brusque, but charming, waitresses who don't suffer fools gladly.

On the back wall of the bar, there's a display of photographs collected for the most part by the late Pascal Radosta, the nephew of founder Frank Manale. Among the signed, framed pictures of boxer Jack Dempsey, basketball great Pete Maravich, comedian Jack Benny, and football coach Bear Bryant, is a faded portrait of a slight man in a dark suit and a skinny tie. A wide grin creases his face; his hands are raised in a mock boxer's stance. He is Vincent Sutro, father of one of New Orleans' signature dishes: barbecue shrimp.

For the uninitiated, barbecue shrimp is a culinary misnomer of the highest order: no smoke, no grill, no nothing other than head-on shrimp bathed in a buttery sauce tasting of black pepper, maybe a bit of rosemary, perhaps a slug of Worcestershire sauce. It's sloppy, oily, and flat-out delicious stuff, best enjoyed with a silly bib strapped around your neck.

It is also the dish upon which Pascal's has staked its reputation. Never mind that the menu is chock-full of other good things to eat like shrimp remoulade and oysters Bienville. Or that the stand-up oyster bar is one of the best in the city. And Thomas Stewart is the hippest shucker in the land. Never mind that Sutro, the father of barbecue shrimp, wasn't a New Orleans native but a Chicago boy. During the 1950s he played the horses down at the Fairgrounds racetrack and liked to stop by Pascal's kitchen on Sunday afternoons to talk sports with the cook, Jake Radosta. One day Sutro came in the door waxing poetic about a dish he ate in a Chicago restaurant. Jake went in the kitchen and tried to replicate it. The rest is good, greasy history.

1838 Napoleon Avenue / 504-895-4877

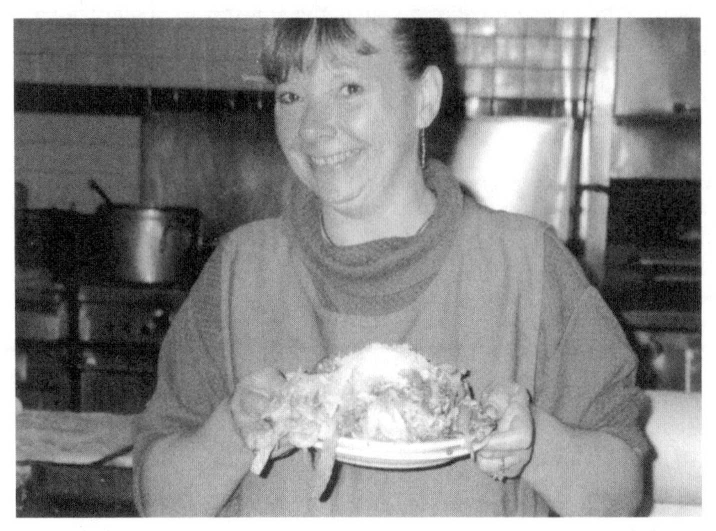

A wop salad and a smile courtesy of Rocky and Carlo's.

ROCKY AND CARLO'S

First you must understand that this is a family business. Rocky Tommaseo and Carlo Gioe were childhood friends in their native Sicily. When Rocky's family came to the U.S. soon after World War II, Carlo's family followed. Rocky married Carlo's sister. Carlo married Rocky's. In 1965 the two patriarchs opened a restaurant in the working-class suburb of Chalmette. And today they remain a close-knit family, turning out wondrous Sicilian-style Louisiana favorites.

The sign out in front of the beige brick building proclaims, "Ladies Welcome." Was that ever in doubt? Out in the parking lot, two pickups sport "David Duke for President" bumper stickers. To make matters worse, they look new. Inside, the dining room, like the building in which it is housed, is large, nondescript, and functional. Video poker machines clang and clamor. The corner television set is turned to *America's Funniest Home Videos.* Cigarette smoke hangs thick in the air, like a low morning fog.

Long a hangout for local refinery workers, Rocky and Carlo's has seen more than its share of fights. Today the only violence you are likely to witness is if you try to break into the line which snakes backward from the steam table to the door.

"Gimme a baked macaroni, brucceloni, a side of red gravy, and a Wop salad," says the roughneck in line just ahead of me. "And make it snappy, will ya, honey? I got to get back to the refinery."

You're hip. You're familiar with the strange lexicon that native New Orleanians use to describe their foods. You know what the counterman means when he asks if you want that poor boy dressed. You know what olive salad is and why it is essential to a good muffuletta. Even tasso ham doesn't throw you for a culinary loop. But Rocky and Carlo's will.

Baked macaroni, brucceloni, a side of red gravy, and a Wop salad. Speak these words and you will be rewarded, as was my friend the refinery worker, with a decadently cheap meal that you will never be able to finish, much less duplicate. Oh, but you will try to finish. Who wouldn't? The brucceloni—fork-tender beef, stuffed and stewed—would be the envy of any uptown New Orleans restaurant, as would the deftly fried, corn-flour-crusted oysters and shrimp. Lavished with garlicky red gravy (known to outlanders as tomato sauce), you quickly decide that the gargantuan helping of baked macaroni may be the best thing on your oversized plate. That is, until you taste the Wop salad.

The first bite explodes in your mouth. Like steam rising off a Louisiana blacktop after a summer shower, the smell of onions, olives, garlic, cheese, peppers, oil, vinegar, artichokes, and giardiniera seems to hover over the bowl of lettuce. The resulting oily, pungent morass of vegetables belies description. Political correctness be damned, you'll love this Wop.

613 West St. Bernard Highway (in Chalmette, a fifteen-minute ride from the French Quarter) / 504-279-8323

Casamento's

New Orleans is a city of great oyster bars. Felix's and Acme on Iberville Street in the Quarter have their proponents, but I prefer Casamento's, for both the quality of the cold, salty jewels they serve on the half shell and the unique atmosphere.

Thanks to the gleaming ceramic tile that covers every surface save the ceiling, sitting down to a meal at Casamento's can feel a bit like eating in a Paris metro tunnel. Indeed there's a vaguely art nouveau feel to the room: cream- and celadon-hued tiles on the oyster bar; green tiles in a pattern reminiscent of fleur-de-lis on the dining-room

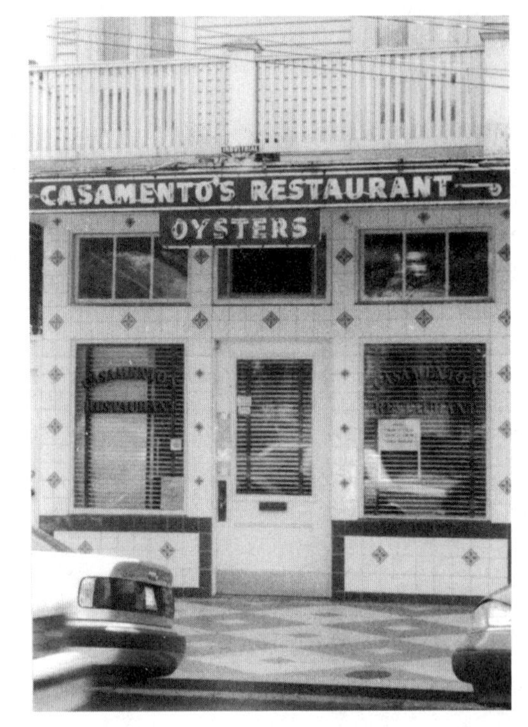

The façade only hints at the wonders of the tile art within.

floor; a blue flower tile pattern on the kitchen floor. Even the courtyard alley out back (where the bathrooms are) is blanketed in tile.

Like the families that opened Rocky and Carlo's, and Pascal's Manale, the Casamentos are of Italian stock. Joseph Sr. arrived in 1914 at the age of twenty-six from the island of Ustica near Palermo. Once in New Orleans he worked his way through a series of French Quarter kitchens before opening his own oyster bar in 1919.

On a recent visit I asked his son, an irascible septuagenarian also known as Joseph, what inspired his father to cover every conceivable surface with ceramic tile. "At first there was just tile on the floor," he told me as he worked at the front bar washing glasses. "After a while he got tired of painting the place over and over again, so he tiled it. That was back around 1949. We closed for two months that summer to do the walls and he figured that was a good thing to do, so we started closing for the summer. We still do. People don't eat as many oysters then."

Today, the dining room looks much like it must have in his father's day—and the food, well, the food is also little changed. Daube of beef with spaghetti, hand-cut fries, gumbo, fried soft-shell crabs, fresh-shucked oysters, and an unlikely fried oyster loaf served on what the restaurant calls pan bread. "We just take a loaf of Sunbeam bread and slice it out longways," Joseph explained to me. "It's what we've always done, what my father did before me. I got no reason to change."

4330 Magazine Street / 504-895-9761

Uglesich's

Anthony Uglesich's father, Sam, arrived in America the same way generations of his Croatian countrymen had done before him. He jumped ship. Back in 1919 he tried it in New York Harbor and was caught. In 1920 he tried again, this time in the waters just beyond New Orleans, and swam to shore.

In 1924 Sam opened a little place over on South Rampart Street. Like many of his fellow Croatians, he earned his living from the sea. Some worked the oyster beds, poling small skiffs through the wetlands south of the city, and some, like Sam, took to selling their harvest. By 1927 he relocated to the spot where, until recently his son still carried on the family business. "Back then he was just serving raw oysters and fried-oyster sandwiches, that sort of thing," says Anthony, who began working alongside his father in the early 1950s when he was still a teenager. "When my father passed away in 1975 it was like losing my best friend. We were that close."

In the intervening years, Anthony and his wife, Gail, won a reputation for serving what may well be the best seafood in the city. Inspired by Paul Prudhomme who brought Louisiana food to the fore in the late 1970s and early 1980s, they began adding items to the menu: first in 1975, a grilled trout with shrimp, later more exotic fare like fried green tomatoes topped with shrimp remoulade. No matter what you ordered, Anthony would serve you only the freshest seafood possible. When you ordered a poor boy, the oysters were shucked then and there, rolled in meal, and fried to a crisp. And almost all the seafood was local. "I don't use any imported stuff," Anthony told me. "And I'm willing to pay for good quality. My suppliers know that; they respect that. I know whether a sack of oysters is any good when it hits the floor."

The cement-floored little cubbyhole of a restaurant was packed from morning to late afternoon, crowded with tourists, local gourmands, and a good measure of big-name New Orleans chefs who braved what even Anthony admitted to be a questionable neighborhood. I can still recall my first visit back in the early 1990s. Along with a pack of friends, I was traipsing down a forlorn side street, looking for the restaurant when a police car screeched to a stop alongside and the driver shouted, "What the hell do you think you're doing here?" When I told him we were headed for Uglesich's he smiled and said, "Well, follow me; it's just a block down."

Before they closed the doors in 2005, Anthony and Gail had been experimenting with some different takes on Louisiana cookery. Inspired in part by the influx of

Vietnamese and other Asian immigrants—many of whom now work the oyster beds like the Croatians of an earlier day—ginger and black bean paste began to show up in a number of dishes. "I still cook like my father did—with a lot of olive oil—but I also love this stuff called Sambul Oelek," Anthony told me. "We use it in a dish called Shrimp Uggie. It's got nice heat, a great chili taste. We've been playing around with it a lot. You know my wife does maybe 70 percent of the cooking, but I'm the taster," he said, patting his belly. "Guess that's why she's still just a little skinny-winny and I'm not."

N.B.: As this edition went to press, Uglesich's remained closed, but rumors swirled of a post–Hurricane Katrina return. Chances look very slim, but devotees of Shrimp Uggie keep hope alive.

1238 Baronne Street (if you want to do a drive-by)

The Baquet Family

New Orleans can claim a number of restaurant dynasties, where generation after generation of the same family has earned their living at the stove or on the dining-room floor. Among the surnames that come readily to mind are the Alciatores of Antoine's fame; the Brennans of Commanders Palace and not a few other restaurants; and the kith and kin of the Manale family, still at the helm at Pascal's Manale.

No less important is the Baquet family, proprietors of the late, lamented Creole Soul restaurant, Eddie's, and a number of other progeny including a short-lived lunch counter in the old Kraus Department Store on Canal, where at the top of the escalator behind a selection of ladies hats whose taste even Minnie Pearl would have questioned, I once ate the best plate of red beans and rice I've ever tasted.

Not long ago I sat down with Wayne Baquet, Eddie's son, to learn a bit more about the family's history. "It all started with my uncle Paul back in 1947 at a place called Paul Gros Chicken Coop," Wayne told me. "My father, Eddie Baquet Sr., worked with him, but it was his sister Ada Baquet Gros who really set things up. Back then my father was a mail carrier by day and worked at the restaurant at night."

In time Eddie Baquet opened his own restaurant. "It opened up November 1,

1965," Wayne told me. "Our family lived in the back. People said we'd never make it; they said a restaurant would never work in the Seventh Ward, because all the Creole blacks were such good cooks, nobody ate out. They were right, too. We didn't do much business as a restaurant so we started selling poor boys."

It wasn't until Wayne came back to work for his father in 1972 after a stint in retail that the restaurant business took off. "That's when we started doing things like serving red beans and rice every day rather than just on Monday," said Wayne. "Sometime along in there Richard Collin wrote us up in the paper and all the white folks started coming and we were rolling."

And so it went. All of New Orleans called on the Seventh Ward restaurant run by Eddie Baquet, lured by the promise of peerless beans and rice, juicy pork chops perched atop a mound of oyster dressing, and dark, dark seafood gumbo full of spiny crab claws. Along the way, a number of branch restaurants opened and closed, including my favorite lunch counter.

After Eddie's death, the restaurant's popularity continued to soar, even as the surrounding neighborhood went into decline. But in late 1999 the family closed the doors on the original. In the intervening years Wayne Baquet opened a restaurant called Zachary's on Oak Street, but the run was comparatively short. And then, in January of 2005, Wayne pulled a nine-lives move, opening Li'l Dizzy's, a brick-walled café with a buffet at back right and an oversized oil portrait of Dizzy Gillespie above the mantel. It's open for breakfast but the place shines at lunch, when white beans and rice, shrimp and okra gumbo, and stuffed bell peppers are the standouts. More than likely, Wayne Baquet will meet you at the door. And at some point in your meal, he will lay his slogan on you, "Always hot and straight from the pot," as if it's the secret of all culinary secrets.

LI'L DIZZY'S / 1500 ESPLANADE AVENUE / 504-569-8997

Austin Leslie

The Strange Career of Austin Leslie

Long a favorite with New Orleans natives, Chez Helene gained national fame when *Frank's Place,* the short-lived but critically acclaimed situation comedy inspired by Austin Leslie's neighborhood restaurant, aired on CBS in 1987. Though the series lasted just one season, to this day it is heralded as one of the only network television shows to paint an accurate portrait of black life. In the series Tim Reid played the part of Frank Parish, a Boston professor of Renaissance history who inherits a funky little restaurant, Chez Louisiane, from his father, thus prompting a sojourn in New Orleans and a discovery of his cultural heritage.

Chez Helene gained national fame when "Frank's Place," the short-lived but critically acclaimed situation comedy inspired by Austin Leslie's neighborhood restaurant,, aired on CBS in 1987.

By the time *Frank's Place* debuted, Leslie was already a veteran of twenty-plus years at the stove. He got his start cooking at that New Orleans institution, D. H. Holmes Department Store on Canal Street. (Readers might recall D. H. Holmes from one of the opening scenes of John Kennedy Toole's comedic masterpiece *A Confederacy of Dunces.* The novel's corpulent, flatulent, overeducated, antihero, Ignatius J. Reilly, inhaled their teacakes like breath mints.) In later years Leslie cooked at any number of local restaurants before taking over the stove at his aunt Helen DeJean Pollock's restaurant, perfecting recipes for New Orleans standards like red beans and rice, jambalaya, oysters bordelaise, and a bread pudding without peer, studded with pineapple, gilded with whiskey sauce.

Not long after *Frank's Place* was canceled, Chez Helene itself closed. While all of New Orleans seemed to be scratching their heads and wondering why Leslie set off for, well, where else but Denmark, where he worked for a number of years cooking classic Creole dishes in the great white north. (It seems folks there love New Orleans food and music. A while back, I met a fellow from the New Birth Brass Band who told me that when his band played a gig there a couple of years ago, he stayed with Leslie.)

Toward the end of his career, Leslie manned the stove at an Uptown New Orleans restaurant, Jacques-Imo's, on Oak Street. He was in his element, for Jacques-Imo's is a hopping joint, filled for the most part with boisterous locals. (It's a bit rakish, too; the bar tables are from a Popeye's Fried Chicken outlet and sport the company's golden coat of arms.)

Sadly, Leslie died in the wake of Hurricane Katrina. Jacques Leonardi, the proprietor of Jacques-Imo's, pledges to keep the memory of Leslie alive. Stop by for dinner, and you'll likely spy Leonardi at the bar, wearing hot-pepper-print shorts, hugging every other patron, and telling tales of his friend's time at the fryer.

See Austin Leslie's **Fried Chicken** and **Shrimp Creole** recipes on pages 160–62.

Tee Eva's

Eating street food is one of the peculiar joys of New Orleans life. In days past Creoles of Color balanced baskets full of *callas* (sweet, fried rice balls) on their heads, calling out to passersby, *"Belle cela, tout chaud."* More recently, Lucky Dog hot dogs have been the street food of choice, sold by itinerant vendors in the French Quarter. (Of the latter I possess firsthand experience, having worked a Lucky Dog cart for three nights, culminating in New Year's Eve 1997, on assignment for the *Oxford American* magazine.)

Down on Magazine Street, Eva Perry runs a little walk-up stand that dispenses some of the finest street food in the city: snowballs drenched in a mind-boggling array of curious syrups including Creole cream cheese, watermelon, and wedding-cake flavors; tiny tins filled with pecan pie, sweet potato pie, and sweet potato–pecan pie; and dirty blonde pralines, thick with pecans.

Eva is a sweet and happy soul, a beacon of joy on a down-at-the-heels stretch of Magazine Street, likely to break into a chorus of Little Richard's "Tutti Frutti" when asked which flavors of snow cone syrup she has in stock. Always cordial she concludes each transaction with a benediction of sorts. "Thank you and God bless," she says to one customer. "Eat up sweetie, and tell your mama and them hello for me," she says to another.

"I'm a river lady," she says by way of explanation. "I was born on Glendale

Plantation in St. Charles Parish. My grandmother taught me how to cook and taught me how to act. I was raised to say 'yes ma'am' and 'no ma'am,' to give everybody you met a smile. Even a dog should get a smile, a little, 'Hi puppy, how do you do.'"

4430 MAGAZINE STREET / 504-899-8350

Willie Mae and company at the bar in the days when beverage mattered more than bird.

WILLIE MAE'S SCOTCH HOUSE

In 1957 or thereabouts Willie Mae's Scotch House, a corner tavern, opened in the Treme neighborhood of New Orleans. The proprietor then, as now, was Willie Mae Seaton. Born in Crystal Springs, Mississippi, in 1916, Seaton had moved south in 1940 with her husband in search of work. He won a job in the shipyards; she earned her keep first at the bar, then in the kitchen. (While tending bar, she won neighborhood fame for a signature cocktail of Johnny Walker Black and milk.)

By 1972 Seaton converted a beauty salon in the front half of her double-shotgun home into a seven-table restaurant. Working in concert with her daughter, Lillie Mae Seaton, she honed a repertoire of country-come-to-town standards: deep-fried, paprika-spiked chicken, sheathed in a diaphanous crust; white beans, chocked with pickled pork; and, on occasion, bread pudding that limns the Platonic ideal.

Over her career, Willie Mae Seaton earned a reputation for forthright cookery of unimpeachable quality. She has done so quietly, one platter of deep-fried chicken at a time. And in the process, she has transformed her restaurant from a place where one eats to a place where one belongs. Assisted by her son, Charles Seaton, and his granddaughter, Kerry Seaton-Blackman, she is a stalwart of New Orleans tradition, a keeper of the city's culinary flame.

Like many citizens of the Crescent City, Willie Mae Seaton's life went topsy-turvy in the wake of Hurricane Katrina. She lost her six-table restaurant to flood waters. And, living as she did in a double-shotgun with the restaurant on one side and bedrooms and the like on the other, she lost her home. As this book goes to press, volunteers are working to rehab her home and reopen her kitchen. And Seaton vies to soon stand tall by her stove and fry again. My prayer is that by the time you hold this book in your hands, the work of those volunteers and the dreams of that determined lady will have taken wing. (And drumstick, too.)

2401 St. Ann Street / 504-822-9503

Shreveport

Herby K's

In a derelict neighborhood where most of the other businesses either burned up or were boarded up long ago, this Shreveport institution endures. The menu is short: soft-shell crabs, seafood gumbo, fried oysters, fried shrimp, and not much else. The prices are ridiculously low. And the atmosphere is a heady mix of flea market castoffs and family heirlooms. Don't expect pretense, and you won't be disappointed.

Famous as the home of the shrimp buster—a faux sandwich of four butterflied shrimp perched atop buttered French bread and served with a side of garlicky cream sauce—Herby K's is as appreciated for the eccentricities of its ribald staff as for its frosty cold fishbowls of beer and delicately fried seafood.

Though there is a tree-shaded beer garden on the side of the building, I prefer to sit inside at one of the four booths or six stools. Inside you're a part of the action, free to trade jokes with the owner, reminiscences of meals past with a fellow patron, or insults with a waiter. On my last trip, my waiter, "Killer," warned the four shrimp on my plate that I would be eating them. When I asked why, he said, "They were alive

An early view of Herby K's, soon after Prohibition was repealed.

yesterday; don't you think they deserve the courtesy?"

Owner Janet Bean is a font of Herby K's lore. Given the least bit of prodding, she'll spin stories of the days when Herbert Busi—known to one and all by the nickname Herby K—ran the place. "Herby K was born in the house next door back around 1902, and kind of fell into this business after college," she told me. "As best as we can determine, Herby K's opened in 1936, though the same building had housed a sandwich shop and a confectionery before that. This was an almost exclusively Italian community then, and it prospered until they put the interstate through."

Though the neighborhood is now far from prosperous, Herby K's—like the Big Apple Inn in Jackson, Mississippi—carries on a legacy of good food that is in large part attributable to the long service of key employees. "Gary Hines has been with us since 1981," Janet told me. "His wife, Belva, has been here since back around 1976. And his mother—Ms. Gracie Bryant—she's been here since around 1958. She's got the most important job in the place. She flattens the shrimp for the shrimp busters."

1833 Pierre Avenue / 318-424-2724

Jim Romero, a man's man and a damn fine baker to boot.

Youngsville

JIM'S KOUNTRY PIES

There's a portrait of somebody's grandmother painted on the front door, her hair in a bun, wire-rim glasses perched on her nose. But take a step inside this tiny country cabin and there's no little old lady to be found. Instead, you'll spy Jimmy Romero, a big man, burly even, shrouded in a fog of flour, rolling out crust for one of his decadent pecan pies. Granted, in other parts of the South men have looked down on cooking, dismissing it as "women's work." But not in Cajun Country. Here, real men cook, always have.

Back in 1987 Jimmy quit the carpentry business, hanging up his hammer and chisel for good. "I'd always loved to bake," he tells me on the day I come calling. "I'd get off work at the carpentry shop and head for the kitchen. Now I get to do it all day long."

Jimmy takes his baking seriously. He'll drive a good forty miles to get the jumbo eggs he prefers. He picks his own blackberries and peels his own sweet potatoes.

And he knows that he does good work, but he's always surprised, even honored, when someone comes driving up unannounced. "This is way out in the country," says Jimmy. "I bake a good pie. I know that, but when folks drive over from Lafayette or New Iberia just to get one of my pies, well, I get so proud I almost pop."

3606 ROMERO ROAD-COTEAU / 337-365-7465

Fried Chicken

from Austin Leslie

Serves 4 to 6

This recipe, adapted, like the one that follows, from the *Chez Helene House of Good Food Cookbook*, is a keeper. The evaporated milk adds a touch of sweetness. And the chicken emerges from the oil with a proper mantle of crust. Some may consider ditching the dill pickles. Don't do it. I believe they are ideal foils for the bird beneath.

1 chicken (3 to 4 pounds), cut into 8 to 10 pieces
2 tablespoons salt
2 tablespoons freshly ground black pepper
1 12-ounce can evaporated milk
1 cup water
1 large egg, beaten
1 cup all-purpose flour
Peanut oil, for frying
1 garlic clove, very finely chopped, for garnish
1 bunch parsley, finely chopped, for garnish
10 pickle slices

Place the chicken in a bowl and season with salt and pepper. Refrigerate uncovered for at least 1 hour and up to 24 hours. Remove from the refrig-

erator. In a large bowl combine the evaporated milk, water, and egg. Place the flour in a shallow bowl; set aside.

Pour the oil into a high-sided cast-iron skillet or Dutch oven to a depth of at least 3 inches. Heat over high heat until it reaches 375° F. Dip the chicken pieces into egg wash, then dredge in the flour. Shake off excess flour, and slip the chicken into the hot oil without crowding, starting with the dark meat. Reduce the heat and cook, maintaining a temperature of between 325° and 350° F, until the juices run clear when pierced with a knife, 10 to 12 minutes. Remove to a wire rack or plate lined with paper towels to drain. Transfer to a serving platter and garnish the chopped garlic and parsley. Top with pickle slices and serve immediately.

Shrimp Creole

from Austin Leslie
Serves 8 to 10

Leslie's reliance upon red wine reminds me of the great Buster Holmes, who once ran a café on Burgundy Street in the French Quarter Café. Holmes was famous for red beans and rice. And if my memory serves, his secret ingredient was, you guessed it, red wine.

¼ cup bacon drippings
¼ cup all-purpose flour
1½ cups chopped onions (about 1 large)
1 cup chopped shallots (about 4)
1 cup chopped celery (about 2 stalks)
1 cup chopped bell pepper (about 2)
4 cloves garlic, finely chopped
1 16-ounce can crushed tomatoes
1 8-ounce can tomato sauce
1 6-ounce can tomato paste
3 bay leaves

1 tablespoon fresh lemon juice
1 teaspoon Worcestershire sauce
1 teaspoon fresh thyme leaves
2 cups dry red or Burgundy wine
1 cup water or shrimp stock
1 tablespoon sugar
1 teaspoon salt
1 teaspoon freshly ground black pepper
Tabasco sauce
4 pounds large shrimp, peeled and deveined
½ cup freshly chopped parsley
Cooked rice, for serving

Heat the bacon drippings in a large saucepan over medium heat. Blend in the flour, and cook slowly, stirring until the bacon drippings and flour foam. Cook, stirring gently, but constantly until the roux is rich dark brown, 18 to 20 minutes.

Add the onions, shallots, celery, bell pepper, and garlic. Cook until the onions are translucent, 3 to 5 minutes. Add the crushed tomatoes, tomato sauce, and tomato paste. Reduce heat to low and simmer until the flavors are well combined, about 15 minutes. Add bay leaves, lemon juice, Worcestershire sauce, thyme, wine, water or shrimp stock, sugar, salt, pepper, and Tabasco to taste. Simmer for an hour, stirring occasionally.

Add shrimp and cook just until the shrimp is pink but still tender, 3 to 5 minutes. Add parsley and stir to combine. Taste and adjust for seasoning with salt and pepper. Serve immediately on cooked rice.

MISSISSIPPI

A vein of spicy pork, wrapped in a cornhusk and tied in a bundle of six. Pork cracklins rendered in woks by Chinese folks from Clarksdale, their accents as thick and sweet as molasses. Plate lunches from Peggy's of Philadelphia, served on a makeshift buffet tacked up in the hallway. Welcome to Mississippi, my adopted home. If you like, meet me for dinner on Sunday night out at Taylor Grocery in rural Lafayette County, where fresh catfish is rolled in spiced meal and fried in roiling oil, and hushpuppies with the sweet scent of corn arrive steaming at the table.

Amory

Bill's Hamburgers

There may not be a business in the South with a more tangled family tree than Bill's, an Amory institution since 1929. Bob Hill was the first man to fire up the grill down in the Vinegar Bend neighborhood, infamous hereabouts for illicit whiskey making. He called his burger stand Bob's.

In the 1930s Bill Tubb joined the enterprise, and the two worked hand in hand, cooking freshly ground burgers on a flattop grill, smearing on a bit of mustard and adding a slice of onion before stuffing the whole affair in a homemade bun from Toney's Bakery down the street. In 1955 Bill and Bob had a tiff, and Bob's Hamburgers moved down the street and soon failed in its new location. Meanwhile, Bill plastered his name on the brick façade formerly occupied by Bob's and never looked back.

Through the years, the good citizens of Monroe County have come to dote on the burgers served from the little grill at 310 North Main Street, no matter the proprietor, no matter the name. Sure, there have been some changes through the years. French fries made their debut in 1984, cheeseburgers in 1994. But among the cognoscenti, it's consistency and community that have mattered all along. "We still grind our meat fresh every day," onetime owner Greg Maples told me. "And we still don't offer lettuce or pickles or any of that other mess."

Old-timers remember the days when the gin was still running across the way, and farmers, flush with cash from selling a bale of cotton, would pick up a pasteboard box of twelve wax-paper-wrapped sandwiches for the family. Others recall the time when most everybody asked for extra gravy on their burgers, and the cook obliged, dipping the bun into the grease that pooled on the side of the grill. "That was back before they discovered cholesterol," offers a man dressed in overalls, seated at one of the fifteen-odd stools that are the little café's only seats.

And most everyone recalls the reign of Junior Manasco, who, until his death in 1994, served as a sort of unofficial ambassador for Bill's, working the counter, grabbing drinks for customers, handing out Tootsie Rolls to children. "People would come in just to see Junior," said Greg. "He was what you might call slow, but, you know, he never really missed a beat. He was the heart and soul of this place. Just to see him smiling behind the counter made you happy, made that burger taste all that much better. And you can bet that you'd never get that sort of thing at a McDonald's."

310 North Main Street / 662-256-2085

GULF COAST POOR BOYS

All poor boys are not created equal. In New Orleans, origin point of the fabled sandwich, they prefer their fried shrimp cradled in a crusty taper of fresh-from-the-oven French bread that shatters with the first bite. But along the Gulf Coast, westward through Biloxi, Gulfport, and Long Beach, the emphasis is oftentimes less on the quality of the bread and more upon the texture that the bread achieves when toasted.

It's common hereabouts for cooks to slit a loaf open, maintaining the hinge between bottom and top, and toast the interior crumb on a flattop griddle. I've seen that done at BP convenience stores in Gulfport and at roadside stands in Biloxi, too. The effect is comparable to a Cuban sandwich, pressed on a *plancha*.

Post–Hurricane Katrina, however, the best Gulf Coast poor boys I've eaten showcase an uncanny reverence for the original form. At New Orleans Style Seafood Poboys, set in a former fast-food outlet, just north of Biloxi in D'Iberville, Linda Dao and Tom Nguyen offer two menus to patrons. The yellow one features *cha gio* (spring rolls) and *com ga nuong xa* (chicken with lemongrass), while the orange one boasts fried shrimp, oyster, or soft-shell crab poor boys, along with potato salad and onion rings.

Although I like their *pho* (beef noodle soup), I'm crazy for their poor boys, especially the shrimp version, overstuffed with corn flour–fried crustaceans, the whole affair nestled in a crackly loaf from the ovens of the local Vietnamese-owned Le Bakery. (The shrimp, by the way, are caught by Linda's father; during shrimping season, you can spy him in the parking lot, selling head-on twelve-counters from the tailgate of his pickup.) If you ask nicely when you order your poor boy, Linda will, at no additional charge, give you a mountainous platter of the bean sprouts and basil and other herbs that are traditionally served with *pho*. Though she will look askance when you do it, I like to tuck a thatch of those herbs inside my sandwich.

NEW ORLEANS STYLE SEAFOOD POBOYS
10271 D'IBERVILLE BOULEVARD / D'IBERVILLE / 228-392-8683

Clarksdale and the Mississippi Delta

CHAMOUN'S REST HAVEN

If you accept novelist Richard Ford's contention that the Mississippi Delta is the "South's South," that this flat patch of fecund farmland stretching along the Mississippi River from Vicksburg northward to Memphis, Tennessee, is the most Southern place on earth, then you must be willing to embrace a South that is more than the sum of its African and Anglo-Saxon ancestors, for here, Lebanese and Chinese, Jew and Syrian, Italian and Mexican peoples have lived for generation upon generation.

Most came to the South in search of work at a time when labor was needed to bring in the cotton harvests. The first Chinese came as indentured servants, the first Italians were lured to work as laborers on a plantation located in Sunnyside, Arkansas, just across the river. Lebanese began arriving in the late 1800s, and many soon took to peddling dry goods from door to door. Chafik and Louise Chamoun arrived in the United States in 1954, where Chafik's grandparents had long run a dry goods store in the town of Clarksdale. "I started out selling door to door to people out in the country, selling a line of flavorings and such made by the Rawleigh company," Chafik says. "But before long I had my own grocery store."

Chafik was a good merchant, a sound businessman, but in short order his wife's talent in the kitchen overshadowed any specials he might run on cornmeal or canned tomatoes. Locals recall taking notice of the kibbe sandwiches that Louise prepared for the family luncheon, watching Chafik eat them at the counter and asking if they might try one, too. Before long Chafik was moving aside the shelves full of tinned sardines and sacks of sweet potatoes to set up tables on which to serve a burgeoning lunch trade.

In 1990 the Chamoun family gave up the grocery business for good when they moved their operation down the road to the Rest Haven, a local institution opened in 1947 by another Lebanese family, the Josephs. It's a vaguely modern place, outfitted with leatherette booths and tile flooring that would look at home in any small-town Southern café—that is until you take a look at the menu and realize that this may well be the only restaurant in the land where you can get an order of skillet-fried chicken with a couple of dolmathas on the side and a little bowl of hummus to begin your meal. Dessert is, of course, coconut cream pie, topped with a towering meringue.

419 NORTH STREET / 662-624-8601

Kim's Pork Rinds

Kim Wong, a sixty-something-year-old native of Guandong Province in China, followed his father to America in 1949. His father, Duck Lee Wong, had made his way to the Mississippi Delta in the early years of the twentieth century. "My father moved here to find work, to become a part of the American dream," Kim tells me. "By the time I came over, he was running a store called the Joe Bing Company in Friar's Point, Mississippi. After I finished school, I joined him and helped run the store."

By the 1960s Kim had moved the family enterprise to the town of Clarksdale, where he operated a restaurant and grocery store, and supplemented his income by teaching karate lessons to local kids at night. The restaurant did fine, serving both Southern fried chicken and Guandong-style wok-fried sweet-and-sour pork, but it wasn't until 1985, when the Wong family hit upon selling pork cracklins by the bag, that the family fortunes soared.

For years, Kim's wife, Jean, whom he met in Hong Kong, rendered lard from pork to use in the Southern-style biscuits that the restaurant served for breakfast, but tossed away the cracklins that settled to the bottom of the wok. "Back then, the fresh cracklins were only available when somebody killed a hog, so we just started putting ours in Ziploc bags, and selling them by the register," Kim recalls. "People loved ours because they were available year-round and they cooked up crisper, too. Woks make the difference. They cook the cracklins more evenly in less oil. Two years later we closed the restaurant because we needed more warehouse for the cracklin business. The old buffet line still sits over in the corner where we left it."

Today, a dozen or more monster woks line the kitchen of the Clarksdale facility and the Wong family turns out a wide variety of products. "I'm really proud of my chicken cracklins," Kim says. "When everybody started talking about how they couldn't eat pork, we started frying chicken skins. They've been doing real well."

417 Third Street / 662-627-2389

A map of Mexico points the way at Jack's in the community of Flowood.

Hot Tamales in the Land of the Blues

So what is this food—tamales—so often associated with Mexico, doing in the Mississippi Delta? you might ask. *Isn't this just an aberration? Like finding curried conch in Collierville, Tennessee, or foie gras in Fort Smith, Arkansas?*

No, it's just not that simple. Tamales have been a menu mainstay in the Mississippi Delta for much of the twentieth century. Indeed, along with catfish, they may just be the archetypal Delta food. Mississippi bluesman Robert Johnson sang about them in the song "She's Red Hot," recorded in 1936. Hodding Carter, always a moderating force in Mississippi race relations, began his book *So the Hefners Left McComb* with an ode to the symbolic importance of tamales. He tells us that the Hefners left McComb, Mississippi, after breaking the 1960s de facto laws against eating with interlopers. The Hefners' great crime? They shared hot tamales, from Doe's restaurant in Greenville, with civil rights workers.

White and black Mississippians recall that tamale vendors traveled the streets of their youth. Author Shelby Foote, a native of Greenville, Mississippi, remembers two African American tamale vendors, "Stanfield and one they called 666," selling tamales during the 1920s: "They sold them out of lard buckets," Foote recalls. "They wrapped them in newspapers and sold them for fifteen cents a dozen. Hell, we were eating them before we ever saw a Mexican."

And why not? Tamale ingredients are few and readily available in the South: cornmeal, pork or beef, and a few spices. All one need do is steam the mixture in a corn husk, a sleeve of butcher's paper, or, *heaven forbid*, a coffee filter (I've seen it done), and you have a Delta tamale.

As best as I can determine, tamales came to be a Delta favorite sometime in the early years of the twentieth century when Hispanic laborers began making their way up from Texas by way of Arkansas to work the cotton harvest. Imagine the scenario: It's an unseasonably cold November day. Two laborers sit side by side in a cotton field, unpacking their lunch pails. One, an African American, has a sweet potato, a slice of cornbread, and a hunk of side meat. Though they were hot when he packed them at sunup, by lunchtime they're cold.

The Hispanic laborer unpacks a similar pail—probably a lard bucket lined with crumpled newspapers—but his lunch emerges from the bucket still warm, because tamales, packed tightly, have wonderful heat-retention qualities. In essence, the cornmeal-mush jackets serve as insulation. The African American laborer casts an envious eye over at his co-worker's hot lunch, begs a taste and then a recipe. Soon both men are heading to the field, their pails packed with tamales. When the cotton harvest is over, the Hispanic laborer hops a train bound for Texas, and the African American, in need of income between seasons, starts selling tamales at rent parties and from a cart he pushes down the main drag on Saturday nights.

All supposition aside, rather than fret about the origins of Delta tamales, most Mississippians would rather eat them. Visit any of these purveyors of culture and cuisine, and you'll be inclined to do the same.

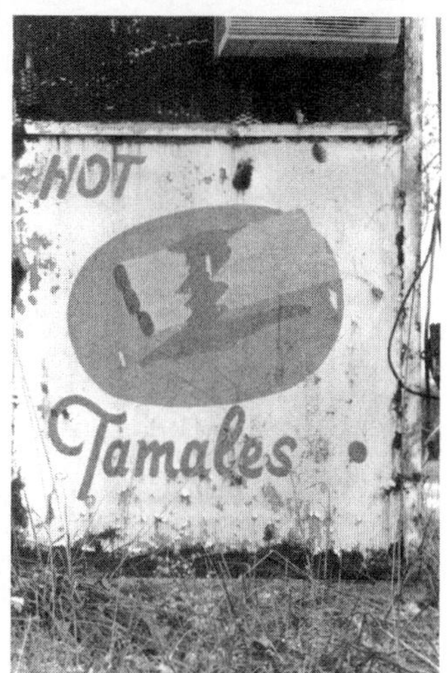

Delta Hot Tamales

OSCAR'S TAMALES

Oscar Orsby once boasted that he sold "hot dogs as long as Fourth Street and pork steaks you don't need no teeth for," but he didn't have to brag about his hot tamales. All of Clarksdale, Mississippi, knew they were some of the best in town.

Until recently Orsby backed his converted pickup into a parking space at the corner of Fourth and Yazoo Streets, flipped the circuit breaker on his personal electric meter, plugged his little two burner stove into a socket on the utility pole, and sold hot tamales to anyone with a few quarters jangling in his pocket. Since Orsby retired, Hick's Tamales seems to own the franchise in Clarksdale.

305 SOUTH STATE STREET / 662-624-9887

THE KOOLICKLE

I first noticed Koolickles in 2005, while traveling the Delta with a friend. We had planned to make it down to Yazoo City before noon to catch piano player Jamie Isonhood's regular Saturday morning gig at the Sunflower Grocery. (He plays on a catwalk above the frozen-food section.) But we overslept and decided, instead, to drive about aimlessly.

It was midafternoon when we hit Shelby. We were hungry. (In my experience, breakfasts of cold tallboys and hot tamales don't quite cut it.) And we were thirsty. For a half hour or so, we sat at the bar in the Dew Drop Inn, drinking more beer and watching the proprietor hack a wild catfish into steaks with a knife that, in the right light, might be taken for a machete.

No food appeared forthcoming, so we exited and ambled over to a small blues festival, staged against a backdrop of the old train depot. Judging by the listlessness of the crowd, the celebration was either just starting or had just ended. But there was food to be had, served from white pop-up tents by local church groups and civic clubs.

I fixed on ferreting out local eats. Hot tamales, check. Fried buffalo fish, check. Spaghetti with a black pepper–shot ground-beef bolognese, served as a side in the

manner of macaroni and cheese, check. All old school. But two of the tents advertised Koolickles, a delicacy that had, heretofore, never graced my maw. I ordered one strawberry-flavored Koolickle and, for good measure, one grape.

Before I tell you of the taste, I should tell you that in the interim I have eaten another dozen or so Koolickles, all in the service of research. In conversations with convenience-store clerks, I have tried to plot their history. In an attempt to establish their bounds of distribution, I have quizzed innumerable friends. For the most part, I've come up empty. But I am not dissuaded. Modern folk foods like this garner little notice, little respect, until they go national. Think Buffalo wings. Think fish tacos.

As of this writing, here's what I know: Dill pickles steeped in Kool-Aid seem to be a Delta phenomenon. And they seem to be of fairly recent divination, certainly not predating the Carter administration and likely not coming before Clinton. Although some makers call for piercing the pickles with a fork before submerging them—and a precious few have been known to hollow pickle centers out and secret peppermint sticks within—the most common method of preparation is to simply empty a gallon pickle jar of its brine and pour in an equal measure of sweetened Kool-Aid. Wait a couple days and you have what are variously known as Southern sweet pickles, Kool-Aid pickles, and, in the most pleasant of coinages, Koolickles.

Lately I've been inclined to eat my Koolickles at one of the Double Quick stores in Indianola (for no other reason than the knowledge that managers from the various stores comprise a singing group, the Double Quick Gospel Choir) or at Big Jim's on Highway 61 in Clarksdale, which is, of course, across the road from a Double Quick.

The setting at Big Jim's is part of the appeal. The sides of the walk-up are plastered with various flotsams, including a bas-relief of a black Santa Claus. A sign advertises hog maws, hot tamales, and various burger riffs. And a red light mounted to a pole revolves day and night.

As for the pickles—which remind me of the ones I first tasted in Shelby—they are textbooks of the form. Pulled from a jar of strawberry Kool-Aid, they emerge a mite shriveled, their color a marriage of green and red. The taste is confusing, at once sweet and tart and salty. Truth be told, they may be a once-in-a-lifetime eat for many. But in my book their presence on the byways of the Mississippi Delta serves notice that throughout the South undiscovered tastes hover on the horizon.

BIG JIM'S / 1700 STATE STREET / 662-645-5600

Solly's Hot Tamales

Just up the bluff from the Mississippi River, Solly's Hot Tamales has been serving generations of Vicksburg residents. Open since 1939, this little storefront serves a subtly incendiary bundle of corn and pork at 1921 Washington Street in Vicksburg.

1921 Washington Street / Vicksburg / 601-636-2020

White Front Café

On a nondescript stretch of road in the sleepy nondescript Delta town of Rosedale, the White Front Café serves what may be the best tamales in Mississippi. Since the death of owner Joe Pope, his sister Barbara Pope has taken up the reins. Stop by late in the afternoon or early in the evening and you'll have the best chance of finding someone at the stove, keeping a watchful eye on a pot of simmering tamales.

902 Main Street / 662-759-3842

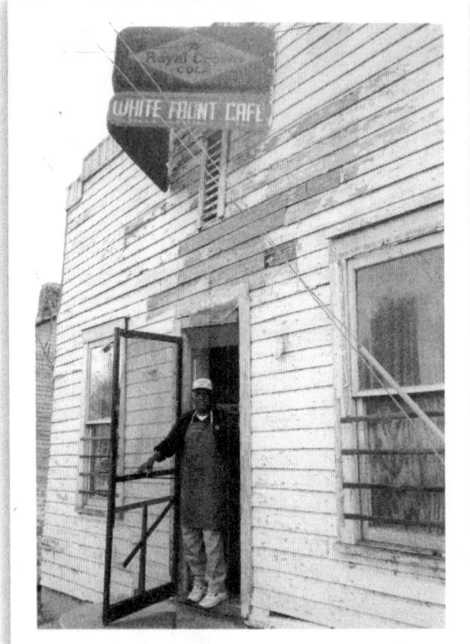

The late Joe Pope, awaiting his public.

Cleveland

Delta State Fighting Okra

A few years back, on a drive through the town of Cleveland, Mississippi, a roadside apparition appeared. Plastered on the side of a hulking, late-model station wagon, were the words "Delta State University Fighting Okra—We're No Ordinary Vegetable." I made a hard right turn into the parking lot and started asking questions.

Here's the story I was told: It seems that a few years back, the football team couldn't get an ample supply of their traditional kelly-green jerseys. But their supplier had a great deal on an earthier brownish green. Strapped for cash like many colleges, Delta State opted for the okra-green jerseys. Soon after, from high in the grandstand, a local pundit was heard to observe, "Well, I'll be damned. Don't they look like a mess of okra wrigglin' around down there?"

More recently, a friend sketched a somewhat similar story. But he ditched the uniform angle and moved the action from a football field to a baseball diamond with an okra patch in the outfield. Same kind of okra epiphany. Same results, the coolest (and slimiest) name in sports.

You, too, can share the vision. Show the world that you're okra and you're proud with a fine, all cotton T-shirt. The Delta State University bookstore (662-846-4640) always seems to have a good stock.

Corinth

White Trolley

Over in Lexington, North Carolina, people know them as bread burgers. I've heard folks all over the South call them wish burgers, as in, *I wish there were more meat.* But nowhere else have I seen these little beauties consumed with such zeal as they are in the northeastern Mississippi towns of Corinth and Booneville. In Booneville they're known as dough burgers and they resemble ground-beef pancakes. Around Corinth, they're called slug burgers, and, unfortunate name aside, folks swear by these faux hamburgers fashioned from ground beef and various fillers, including soy. (Corinth also holds an annual slug-burger festival where they crown a slug-burger queen. My wife, Blair Hobbs, was honored to teach creative writing to Mia Knighton, the first queen so crowned.)

General consensus is that the best slug burgers in Corinth come from the White Trolley, a blond-brick rectangle out on the highway at the edge of town. Seating is at one of the fifteen-odd stools that face the counter, which, by the way, is lined with a dazzling display of snack cakes and honey buns, Moon Pies and Break cakes. I consider ordering a baloney burger (fried baloney on a bun) or a double dog (two hot dogs, split along their length and fried until they curl up, again served on a cottony white bun) but succumb to the pull of curiosity and order a slug burger and a side of Tater Tots.

While I'm waiting, I ask the elderly woman next to me how slug burgers came to be so popular around here. "You can't remember that far back, but back during the Depression meat was awful expensive," she says. "And after that World War II came along and they got to rationing out our meat. Folks around here were poor. I guess we got used to doing without and never thought better of it."

As she talks I can hear oil cracking and soon my burger emerges from the kitchen, topped with a healthy dollop of mustard and a scattering of hacked-up onions. It looks and tastes a bit like a pig's-ear sandwich, floppy, meaty, and vaguely cartilaginous. I chase each bite with a Tater Tot and the whole affair goes down just fine.

1215 Highway 72 East / 662-287-4593

Greenville

A joint, pure and simple.

Doe's Eat Place

Like Lusco's over in Greenwood and Taylor Grocery just south of Oxford—not to mention Shadden's Barbecue in Marvel, Arkansas; Joe's Dreyfus Store in Livonia, Louisiana; and hundreds of other spots on the Southern culinary map—Doe's Eat Place began life as a grocery sometime between the world wars. Back then Carmel Signa stocked the shelves of his home with tinned sardines, hoop cheese, and a few staples of the Italian tradition like cans of Roma tomatoes and sleeves of dried spaghetti. Neighborhood folks—fellow immigrants for the most part—were his first customers. The Signa family bunked in back.

By the late 1940s Carmel's son, Dominick, had taken over, and, as was the fashion in the Delta—both then and now—began rolling hot tamales and selling them by the bundle to passersby. Soon neighbors were showing up at the kitchen door, tin pots and pans in hand, to collect a dozen or two for a dinner. While waiting for Dominick to fish their reward from the pot, customers caught wind of the stuffed eggplant swimming in tomato sauce that Dominick's wife, Mamie, had left simmering on the back burner, and soon they were inquiring if she might be willing to make up a few more of those for tomorrow night's dinner. She was.

Before too long folks started plopping down right in the middle of Mamie's kitchen to eat her eggplant, and Dominick began broiling gargantuan beefsteaks, first for the local folks and later for the masses. As improbable as it may sound, in the intervening years, what was once the Signa family home and grocery has been transformed into a temple of gastronomy, recognized as one of America's great steak houses. And a seat in the kitchen, at a rickety oilcloth-draped four-seater by the stove, is as hard won as a chef's table at a four-star restaurant in New Orleans or New York.

Though branch locations have opened in recent years—in Little Rock, Arkansas, Oxford, Mississippi, and elsewhere—the original Doe's remains, as ever, a clapboard and cinder-block heap at the corner of Nelson and Hinds Streets—butt-sprung and busted—but nonetheless famous throughout the South for massive hillocks of prime beef broiled to perfection, and hand-rolled hot tamales, bursting with grease and spice.

502 Nelson Street / 662-334-3315

Greenwood

Lusco's

Butter pats no longer cover the pressed-tin ceiling. The menu, once recited by a waitstaff that was old, dignified, and black, is now handed out by waitresses that are young, perky, and white. Over the past few years, this Delta dowager has undergone many a change. Yet Lusco's remains one of the most popular and peculiar restaurants in Mississippi.

According to third-generation owner Karen Pinkston, who has operated the restaurant with her husband, Andy Pinkston, since 1976, the secret to the restaurant's success can be attributed to sage words of advice offered by a longtime customer. "When we took over, he said to me, 'Change, but change gently.'"

To the denizens of the Delta, any change is suspect. Take those butter pats. "For years, people would use their knives to catapult the little pats up onto the ceiling," explains Karen. "It wasn't so bad during summer. But during the winter, when we turned the heater on, those little pats would come unglued and go splat! Right on somebody's nice dress . . . Tradition or not, we just had to put a stop to it."

Long the haunt of wealthy Deltans who made their way to the wrong side of the tracks for a little dining, drinking, and slumming, Lusco's still looks as though it has never escaped the Depression during which it was born. "Andy's grandparents opened on the same day in 1933 that President Roosevelt was inaugurated," says Karen. Once at the center of Greenwood life, Lusco's now shares the block with a collection of boarded-up and soon-to-be-boarded-up brick-fronted businesses, including L.C.M.C. Mortuary Products.

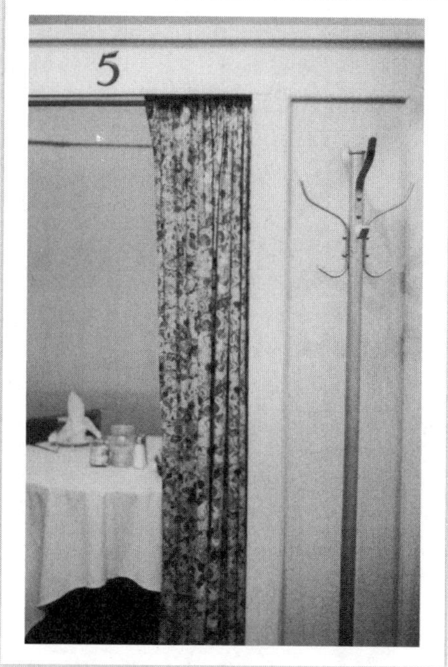

The No Tell Motel of restaurant spaces.

Though the restaurant was started by first-generation Italian immigrants, it was illegal hooch, not tasty Italian food, that lured the Delta gentry to Lusco's. "During Prohibition folks came to drink Poppa Lusco's home brew in the back booths. But Lusco's didn't serve any riffraff," Karen says. "Back then it was mainly a grocery store. The food was kind of secondary; people showed up to dance, drink, and hide out."

Thanks to ten-foot-high wooden partitioned "booths" with curtained fronts—the preferred seating—and a waitstaff that tells no tales, hiding out was (and is) easy at Lusco's. But food is no longer an afterthought. Andy Pinkston is a stickler for the perfect steak: "We use certified Angus from Buckhead Beef in Atlanta. And I don't sear my steaks; I broil them. Steaks should be tender, not crusty."

Served with Lusco's Special Salad (a pungent oily mix of greens, capers, ripe olives, and anchovies) and a heaping helping of hand-cut fries, the T-bones, rib-eyes, and sirloins are superb. Yet the steaks pale in comparison to the house specialty: luscious, dove-white, broiled pompano. Served whole and slathered with Lusco's lemony fish sauce, the broiled fish often overlaps the magnolia-laced platter on which it is presented. Of special note is the broiled shrimp. The shrimp are plump and juicy, if just a tad overcooked, but the raison d'être of this delectable dish is the sauce itself. Available in mild, hot, or *"hoteeee"* versions, it tastes of vinegar,

cayenne, and an ineffable mixture of spices, all swimming in the thinnest and butteriest of emulsions.

And yet as tasty as the food may be, it is the unique atmosphere, at once shabby and genteel, libidinous and chaste, that remains the primary draw. On a typical Saturday night the restaurant is filled to capacity. In the cavernous front waiting room, beneath a covey of stuffed ducks, society swells take occasional nips from hip flasks, while dirty, brogan-wearing farmers of indeterminate age and wealth pace the cracked linoleum floor, stopping by the cash register to chide the hostess about seating another party in their favorite booth. In the corner a clutch of tourists lounge on rickety sofas.

As you walk the dimly lit hall toward your booth, snippets of conversation float upward. Booth curtains ruffle briefly, revealing glimpses of courting couples locked in embrace. Toward the front a family of six holds hands, heads bowed in prayer. In the far booth a group of college students drink heavily and whoop loudly. At moments like these you realize that, though Lusco's has endured slight changes, it remains as hidebound as ever. That is, until you notice the sign: "Butter pat flipping is considered malicious mischief. Violators will be prosecuted."

722 CARROLLTON STREET / 662-453-5365

Hattiesburg

Leatha's

Leatha Jackson stands proud at the door to her smokehouse.

For reasons still somewhat unclear to me, Mississippi lags behind other states of the Black Belt South in both quantity and quality of barbecue restaurants. Spooney's over in Greenwood smokes some good pig as does Westside Bar-B-Que in New Albany. And there are a good half-dozen other joints scattered about the state that do a decent job with ribs and shoulders. But the state lacks critical barbecue mass.

Now if you ascribe to the notion that, at least in the Deep South, the best pitmasters have often been African American, then this dearth of great barbecue in the state with the highest percentage of black population just doesn't compute. Chalk it up to a legacy of poverty and prejudice if you like, but, for me, neither wholly explains the situation.

One notable exception is Leatha's, an African American–owned smokehouse of the highest order, set among the piney woods of southern Mississippi. Pork or—heaven forbid—beef ribs are the draw and they're a paragon of the pitmaster's art. Charred just slightly after a five- to six-hour turn on the huge upright smoker that for the longest time set in a tin-roofed shack across the way, they fall from the bone with the slightest tug. And the sauce, served on the side in a coffee cup, is sweet and catsupy, but balanced with a bit of heat. Fresh-cut fries, regrettable brown-and-serve rolls, and a fat bowl of coleslaw complete the feast.

Leatha Jackson has been the proprietor here since 1974, and an audience with her is not to be missed. After I finish my ribs, Mrs. Jackson, pulls up a red metal folding chair and starts to talk. "I picked cotton when I was a child, until I got just about fed up with it and left that mess behind," she tells me. "I got a ride on a log truck and I

was gone. That was back around 1948; I guess I was twenty-five or so. Now I got my own place and I got my children with me. God has most definitely blessed me. My daughters live right alongside me. That's my son, Larry, over there. When we get crowded, he'll go from table to table singing for folks. Some people come just to hear him sing."

Sensing an opening, Larry sidles over. "I can sing Michael Jackson, Duran Duran, Elvis, most anybody," he says. "I've won twenty-nine trophies for my singing. Want to hear me sing, mister?" I tell him that I would love to hear him sing. At that Mrs. Jackson just beams, and Larry breaks into a rousing rendition of Boy George's "Karma Chameleon."

6374 Highway 98 West / 601-271-6003

Jackson

Big Apple Inn

Each morning this Farish Street institution, open since 1939, buys about 300 pig ears from a local butcher, slices them in half, and tosses them in huge pressure cookers where they stew until soft. Locals munch them morning, noon and night.

On my last visit, Gene Lee Jr., great-grandson of founder, Big Juan Mora, was still aflutter after a recent stopover by a film crew from the *Ripley's Believe It or Not* television show. It seems they had never heard tell of a pig's-ear sandwich before and spent a day filming at the restaurant. By the time you read this, all the world will surely know of this peculiar porcine delicacy thanks to this unprecedented gastronomic scoop scored by the dogged investigative *Ripley's* team. Trouble is—as most Southerners know—there's nothing so special about a pig's-ear sandwich. We Southerners have long consumed every part of the hog but the squeal. Trotters and maws, lips and lights, we eat it all, and though, these days, such delicacies show up less and less often on restaurant menus, the Big Apple is not the only pig's-ear sandwich purveyor south of the Mason and Dixon.

That said, the Big Apple is a joint worth knowing about, a vestige of the day when Farish Street, like Auburn Avenue in Atlanta or Beale Street in Memphis, was the black business address of import. Today, Farish Street is, for the most part, a rather forlorn thoroughfare, chockablock with abandoned storefronts, but the Big

Apple seems to be always pulsing with life, its Wurlitzer Americana jukebox booming forth with the sounds of Jesse Graham singing "Do Me Baby" or Bobby Blue Bland crooning "Twenty-Room House." And though the pig's-ear sandwiches are indeed good, I prefer their curious smoked sausage sandwiches, made from link sausage pulled loose from its casing, sizzled on the grill, and served on a cottony bun drenched in mustard, slaw, and hot sauce. Could it be the only one like it available in the South?

509 North Farish Street / 601-354-9371

Bully's Soul Food

I can spot a plate of processed turnip greens at twenty paces. Ragged, leathery leaves reduced to a mulch worthy only of cattle fodder; pale white bulbs sliced into rectangular bits of regularity: these are the telltale signs that your greens came from, at best, a freezer bag, at worst, a can. And sadly, such as this is what you'll find on your plate at many restaurants that purport to serve Southern cooking. Some even go so far as to tout their product as homemade, when all they've done is doctor up the stewpot by tossing in a smoked jowl or trotter and a couple of rooster peppers.

Not so the greens served at Bully's Soul Food, a north Jackson joint in business since 1982. "All our greens are fresh," proprietor Ballery Bully tells me. "If we can't get it fresh, we won't serve it. And we like to serve a variety. Monday through Wednesday we'll go with just two greens on the menu, but toward the weekend, we usually have three."

I visit Bully's on a weekday and yet there are still three varieties to be had: mixed greens with turnips and mustards, collard greens, or cabbage. I order a bit of each along with some oxtails, and lean back in my chair to survey the surroundings. Soft-focus oil portraits hang on the walls: Jesse Jackson in a meditative pose, Malcolm X in a dark suit and skinny tie, his eyes fixed with determination. Through the barred windows I can see a freight train rumbling by. In the corner sits an elderly lady, a garbage bag of greens at her feet. She's pulling collard leaves from the bag one by one, stripping the spine and tearing away any blemish spots.

A few minutes pass before Ballery comes barreling out of the kitchen. In his hands is a beige plastic lunch tray, piled high with greens and oxtails. The oxtails are good, if a tad greasy, but the greens are near perfect: golden-hued shards of cabbage studded

with pork fat; dusky collards stewed with a few strips of sweet onion; a messy melange of peppery mustard greens and sharp turnips. It's all good, all fresh, all suffused with the sweet scent of smoked swine. "A while back, we tried cooking our greens with smoked turkey, for those folks that are so health-conscious," Ballery tells me. "But that started costing more than pork, and besides, nobody came back asking for those greens that didn't have the pork in them. Some things just shouldn't be fooled with."

3118 Livingston Road / 601-362-0484

Crechale's

For the longest time, most of the great cooks of the South lived and worked among us, their names known only to their family and friends. Like the Pullman car porters of the railroad age and the barbecue pitmasters of plantation days, these African American cooks toiled in sweaty, greasy obscurity, tending the fryer, the broiler, the grill. Generations of Southern restaurateurs staked their reputation upon the talents of these experienced cooks, though you'll find little record of their time behind the stove.

A case in point is Crechale's, which has been in business since 1956. For more than a quarter of a century, a sisterhood of African American cooks—the Thomas siblings—has ruled the roost at this swank roadhouse, famous for sweet, fried onion rings sheathed in an ethereal crust, peculiar cocktail sauce spiked with pickle relish, and well-marbled steaks broiled to perfection.

Martha Thomas has worked in the kitchen since 1969, her twin sister, Red Thomas, since 1967. Another sister, Diane Marshall, has been at it since 1975. More than 100 combined years behind the stove at Crechale's frying some of the best shrimp that've ever crossed my palate, and yet the Thomas sisters remain, for the most part, unrecognized.

3107 Highway 80 West / 601-355-1840

Mayflower Café

The cognoscenti call this Greek-owned, Depression-era diner in downtown Jackson a "poor man's Galatoire's." The reference points are twofold. First, the Mayflower serves Gulf-fresh seafood of similar quality as the century-old New Orleans standard-bearer, at a significantly lower price point. Second, although both dining rooms are devoid of pretense, inspiration for the mirror-lined Galatoire's comes from the bistros of France while the look of the neon-haloed Mayflower, with its porthole windows and leatherette booths, is Vegas-cum-Vicksburg.

Another consideration is the Mayflower bathrooms. They are reached by exiting the building, walking down the street and up a steep flight of stairs to a rabbit warren of rooms, one of which is carpeted, in the manner of a litter box, with old newspapers. But I digress.

Recently, I ate a fillet of wild redfish at the Mayflower. Swabbed in a mix of Worcestershire sauce and butter, it was accompanied by a brace of hand-cut fries and preceded by a salad of iceberg and feta and black olives. Before that I sipped an okra-muddled gumbo. Between bites of pearlescent fish, I dragged fries through a puddle of curry-spiked Cumback dressing, which Jerry Kountouris makes according to the recipe handed down by his late father, Mike Kountouris, born on the Greek island of Patmos.

That meal conjured the cookery of New Orleans, but it sang, too, of a uniquely creolized Mississippi. It taught me a lesson I should have already known. Of Africans who arrived in Mississippi knowing okra as *gombo*, its Bantu name. Of Vietnamese who, in the wake of the American exit from their homeland, arrived in Biloxi to pull nets of shrimp and strings of fish from the Gulf of Mexico. Of Greeks who have provided the muscle and intellect for generations of Jackson restaurants, from the Rotisserie Grill and the Black Cat Café to the Mayflower.

123 West Capitol Street / 601-355-4122

For a riff on Mike Kountouris' **Cumback Dressing** recipe, see page 189.

Cumback Dressing

Cumback dressing, the Jackson condiment of choice, is a pale orange local favorite that upon first blush appears as peculiar to outlanders as the mustard-based barbecue sauces of central South Carolina or the remoulade sauces so popular in New Orleans. At Crechale's they serve a pickle-relish-spiked version, and every table in the joint is set with an old catsup bottle, stripped of its label and filled to the top. At the Mayflower a stubby bottle of Cumback dressing hits the table when you do, filled with a red-flecked orange slurry brightened by a hint of curry. At the Cherokee Inn it's more of the same, with a punch of garlic to boot. Most every local restaurant serves it in some form or fashion. Locals pour it on their salad greens, slather it on hamburgers, and use it as dunking sauce for everything from fried chicken to French fries to fried shrimp.

In its simplest form, Cumback is nothing more than a smoothly pureed Thousand Island dressing, spiked with a bit more chili powder, perhaps an extra teaspoon or two of garlic salt, but share that observation with a native of Jackson and you're liable to raise a ruckus. Among the culinary cognoscenti hereabouts, it is considered to be a Jackson original, as common as catsup, but with no known progenitor. "Cumback is Jackson restaurant history in a bottle," my friend Randy Yates of Oxford's Ajax Diner once told me. "You can trace the history of eating places in Jackson by tracing the changes in Cumback dressing as it moved from one place to the next, from one Greek-owned restaurant to the next." My friend Malcolm White points to the now-defunct Rotisserie restaurant as the origin point, postulating that they made a Cumback dressing as early as the 1930s, and that from there it spread first to the Black Cat and later to the Mayflower. His theory gains credibility when you take note that by the early 1950s Duncan Hines' *Adventures in Good Eating* was touting the Rotisserie as "Home of the KUMBAK salad dressing."

McComb

Dinner Bell

Round-table dining may not be exclusive to Mississippi, but it is here that this peculiar dining custom reaches exalted heights. Over in Vicksburg there's Walnut Hills, set in an 1880 vintage home. Down in Columbia the Round Table has been packing them in for years.

Until recently, the Mendenhall Hotel, a circa 1915 railroad hostelry in the county seat town of Mendenhall, was the grandfather of them all. But the Mendenhall, once a favorite of M. F. K. Fisher, is now shuttered, leaving the Dinner Bell in McComb as the standard-bearer of a tradition that calls for serving all-you-can-eat midday meals from lazy Susan–style tables, which were likely solutions to the "boardinghouse reach"—long the bane of mannered Southerners who looked with disdain upon itinerant drummers who reached across a crowded table to snag a bowl of black-eyed peas, a casserole dish of creamed spinach, or a platter of country ham.

In Mississippi boardinghouses, long-armed extensions have long been unnecessary, for while the bottom tiers of the lazy Susan tables remain stationary the buffets spin by on the top tiers like carousels of calories. And at the redbrick Dinner Bell, in business since the early 1950s, that carousel includes fat butter beans in potlikker, sweet potato casserole dotted with marshmallows, and sage-laced chicken and dumplings that owing to the richness of the poaching stock shade more toward yellow-green than pasty white. And let's not forget the house specialty, fried cornmeal-coated disks of eggplant, raspy on the outside and creamy at their core, quite frankly, the best you'll ever taste.

Twenty people can take seats at the Dinner Bell's back table. And on a recent Sunday, each chair was full. Over the course of an early lunch, I learned from an aging regular how to expertly spin the lazy Susan, how to use English to get the casseroles and bowls I desired. He worked the thing like it was a roulette wheel and a C-note was riding on the proper placement of the eggplant. As for me, I was happy to accept what fate spun my way, although I will admit that the best of my spins landed a bowl of stewed okra and tomatoes that I quietly removed from the rotation.

229 Fifth Avenue / 601-684-4883

Philadelphia

PEGGY'S

Ask Peggy Webb why she's never hung up a sign to advertise her restaurant, and she's likely to tell you much the same thing she told me. I ducked my head back in the kitchen and found her standing at the stove in a flour-dusted blue apron, dipping battered pork chops into a cast-iron pot burbling with hot oil: "Honey, people show up here often enough when we're not open, looking for me to fix them some food. You know it would only get worse if I put up a sign. We live here; I've raised three children in this house. You're standing in *my* kitchen. No, we don't need a sign."

Since 1961 Peggy and her husband, Don, have been welcoming local folks to lunch in their modest, stuccoed home, just off the town square. Seating is communal style, at one of six tables scattered about the floors of the family's former living and dining rooms. A hostess brings your iced tea, a basket of cornbread, and a roll of silverware. You step into the hallway where a board Don tacked up across the walls serves as a makeshift buffet.

Arrayed on a collection of electric hot plates are big, metal pans of sweet, rosy ham on Monday; crusty fried chicken on Tuesday and Friday; soupy beef tips on Wednesday; and salty, fried pork chops on Thursday. Sweet creamed corn and butter beans in a pale green potlikker are among the vegetable offerings. Caramel layer cake is the dessert of choice.

If it's your first visit to Peggy's, a call for the check will bring a chortle or two from your tablemates, for, when it comes to settling up, you're on your own. Just toss your six dollars in the basket near the entrance, making change if need be. Short on cash? If Citizen's Bank of Philadelphia is your financial institution of choice, then you can just scratch out payment on one of the counter checks stacked alongside the basket.

512 BAY STREET / 601-656-3478

Taylor

TAYLOR GROCERY

Back in the dark days, when Taylor Grocery closed in the spring of 1997, a heavy sigh could be heard to drift across the hill country of northern Mississippi. Famed for serving crisp-fried, sandy-brown catfish in a woebegone, tin-roofed old country store, the avant-funk restaurant had won an army of admirers throughout the years. When those screen doors slapped shut, and the big metal sign—the one that pleaded with passersby, "Eat or We Both Starve"—was hauled inside, a large chunk of Lafayette County history was missing from the landscape.

It was a tradition, a rite, a pilgrimage of import. Rain or shine, win or lose, generations of Ole Miss football fans had made their way down the two-lane blacktop that snaked from Oxford nine miles south to the little hamlet of Taylor, toddies in hand, fried catfish and hushpuppies on their mind.

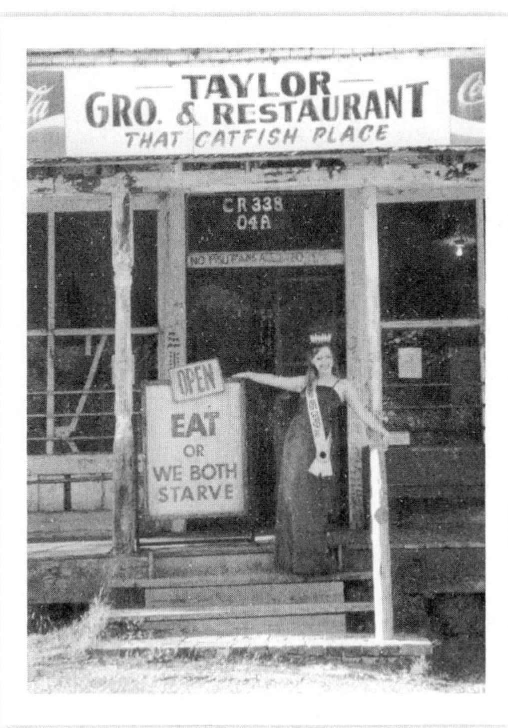

Miss Catfish 2000, Jessica Perkins, just can't get enough of that good fried fish.

No one seems to remember when the first string of Taylor catfish was bathed in milk and eggs, rolled in meal, and tossed in a skillet burbling with oil. Maybe it was sometime in the early 1970s; that seems to be the era most often cited. This much is clear: by the early 1980s tiny Taylor was the catfish capital of a state that was plumb catfish crazy. Politicos and starlets, musicians and writers, adventuresome gourmands and just plain folks; they came by the carload, by the busload even, intent on tasting something authentic, something real, something that smacked of

Mississippi. No matter the occasion, Taylor catfish was the destination restaurant of choice. Weddings and divorces, births and deaths; at the rickety tables set with dull flatware and paper napkins, good times were celebrated, bad times salved.

But it was on football game weekends that the place really came alive. Fraternity boys, tight on Jim Beam, sorority girls, pink bows fixed in teased, henna-colored hair—they came, they ate, they scribbled doggerel on the white plaster walls: "John Loves Jessica," "Tammy Digs Tommy," "Mississippi State Sucks," "Archie Manning for Governor," "William Faulkner Can Kick William Shakespeare's Ass!"

Soon "that catfish place" was as prized for the graffiti that covered the walls as for the sweet white fish that emerged piping hot from the skillets of owner Mary Kathryn Hudson. Some folks will tell you that it all began on the eve of the Ole Miss–Georgia game back in 1979, when Willie Morris and Senator Thad Cochran took pens in hand. No matter, in the ensuing twenty years, barrel after barrel of ink was spent, to the point where Willie and Thad's doodles were long ago eclipsed by Tammy and Tommy's. Taylor Grocery was a democratic institution, in the truest sense of the word.

And then it was gone: doors locked, cast-iron skillets stowed away. Mary Kathryn retired. Soon locals were carping that though you could get a decent plate of sushi up the road in Oxford, a heaping platter of bone-in, honest-to-goodness fried catfish was getting about as scarce as chicken teeth. And they were right.

Enter Lynn Hewlett. Turns out, he bought the place soon after it closed in '97, and has since been working to reopen it, albeit with a few changes. He grew up in the community, three doors down from Taylor Grocery, to be exact. His grandfather owned the little general store next door. This is his place. These are his people.

"I did my best to remodel the place—to fix it up so that it would satisfy the Health Department—in the least obtrusive way possible," Lynn says, his arms sweeping wide to take in the restaurant. From the looks of things, he has succeeded. The walls have been patched in places, but with an eye for saving as much of the old graffiti as possible. The open kitchen has been enclosed. The old bathrooms have been reworked. But the heart and soul of the place remains intact. "We want to pay homage to the history of this place, to Mary Kathryn who cooked here for so long," says Lynn. "She'll get free catfish any time she wants it. I hope we can fix it to suit her."

HIGHWAY 338 / 662-236-1716

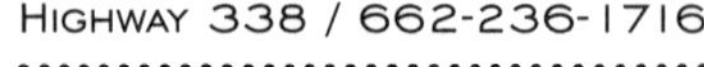

Cumback Dressing

an homage to Mayflower Café

Makes about 4 cups

At the Mayflower, the café that inspired this recipe, they bring a bottle of their housemade concoction out when you they serve your salad. I recall that it's always cold from the refrigerator. And it's always a welcome accompaniment to my salad. But I like it better as a dipping sauce for my French fries.

2 large garlic cloves, peeled
1 large or 2 medium onions, grated
1 cup mayonnaise
½ cup chili sauce
½ cup catsup
½ cup mustard
½ cup vegetable oil
1 tablespoon Worcestershire sauce
1 teaspoon finely ground black pepper
Dash of paprika
2 tablespoons water

Place the garlic and onion in a blender and puree until mixed. Add the mayonnaise, chili sauce, catsup, mustard, vegetable oil, Worcestershire sauce, pepper, paprika, and water. Blend until well combined.

NORTH CaRoLiNa

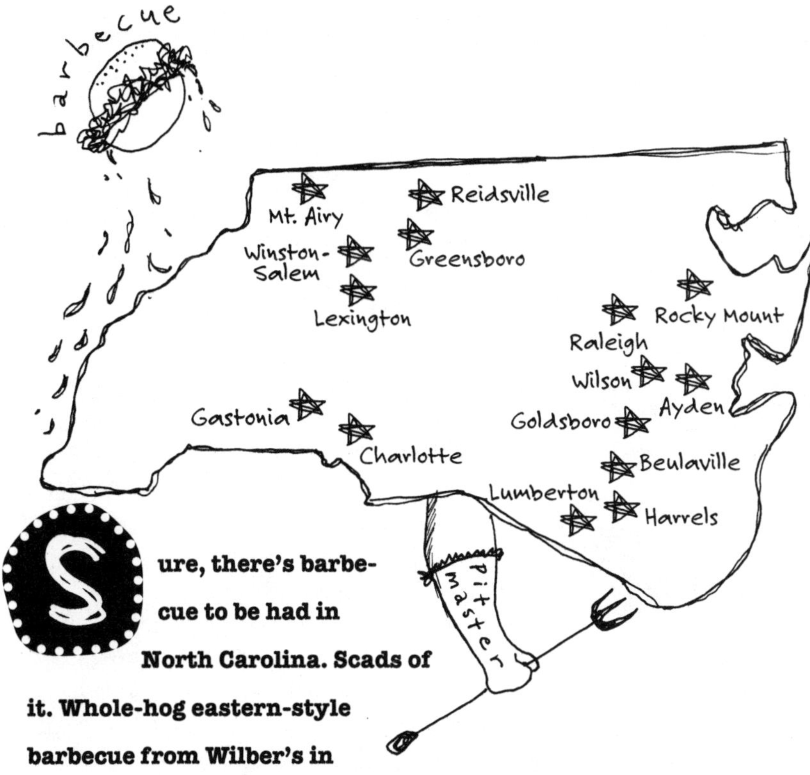

Sure, there's barbecue to be had in North Carolina. Scads of it. Whole-hog eastern-style barbecue from Wilber's in Goldsboro, western-style sandwiches of minced pork shoulder napped in a tomato-vinegar slurry from Wayne Monk's Lexington Barbecue. But the Tar Heel state is also home to a bit of food history worth pondering, for it was at a Woolworth's lunch counter in the town of Greensboro that the sit-in movement took flame, when in 1961 four African American students asked to be served a cup of coffee alongside their fellow white citizens. Think about that. Chew on that. And then join me at Charlotte's Coffee Cup for a slice of pie.

A North Carolina 'Cue Primer

When it comes to barbecue, North Carolinians fall into two camps: devotees of eastern-style or western-style barbecue, with the latter often labeled Lexington-style in deference to the Piedmont city that most accept as the capital of 'cue. Along a line that runs roughly approximate to Highway 1, which traces a route north and south from the town of Raleigh, the state divides into two factions, and allegiances are drawn based upon the relative merits of eastern vinegar-pepper sauces versus western tomato-spiked concoctions, and eastern whole-hog versus western shoulder-meat barbecue. Easterners go so far as to argue that since their sauces tend to lack even a kiss of tomato, theirs is the oldest style, dating back to the days when popular belief held that the tomato was poisonous. Westerners counter that everyone knows tomatoes are God's gift to smoked meat.

Guess what their specialty is?

Though there are myriad variations in the different styles that a local might be willing to spend an afternoon explaining—like the tendency of eastern aficionados to offer boiled potatoes dusted with paprika on the side and the western habit of serving a reddish coleslaw shot through with barbecue sauce—the novice eater is advised to stick to analysis of meat and sauce when trying to get his geographical bearings. A peek around back of the building might also be in order, especially when you are in the eastern part of the state, for, of late, many of the state's venerable smoke shacks have taken to cooking on thermostat-controlled pits. When in doubt don't just look for a pile of hickory stacked by the pit. Instead, bend down and take a look at the woodpile. Are there cobwebs collecting between the split logs? If so you might be staring down at what amounts to little more than window dressing for one of those heretical gas- or electric-fired ovens.

Ayden

Still life with pig and cabbage.

Skylight Inn

The late Pete Jones claimed lineage in the barbecue business dating to the days of his great-great-grandfather, Skilton Dennis, who was widely recognized as hosting one of the first commercial barbecues in the state. In February of 1830, he dug a pit and smoked a few pigs for a Baptist church convention, serving the assembled masses from the back of a wagon. "The TV folks say the date was February 14, but you never can tell about what they say," Pete once told me.

Pete, a chain-smoker with the scarred forearms of an experienced pitman, died in 2006. He had been in business for himself since 1948. But his instruction in the ways of the pit started at the age of seven under the watchful eye of his uncle, Emmett Dennis. "I guess if anybody showed me how, it was him," Pete told me.

Today, his nephew Jeff Jones runs a smoke shack that seems little changed from the days when the elder Jones shoveled his first load of hickory and oak embers onto an iron grate covered with a splayed hog. "We still cook all night—get through around 9:15 in the morning," Pete liked to say. "Somebody's got to be here with the meat. They got to add coals every thirty or forty minutes if they want to do it right. We go slow, but we don't go at one temperature; it just depends. And we put our coals around the pig, never under it—that is if you want to do it right." With that kind of schedule it should come as no surprise to you that Pete lived across the street.

The restaurant is a no-frills operation, a stop-sign-shaped brick building on the outskirts of town, hard by the local airstrip. There's no sign out front. Indeed the only thing likely to catch your eye is the rustic rendition of the U.S. Capitol dome—made with vinyl siding, wood, and tin—that Pete had mounted up top when *National Geographic* magazine declared his place to be the barbecue capital of the world back in 1984. Pete's rationale was simple: "You've got to have a dome if you're the capital, now don't you?"

Choices are limited: small tray, large tray, or sandwich; that's about it. And trays are the way to go, for they combine a cardboard boat of sweet, moist 'cue, topped with a slab of grainy cornbread suffused with meat drippings, and another tray of brightly-flavored coleslaw, each layer separated from the other by a sheet of wax paper, and the whole affair balanced precariously on the counter while you fish in your pockets for cash. A sauce tasting of red pepper and vinegar sits on the table, but most folks forgo any further adornment. No matter how many times I visit, my eyes are always drawn to the fellow stationed behind the back counter, wielding a cleaver, hacking the meat to pieces, and tossing bits of crispy skin with dove-white tenderloin, working all the while to get the right mix of fat and lean, crunchy and soft meat.

Noting that the chopping block is almost concave, I once asked Pete how often he had to buy a new one. "If I tell you about that," he said, "I'll have to tell you about the midgets." I told Pete that I was game and we were off on a thirty-minute romp of a story. Along the way I learned that Pete sold the concave chopping blocks for fifty dollars per and that his best customers were a pair of midget Florida real estate developers who, enamored of his barbecue, liked to take the blocks, top them with Plexiglas, fix them with legs, and use them as coffee tables. "Last time they were in, I posed for a picture with them," Pete said. "I got down on my knees and I was still taller than the little fellers. One of them looked up at me and said, 'We've had our pictures taken with the president before, but this is the first time we've gotten a picture with a king, the king of barbecue.'"

1501 South Lee Street / 252-746-4113

Beulaville

Ann's Wagon Wheel

Though collards are revered throughout the Southland, with some folks going so far as to argue that a sip of murky potlikker from the bottom of the kettle is the first line of defense in curing a head cold, or a poultice made from collard leaves and a flour sack the perfect balm for arthritis, the citizens of North Carolina have a peculiar affection for the crucifer.

Jazz great Thelonious Monk, a native of North Carolina, wore a collard leaf in his lapel when playing New York clubs. Archibald Leigh, a black American expatriate living in Paris, penned a poem for the 1984 collection of *Leaves of Green: The Collard Poems,* a wide-ranging compendium of more than 300 efforts. Commissioned on behalf of the Ayden, North Carolina Collard Festival, the pamphlet included poetry by such established literary figures as Fred Chappell. Leigh, for his part, claimed for collards a righteous and proud blackness, calling them "colored people's greens."

What's more, the state boasts a number of distinctive styles of collard cookery. For the longest time, the Wagon Wheel was base for a comparatively unconventional camp. Rather than strip the leaves from the tough stems, Wagon Wheel cooks chopped the leaves whole. And there was no smoked swine bobbing in the pot. Instead the Wagon Wheel, still a modest clapboard building on the outskirts of town hard by a trailer park, cooked exclusively with fresh pork backbones. And they tossed stewed cabbage into the mix to cut the bitterness. Last, the collards were whipped into a state that borders upon a puree, leaving not a trace of the traditional leaves of dusky green swaddled in a puddle of potlikker.

Eaten with a side of cornmeal dumplings swimming in backbone broth, they were a platonic dish of the highest order, worthy of gassing up the Humvee on a Wednesday morning and barreling across the countryside. A few years back, the Wagon Wheel changed hands. It's now formally known as Ann's Wagon Wheel. And the collards now lack the sweetening effect of cabbage. Some locals say this allows the true essence of the collards to shine through, but I would be lying if I didn't tell you I missed them.

169 Highway 111 / 910-298-4272

Charlotte

Coffee Cup

From the outside, the Coffee Cup, with its cinder-block walls and barred windows, looks like a Cold War–era bunker. Set on an industrial side street where forklifts have been known to share the road with commuters, the restaurant is Charlotte's premier purveyor of plate lunches, the kind of place that draws white-stocking attorneys and blue-coverall-clad mechanics alike.

It's also the spot to which a native of Charlotte is likely to point when asked whether the civil rights struggles of the 1950s and 60s paid any real dividends, for here, where black Southerners once were served only at the take-out window, what is arguably the city's most integrated crowd sits down to plates of skillet-fried chicken and creamy macaroni and cheese, buttery mashed potatoes, and earthy black-eyed peas.

Until recently, Chris Crowder still ruled the roost at the Coffee Cup. A North Carolina native, an African American of farm stock, she'd returned home from New Jersey in the 1960s when her aunt, Myrtle Heath, bought the place and offered to put her to work as a waitress. At a juncture in the South's history when many blacks were fleeing for Chicago and Detroit, Crowder picked up a cork-lined tray and an order pad and waded into the fray.

In the intervening years, she didn't budge one whit. After her aunt retired in the early 1980s, she bought the place with a fellow waitress named Mary Lou Maynor. Mary Lou was white, Crowder black, and as Charlotte grew, their customers became a kaleidoscope of nationality and ethnicity. A few years back Mary Lou passed on, and though the Coffee Cup no longer claims a biracial management team, there are lessons still to be learned from a lunchtime trip to this Charlotte institution. Ask about the sign that was once posted on the back wall, the one that read, "Bathrooms Are Outside," and you're likely to get a history lesson: "They're out there because white folks put them out there, back when black and white people weren't supposed to eat or sleep or go to the bathroom in the same place." Crowder told me: "I keep them there so we don't forget where we came from."

914 South Clarkson Street / 704-375-8855

Price's Chicken Coop

Thinly battered, well-salted deep-fried chicken, dumped unceremoniously from cook baskets and served with hushpuppies, coleslaw, a marshmallowy white bread roll, and a jumble of so-called Tater Rounds. That's what you get when you quit the more well-traveled and gentrified precincts of Charlotte's Uptown neighborhood for this South End favorite, in business since 1948 as a chicken market, since 1952 as a kinda-sorta restaurant.

The exterior is a plane of redbrick, fronted by plate glass windows which, when the place is bursting at the seams—and it almost always is—fog with clouds of chicken grease. The white cinder-block interior is utilitarian. There may well be an air-conditioning unit in use somewhere but, come summer, it's no match for the combo of roiling oil and broiling Carolina sun. And there are no seats. Most meals are eaten in the front seat of cars or vans parked at the curb or, for those with a bit of lolling-about time, beneath the boughs in nearby Latta Park.

If you desire a meal of chicken parts, you're in the right place. The menu, printed on the top of the white pasteboard boxes in which Price's serves their birds, boasts quarter chickens, chicken livers, and chicken gizzards. (They also dish burgers and barbecue sandwiches, but no one is fool enough to order them.)

I once believed that in the cookery of fried chicken a cast-iron skillet was elemental. I claimed a seat in the skillet-fried pew alongside Calvin Trillin, who once observed that a "fried chicken cook with a deep fryer is a sculptor working with mittens."

But after a decade of traveling the South, eating at the likes of Price's—not to mention the fabled Willie Mae's Scotch House in New Orleans—I've tasted my share of wonderful deep-fried bird and have, in the process, come to see the error of my ways. I now believe that skillet-fried chicken is not inherently superior to deep-fried chicken. Nor is the inverse true. (The two are, however, different. So keep this in mind: If you like a crust that clings to the meat and offers a bit of chew, you're in the skillet camp. If you like a brittle crust that shatters upon first bite, you're a deep-fried fan.)

One more thing: When you step to the counter at Price's, have purse or wallet in hand and your order settled, for the white-jacketed employees brook no fulminating and fumbling. There is, however, a payoff in the harried exchange of cash and drumstick. Standing amid the rugby scrum of hungry supplicants, waiting for your box, you will recognize a place that matters deeply to this ever-evolving New South metropolis.

1614 Camden Road / 704-333-9866

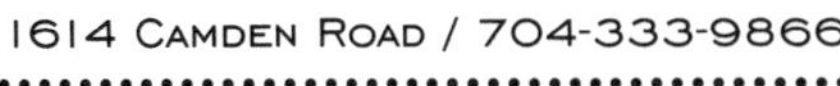

Gastonia

R. O.'s Bar-B-Cue

Slaw is a many splendored thing. I've eaten apple-studded stuff in Arkansas. Buttermilk-glazed in Texas. Mustard-laced in Tennessee. Bacon grease–doused in Kentucky. And here, in the Piedmont of North Carolina, I've eaten what some, owing to a pour of barbecue sauce, call bloodshot slaw. Yet none of these variations on a theme strike me as more distinctive or more curiously compelling than the almost puree of cabbage, catsup, mayonnaise, pickle relish, and spices served by Robert Ozy Black, his wife, Pearl, and their descendants since 1946.

R. O.'s began as a barbecue drive-in. And so it remains. Carhops, callow men with pencils tucked behind their ears, still work the blacktop. And barbecue sandwiches of sliced pork are still popular. (So are sandwiches of liver mush and eggs on white toast, but I digress.)

Hereabouts, slaw has supplanted barbecue as the center-of-the-plate focus. On a recent visit, I watch people drizzle it on hushpuppies, smear it on saltines, and use it as a dip for onion rings. Between pulls on a Cheerwine, one woman eats the stuff with a spoon. A love for slaw has even upended the Gastonia sandwich paradigm. In conversation with locals, I learn that the best meat to get as a slaw accessory is not barbecue pork but a flattop-cooked burger.

Later that same afternoon, I stop at Black's Barbecue, south of town. The same tenets hold true: carhops, slaw, and burgers. Although the slaw at Black's is a mite coarser, perhaps a bit spicier, it is undoubtedly born of the same palate.

Sitting at table in Black's, I conclude that the tradition will remain hyper-local. Sure, R.O.'s now sells its slaw in area grocery stores and has plans to expand nationally. But exceptional of displaced Gastonians pining for a taste of home—and acknowledging my own acquired taste for the stuff—the consistency and flavor of this sort of slaw does not strike me as a food outlanders will come to claim as their own. As I dip my fry in a pool of the slaw that drips from the backend of my burger, I take heart in that realization and rationalize a loop back to R. O.'s, where I will pick up a to-go quart.

1318 West Gaston Avenue / 704-866-8143

Goldsboro

WILBER'S

Wilber's is a devoutly Democratic institution. Tacked to the knotty oak paneling are black and white photos of FDR and other gods of the yellow-dog pantheon. It's a vestige of the day when North Carolina was a one-party state. Much has changed since the Republicans began luring rural Southerners into their lair. But Wilber's has not.

On my most recent visit, after wolfing down a sandwich of moist, chopped pork flecked with bits of red pepper and doused with a splash from the cruet of thin vinegary sauce they keep on every red-checked tabletop, Dennis Monk—owner Wilberdean Shirley's son-in-law—took me on a tour of the pit house out back, where whole hogs spend eight or nine hours on racks of steel rods perched above a bed of smoldering hardwood coals. Of the infernal pit room, Rick Bragg once observed, "It would seem a little bit like hell, if it didn't smell so good."

Not too long before my visit Wilber's lost the services of its pitman, Ike Green, a veteran of nearly thirty years on the job. "He was still working the pits on a Thursday," Dennis says. "But by that next week he was gone. It was a big loss. We're still trying to figure out what to do."

When I tell Dennis that judging by the quality of the barbecue I just ate, Wilber's has coped just fine, he smiles and allows that it's all about wood smoke and pig meat. "Ever since my father-in-law bought this place back in '62, salesmen have been calling on him, trying to get him to switch to gas and electric cookers. They like to have worried him to death. Some people will tell you that—like the old tobacco barns where they cured the leaves with wood smoke—before long this will be gone, but Mr. Shirley doesn't buy that. As long as we got wood to use we'll be cooking with it. We use oak and hickory for the most part, and with all these storms that have come through lately—Dennis, Floyd, Fran—we should be cooking for a while."

HIGHWAY 70, FOUR MILES EAST OF TOWN / 919-778-5218

Greensboro

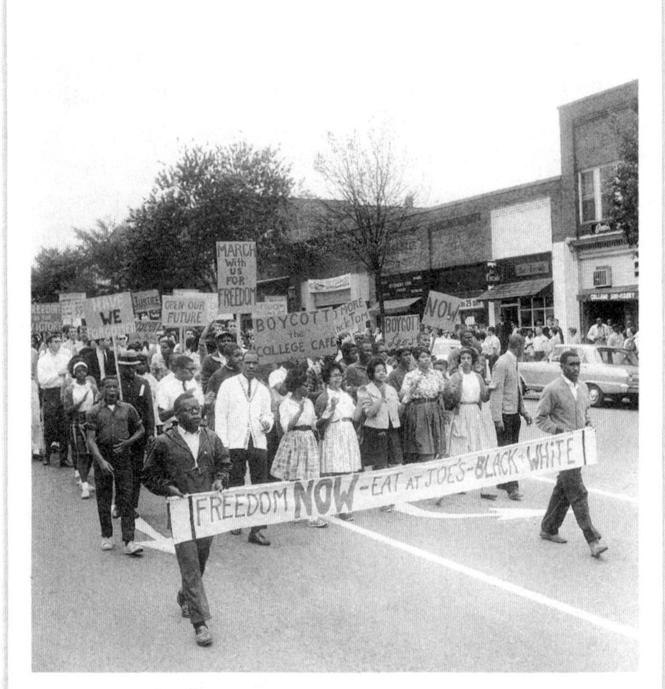

Inspired by students in Greensboro, sit-ins and marches soon spread to nearby Chapel Hill (pictured here).

Woolworth's Lunch Counter

On the afternoon of Monday, February 1, 1960, four black college students—Ezell Blair, Joseph McNeill, David Richmond, and Franklin McCain—took seats at the long L-shaped lunch counter that ran along the back wall of the Woolworth department store in downtown Greensboro. Like other customers on that sunny winter day, they sat on chrome-backed swivel stools and pondered the menu choices: a chicken salad club sandwich for fifty-five cents, a roast turkey dinner for sixty-five cents, and a slice of layer cake for fifteen cents.

The four students ordered coffee. A black waitress refused, for the seats they had chosen were in the "whites only" section of the lunch counter. The white manager, Clarence Harris, stepped into the fray, and rather than raise a ruckus or call the police, he did nothing. The students kept their seats, stood their ground, but were not served. And when the store closed for the night, the four freshmen from North Carolina Agricultural and Technical College bid Harris a civil good night, promising to return in the morning. Surely they took note of the Woolworth slogan, "Everybody's Store," emblazoned on signage posted throughout the building.

The students had read Gandhi. They knew of Martin Luther King Jr. and Rosa Parks and the Montgomery Boycott. The question was quite simple: why couldn't they take a seat beside their fellow white citizens and order a cup of coffee, a slice of cake? "It was put up or shut up time," McCain later recalled. "We were compelled to take an extra step to do something . . . and that 'do something,' as the world knows, turned out to be the sit-in movement . . . the tactic of well-mannered, well-dressed, courteous, polite kids just sitting there, well it just left people perplexed."

On Tuesday the four students returned, accompanied by more than twenty others. On Wednesday there were nearly eighty students in attendance. By Thursday more than 100 students gathered in protest at the lunch counter, including a handful of whites. Within two weeks, students in eleven other cities would launch similar protests.

Nearly six months passed before the Greensboro sit-ins came to a close on the afternoon of July 25, when three black Woolworth's employees were served at the previously segregated lunch counter. Though the Civil Rights Act of 1964, with its provision for nondiscriminatory practices in public accommodation, was still nearly three years away, the initial blow had been dealt, the first chink in the armor of restaurant segregation exposed. One year later, the *New York Times* would declare that the Greensboro sit-ins were the spark that, combined with "stand-ins at theaters, kneel-ins at churches and swim-ins at beaches," defined the "proportions of a national movement."

Today the Greensboro Woolworth is closed, the lunch counter enrobed in dust. Though a small section of the actual counter and four stools has been acquired by the Smithsonian Institution's National Museum of American History, the store remains almost wholly intact. On a recent visit, as my heels clacked on the marble floors and my eyes swept wide to take in the enormous length of the fabled lunch counter, I talked with Hurley Derrickson, an official with Sit-In Movement Incorporated. "We hope to have our International Civil Rights Center and Museum open here," he told me. "One of my favorite features will be a Hall of Civil Rights Leaders similar to the Hall of Presidents at Disney World. I can imagine Gandhi introducing King, who introduces one of the Greensboro protesters. There will also be a lunch counter, of course, where you can order food similar to what the protesters ate. Or should I say you can order food similar to what they would have eaten?"

132 South Elm Street / 336-274-9199

Harrels

Garfield Cromartie
Liver Pudding Maker

"Now I'm just piddling, making a bit for these people. Ain't nothing to it."

For those in need of a definition, liver pudding is the peculiar Carolina puree made of pork parts and cornmeal (some use rice). The product varies from region to region, and though there are no hard-and-fast rules, it can be argued that the farther north you travel, the more cornmeal you will encounter, and the closer to the South Carolina coast, the more likely you are to find rice.

Liver pudding is first cousin to the scrapples of Virginia and the Eastern Seaboard, kissing cousin to souse and head cheese. It is, in the most indelicate of terms, a mixture of every part of the hog but the squeal, and North Carolinians of a certain vintage can't get enough of the stuff. And legion are the North Carolinians who can't get enough of the pudding that Garfield Cromartie has been stirring up since the 1930s.

Born in 1916, Cromartie is the grand old man of liver pudding makers. "I grew up watching other folks make it," he tells me, his eyes glinting from thin slits set deep in a wizened black face. "We grew corn, tobacco, cotton, and cucumbers on the farm, working on shares, and I started traveling around to kill hogs for folks during the winter. I would show up, scald him, cut him up, and make the pudding, souse meat, and cracklins and then move on."

Unlike some brands that give off a canned-cat-food smell at twenty paces, Cromartie's liver pudding is subtle, sophisticated even, with a consistency not unlike paté. I tell him as much and he scoffs, "Now

I'm just piddling, making a bit for these people. Ain't nothing to it. I got my seasoning set in my head and that's what I use, a little bit of salt, black pepper, red pepper, sage . . ."

When the Moore family opened a retail outlet for their Clear Run Farms back in 1994, Cromartie came on board to teach them the fine art of pudding making. "He's trained me how to make it his way," says Joan Moore," but there are a few things he still won't let me do. He's got his own paddle for stirring the meat and his own ways. I follow him as best I can."

HIGHWAY 421 AND 41 / 910-532-4470

Lexington

LEXINGTON'S BARBECUE FAMILY TREE

"You could eat at a white-owned barbecue restaurant," Calvin Trillin once wrote. "But that's kind of like going to a gentile internist. You're not playing with the odds."

Trillin almost got it right. In the Deep South, where black pitmasters reign, their abilities linked to those bleak times of slavery, his words ring true, for even if the barbecue joint is white-owned, you can be sure that in most cases, there has been a black hand on the pit shovel, a black arm flexing to heft a load of oak into the firebox.

But here in the Up South, where plantations were fewer and the slave population smaller, barbecue has always been different. Here the tradition of barbecue stands dates back as far as the early years of the last century, and the best restaurants of the modern day are still, for the most part, run by white men, heirs to a legacy of open-pit cookery done in the hollow back behind a courthouse when the county magistrate court was in session, or in a fallow field come corn-shucking day.

Among present-day proprietors of Lexington-style barbecue spots, most folks look to Sid Weaver when talk turns to the past, for he is believed to have been the first man to cook barbecue commercially hereabouts, when in 1919 he erected a tent at the corner of Center and Greensboro streets in downtown Lexington. At first he opened only when the Davidson County Court was in session, but in time he erected a more permanent structure of timbers and tin with a canvas top. Beneath his feet, he spread wood chips and sawdust to soak up the grease from the pits. His sister-in-law, Dell Yarborough, and wife, Vergie, stirred up the slaw and Worcestershire-spiked sauce.

By 1923 there was competition for the court day barbecue trade when Jesse Swicegood, a farmer from a nearby community, opened his own stand just across the way from Weaver's. In his self-published book full of wonderful oral histories, *Barbecue, Lexington Style,* veteran pitman Johnny Stogner tells us that the two men's "wood piles were adjacent to one another." By 1938 Weaver retired, selling his business, which was by then located in a block building, to a gentleman named Alton Beck, though he continued to run a virtual barbecue stand from a pit in his backyard until his death in 1948. Swicegood also retired in 1938, selling his business to a native of Shelby, North Carolina, named Warner Stamey, who, further complicating matters, hired Weaver's sister-in-law, Dell Yarborough, to make the slaw and sauce.

Today, there are more than twenty barbecue stands in the 17,000-person town of Lexington, and I would make a strong argument that, though the family tree may be tangled and the lineage unsure, you could trace every single one of them to those rickety tents first erected by Weaver and Swicegood so very long ago.

Lexington Barbecue

From the road, Lexington Barbecue looks like an oversized dairy barn with a six-chimney nuclear reactor tacked onto the backside. Morning, noon, and night, wisps of blue billow forth from those stacks, an infernal torrent of sweet hickory and oak smoke. The interior is as plain as mud. In a land of country-cute pig parlors festooned with gewgaws and whatnot, Wayne's place is almost drab. The only decorations are a few paintings of old barns tacked to the pine-paneled walls.

The back end of the business where the fires burn day and night.

Locals still refer to this Piedmont institution by its original name, "Honey Monk's," in deference to proprietor Wayne Monk, who first fired up the pits back in 1962. You can usually find Wayne up front, scuttling back and forth between the kitchen and the counter, loading up the waitresses with paper trays piled high with sublime, coarsely chopped, smoked barbecue and sweetish slaw, tinted a ruddy hue by way of a good slug of vinegary barbecue sauce. Hushpuppies—crusty, creamy, and tasting of little more than corn and salt—come free for the asking.

I order a "brown" tray—chopped meat from the outside or "bark" of the shoulder, the smokiest stuff—polish it off in short order, and convince Wayne to take a few minutes to define for me what folks mean when they refer to Lexington-style barbecue.

"We use shoulders," he says. "Further east you'll see folks cooking whole hogs, but here it's just the shoulder. We cook ours for around nine hours or so over oak and hickory coals. Slaw here is simple. Mine has vinegar, salt, pepper, sugar, and a few other things; I learned it from Mrs. Dell Yarborough, sister-in-law of Sid Weaver, the guy lots of folks think started it all. The sauce has a little tomato in it, while you wouldn't be likely to see that in the eastern North Carolina. Oh, and hushpuppies, you gotta have hushpuppies. There's not much else to say."

Indeed he's right. For those who ascribe to the less is more school of barbecue cookery, this is a pork palace of the highest order, and Wayne Monk is the crown prince of the pits.

10 Highway 29 & 70 South / 336-249-9814

How the Hushpuppy Joined the Pig on the North Carolina Plate

While elsewhere in the South, hushpuppies—those little fried nubs of cornmeal batter—are thought of as a side dish best served with fried catfish or perch, shrimp or oysters, in North Carolina they are a fixture on barbecue restaurants' menus. As a native of Georgia, where white bread and slaw, Brunswick stew, and maybe baked beans, are the traditional accompaniments, such a pairing left me scratching my head and wondering why.

Wayne Monk of Lexington Barbecue put me on the trail of the first man to marry smoked pork and fried cornmeal. "The story goes that Warner Stamey was the first man to start serving hushpuppies with barbecue around here," he told me. "I worked for Stamey myself way back and I've always thought he was the first."

In a later conversation with Johnny Stogner, author of *Barbecue, Lexington Style,* I refined my understanding. "Stamey was the greatest Lexington-style barbecue entrepreneur," Stogner said. "He would travel around and talk to the old folks out in the country and see what they were up to, how they cooked. He picked up the hushpuppies from someplace down east, I'm sure of that. That was back in the early '50s. Now the hushpuppies had been popular in fish camps for a long time, but I'm pretty sure that by the time he brought them back up this way, there was a fellow already serving barbecue and hushpuppies down east, but I can't recall his name. Mr. Stamey got around to a lot of places."

Today, Stamey's flagship restaurant in Greensboro is run by his son Keith and grandson Chip. Asked about how hushpuppies came to be on the same plate as barbecue, Keith said, "My dad was great friends with the fellow who ran a fish camp called the Friendly Road Inn here in Greensboro, and I'm pretty sure he picked up on it there. Back then they used a hand-cranked little device to make the hushpuppies, but now we use a donut machine with a little extension on the nozzle that cuts the hushpuppy donuts in half as they drop into the oil. I wouldn't say my dad was the first, but I would say he was one of the first. Either way, I take after the old men of Lexington; I like my barbecue with bread."

Lumberton

FULLER'S

The contributions of Native Americans to the Southern larder may be among the most overlooked aspects of Southern culinary history. Despite a tendency toward knee-jerk genuflection at the first mention of corn, modern Southerners are, for the most part, unaware of just what constitutes a traditional Native American meal. Perhaps that is because in a day when restaurants function as museums of home cooking there are precious few places where one can sample fry bread and venison, squash and succotash.

Sure, you can travel to the Tee Pee Restaurant on the banks of the Oconaluftee River in the Great Smoky Mountains, where on the first and third Thursdays of every month the restaurant offers "Indian Food Dinners," derived from the Cherokee tradition, but the meal is better appreciated as an example of culinary voyeurism than immersion.

A better idea might be to light out for the town of Lumberton, epicenter of the land of the Lumbee Indians, a tribe with a storied history. Theirs is the largest tribe of Native Americans east of the Mississippi River, and the largest in the country not fully recognized by the federal government. Once known as the Croatan, the Lumbees are believed by some to have intermingled with English survivors of the Lost Colony in the 1580s and later with enslaved Africans. Though the town is chockablock with Lumbee-owned businesses, I know of no other restaurant that pretends to serve food of the kind savored in local homes.

As would befit a modern restaurant run by Native Americans, the daily buffet is a study in assimilation and adaptation featuring fatback and fried chicken, liver pudding, smoked pork ribs, and gleaming yellow strands of chicken and pastry. Collard greens and mashed rutabagas, steamed cabbage and green beans are also piled high. Come summer you can count on yellow squash, white corn, and fat butter beans. But the best thing on the buffet—indeed the single overtly Native American item served—is the fry bread: floppy disks of fried cornmeal that are just a tad greasy and pleasantly chewy.

I ask Karen Locklear, whose parents, Fuller and Delora, first opened the restaurant back in 1987, why there were so few dishes that I might identify as Native American. "This is what we eat at home," she tells me. "You're forgetting that what you might see as Southern, we see as Lumbee—things like squash and corn and

greens. Our people have been here a long time. Our food is a reflection of that history, even our barbecue. We've been smoking meat forever."

3201 North Roberts Avenue / 910-738-8694

Mt. Airy

Snappy Lunch

Like a thousand other small town cafés scattered about the South, Charles Dowell's Snappy Lunch is a simple place—dowdy even—outfitted with a couple rows of tight plywood booths and a trio of orange swivel stools facing a short counter. From a perch at the front window, Dowell, attired in his trademark white shirt, white apron, and white paper hat, can tend to the grill and watch the comings and goings of his neighbors as they walk along Mt. Airy's Main Street. Next door, a couple of tourists on a pilgrimage to the hometown of TV icon Andy Griffith peer into the window of Floyd's City Barber Shop, in hopes of catching a glimpse of Goober or Gomer or maybe even Otis.

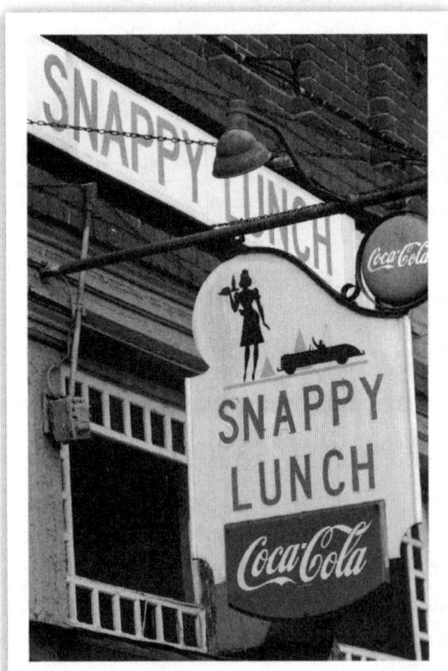

Inside, you'll find the mythic Tenderator.

"This place opened in 1923," Dowell tells me. "Two brothers-in-law named George Roberson and Ben Edwards were the ones. I came along in 1943. Back then we used to have a beer joint on either side of us and our customers were almost all men. About all we sold were hot dogs, hamburgers, and bread burgers. No breakfast, no nothing. By '51 I bought half of the place, by '60 I had the other half. I guess that you could say that over the course of the past forty years, I've made this place my own."

Truth be told, not only has Dowell made this place his own, but after years of grill work he has claimed his rightful rank in the Southern culinary firmament, alongside fabled fry cooks like Deacon Burton of Atlanta and Hap Townes of Nashville. His accomplishment? Nothing less than the reinvention of the pork chop sandwich, a longtime favorite of Southern trenchermen accustomed to wolfing down a thin, bone-in chop slapped between two slices of thin, cottony white bread.

Dowell starts with boneless loins of pork, feeding them through a device called a Tenderator, which, with its rotating spines, looks like a miniature version of an old cotton gin. Slide a slice of tenderloin in the top and it slips out the bottom perforated and tenderated, the soft pink pork flesh billowing open like an accordion. "I found the thing in a restaurant supply house back around 1988," he tells me, proving that the best Southern foods do not always claim the longest lineage. "At first I didn't buy it because I already had a cuber. In fact I went back three times before I took it home. Now I couldn't do without it."

Next comes a quick dip in a batter of flour, milk, water, salt, and sugar, and a baptism in a shallow pool of hot oil, where the thin beauties burble and spit until they reach a crusty brown. Served on a bun piled high with a slice of tomato, a smear of mustard, chopped onions, slaw, and chili, the pork chop flops out the sides like a pair of elephant ears.

Dowell plops a sandwich down in front of me and I take a bite. It's among the best things I've ever eaten—and among the sloppiest. Dowell looks at me, sizes up the contentment in my face and says, "Wouldn't you think that by now somebody else would have caught on to how you do this? I don't want McDonald's running me out of business," he says modestly, "but this isn't all that complicated."

125 North Main Street / 336-786-4931

Raleigh

Farmer's Market Restaurant

Come fall, the stalls at this state-run market are filled to overflowing with the bounty of North Carolina farms: bins of Beauregard sweet potatoes, flats of starburst squash, bushels of hen-peck mustard greens, and baskets of blue-top turnip greens. In the spring, farmers display pyramids of lustrous heirloom tomatoes with curious

appellations like Crimson Cluster and Aunt Ruby's German Green, White Queen, and Brandywine. By summer, there are watermelons by the score: yellow melons and rattlesnake melons, Crimson Sweets and Jubilees.

And no matter the season, you can rest assured that the on-premises restaurant—the one set in that unfortunate octagonal concrete guardhouse of a building by the front gate—will be serving the best of what's fresh and local. On the day I visit, the cavernous dining room is packed. The few people not tucking into plates of chicken and pastry (known elsewhere as chicken and dumplings), or fat salmon croquettes flecked with bell pepper, are studying the barely legible mimeographed menu, debating the relative virtues of pork backbone with rice and fried chicken, navy beans and steamed cabbage, collard greens and stewed squash.

The clock on the wall says, "We serve fresh vegetables 12 months of the year." My waitress's T-shirt promises, "Food so great you'll think we stole your mama." Who am I to argue? I dig into my breadbasket. Over in the corner, I spy Jim Graham, onetime North Carolina commissioner of agriculture, working the crowd, slapping backs and buttering biscuits as he goes.

I'm soon buttering biscuits, too, gilding the brown beauties with a squeeze from a bottle of molasses, and singing the praises of the unnamed cook. These are among the best biscuits I've ever tasted: soft, snowy centers capped with a butter-crusted mantle. When split open, a puff of steam floats upward like a sweet kiss from the baker. Indeed the biscuits are good enough to make me forget all about those fresh vegetables. I butter another and push aside my plate of chicken, collards, and cabbage.

When I ask my waitress whom to thank, she points the way to the kitchen and says, "It's Annie Mae Jones you want to see. She's been working here one way or the other since the '70s." I find Mrs. Jones up to her elbows in flour, surrounded by spent cartons of buttermilk. As she works, her glasses keep slipping down her nose, and each time she tries to push them back up, her black face is splotched once again with white flour. Lacking much else to say besides thank you, I ask her to reveal the secret to her biscuits. She smiles, plants her hands on her hips, and says, "Ain't no secret to it. It's just soul power."

On my way out I stop and talk to Mr. Graham. When I tell him how much I like Mrs. Jones' biscuits, he, too, smiles and points to the Jim Graham special, made with mayonnaise, onion, tomato, and streak-o-lean, all piled high atop one of Mrs. Jones' biscuits. "I can eat those by the carload," he tells me.

1240 Farmer's Market Drive / 919-833-7973

MECCA

Top left, behind the bar, above the wall-mounted fridge, is a portrait of Franklin Delano Roosevelt. Look closely and you'll see the nicotine shadings that soften the brushstrokes, the lint-ball fuzz that haloes his head. Roosevelt's smile is slight, even wry. He appears omniscient, by which I mean that our Depression-era savior looks like he has witnessed every deal done, every back slapped, every glad hand extended since the day Mecca Restaurant, a pol's warren in downtown Raleigh, opened in 1930.

Pull back from Roosevelt to take in the whole of the space and you'll find a restaurant little changed since Greek immigrant founders Nick Dombalis and his brother-in-law Nick Bougadis threw open the doors and staked a claim to the motto "He profits most who serves the best." Wooden booths, embellished with scrollwork and fixed with coat hooks, hug the walls. Swivel stools front the counter. The cash register doesn't chirp and bleep like new computer models; it churns and grinds as gears engage in the manner of a vending machine.

Now operated by Paul Dombalis, grandson of Nick, and Floye Dombalis, mother of Paul, the restaurant still tips its hat to Greek roots by way of lemon herb chicken, a Friday special, as well as an everyday salad with feta and olives. But, in large part, the menu is defined by ethnic assimilation and various quirks.

Among the latter are the Garry Dorn Burger (veal cutlet, catsup, onion, and tomato), a sandwich of so-called Danish ham, a barbecue plate of "young North Carolina pig," and a New England Clam Chowder which is, counterintuitively, given top billing. Assimilation, however, is the real story, for grilled chicken and Greek salad excepted, the eats proffered by the Mecca cooks are irreproachably Southern.

On a recent visit, my plate lunch included thinly battered and expertly fried chicken, ropy turnip greens, rice napped with gravy, and, best of all, earthy field peas jumbled with snaps. The presence of the field peas—and even more so the inclusion of those snaps—signaled that I was in a restaurant where old-school cookery and produce are valued. Corroborating evidence came when I noted home-grown tomatoes and sliced cucumbers among the tail-end-of-summer vegetables of the day.

13 EAST MARTIN STREET / 919-832-5714

Reidsville

Short Sugar's Drive-In

"You'll find a few nicknames here and there, but nowhere, I'll venture, are they as common and well-considered as in the South," observed journalist Robert Coram. "One episode, one physical or mental aberration, one mistake, one peculiarity, and you get a nickname hung on you that will last for years."

An awful tall chimney for a short place.

Perhaps, while musing poetic about nicknames, Coram was thinking of the late Eldridge Overby, who was killed in a June 1949 car crash two days before he and his brothers Johnny and Clyde were to open a barbecue and burger shop called Clyde Brothers Drive-In. It seems that years before, Eldridge's girlfriend pinned him with the moniker. "He was called Shorty by everybody," present-day proprietor David Wilson tells me. "And when she went into one of his hangouts and asked, 'Where's my Shorty Sugar?' it just stuck." In tribute, the brothers Overby called their new business Short Sugar's.

I arrive at such an early hour that most folks are seated at the low counter, coffee cups in hand, staring down a platter of eggs, biscuits, and bacon. But without hesitation, my request for eggs, biscuits, and barbecue is honored, and soon I can hear the sound of cleaver meeting cutting board. In no time, a plate of eggs, grits, and chopped, smoked ham brightened by a thin, sugary, vinegar-based sauce is set before me. Biscuits, split and toasted in a flattop press, are piled on top; a sliced beefsteak tomato is served on the side.

The sauce is sweeter than I expected, the marriage of grits and barbecue reminiscent of the dishes of grillades and grits I sampled in Louisiana—which is to say it is delicious. When I ask David whether he considered my request to be odd he shakes

the idea off with a smile. "I've seen just about everything," he tells me. "Some people want their biscuits burned. Other people want barbecue omelets."

I leave in the company of David by way of the roofing tin–topped pits, where the pork I just ate spent the last twelve to thirteen hours over a smoldering hickory fire. Rick after rick of wood is stacked by the door and the firebox is propped closed by a broom handle. David pops the door open and scoops up a shovel full of coals to feed the fire. Smoke swirls lazily from the pit door and I bid good-bye.

1328 SOUTH SCALES STREET / 336-342-7487

Rocky Mount

HARDEE'S AND THE FAST-FOOD BISCUIT

Can you imagine a person of Jewish descent eating one of those sausage-stuffed Bagelwiches that Burger King used to hawk? Or a Frenchman downing a Croissanwich enrobed in a caul of melted American cheese? Of course not. So why do we Southerners accept the fast-food biscuits proffered by the national chains?

Perhaps there is some solace to be found in learning that at least the roots of the fast-food biscuit are Southern. The North Carolina–based Hardee's chain is generally credited with popularizing the homemade-style biscuit in the late 1970s, when franchisees Jack Fulk and Mayo Boddie began baking biscuits the size of an infant's head and selling them to morning commuters. By 1977 Fulk left Hardee's, striking out on his own with a chain of Bojangles Chicken and Biscuit restaurants.

Today, Hardee's and Bojangles—as well as smaller North Carolina–based chains like Biscuitville—still bake a better product than McDonald's or Burger King, but I can't eat one without a twinge of guilt, for with each pan of faux homemade biscuits that emerges from a fast food restaurant's convection oven, we edge a bit closer to the culinary and cultural precipice. Call me cranky if you wish, but I've got a rolling pin and I'm prepared to use it.

Wilson

The Pitmaster

Dressed in blue overalls, a gimme cap pushed back on his head, Ed Mitchell is a barbecue evangelist. With his full beard and lumberjack frame, he musters an Old Testament gravitas, leavened by a modicum of Jesse Jackson populism. Here's the pitmaster's plan:

By contracting with farmers to rear hogs for a nascent chain of barbecue restaurants, Mitchell hopes to rescue the small North Carolina farmer from the brink of extinction. What's more, Mitchell wants to return great pork—the round-flavored pork he knew as a child, before the industry embraced confinement pens and waste lagoons and lean-generation genetics—to working-class eaters.

Like any good barbecue man, Mitchell has, while running a barbecue restaurant in his hometown of Wilson, honed a repertoire of techniques. He has learned to bank his pits, to stack them with charcoal and hickory so that the temperature holds steady through the night. And following his mother's lead, he soaks his wood in a salt-and-pepper-spiked vinegar solution that when ignited perfumes the pork with more than mere smoke.

But Mitchell's true talent is selling eaters on the import of ideas. For him, it's a crusade. Sure, he cooks some of the best eastern-style Carolina barbecue you will ever have the pleasure to eat. And his vinegar sauce is a well-balanced concoction, perfect for pig or chick. But years from now, when Ed has passed on, he will—hopefully—be remembered as the man who showed working-class Southerners a way back to cooking honest pigs. Mitchell knows the path won't be easy. But you can see the determination in his face. And you can, if you like, taste the future he promises at this, the first in what he hopes will be a host of restaurants.

6228 Ward Boulevard / 252-237-8645

For the Pitmaster's version of **Eastern North Carolina Sauce**, see page 217.

Winston-Salem

Texas Pete Hot Sauce

Southerners like it hot. Maybe that's attributable to a latent taste for the heat of the islands, introduced by slaves who underwent a period of seasoning in the Caribbean. Maybe it's fueled by a secret wish to sweat during the swelter of summer, when the scorch of a habañero or jalapeño induces the body to cool down. No matter, we Southerners are a hot-sauce-mad people. Few are the restaurants which can't produce a couple of bottles on demand; many are the spots where tables are set with a couple of different brands.

Although Tabasco, a product of Avery Island, Louisiana, is my favorite, it does not have a lock on the Southern hot-sauce market. Even in Louisiana, there are pockets of Crystal hot-sauce lovers in New Orleans, and up around Monroe you'll

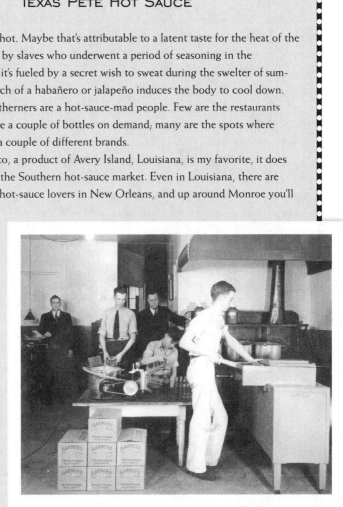

The Garner family at work, packing bottles of their heady Texas Pete hot sauce.

find a strong contingent of Panola pepper sauce fans. You have to travel farther north and east, though, before another maker truly comes to the fore, but by the time you cross the border into North Carolina, the comparatively viscous and somewhat milder Texas Pete is oftentimes the favored brand.

Despite a name that conjures up images of roping and riding along the Rio Grande, Texas Pete is a North Carolina company born and bred, still run by the family of founder Thad Garner.

It seems that back in 1929 when Garner graduated from high school, he bought a barbecue stand in Winston-Salem called the Dixie Pig. In time he developed such a strong reputation for barbecue sauce that he was selling it by the gallon to his competitors. And when some folks started clamoring for a hotter version, Garner obliged, packing it with peppers and selling the new sauce by the bottle.

The barbecue stand soon folded when traffic was diverted by a new rail line, but by then no one cared because the sauce was flying off grocery store shelves, with sales boosted in part by a catchy new name, Texas Pete, dreamed up by Thad's father, Joseph, in a brainstorming session. "Everybody got involved about then," says Ann Riddle. "That was back in the days when Uncle Thad's father, my grandfather, took off on the road in a seven-passenger Cadillac selling hot sauce. Back then, he wouldn't come home until he ran out of bottles to sell."

Eastern North Carolina Sauce

from the Pitmaster
Makes about 1 quart

The simplest of eastern Carolina sauces comprise just vinegar and red pepper. And so in some quarters this sauce would, despite hewing to the prevailing gestalt by forswearing tomatoes, be considered heretical. No matter, I love this stuff. And I believe with all my heart that there is no finer swab for smoked pork.

1 quart apple cider vinegar
½ cup crushed red pepper flakes
1 tablespoonful sugar
1 tablespoonful salt
1 tablespoonful freshly ground black pepper
1 teaspoonful cayenne pepper

Pour out an inch of vinegar from the quart container. Add the dry ingredients, replace the cap, and shake vigorously. Use liberally as a mop and a sauce. This sauce may be stored for up to 3 months without refrigeration.

SOUTH CaROLiNa

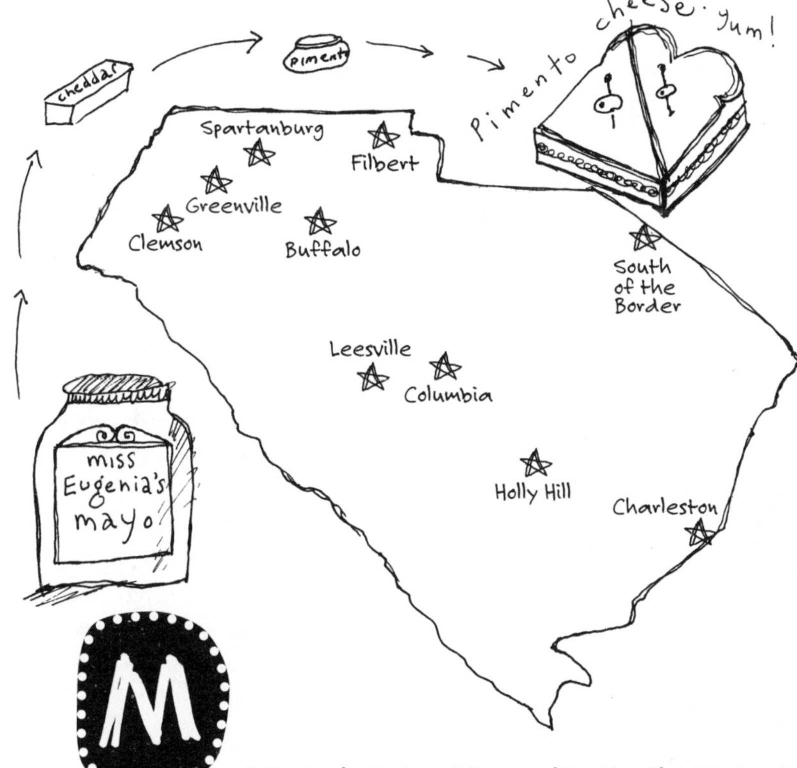

Meet Eugenia Duke of Greenville, the first lady of mayonnaise. Revel in a perfect pimento cheese sandwich, slathered with Eugenia's eggy spread. Better yet, try a pimento cheeseburger in Columbia, where they smear on the stuff with a heavy hand. Take a summer excursion with me to the little community of Filbert—to the roadside vegetable stand of author Dori Sanders—where we sample peaches with bright, sweet, hopeful names like Starlight, Sunhigh, and Georgia Belle. And don't forget to try a bottle of Blenheim's Ginger Ale, the three-sneeze-fit strong stuff now bottled at South of the Border.

sweet peach!

Buffalo

Midway B-B-Q

There's a fine spray of sawdust covering the concrete floor at this combination barbecue joint and butcher shop—a vestige of the days when the blood from eviscerated cow and pig carcasses spilled onto the floors, and sawdust was thrown down to soak up the mess.

Proprietor Jack Odell doesn't slaughter his own animals anymore (a packing house does it for him), but he does haunt the local auction houses, personally selecting the pigs and cows that will eventually end up on his pits or in his kettles. And what Jack doesn't smoke or stew he sells at his butcher counter, where souse and liver mush, cracklins and country sausage are piled high. "I look for the top end, the cream of the crop," he says. "Otherwise my barbecue will end up as tough as whit leather."

As you might expect Jack's barbecue is indeed tender, if minced a little fine and sauced a little heavily for my taste. But it's the beef hash and chicken stew that keep the regulars coming back. Ropy and rich with sweet butter and mild onions, Jack's hash is a paradigmatic dish, a standard by which all others might be judged. And the chicken stew is without peer, a localized specialty that deserves wider notice: a thin buttery milk emulsion, suffused with strands of tender bird and laced with the pleasing bite of black pepper. I can't think of any place I'd rather be than seated in a ladder-back chair at one of the red and white gingham-flocked tables in Jack's dining room, with a bowl of that steaming white stew in front of me, a pile of saltine crackers at the ready.

If you happen to be driving into Midway around lunchtime, be sure to listen out for the daily dinner report from Jack's grandson-in-law, Jay Allen, broadcast live on WBCV at 11:05. That's how I found this Upstate treasure. "Yes sir, we got chicken stew today, piping hot and creamy," came the siren song. "And just look at Shirley over there rolling out that pie crust. Now you know we don't allow any tipping at Midway. No, we'll accept compliments and constructive criticism, but no tipping. Say, did you know we've got the largest display of fatback in the state?"

811 Main Street / 864-427-4047

Charleston

Bowen's Island Restaurant

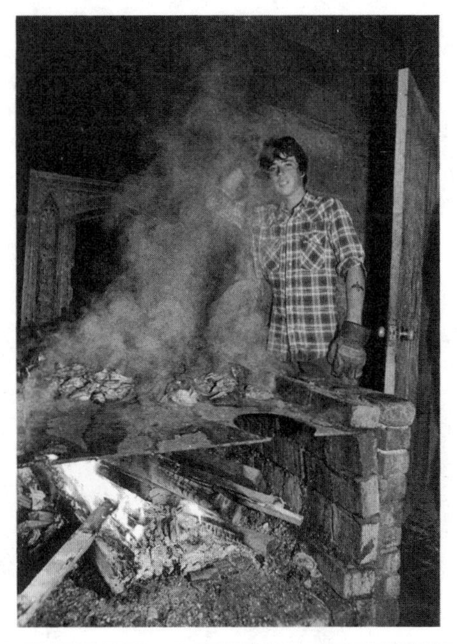

Scene from Bowen's before they went to gas.

Drive the lane that branches off the road from Charleston to Folly Beach, South Carolina, and as you wend through a thicket of palmettos onto Bowens Island, you will spy a dock jutting into the marsh. At the heart of the island is a restaurant, a cinder-block bunker ringed by oyster middens. Decorations include decommissioned televisions scrawled with graffiti, a jukebox or two, and a rusted-out hair dryer liberated from a beauty parlor.

Spray-painted on the side of the building are portraits of Jimmy Bowen and Sarah May Bowen, the husband and wife team who in the 1940s bought the island and, in what seemed a quixotic move, constructed their own causeway to the mainland. Alongside is an aerosol-rendered likeness of John Sanka, the cook who worked with the Bowens for more than thirty years.

Generations of Charlestonians have made the pilgrimage to sit at tables covered with yesterday's newspaper and piled high with today's catch. They come for oysters—pulled from local waters by pickers Victor Lafayette and Nell Walker—served without pretense.

Present-day proprietor Robert Barber, a grandson of the Bowens, takes that responsibility seriously. Barber's staff, among them counterman Jack London and oyster cook Henry Gillard, serve as guardians of Bowen-family tradition and curators of imperiled Carolina folkways. In those roles they dish the house specialty: clusters of oysters, harvested by hand from the Folly River, steamed on a gas-fired griddle under cover of a burlap sack, heaped by the shovel onto *Charleston Post and Courier* place mats, and washed down with cold beer.

1870 Bowen's Island Road / 843-795-2757

Jestine Matthews
An Okra Education

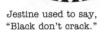

Jestine used to say, "Black don't crack."

"I keep this for educational purposes," Dana Berlin Strange tells me as she retrieves a mason jar of pickled okra from the corner cupboard of her restaurant, Jestine's Kitchen. "A lot of our customers aren't from the South, and they always seem to be asking, 'What is okra? What does it look like?' I show them the jar and tell them it has the skin of a peach and the shape of a hot pepper. I try to help them understand."

As we talk, seated at the back of her corner restaurant, it occurs to me that, for Strange, the white proprietor of a restaurant named in honor of her family's black housekeeper, helping tourists understand okra may be the least of her worries in a town where most everyone has come in search of an Old South where magnolias and mint juleps hold sway.

> "A lot of our customers aren't from the South, and they always seem to be asking, 'What is okra? What does it look like?'"

"I never imagined I would own a restaurant," she tells me by way of explanation. "But when Jestine fell sick at 110, I knew I had to do this, to open this little diner so that people would know about Jestine, so that she would know about the restaurant before she passed."

As the early lunch customers start to trickle in, Strange makes her way across to the front of the room, burping her infant son, Berlin, as she goes. For the next couple of hours she will serve as hostess: seating customers and taking drink orders, all the while exchanging reminiscences with her customers about the woman for whom the restaurant is named, the black woman this white Southern Jew knew as "my Nursey."

"My grandparents owned a clothing store in town, and met Jestine when she was in her fifties," recalls Strange. "They basically said to her, 'If you'll help raise our child, we'll take care of you for the rest of your life.' I guess the joke was on my grandparents; they've been gone for years and Jestine lived until this past December . . . Jestine was my mother's companion. And when my mother had me, she started taking care of me."

Soon the tables are packed with customers, the air heady with the

scents of what the restaurant advertises as "Southern food with lots of soul." As Strange works to seat customers and bus tables, she expounds upon her rationale for the restaurant's existence. "People come in here and tell me that they had a Jestine," says Strange. "Maybe not a 112-year-old Jestine, but they had someone who took care of them when they were growing up. I'll be walking through the dining room and see a tear or two or they'll call me over and tell me, 'We're so glad you did this; we had a Jestine.'"

"People come in here and tell me that they had a Jestine. Maybe not a 112-year-old Jestine, but they had someone who took care of them when they were growing up."

There are those that label Strange a paternalistic profiteer, yet she is unrepentant. "I've had people question my motives. I've had people ask if Jestine was my parents' slave. How could they think I'd be that way? I loved her," she argues, her voice crackling with indignation. "I could have named this place after my mother. You can't get much more Southern than Shera Lee's Kitchen . . .

"As it is, the recipes we use are Jestine's. We kind of whiten the food up a bit. But we don't have chefs. Jestine is the chef," explains Strange as she piles a table high with mashed potatoes and gravy, green beans and okra gumbo, red rice and fried chicken.

"Now I'm looking for a Jestine for him," she sighs, her eyes cast wistfully back to the bassinet at the rear of the room where baby Berlin sleeps.

251 MEETING STREET / 843-722-7224

MARTHA LOU'S KITCHEN

There's a scrap yard next door, chockablock with rusting pickup trucks and busted refrigerators. Sea gulls circle overhead, in search of scurrying prey among the wreckage. Twisted metal spirals upward from the center of the lot, dull and scarred, looming over the tiny pink cinder-block building that is home to Martha Lou Gadsen's café.

Inside, Martha Lou stands in front of the fry basket, a pair of tongs in hand, fishing—forgive me—a golden brown whiting fillet from the roiling oil. It's Wednesday, so there's a pot of chitlins and hot peppers simmering on the back burner, and lima beans, soupy and rich, bubbling in a battered aluminum pan on the front burner. In the oven a tray of macaroni and cheese burbles and spits. Yesterday she served okra soup, tomorrow she'll have giblet rice, Friday there's red rice. Every day you can count on pork chops and fried fish.

The phone rings. Her son picks it up and I eavesdrop on his end of the conversation. "What kind of chicken you want?" he asks. And then after a pause, "I said what kind of chicken you want? White meat, dark meat, blue meat, green meat. What you gonna have?"

I order a fried pork chop, lima beans, rice, and, for good measure, a side of macaroni and cheese before taking a seat at one of the two vinyl booths that line the wall. Above me is a mural of the Charleston market, rendered in a colorful, almost Haitian manner. In short time Martha Lou returns with a plastic plate, quaking beneath the weight of my lunch. She catches me staring at the mural and points to the one alongside. "That one's of Mosquito Beach," she offers, "where we all used to hang out after hours, back when the beaches were segregated." Martha Lou sets my plate down, slides into the opposite seat, and without much prompting, shares her culinary philosophy. "I believe in fresh foods," she says. "And I believe in seasoning my food. I don't like seeing people reach for the salt and pepper shaker."

One bite of the lima beans and I'm a believer. They are assertively, even aggressively seasoned, spiked with a healthy dash of salt and what tastes like a half-shaker of black pepper. The pork chop is juicy, sheathed in a thin, brittle crust. The rice is perfect, each grain separate, distinct. But the macaroni and cheese is in a class all its own. A paragon of Southern Soul cookery, it takes my breath away and sends me reaching for my tumbler of water. While most mac 'n' cheese is rather anemic stuff—limp elbow noodles swimming in a neon-orange soup of American cheese and condensed milk—Martha Lou's rendition is a burnt ochre in color, shot through with black pepper, firm at the center, crunchy on the top, and stupendously salty. I look up at Martha Lou and she smiles. "See what I mean?" she says. "I told you I liked my food seasoned."

1068 Morrison Drive / 843-577-9583

The Rice Kitchen

Charleston was once rice-obsessed. Planter whites built their antebellum fortunes on the grain they called Carolina Gold. Laboring blacks supplied, under force of violence, African-honed expertise. Pithy locals, cognizant of their hidebound ways, were fond of asking, "What do the Chinese and Charleston natives have in common?" The answer came quick: "They eat rice and worship their ancestors."

In 1860, when the total national rice crop was 5 million bushels, 3.5 million of those bushels were harvested along the South Carolina coast. That was the height. The decline, in the wake of the Civil War, was swift. By 1901 only 35,000 were planted. By 1920 the total rice acreage did not top 500. "Charleson had a mere handful of good restaurants then," my friend John Martin Taylor has observed, speaking of the decades that followed the early twentieth-century decline. "Other than a couple of joints, none of them served rice in any form."

Today, however, South Carolina is in the midst of a rice renaissance. Charleston is chock-full of restaurants that aim to be temples of rice culture. And rice cookers, bulbous aluminum double boilers, ideal for steaming the local crop, remain fixtures in Charleston kitchens. Even the cultivation of rice is on the rise. Carolina Plantation Rice grows an aromatic variety on the Pee Dee River, while Specialty Foods South sells true Carolina Gold rice. Anson Mills, on the other hand, both grows and sells true Carolina Gold.

Anson Mills / 803-467-4122
Carolina Plantation Rice / 843-395-8058
Specialty Foods South / 843-766-2580

TONY THE PEANUT MAN

Street vendors were once ever present on Southern streets. In Canton, Mississippi, Frank Owens walked the courthouse square, selling pecan, chess, and blackberry pies from a cut-down cardboard box. In Lufin, Texas, a tamale vendor known as Hombre worked high school football games. In the French Quarter of New Orleans, Louisiana, Sam De Kemel peddled four-for-a-nickel waffles while wearing a white chef's toque and playing a bugle.

Reform movements geared toward improvements in public health introduced onerous regulations and wiped out most of them. The fast-food industry finished off the rest. Or so I thought. Of late, I've begun to spot a few retro renegade operators. I've met a man who vends red velvet cakes from the trunk of his car. I've met a woman who sells pimento cheese sandwiches from a basket bolted to the front of her ten-speed. I've met a passel of hot dog vendors. (For a year I, too, owned a weenie wagon.) But no one has honed a shtick like Tony the Peanut Man, peddling sacks of peanuts since 1991 in Charleston, South Carolina.

He wears a bow tie, fixed tight around the collar of a T-shirt. The front is blazoned with his own smiling mug. The rear boasts his slogan-cum-song, "Got some boiled / Got some toasted / Got some stewed / Got some roasted," which, when he's selling—and he's always selling—wizened Tony sings with the bravado of a pubescent opera star.

On his head is a baseball hat, woven in the Gullah-style from sweetgrass. "I do the market," he tells me, referring to the City Market, where local women of African descent have long sold their signature baskets to tourists. "I do most anything to make a buck. Gotta move. Gotta sell."

Tony Wright's salt-roasted peanuts are good. And his boiled peanuts are great; they have that telltale dank earth taste. If you can't find him at the market, he's probably working a high school football game. Or a college basketball game. The local Piggly Wiggly sells his canned peanuts. But Tony is worth tracking down. If you don't meet the man you won't hear the song, a ditty that links him to generations of African American vendors past, people like the late Ben Campbell, the Charlestonian Tony modeled his pitch after, the man all remember as the King of Peanuts.

843-343-6362

Clemson

Clemson Blue Cheese

A slice of rat cheese (called hoop cheese in more polite circles) and a couple of saltine crackers has long been a snack time Southern favorite. Look on the counter of an old country store—or a modern convenience store for that matter—and you're likely to spy a luminescent orange round of the sharp stuff, encased in a red plastic mantle. It's the prime ingredient in pimento cheese, that heavenly concoction known by many as the house paté of the South. But it's not the only cheese in town.

Since the 1940s, Clemson University's agricultural school has been turning out a blue-veined cheese, sweet, creamy, and piquant enough to give the folks in Roquefort a run for their money. Originally aged in nearby Stumphouse Tunnel, an abandoned antebellum train tunnel, the cheese is now a marvel of high-tech ingenuity, crafted in a climate-controlled ceramic-tile kitchen and lorded over by any number of card-carrying doctors of dairy science.

To pick up a wedge or wheel of Clemson Blue you have to wend your way through campus, past innumerable nondescript low-slung redbrick buildings until you reach equally nondescript Newman Hall, home to the Clemson Ag Sales Center, where, in addition to selling cheese, they mix up a fine milkshake.

118 Newman Hall / 864-656-3242

Columbia

Pimento Cheeseburgers

If there is one dish that defines Columbia, it is the pimento cheeseburger. Sure, the Varsity over in Atlanta, Georgia, serves them, as does the Delta Sandwich shop in Augusta, Georgia, but it's here that this Southern twist on the national dish gets the most grill play.

Locals remember the 60s-era Dairy Bar as the place that popularized the slathering of pimento cheese on a hamburger. My friend Bobb Dixon recalls that the Dairy Bar "made their own pimento cheese and spread it over a very thin but barely griddled patty. The combination was melt-in-your-mouth meat. It was heaven. I say 'was' because they moved to Main Street and then retired. The current versions available around town are okay, but not the same."

Tim Shealy, whose grandfather opened what was Shealy Sandwiches down on Assembly Street back in 1940, also remembers those Dairy Bar pimento cheeseburgers. "Used to be that we didn't serve a pimento cheeseburger out of respect for the people that owned the Dairy Bar," he told me. "That was their sandwich, just like ours was the MOC, the mustard, onion, and chili burger. Hell, both of 'em were real popular before cholesterol was discovered."

Until recently, Tim sold a slew of pimento cheeseburgers at his little lunchroom. "We use four different cheeses in ours," Tim told me. "People can taste the difference; it's rich and sharp. We just can't make enough of the stuff." With Tim's spot now closed, the keeper of the Dairy Bar flame is Eddie's, where they cook their burgers on a flattop and stir up their own pimento cheese blend. Or you might try the filet mignon–capped "French Quarter Pimento Cheese" served at the nearby Mr. Friendly's, a trendy place that advertises itself as a "New Southern Café."

Eddie's / 1301 Assembly Street / 803-779-6222

Cromer's P-Nuts

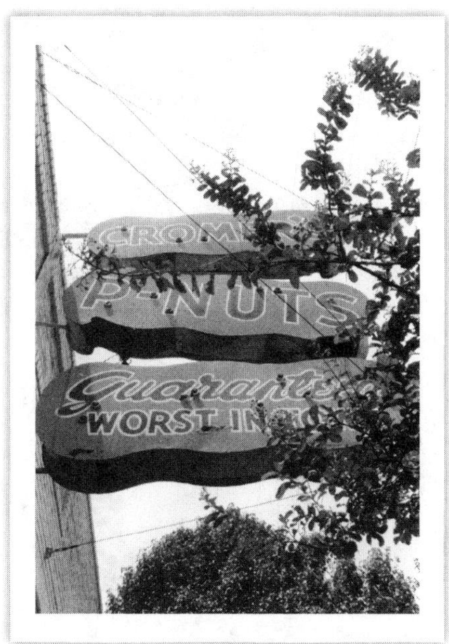

A beacon of good taste and good humor for peanut lovers.

"Guaranteed Worst in Town"—now that's the kind of slogan you don't want to live up to.

Yet, if you visit the Cromer's P-Nut store, that's just what you'll see, hanging high above the entrance, outlined in neon.

"It began as a joke back around 1937," the late J. D. Cromer Jr. told me a few years back. "When Dad—he was J. D. Sr.—started selling peanuts down here at the curb market, well he did all right, and before you know it, there's another fellow setting up across the street. Well, this fellow was a loud cuss, and whenever a customer would come by our stand, he'd yell, 'Don't buy those. Mine are best! Mine are best!' Dad got irritated with the guy and grabbed a piece of cardboard and scribbled 'Worst in Town' on it and set it down. Well, the slogan stuck and business picked up."

At some point along the way, Cromer's expanded upon this early marketing strategy, posting signs that pleaded, "If you find a good p-nut in your pack, please return our mistake."

Today, there's a little less hucksterism and hustle evident, and the once dowdy building where the peanuts were roasted has been exchanged for a new brick box, but if you take a look around back you'll soon learn that a few relics remain from those early days, including one of the old retrofitted coffee roasters in which J. D.'s father cooked his peanuts. It's still in use today, a bulking black metal and chrome affair that has a passing—if unappetizing—resemblance to an iron lung. Rest assured that the peanuts that emerge from a tumble inside are as good as ever, sweet, salty treats that belie Cromer's jestful promise.

1055 Berea Road / 803-779-2290

Maurice Bessinger's Piggie Park

Like the late J. D. Cromer Sr., Maurice Bessinger is a showman of the old school, a regular P. T. Barnum of the barbecue world who has been tending the pits in West Columbia since 1955. Give him a minute and he'll take an hour to tell you just how good his "gourmet" pork barbecue and "secret heirloom" mustard sauce are. Low in cholesterol and fat, too, God's own health food. And while we're at it, did you know that God was the original pitmaster? That's a fact, says Bessinger: "All the Old Testament sacrifices were cooked with wood, and that was ordained by God."

Home of right-wing politics and right good 'cue.

The restaurant is a sprawling behemoth built, like many drive-ins of an earlier era, in a hub and spoke pattern, with the dining room and pits at the center and little corrugated-tin-topped awnings radiating outward. Carhops still work the parking lot, but you have to hike inside, past cord after cord of hickory wood, to get the full effect.

Just inside the door sits a pile of pamphlets and newspaper clippings, some attesting to Maurice's barbecue acumen, some pleading that you had best heed the word of God or spend the rest of your days in Hell, and others arguing for the sanctity of Confederate heritage. If you're lucky, you'll spot the big man himself—Maurice—behind the counter, his white hair shining bright beneath the heat lamps. The day I was there, he beamed a smile that would make a TV weatherman proud and pronounced, "I'm going to make barbecue the hamburger of the twenty-first century. With God's help, I will."

All proselytizing aside, you have to admire Bessinger's way with a ham. Cooked up to twenty-four hours over hickory coals, the meat comes out tender and smoke-suffused, with a bark that is dark and sweet, almost caramelized from the heat of the pit. And the sauce—a heady concoction of mustard, soy sauce, brown sugar, and vinegar—is a joyous taste revelation for those barbecue hounds of the vinegar or tomato camps. Side dishes of slaw and hash are good as well but, comparatively, don't rate even a hosanna.

4411 DEVINE STREET / 803-782-9547

Maurice Bessinger An Ill-Fated Flirt with Politics

Like Lester Maddox over in Georgia, Maurice turned his attention away from the food business for a few years, trading in his pit and tongs for a stump and a megaphone. At one point in the 1960s, he even took to riding a white horse and touting the virtues of a group called the National Association for the Preservation of White People. His racially charged antics fanned the flames of intolerance in South Carolina, and won him a good measure of scorn and ridicule. In 1974 he ran for governor and lost.

It was all a mess really, a sad mistake as Maurice tells it. By the late 1970s he had undergone a religious conversion, erecting a mission in the midst of Piggie Park, right beside the pits, where on Wednesdays he still leads a Bible study class from 11:30 to 1:00. "When you have a truly religious conversion, you don't see black and white, you don't see rich and poor," he told a reporter a few years back. But these days Maurice is backsliding, writing "God and Country" editorials in the local newspaper and flying his Confederate flag high for all to see.

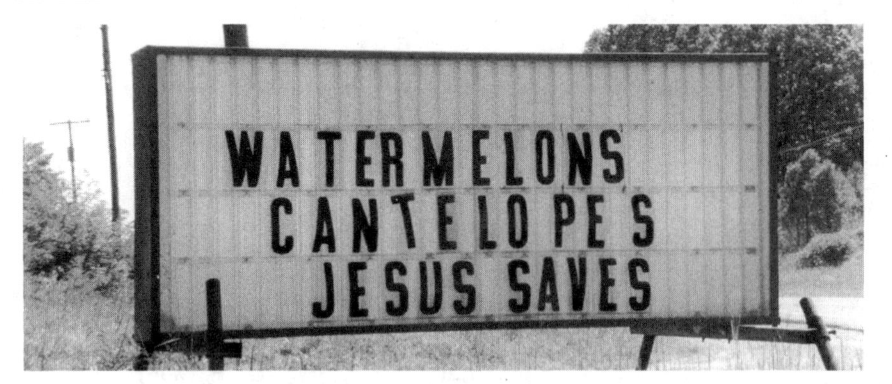

Do you believe in farm-fresh produce?

Filbert

Sanders' Peach Shed

Peach sheds, tomato stands, and truck farm stalls; peanut shacks, apple barns, and farmers' markets: no matter the name, they are a fixture of the Southern roadside. Most are cobbled together from scrap lumber with a strip of roofing tin tacked on top. Some are nothing more than a tarp thrown over the bed of a pickup truck to ward off summer showers. A precious few are sturdy structures built of cinder block and asbestos shingles.

Traveling the country roads of South Carolina in the summertime, when the peach trees begin to bear their lush, flesh-colored fruit, it seems as though with each curve you take, another peach stand comes into view, stacked high with wire and wood-slat baskets full of sweet, fluent peaches.

As pervasive as peach stands may be, there are a few spots that are truly exceptional, stands where the peaches are juicier than you ever imagined, the proprietors warm, welcoming, as sweet as the product they proffer. In the York County community of Filbert, Dori Sanders and her family run just such a place, an open-air market hard by Highway 321. Though Sanders is famous in Southern literary circles as the author of the novel *Clover* and the cookbook *Dori Sanders' Country Cooking*, come late May she still takes to the orchards, harvesting Sunhighs and Georgia Belles, Blakes,

Albertas, and Redskins. Longtime customers with a yen for a certain variety look for the cardboard signs tacked up to announce the projected date of first picking.

"Our first peach of the summer is called Starlight," Sanders tells me. "It's a white peach, sweet as can be. They usually come in just before Memorial Day and from then on out we're picking peaches until September. In the fall, we've got greens in profusion: mustard, rape, and turnip, every kind of green you can imagine. And sweet potatoes; we've got white sweet potatoes, my favorites. There's nothing fancy about our little farm shed. No air conditioning, no refrigeration, no nothing. Just fresh fruits and vegetables, straight from our farm."

HIGHWAY 321 BETWEEN YORK AND CLOVER / 803-684-6062

For Dori Sanders' **Peach Cobbler** recipe, see page 241.

Greenville

Eugenia Duke The First Lady of Mayonnaise

Take a look in the refrigerator of a good Southern cook, and chances are that front and center between that jar of Osage pimentos and a twelve-pack of Coke, just to the left of Aunt Ruth's pickled okra, back behind the dilly beans Uncle Sam put up last spring, you'll spot a bottle of Duke's mayonnaise. It's the South's favorite condiment, whipped white gold sold in squat glass jars affixed with a simple yellow label.

Though the business is now owned by a Richmond, Virginia–based company, Duke's mayonnaise still has strong ties to Greenville, the city of its birth. "We still make it here," Duke's employee Kathy Morgan told me. "Now don't think we've got the three witches from *Macbeth* out back stirring it up. We got rid of them years ago. We've got machines that do it now."

"Now don't think we've got the three witches from 'Macbeth' out back stirring it up."

That may well be the only thing that's changed about the making of Duke's since Mrs. Eugenia Duke mixed up her first batch down on Manly Street sometime in the early years of the twentieth century. Eugenia got her start making sandwiches and selling them to local drugstore soda fountains and corner groceries. She baked her own bread, roasted her own meats, and most important, whipped up a fine mayonnaise, which she slathered on with a heavy hand. Unlike the commercial versions that were coming on the market, Eugenia didn't use a drop of sugar, nor did she whip in egg whites as filler. And thanks to her use of cider vinegar, her mayonnaise had a pleasing tartness others lacked.

By the time of World War I, Eugenia had expanded her business, selling sandwiches to servicemen stationed at nearby Fort Sevier, many of whom returned home after the war with a taste for her mayonnaise. Soon soldiers were writing her asking that a jar or two be shipped to faraway Georgia or Virginia, and Eugenia was in the mayonnaise manufacturing business. But her reign would be a short one. In 1920 she sold the sandwich company and in 1929 she sold her mayonnaise business, lock, stock, and egg dasher, to the C. F. Sauer Company. Last anyone saw of Eugenia, she was hightailing it to California, a sack of money in tow.

Bar-B-Q King: The Infernal Machine that's Killing 'Cue in the Carolinas

I've got a friend, a typically mild-mannered fellow, who has some rather unseemly things to say about the inventor of the Barbecue King electric smoker. "Maybe we ought to hang the son of a bitch in effigy right out front here by the pits," my friend said, as he unloaded cord after cord of wood from the bed of a weary old pickup. "That damn electric smoker has done more towards killing off barbecue in the Carolinas than the health department and the IRS put together."

The object of my friend's scorn, the Barbecue King electric smoker, is the invention of Bob Wilson, a onetime pitmaster, who, while running a Greenville barbecue joint called the Smoke House, devised what he thought was the perfect replacement for an open pit. (Now, in Wilson's defense, this was the 1950s when *faster, cheaper, easier* was the mantra of the day, but don't tell that to my friend.) What Wilson built for himself, and later sold to friends and then a host of customers, was an electric-fueled pit, an extra-large oven really, to which he added little smoke boxes where wood chips would smolder, theoretically infusing the meat with a smoky taste. Wilson peddled a slew of the things. He even sold one to President Eisenhower and was granted the honor of preparing a barbecue dinner at the White House. Soon, there were competitors on the market, brands like Bar-B-Q Buddy and Bar-B-Q Slave.

Now the first time I came across one of these heretical beasts was at Little Pigs Barbecue in Anderson, where pitmaster Joe Dukes was kind enough to show me how the thing worked. Joe's was a rotisserie-like model, outfitted with all manner of switches and toggles, connected presumably to internal heat sources which released, according to the labels on the stainless-steel box, either grease smoke or wood smoke. When I asked Joe about what type of wood chips he used to generate the smoke, he fixed me with a look that was somehow both conspiratorial and apologetic and said, "We don't use any smoke these days. People don't have a taste for it." I thanked Joe for his time and exited.

In 1986, perhaps in response to this blight upon barbecue, the South Carolina legislature passed a Truth in Barbecue Law, requiring that restaurants post a state-issued sticker advising patrons as to whether they cook with wood or not. Said South Carolina State Representative John Snow, "If you're eating barbecue, you deserve to know exactly what you're getting." I didn't see any stickers in my travels, but at more than half the South Carolina barbecue houses I visited, there was not a cord of wood in sight.

Holly Hill

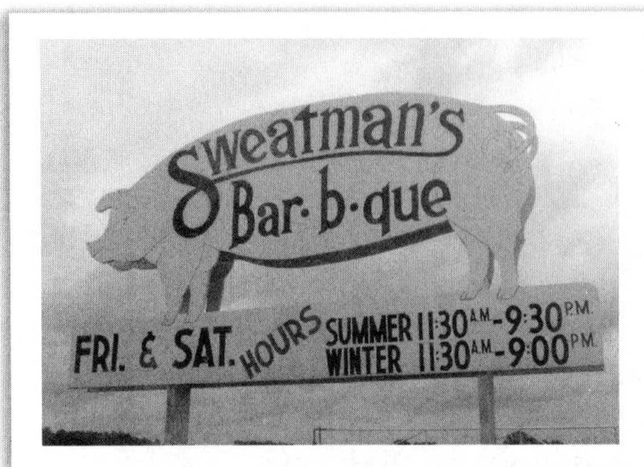

A beacon for the barbecue bereft.

SWEATMAN'S BAR-B-QUE

Bub Sweatman's family has been making barbecue as long as anyone in this part of the state can remember. As far back as the 1910s there always seemed to be a weekend barbecue at the old Sweatman homeplace. The men would dig a hole in the ground, burn down some oak limbs until they were white and smoldering, and throw a pig on the grate, staying up all night telling stories and stoking the fire. In the morning the men would wash up, maybe take a nap, while the women set to work picking meat from the bones and stirring up kettles of hash and pots of rice. By midday, the whole county seemed to be gathered in their backyard. And so it went weekend after weekend, year after year. It wasn't until 1977 that Bub staked a claim to barbecuing as a business. "Until then, well, we just cooked hogs for friends," he told me a few years back. "That was just what we did on the weekend. Still do. Some people go bass fishing; we cook hogs."

Set in a weathered old farmhouse with a wide, welcoming front porch, Sweatman's, like many of the best pits in the state, is a weekends-only operation. And it's a far piece out in the country to boot. But that doesn't dissuade the faithful. By 10:45 Friday morning the packed-sand parking lot starts to fill with late-model pickups and import econo-boxes alike. Above, an almost solid canopy of pecan trees gives needed shade to the old home, bleached pale by the unrelenting rays of the summer sun. Around back, clouds of smoke hang heavy in the sky above the cinder-block pit house where split whole hogs have spent the night on a pit stoked with oak coals.

Up on the porch there's a crowd of folks milling about, stomachs rumbling, waiting for Sweatman's to open. A little before 11:30 someone unlatches the door and the feed is on. Down the wide hallway we pour, headed for the buffet in back where crusty ribs and tender chunks of pulled pork wait alongside cauldrons of thick, pungent hash and dove-white rice. While most buffets are bad news, stew pots really, where the meat turns to mush and rice turns to gum, business is so good at Sweatman's that you can be assured what sits before you has been there only a matter of moments. There are even pork rinds, oily treats fried to a teeth-shattering crispness, best slathered with a little of Sweatman's mustard sauce, a mellow concoction with a sneaky vinegar kick.

Plates piled high, we retreat to what was once the family living quarters and is now a warren of smaller dining rooms simply furnished with trestle tables and calico curtains. I sink my fork into a mound of sweet pork just as my neighbor one table away bows her head to say grace.

HIGHWAY 453 BETWEEN HOLLY HILL AND EUTAWVILLE / NO PHONE

Leesville

SHEALY'S BAR-B-QUE HOUSE

Though touted as a barbecue joint, this gray ranch-style roadhouse is better appreciated as a reliquary of country cooking where they use every part of the pig but the squeal, every cut of the cow but the moo.

This is one of the few places around where during the winter, on Thursdays, you can taste liver nips: dumplings made from beef liver, sage, and flour, boiled in beef stock. On Fridays the *specialité de la maison* is potmeat, which the buffet attendant told me is "similar to hash but not chopped up so much. With potmeat you can still pick out pieces of ear, tongue, that sort of thing." And day in, day out, you can count on great slabs of fatback and little nubs of cracklins to be piled up high on the forty-item buffet beside more traditional offerings like fried catfish and creamed corn, stewed tomatoes and fried chicken.

Victor and Sarah Shealy, who opened the ranch-style roadhouse in 1969, are of Pennsylvania Dutch stock and their cooking shows it. Like many of the natives around here and Orangeburg to the south, theirs is a cuisine that makes ample use of offal: gizzards are wrested from chicken carcasses, livers from cows, tongues from pigs, and testicles from lambs. It is a cuisine of frugality, honest, simple, and good.

The barbecue, by the way, is cooked on one of those infernal gas cookers. "We use whole hogs," the pitmaster told me. "But we don't cook over wood anymore. We found out that after we chilled the meat, most of the smoke flavor was gone. So we switched to gas. It's easier and no one seems to be complaining." I would have told him exactly what I thought of his damned gas cooker, but my mouth was full of liver nips.

340 East Columbia Avenue / 803-532-8135

South of the Border

Blenheim Ginger Ale

Just south of the North Carolina line, nestled among the apocalyptic commercialism of South of the Border, the ticky-tackiest tourist trap this side of Tijuana, is a nondescript brick and aluminum-siding building that turns out the spiciest libation I know of—Blenheim Ginger Ale.

Like a slap in the face from a spurned lover, Blenheim commands your attention. I can still remember my first bottle. With the first swallow, my neck went loose, my lips went numb. This was not a *soft* drink. And though Blenheim is indeed pungent stuff, its taste is not solely defined by heat. There is pleasure as well as pain. Take a second sip and your palate, indeed your whole body, comes to life. Locals claim that "it's good for what ails you," and they may well be right.

Created in the 1890s by a doctor who added Jamaican ginger to the local spring water curative in an attempt to mask the taste, the resulting concoction quickly built a reputation as a digestive aid. Bottled since 1903, Blenheim has, until recently, avoided any attempts at modernization. Until the early 1990s, each bottle was taken off the production line and shaken by hand to mix the granulated sugar into the ale. That laborious process ended when the Schafer family, owners of S.O.B., bought out the bottler. The old plant was closed and production moved to its new home amid the faux Mexican façades of South of the Border.

Despite the efforts of the Schafer family, Blenheim Ginger Ale is still not widely distributed. In fact, it's damn hard to find—so hard that if you want to be assured a steady supply, you had best stop by the bottling plant. Until recently this was a simple proposition. You needed only to find Blenheim, South Carolina, and you had found Blenheim Bottling Company. Now, with the company's acquisition by the South of the Border folks, things are a bit more difficult.

It seemed easy enough. I called ahead for directions. "You can't miss us," they said. "Take the South of the Border exit. We're right across from the observation tower," they claimed. With the world's tallest sombrero as my guide, I couldn't lose my way. Or so I thought . . . I stopped and asked directions. Numerous times. Everyone tried to help: "There, through the Ape's thighs, to the right. Just beyond Pedro's Pleasure Palace. Yea, that's it. A little farther. No, turn left, not right, at the thirty-foot gorilla." I was lost, hopelessly lost—that is until I rolled down my window, caught a whiff of spice in the air, and began sniffing my way toward the land of ginger and fizz.

843-774-0322

Spartanburg

Beacon Drive-In

Founder J. B. White, who opened the Beacon back in 1946, sold the place a few years back. And, as you might expect, there have been a few changes. No longer are Easter services held at sunrise in the asphalt parking lot. Revivals, once staged each Sunday in August, complete with a gospel band and throngs of worshipers, have been discontinued. And the gang of curbhops that once worked the lot has dwindled to a few, the most recent loss coming in December 1998 when Thomas Bird retired after fifty-two years of service.

And yet, much has endured. J. C. Stroble, a veteran of more than forty years, is still perched at the end of the counter, ready to take your order. "Let's Don't Boogie-Jive. Let's Merchandise!" says the placard hanging above his head. Though a bout with glaucoma has dimmed J. C.'s sight, he's still a fireball of energy, a model of efficiency and economy. "Talk!" he booms as I approach. "I'm ready for you. Come on with it. Tell me! Tell me!"

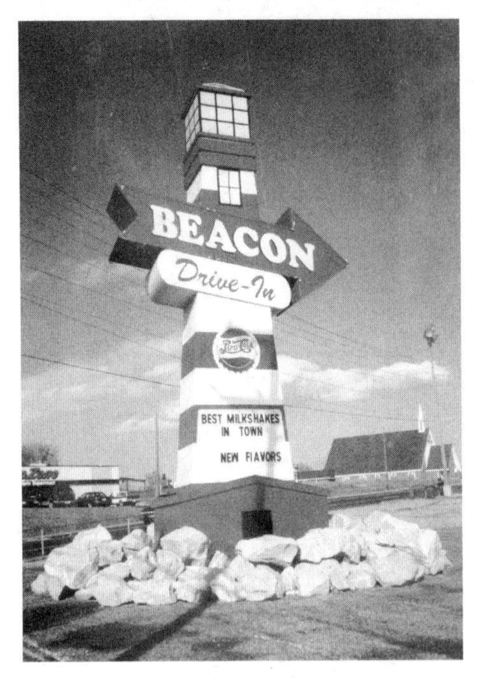

A beacon of grease and goodness.

I sputter out my order, parroting the guy in front of me—"I'll take a chili cheeseburger a plenty"—not really aware of what that means, but somehow sure it's the right thing to do. J. C. calls it down the line, his voice a ringing baritone worthy of a cantor. Thirty seconds later, no more, my order is plopped in front of me on the stainless-steel counter: a soft burger, oozing chili and cheese, barely visible beneath a foot-high tangle of onion rings and fries. It's a bewildering sight, at once appetizing, and, thanks to the sheer quantity of food, vaguely disgusting. (I later learn that back in the days when J. B. was in charge, if a competitor opened nearby, the old man's response was, "Put more meat on the bread, pile more fries and rings on top.")

I slide down the line, past the sign advertising a Pig Dinner—ten scoops of ice cream atop two bananas, the whole affair smothered in a three-foot blob of whipped cream—and snag a tall tumbler of iced tea. I take a seat in the cavernous dining room, hodgepodge of early 1970s greenhouse architecture with malt shop mod touches, and eat my way through the top layer of the greasy onion rings in search of my burger. Found it! The burger is a colossal mess, erupting with chili and cheese, the top bun gilded with a thin skein of grease. It's also delicious.

On the wall opposite my table, there's a banner proclaiming that the Spartanburg chapter of the Full Gospel Businessmen's Fellowship International meets here on the second and fourth Saturdays of each month for breakfast and Bible study. Above the din of the dining room, I can hear J. C. calling out, "I'm ready for you. Come on with it. Tell me! Tell me!"

255 John B. White Sr. Boulevard / 864-585-9387

Peach Cobbler

from Sanders' Farm Stand

Serves 6 to 8

This recipe, adapted from *Dori Sanders' Country Cooking: Recipes and Stories from the Farm Stand,* reminds me of what my mother used to call a dump recipe. As in "dump it in a casserole dish and bake." It's simple as all get-out, but it's not simplistic. And should you consider making it with canned peaches, think of Dori—and think better of it.

½ cup unsalted butter, melted
2 cups sugar
1 cup all-purpose flour
3 teaspoons baking powder
Pinch of salt
1 cup whole milk
4 cups peeled, pitted, thinly sliced peaches
1 tablespoon freshly squeezed lemon juice
Several dashes of cinnamon or nutmeg

Preheat the oven to 375° F.

Pour the butter into a 13 x 9 x 2–inch casserole dish and set aside. Combine 1 cup of the sugar, the flour, baking powder, and salt in a medium bowl. Stir to combine. Add the milk, mixing until just combined. Pour this batter over the butter, but do not stir to combine.

In a small saucepan, combine the peaches, the remaining cup of sugar, and the lemon juice. Bring to a boil, stirring constantly. Once it's reached a boil, pour the peaches over the batter without stirring to combine. Sprinkle with cinnamon or nutmeg. Bake until golden brown, 40 to 45 minutes. Remove to a rack to cool slightly and then serve.

TENNESSEE

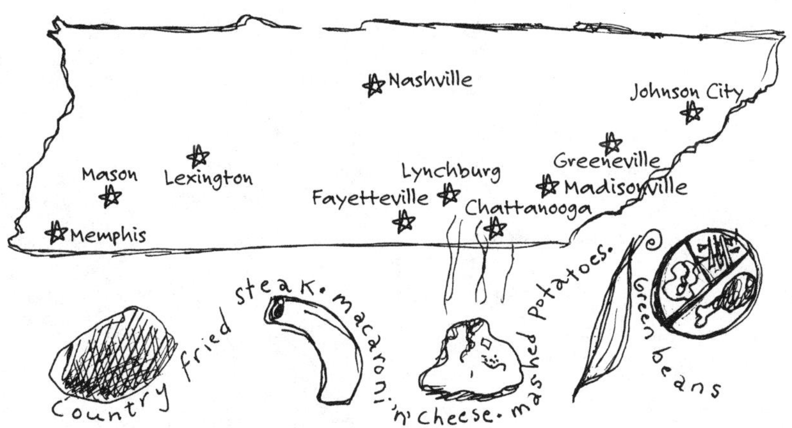

Home of the plate lunch, the meat 'n' three, and the blue plate special, Nashville is the place to be come noontime. At Arnold's Country Kitchen, you can count on garden-fresh vegetables served from a steam table and hoecakes hot from the griddle. South of Nashville in the hamlet of Lynchburg, fine whiskey and fried chicken are to be had, the latter at Miss Mary Bobo's Boarding House just off the square. Should you find yourself in western Tennessee, be sure to stop off in the town of Mason for a platter of Gus's fried chicken or Memphis for a bowl of Frank Vernon's barbecue spaghetti.

Chattanooga

Krystal

Long before the golden arches spanned the Southland, there was Krystal, a homegrown chain of burger stands patterned after the mother of them all, White Castle Hamburgers of Witchita, Kansas. Founded by Chattanooga businessmen R. B. Davenport and J. Glenn Sherrill, Krystal came of age during the Depression, selling small, square hamburgers on small, square buns for five cents apiece. The first location, a streamlined affair made of porcelain enamel and stainless steel, opened in October 1932 at the corner of Seventh and Cherry Streets.

The business model was almost identical to that of White Castle founded eleven years earlier. Cheap cost, consistent quality, and clean, well-lit surroundings were the hallmarks then and now. Employees ascribed to the Krystal Kreed of operations:

Hamburger Moderne, courtesy of Chattanooga's Krystal Company.

To Operate a Spotlessly Clean Establishment
To Serve the Best Foods Obtainable, Properly Cooked
To Render Quick, Efficient and Courteous Service
To Offer All These at the Lowest Prices Possible

Truth be told, there wasn't anything particularly Southern about the Krystal concept. But in the same way that sliced, white loaf bread and tinned tuna fish came to be appreciated, first for their novelty and later for their economy, Southerners were soon clamoring for Krystals. And as the

Depression ebbed and hundreds of hungry veterans returned from World War II, Krystal hamburgers—steamed on a flattop griddle, sprinkled with onions and pickle chips, and smeared with mustard before being stuffed in a fluffy bun not much bigger than a ladies compact—came to be a lunchtime staple, a gut bomb now fondly recalled by generations of Southerners.

Fayetteville

Slawburger Capital of the World

Just when I was beginning to think that the McDonald's, Wendy's, Burger King cabal had finally run roughshod over the Southland, banishing regional variants on the all-American burger to the dustbin of history, I had the good fortune to spend an afternoon eating my way through the south-central Tennessee town of Fayetteville, where slawburgers are the undisputed local dish of choice.

Sure there are other spots on the Southern map where quirky local burgers are still savored—the pimento cheeseburgers of Columbia, South Carolina, and fried-egg-topped burgers of Roanoke and Charlottesville, Virginia, come to mind—and, yes, folks up around Greensburg, Kentucky, and Gastonia, North Carolina, do serve a similar slaw-capped comestible, but only in Fayetteville does the cult of the slawburger reach such exalted heights.

On the courthouse square, two pool halls sit side by side: Bill's Café & Billiards and Honey's Restaurant & Billiards. Both serve a burger nestled in a bun slathered with a sweet, mustardy coleslaw that resembles chowchow. Walk in the door of either and you'll see a long counter facing a flattop grill. The atmosphere at Bill's is a bit ruder, the air a bit smokier, but the formula is much the same. Both restaurants boast pool tables, though at Bill's the game of choice is dominoes, played with a surprising ferocity.

Honey's, opened in 1923 by Weston Stubblefield, is the older of the two, and the current owners boast that their restaurant is "home of the original pool room slaw." Among locals the subject is a matter worthy of debate, with most folks in one of two camps: those who believe that Mr. Stubblefield first concocted the slaw, and a lesser contingent who claim that Stubblefield's longtime grill cook, Bob Kelso—who once ran a burger joint known as Big Hearted Bob's—was the first man to swab a burger with a fine-chopped mix of mustard, vinegar, sugar, and cabbage.

After finishing my burger at Honey's—a juicy, hand-patted disk stuffed into a toasted bun slathered with their cardamom-yellow coleslaw—I take the advice of proprietor Lee McAllister and make my way down to the local grocery store, intent upon picking up a pint of Honey's Pool Room Slaw to take home. Any doubt I may have had about the primacy of slawburger culinary culture in Fayetteville vanishes when I take a gander at the refrigerator case, where, next to shrink-wrapped packages of hamburger meat, three varieties of hometown slaw are arrayed: Daniel's Pool Room Slaw, Honey's Pool Room Slaw, and Bill's Spicy Slaw, the latter a pinkish version of the yellow norm. I buy one of each.

HONEY'S RESTAURANT & BILLIARDS
109 EAST MARKET STREET / 931-433-1181

Greeneville

BEAN BARN

Beans and cornbread might as well be the state dish of Tennessee: white beans swimming in a beefy stew, as dished up at church picnics in Columbia; butter beans from a cast-iron kettle, served at a fire-department fund-raising dinner down in Sewanee; pinto beans, larded with smoked pork jowl, dipped from a tin pot simmering on the back of the stove in Lexington. With a coarse hoecake or moist slice of cracklin bread for sopping, it's as simple, frugal, and good as supper gets.

Problem is, few spots serve truly great beans every day. Truth be told, in Tennessee you can't even depend upon getting great beans one day a week like you can in Louisiana, where Monday is the traditional wash day, the day you could count on finding that cracked ham bone from Sunday dinner bobbing in a pot of red beans meant for Monday supper.

At least that's what I thought until my friend Fred Sauceman told me about the Bean Barn, in business under one name or another since 1949. Here beans and cornbread are an everyday staple, the house specialty.

"You've got your choice," Jerry Hartselle, the owner since the late 1970s, tells me. "Beans with onions, beans plain, beans with stew, beans all the way." I ask for a bowl all the way and lean close against the counter to watch as my waitress spoons a bit of broth and a single chunk of potato from a pot of beef stew into a plastic bowl. A ladle full of deep maroon pinto beans goes on top of that, and as the darker beef broth floats to the top like an oil spill, she tosses in a handful of chopped onions and plops the whole affair down in front of me. A crusty hunk of cornbread wrapped in a paper towel, and my feast is complete. The beans are perfect, soupy and soft, but with a bit of tooth; the cornbread salty and coarse and not the least bit sweet.

I am so drawn to my bowl of beans that I almost forget to ask Jerry about all the advertising paraphernalia displayed on the walls, transforming the dining room into a tasteful version of a Cracker Barrel restaurant. On a brief tour I had spied old cola bottles by the score, tobacco tins by the gross, and a collection of lard cans that would make a sow blush: Clover Leaf lard from Knoxville, Tennessee; Valleydale lard from Bristol, Virginia; Selecto lard from Knoxville, Tennessee; Azalea lard from Orangeburg, South Carolina. "My bread man got me started collecting that stuff a while back," Jerry says by way of explanation. "He's been collecting the stuff since he was a kid and he got me hooked on it, too. His real name is Jim Hensley, but we call him the Bunny man because he delivers the Bunny brand bread we use."

515 East Church Street / 423-638-8329

Johnson City

Dr. Enuf's fleet of delivery trucks, ever at the ready.

Dr. Enuf

During the late nineteenth and early twentieth centuries, patent medicine products, such as Sagwa from the Kickapoo Indian Company, promised Southerners relief from all manner of ills including catarrh and pulmonary consumption, premenstrual cramps and fatigue. Medicine shows traveled the land, hawking various and sundry cures that were really nothing more than alcohol infused with herbs and roots, boosted perhaps by a bit of cocaine or opium.

But by the middle years of the twentieth century, the popularity of patent medicine was on the wane, as the Food and Drug Administration worked to ensure that manufacturers clearly label their products and refrain from making fraudulent claims of their effectiveness. Today, few inheritors of the patent medicine tradition endure. No more Carter's liver pills, no more Kickapoo salves, ointments, and tonics.

But up around Johnson City, locals are still swilling a citrusy soda known as Dr. Enuf—and claiming it's good for whatever ails you. Introduced to the area in 1949 by a Chicago chemist, the soft drink was initially marketed as a dietary supplement, chock-full of vitamins, packed with energy. Even today bottles read, "Ask your doctor about Dr. Enuf." Rich with 260 percent of the daily requirement of thiamin, 120 percent of the needed potassium iodide, and 90 percent of the required niacin, the fizzy drink attracts today's health-conscious consumers and hedonists alike, with the latter group claiming that, next to a slug of hair-of-the-dog, it's the best cure for a hangover to be found in the hills.

Lexington

B. E. Scott's Barbecue

Ricky Parker hasn't had a good night's sleep since 1989. Like his mentor, B. E. Scott, who opened this roadside smoke shack back in the early 1970s, Ricky is resigned to his fate, content to catch a catnap or three over the course of a long night spent stoking an open-pit with shovel after shovel of smoldering hickory embers.

Ricky was reared here, by the pits. He began his tutelage in whole-hog barbecue cookery back in 1976 at the age of fourteen when Mr. Scott hired him to do a few odd jobs: cutting and hauling wood, chopping cabbage for slaw, that sort of thing. "He used to pick me up from school in the afternoon and then take me home at night," Ricky tells me. "Mr. Scott was like a daddy to me."

Back in 1989 Ricky took over the daily operations of the restaurant, and Mr. Scott retired to his home next door. "He'll still help me out once in a while," Ricky recalls. "If I get so exhausted that I really can't take it, he'll come over and check on the pits while I get a little more sleep. I've inherited a hard life. I know that, but it's the only way. I've spent almost my whole life at this. You know, I got a call from this barbecue place up in New York called Virgil's. They wanted me to come up there for three months to teach them how to do whole-hog barbecue—wanted to pay me $10,000. Three months! They must be crazy. You can't learn how to do this in three months!"

Ricky, like Mr. Scott before him, works two pits: concrete-block rectangles rigged with metal rods on which the splayed hogs rest for twenty-two to twenty-four hours

of slow, slow smoking. And like his mentor, Ricky still caps the primary pit with old pasteboard boxes, stacked layer upon layer to seal in the heat. A second pit, kept at an even lower temperature, is used as a serving line of sorts, where the cooked hogs lie in repose until a customer orders a sandwich or plate. "Barbecue should be served straight from the hog," says Ricky. "If you put it on a steam table it'll dry out. We pull our meat from the pit by hand. And since it's whole hog, we can do special requests. We can serve folks most any part of the hog they want. Some people like the white meat from the tenderloin or middlin', we can do that. Ribs, we can do that, too. Some people want a special mix of outside and inside meat. That's all right by us."

I order just such a mixed sandwich, topped with a bit of coleslaw and doused with Scott's fiery vinegar-based sauce. The meat is tender, subtle, sweet, and smoke-suffused—as close to porcine perfection as I have ever tasted. I look up at Ricky. His eyes are at half-mast, a slight grin creases his face. "If they made me start cooking with gas, I'd just quit," he says by way of accepting the compliment that was forming in my mind.

10880 Highway 412 West / 731-968-0420

Lynchburg

Miss Mary Bobo's Boarding House

For three years—from 1908 when Mary Bobo and her husband took over the Salmon House Hotel just off the town square, until 1911 when Tennessee whiskey distiller Jack Daniel passed away at the age of sixty-one—Lynchburg's two most famous citizens walked the same streets, shopped in the same stores, even broke bread at the same table.

Tales of Mr. Jack crossing the footbridge over Mulberry Creek—a duster coat wrapped tight against the winter chill, a tall hat perched on his head—to eat a midday meal with Miss Mary are legion in this bucolic little burg. And on a cold winter day in the year 2000, with the gas heater in the parlor at full blast and the dinner bell clanging loud enough to wake the dead, you, too, might swear that you caught a glimpse of Mr. Jack out there on that bridge, hotfooting it across the creek for a noonday repast of fried chicken, scalloped tomatoes, and rich, dank black-eyed peas; pot roast, turnip greens, and garlicky cheese grits.

Not too long ago, Miss Mary herself would have been your hostess, but when she passed away in 1983, one month shy of her 102nd birthday, Jack Daniel's great-grandniece Lynne Tolley stepped in. Though roomers had been banished long ago, the tradition of gathering at communal tables for the midday meal was still going strong. Lynne was the perfect choice to take over the reins. She is a native of Lynchburg. Her mother and Miss Mary's daughter were best friends. And what she has helped preserve is the closest thing to a museum of country cooking that we Southerners have.

Nestled in the bucolic burg of Lynchburg, Miss Mary Bobo's is a site to see—and taste.

Each day, perfect strangers gather at one of the wood tables on the ground floor of Miss Mary's clapboard antebellum home, bow their heads in prayer for the briefest of moments, and begin passing bowl after bowl of savory Southern cooking around the table for all to share. For those lucky enough to be seated at Lynne's table, conversation is punctuated by morsels of food history. On a recent trip, seated with a group from the Hermitage, Tennessee, Church of the Nazarene, Lynne shared her theory on why boiled eggs are used in giblet gravy: "Back when you raised your own chickens, if you killed a hen for Sunday dinner, well you would take the eggs from the egg sack and boil them to add to the gravy," Lynne told us all. And when I cracked a weak joke saying that such a dish constituted the "ultimate mother and child reunion," Lynne was kind enough to smile.

295 Main Street / 931-759-7394

Madisonville

Benton's Smoky Mountain Hams

Allan Benton is a pork man who works with salt and smoke, transforming haunches and bellies into ham and bacon that many consider to be among America's best. A visit to his roadside smokehouse, blazoned with the slogan "We Cure Em," offers an audience with a humble master of his chosen craft.

Bend his ear while purchasing a side of bacon or a shrink-wrapped sheath of thin-cut prosciutto-style ham. It's time well spent. Tell Allan you love his hickory-smoked ham and he'll say, "You just made my day." Tell him you think his unsmoked salt and pepper–cured bacon is better than much of the pancetta served at America's new guard salumerias, and he'll answer, "You just turned my grin into a smile." And Allan will mean it. Every word will ring true.

Allan delivers his message with an earnest intent that rocks you back on your heels. Ask him for a brochure, and instead of giving you a catalog, he'll write you a letter, sketching the life of Albert Hicks, the man who founded the company in 1947, the man Allan bought out in 1973. Ask Allan about technique and he'll talk of the maple salt box he and his father crafted, about the dehumidifier he jerry-rigged to draw additional moisture from his hams, about the old cast-iron stoves he uses to burn his perfume wood, about the rub of salt and red pepper and black pepper he applies.

Press Allan for a trick of the trade and he'll tell you, "The secret is there's no secret. Just long hours and patience." Tell him you admire his handiwork, and Allan and his wife, Sharon, invite you to visit Madisonville, where, in a humble block building perched on the cusp of the Great Smoky Mountains, pork makes its leap toward immortality. Hesitate, and in an endearing display of aggressive Southern hospitality, he'll suggest that you take a look at your calendar.

2603 Highway 411 / 423-442-5003

For Allan and Sharon Benton's **Ham with Redeye Gravy** and **Buttermilk Biscuits** recipes, see pages 268–69.

Mason

Does this roadside joint fry the best chicken in the land?

Gus's World Famous Fried Chicken

Hard by the side of Highway 70, sits a hoary shotgun shack ringed by dirt, gravel, and crabgrass. Though old-timers still call it Maggie's in deference to founder Mary Magdalene Vanderbilt, these days her stepson, Gus Bonner, rules the roost.

Despite the best efforts of four air conditioners and as many ceiling fans, the air is thick with grease on a recent summer night. Hot and sweet, it hangs heavy in the air, floating like a bank of clouds, enveloping everyone, everything. Save the one table closest to the kitchen, every seat is taken. Above the rattle and boom of the jukebox, glasses clink, voices strain to be heard. In the far corner, a teenage boy in cutoff shorts and a T-shirt leans against the particleboard wainscoting, working a piece of crust from his teeth with a frill-topped toothpick. Across the way, a group of three businessmen roll up their sleeves, tuck their neckties into their shirts, and peer back toward the galley-like kitchen, hoping to catch a glimpse of a platter of fried chicken headed their way.

Perched like a crane over a pot of sputtering peanut oil, the elfin seventy-something-year-old with the hair-trigger laugh chases two rusty brown thighs around a cast-iron, coffin-shaped cookpot, snags them with a pair of tongs, plops them onto a flattop griddle to keep warm, and then pivots, reaching into a black bus tub filled to the brim with breasts, thighs, wings, and legs, all sheathed in a viscous, chalky, blush-colored batter. As he lowers the next batch, the oil burbles and spits, and Bonner deflects my query with weary aplomb.

"Now you know I can't tell you what's in the batter," he says with a smile. "You ate the recipe . . . People done tried everything in the world to get that recipe, but grab the tub and run. They call up and say they're with the health department and want to know what all I put in that batter. Some of them say, 'You got cocaine in there, don't you?' I told them same I'll tell you: Ain't no drugs in there. Only thing you're addicted to is that fried chicken."

Gus Bonner's family has been selling fried chicken since 1950. And since that first day his stepmother hefted a skillet to the stovetop, admiring customers have beaten a path to their door, in search of the secret to the chicken's subtle heat and ruddy, brittle crust.

For some the path beaten was to the back door. "At first the white folks came around back to get their chicken," recalls Gertrude Bonner, his wife of thirty-six years. "But that was back during segregation, back when black folks had to go to the back door to get a barbecue over at Bozo's," she says, referring to the white-owned barbecue restaurant across the highway.

Today more than three-quarters of Bonner's customers are white. Most are pilgrims of a sort, inveterate eaters on the trail of the perfect piece of fried chicken. After years of searching, of eating their way through a barnyard full of fowl, they find their way to Mason, Tennessee, and to Gus. Gus feeds them, accepts their compliments, sips his beer, smokes his cigarette, and waits.

"You see that sign out front?" Bonner asks yet another admirer who had sidled up to the counter. "It says 'Gus's World Famous Fried Chicken.' We've had folks from Russia, Cuba, Iran; you name it. All of them just alike, just like you. They all want that recipe. Ain't no difference one from the other, black or white, can't none of them get this recipe unless they're willing to pay big money . . . Now go eat your chicken; it's getting cold."

HIGHWAY 70 / 901-294-2028

Memphis

Piggly Wiggly

Until Memphis native Clarence Saunders came along, grocery shoppers presented their written orders to clerks, who then gathered goods from the store shelves. Saunders, a man obsessed with innovation and efficiency, tried something new back in 1916, equipping shoppers with baskets and opening the shelves to browsers. It was, in essence, the first self-service grocery store. And, for reasons still unclear to all, he chose to call his new retail venture Piggly Wiggly.

By the 1920s there were Piggly Wigglys scattered from Spartanburg, South Carolina, to San Francisco, California. Alas, the Depression hit Saunders hard, and soon he had lost control of his burgeoning grocery empire. Piggly Wiggly grocery stores continued to thrive, but without the Saunders' involvement. Undeterred—perhaps smarting a bit from his business failure, maybe buoyed by a touch of megalomania—Saunders returned to the scene a few years later with a chain of groceries called Clarence Saunders Sole Owner of My Name Stores, which were, for a short time, successful. He was back again in 1937 with an automated concept called the Keedoozle, as in Key Does All. It, too, was initially successful, though plagued by repeated mechanical failures. When Saunders died in 1953 he was working to open a new retail prototype, a fully automated precursor to the fast-food restaurant, to be called Foodelectric.

An early self-service Piggly Wiggly grocery.

Calvary Waffle Shop

Jane Barton, whom everyone seems to call the Mayonnaise Queen, has been on her feet since 4:30 this morning. Her gray hair is fashionably coiffed. She wears a paisley smock over Bermuda shorts. Her reading glasses dangle from a gold herringbone necklace. This is her forty-ninth year of service at the Waffle Shop, a Lenten-only canteen set in the basement of Calvary Episcopal Church in downtown Memphis, Tennessee. "I've been making mayonnaise for forty-five of those years," she says. "I took over when the lady who was supposed to make it broke her leg."

Service to Calvary by local belles is a long tradition. The ladies tell of the early years, back in the late 1920s, when the shop bordered an alley known as the Whiskey Chute, the water for washing and drinking was drawn from corner hydrants, and cooking was done on coal stoves. They talk of the grande dames of their day who dressed for midday services in couture and heels but descended to the basement kitchen postsermon, donning protective rain slickers, and stirring up waffles and chicken hash, corned beef and cabbage, shrimp mousse, fish pudding, and tomato aspic, the latter three embellished with a niggardly flourish of homemade mayonnaise.

The waffles alone are worth a pilgrimage. Cooked on home kitchen irons by a crew at the rear of the dining room, within sight of inspirational plaques with messages like "Bloom Where You Are Planted," they are vaguely sweet and almost crisp. Drenched with Calvary hash, a brown sauce stew of dark-meat chicken, they earn a place in the pantheon of comfort foods. But the ladies-who-lunch salads are the exemplars. Order a jiggly wedge of tomato aspic topped with a cotton boll of chicken salad and you will taste the best of white-glove cookery. Plus, they seem to be a bit more generous with the luxe mayo when you order that double-decker.

One more thing to keep in mind: In 2004 Thomas Pavlechko, Calvary's choirmaster, premiered his "Ode to the Calvary Waffle Shop." Sung to the tune of "My Favorite Things" from *The Sound of Music,* it includes such memorable stanzas as:

> Waffles with sausage and hash made with chicken,
> Historic foods that we serve from our kitchen;
> Creole with shrimp and some giblets with rice,
> Gumbo and turnip greens: isn't that nice?

On a recent visit, I was lucky enough to eat aspic as Pavlechko banged out the tune on an upright Kimball and the voices of the congregation rose in tribute.

102 North Second Street / 901-525-3036

Payne's

Local belief holds that in 1922 a man by the name of Hueberger, proprietor of the eponymous Leonard's on South Bellevue Avenue, invented the Memphis-style barbecue sandwich: chopped pork shoulder doused with a sauce, capped with a bit of coleslaw, and served on a cottony bun.

Well, if ol' Leonard invented it, then Emily Payne perfected it. Since 1972 she's been dishing out pluperfect pork shoulder sandwiches capped with a mustardy hot-and-sour slaw.

I can still recall my first visit to Payne's. Located on a forlorn stretch of old Highway 78 and housed in a barely converted filling station, the place showed great promise. I stepped inside. Smoke hung in the air like a fog. The interior was bare, with all the physical and acoustical charm of an elementary school lunchroom. A few tables hugged the side of the building where the grease pits once were. No foolishness at all here, just barbecue. It was lunchtime, the line was to the door, and I was primed to experience the mythical Memphis barbecue about which I had heard so much. I ordered a sandwich. It was cheap, dirt cheap. My spirits and expectations rose. Hell, I was almost giddy. I clutched my number like a talisman and grabbed a Coke from the machine.

Behind the counter I could hear the whack, whack, whack of a cleaver on the cutting board. Okay, so it was chopped instead of pulled. I could accept that. After all, this was Memphis; they do their barbecue a little differently than where I grew up. No matter, at least it was prepared to order. Barbecue dies a miserable death on a steam table.

And then my number was called. The sandwich I retrieved from the counter was huge. Despite a bun the size of a good-sized hubcap, little bits of barbecue had escaped their white bread trappings and were scattered about the flimsy paper plate. Also scattered here and there were seemingly errant bits of coleslaw, but I could forgive them a little sloppiness; barbecue restaurants are concerned with product, not presentation.

This former filling station dishes out one of the best barbecue sandwiches in the land.

I could not forgive them my next experience: I removed the top of the bun, and recoiled in horror. Right there, smack dab in the middle of a perfectly good barbecue sandwich, some fool had put a mess of coleslaw—not on the side, where God intended it to be, but on the sandwich.

Now don't get me wrong; I like slaw. In fact, coleslaw runs a close second to Brunswick stew in my hierarchy of barbecue needs. Oh well, there was little to do but sink my teeth into this heresy on a hamburger bun. Despite myself, I liked it. The meat was well charred and juicy. Little chunks of blackened outside meat added texture, smoke, and the bite of pepper to each morsel. The tomatoey sauce brought with it the welcome heat of red pepper, and soon I was sweating like a stuck pig.

I even warmed to the slaw. This wasn't some sugary, mayonnaise-sodden collection of cabbage. This stuff was assertive in its own way, tasting of vinegar, mustard, and black pepper. It might have tasted better on the side, but since it was already there, I knuckled under.

To tell the truth, I did more than knuckle under. Two days later, I returned to Payne's and, fully aware of what was in store for me, ordered yet another coleslaw-topped sandwich. In the intervening years I have returned many times, and though

I still yearn for the unadulterated sandwich of my Georgia youth, my culinary soul is now rested; I've learned to adapt.

1762 Lamar Avenue / 901-272-1523

Cozy Corner

In Memphis locals like to debate the relative merits of wet versus dry ribs, with those in the dry camp almost invariably touting the Rendezvous as the high holy house of the dry sect. Don't believe the hype. Though Rendezvous founder Charlie Vergos may well have been the originator of the dry style when he took to sprinkling a spiked Greek spice mix over his charcoal broiled spare ribs, Ray Robinson Sr. stole his thunder back in 1977 when he opened this little spot in a rundown shopping center just east of downtown.

Behind the counter his wife, Desiree, can usually be found sitting on a high-back swivel stool, within easy reach of a Rube Goldberg smoking apparatus and a stack of order pads. Inside the restaurant's custom-built Chicago-style smoke box hang link sausages, baloney, ribs, Boston Butts, and, believe it or not, Cornish game hens. Though every smoked item on the menu is tasty, I go for the rib ends. Usually reserved as cooks' treats, these little nubs from the end of the slab are crunchier and smokier than the rest. That is not to say that every darn dish that emerges from Robinson's smoke box is not a paragon of the smoked pork art. It is.

What is more, Cozy Corner is a grand example of the positive culinary effects of the ongoing reverse migration of black Southerners, who, after years in exile, head home, no doubt salivating over the prospect of tasting an honest slab of ribs. Robinson spent his time in barbecue-bereft Denver, Colorado, before returning to Memphis, his birthplace. I asked him one day why he came back. "It was cold up there, son," he said with a sly smile. "It was real cold."

745 North Parkway / 901-527-9158

The Bar-B-Que Shop

Mention barbecue spaghetti outside of Memphis, the town of its origin, and you will get a blank stare or a poor attempt at humor: "How do you keep the little noodles from falling through the grill?"

As served in more than twenty restaurants here, barbecue spaghetti is a simple side dish, served in lieu of beans or slaw: well-cooked noodles are combined with barbecue sauce, the requisite "unknowable ingredients," and variably, a bit of smoked pork shoulder. Ask Bar-B-Que Shop proprietor Frank Vernon what makes his the best and he begins to recite a brief history of barbecue spaghetti:

"I learned from Brady Vinson. Brady was a railroad cook back in the '30s and '40s before he settled back here in Memphis. When he was traveling, he started to experiment with the different foods he came across. Guess that's how he started combining barbecue and spaghetti at his place called Brady and Lil's. That was back in the early '50s. Brady, he was real secretive about how he made everything—especially the spaghetti. When I bought the business from him, he didn't want to teach me how he did things. He wanted to take that to his grave. But he finally taught me how to do everything—how to make the sauce, the ribs, the spaghetti, everything."

Try to dig a little deeper, especially concerning matters of recipe and technique, and Vernon turns cagey. "The base is the thing," he says. "I can't tell you what's in it. The one thing that's in it, I can tell you, is the oil from cooking the meat. You'd be surprised what you can do with a base like that and a few spices and things."

One look at a plate of his barbecue spaghetti and you will have no doubt that oil is a primary ingredient. Indeed, the plate glistens with it. As for the noodles, in the Italian tradition, noodles are cooked until they are al dente—meaning to the tooth. These noodles, on the other hand, are more to the *gum*—they nearly melt in your mouth.

Topped with smoked pork shoulder and a zippy, tomatoey sauce, this culinary hybrid seems an unlikely challenger to the more traditional side dishes. That is, until you taste it. Soon after, you, too, will begin ordering a bowl of barbecue spaghetti as an entree, instead of a side dish. Soon after, you will find yourself in bed, during those precious moments before sleep descends, concocting a recipe for barbecue manicotti.

1782 Madison Avenue / 901-272-1277

Nashville

MYSTERY OF THE MEAT 'N' THREE MECCA

For years I have tried to make sense of why Nashville is so blessed with great plate lunch places, why this middle Tennessee town is a meat 'n' three mecca, with more than a half-dozen great restaurants to choose from, while cities of equal or larger size—say Atlanta or Birmingham or Charlotte—can claim only a couple truly great lunch spots. And then it hit me: Nashville is a country-come-to-town kind of town, drawing backwoods pickers and small-town singers to Music City like bees to a hive. Out of the hills and hollers of Appalachia they came, guitars slung over their shoulders, dreams of a date at the Grand Ole Opry dancing in their heads. And with them came a host of friends and family, in town to trade in the city's markets or visit their congressman at the state capitol. Doesn't it stand to reason that they brought along a taste for the foods of their birth, the foods of the hills—salt-cured ham and skillet-fried corn, kettles of cabbage and pones made of sweet potato? And what is a meat 'n' three restaurant after all, I mused. Why it's nothing more than country cooking come to town, the noonday groaning-board feast replicated for the modern age.

It was a good theory, or so I thought until I tried it out on my friend John Egerton, author of the wonderful book *Southern Food: At Home, on the Road, in History*. Back in 1987 he had pondered the same question and come up wanting. Kind man that he is, John let me down gently. "I like the theory, John T.," he said. "But it just won't hold water, especially when you think about a town like Birmingham, that drew people from the surrounding rural areas to work in the steel mills and coal fields. Why don't they have the same tradition of meat 'n' three restaurants? No, I think this is the kind of thing you just thank your lucky stars for, the kind of blessing you chalk up to unearned grace."

Arnold's Country Kitchen

In fine dining circles, tales of temperamental French chefs are rife. Neophytes who fiddle with the foie gras or diddle with the duck confit are sure to stir the ire of the guy in the white coat and pleated toque outfit. But who would expect such a burst of temper from a guy in a flour-streaked apron, the proprietor of an unassuming little brick rectangle of a restaurant, set amid a row of old redbrick warehouses?

Meet Jack Arnold, a native of the North Carolina hills, with a dedication to fresh, honest foods that, in a just world, would make him as well known a cook as Julia Child or James Beard.

On my first visit to Arnold's Country Kitchen, I caught Jack in a foul mood. Indeed, he was cussing a blue streak. "The damn fools I hired to clean my greens broke them!" he told me, as he worked to stock the serving line with the day's specials. "I told them to strip the leaves. But dammit to hell, they snapped them right in half. I had some really nice purple tops and they just ruined them."

Like Hap Townes who once ran one of the South's best lunchrooms in the shadow of the nearby Nashville ballpark, and the late James Lynn Chandler whose Sylvan Park Restaurant over in west Nashville still wins praise from locals for its vegetable plates and chocolate pie, Jack has spent a lifetime in the kitchen. And with each meal he serves, Jack Arnold makes a convincing argument that country cooking—collard greens and cabbage, fried chicken and meatloaf—is worthy of the respect normally accorded highfalutin French and Italian cuisine.

He started out at the age of twelve, washing dishes. While studying fine arts at Vanderbilt University, Jack managed the campus cafeteria. Since 1983 he has been at the helm here, frying green tomatoes to a crisp, roasting monstrous rounds of garlic-studded beef to a turn, simmering fat butter beans in a swine-scented potlikker, baking pan after pan of macaroni and cheese.

It's all good, all simple, all Southern. Indeed, I would go so far as to posit that Arnold's is among the best two or three plate lunch places in Nashville, which makes it among the best in the South. And, Jack's protestations to the contrary, the greens were great, broken stems and all.

605 Eighth Avenue South / 615-256-4455

Loveless Café and Motel

There has been a restaurant here on the southwestern outskirts of town, by the side of Highway 100, since 1947 when the Harpeth Tea Room opened its doors to the ladies-who-lunch trade. It took the Loveless family—Lon and Annie—to toss aside the tea and crumpets and transform the Loveless into a roadside restaurant and motel complex of modest dimensions and national renown. In 1951 they added a few rooms out back for guests, piled their breakfast plates high with salty country ham and billowy scratch biscuits, and erected a towering blue sign outlined in pulsating pink and green neon to let travelers know they had arrived at the Loveless Café and Motel.

The rooms were nice enough—little connected cabins of the motor court variety, set in a row flanking the restaurant—but it was the food that proved to be the real draw. Old-timers still talk of how Lon would scour the Tennessee countryside in search of the best ham producers, of how he would massage a ham before he sliced it to "work up the juices." Annie Loveless' biscuits were of no less renown, light as clouds with a crusty brown mantle, the perfect foil for a hunk of butter or a dollop of homemade wild blackberry preserves.

In succeeding years, the Loveless has passed on to new owners, first Stella and Cordell Maynard, then Donna and Charlie McCabe, now Tom Morales, and the old restaurant with its plywood-paneled walls and beaded-board ceiling has been scrubbed clean of its pleasant patina of age.

Today the "No Vacancy" sign flashes day and night—the little motel rooms have been shuttered since 1986—and a new generation of proprietors tend the stoves, but the ham and biscuits remain exemplary. On one visit I asked owner Donna McCabe to let me in on the secret to baking those ethereal biscuits. "Our recipe is the secret, same one that Annie Loveless started out with way back," she said with a smile. "And I'm not telling."

N.B.: On weekends, the Loveless can be overwhelmed by ham and biscuits pilgrims. The effects are twofold. Sometimes the biscuits suffer. Other times, it's just a matter of escaping the crowds. Relief waits twenty or so minutes down the road at the Beacon Light Tea Room. Annie Loveless was once the proprietor here, too. And although the dim interior has gone Cracker Barrel Christian, the lard enriched biscuits and center-cut ham steaks remain fitting tributes to her kitchen prowess.

Loveless Café / 8400 Highway 100 / 615-646-9700
Beacon Light Tea Room / 6276 Highway 100 / 931-670-3800

Mayo's-Mahalia Jackson Fried Pies and Chicken

You could order a Soul Bowl of stewed chicken giblets over rice at this walk-up, ringed by a gravel parking lot. Or a tripe sandwich. Or a platter with half chicken gizzards, half chicken livers. You could, taking note of the name, get a three-piece box of fried chicken, spiced and cooked in a manner dictated by the founders of the long-kaput Mahalia Jackson Fried Chicken chain. But such choices are inadvisable. Here, fried pies are, by far, the best food to emerge from the kitchen.

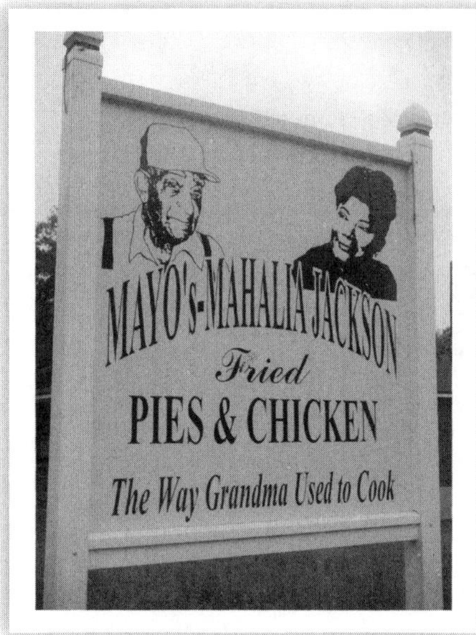

If E. W. Mayo has his way, signs like this will line the South's roadways.

In the 1970s E. W. Mayo bought the last link in a chain of restaurants that in the 1960s aspired to offer an alternative to the franchise of the moment, Minnie Pearl's Fried Chicken. The brand had been built around singer Mahalia Jackson, the woman who sold white audiences on black gospel music. But Mayo didn't do it Mahalia's way. A native of Cottage Grove in northwestern Tennessee, he decided to leverage the recipes of his mother, Eula Mayo, born in 1890, just one generation removed from the yoke of slavery. And as a marker of his ownership and of his mother's reputation for excellence in pastry, Mayo appended the family name to the business.

Mayo is proud of his mother, prouder still of her pie recipe. "My mother invented the sweet potato pie," Mayo, born in 1917, tells me, his voice trembling with braggadocio. "I'm just carrying on what she started."

One bite of a fried sweet potato pie—a flaky crescent of dough bursting at its fork-crimped seams with a cinnamony custard—and you'll know her legacy was entrusted to the right man.

Although Mayo now spends part of his time in a wheelchair, he has grand plans for the future. Visit his home base, near Tennessee State University, and if you lean in close to hear through the Plexiglas partition that separates the kitchen and the two benches where anxious customers disassemble cellophane-wrapped pies, he'll tell you about his plans for more fried pie outlets; maybe he'll even show you the balsawood model of the one that's already in service on Jefferson Street.

2618 BUCHANAN STREET / 615-742-1899

PRINCE'S HOT CHICKEN SHACK

Prince's Hot Chicken Shack will never be accused of false advertising. Housed in a run-down strip shopping center on the northern edge of Nashville, this simple storefront operation serves exactly what it claims: hot chicken. Make that very hot chicken.

Crisp-fried in monstrous cast-iron skillets burbling with lard, before being doused in a fiery torrent of out-of-this-world orange-hued sauce, piled atop a nest of white bread, and crowned with a few pickle slices, the half-bird portions are as generous as the sauce is incendiary. For first-timers, unaccustomed to the uncommon heat of their birds, the good folks at Prince's once had a sign tacked to the wall, serving notice to one and all. It read, "Don't touch the chicken and then touch your eyes."

Today, the cautionary cardboard placard is gone, but the fiery fowl remains a Nashville favorite, a link to the 1940s when founder James Thornton Prince first opened a little take-out joint at Twenty-eighth and Jefferson Streets. His great-grandniece Andre Prince Jeffries runs the place these days, and by all accounts she's got more business that she can handle. On my last visit, the gentleman taking orders was a customer who told me that he "stopped in to pick up a couple of breasts and was trying to help out." When I left, my lips a-tingle from a taste of that great chicken, he was still at the order window, pen in hand.

123 EWING DRIVE / 615-226-9442

SWETT'S DINETTE

Swett's is a pillar of the local African American community, a restaurant that owes it success to the entrepreneurial zeal and pluck of one determined family.

"When my grandfather and grandmother started out back in 1954, they were running what you might call a tavern," present-day proprietor David Swett Jr. recalls.

"They had ten children and when it came time to eat, well, my grandmother would feed the children right there in the barroom. After a while—I guess her cooking must have smelled so good to them that they couldn't resist—customers started asking for the same food my father and the other children were eating. Before long food started outselling beer."

Today, iced tea is the beverage of choice and Swett's is housed in a modern, brick building that bears an unfortunate resemblance to a Shoney's. Inside, mauve laminate tabletops are scattered about a tile-floored dining room and an acoustical tile ceiling looms overhead. But the tradition of good food endures.

Toward the back of the room sits a gleaming stainless-steel buffet line, stocked with a veritable cornucopia of country cooking: pork chops in a rich brown gravy, smothered beef ribs, and juicy chicken thighs sheathed in a soft crust; puffy squash soufflé, pole beans in an oily potlikker, thick mashed potatoes, and ropy batons of stewed okra. A creamy, corny hoecake and a dab of pepper relish from the little tubs set out by the register, and your feast is complete.

"Yea, we've changed a few things since my grandparents' day, but I think they'd be proud of what we've done," David tells me as I plow into my lunch. "My grandfather was a good businessman. People respected him. But he never forgot how it was when he started out. He used to tell me, 'I was a nigger when a nigger was a nigger.' And I think my grandmother would recognize our food as hers. We may not cook with as much pork as she did; we try to be a little healthier. But the feeling is the same; it's all about family."

2725 Clifton Avenue / 615-329-4418

Biscuits: A Short History of a Quick Bread

Baking-powder-leavened biscuits are a relatively recent arrival on the Southern dining room table. Not too long past, wheat flour was a comparative luxury. Cornbread was the staff of life, the staple upon which armies marched and families with more mouths than money doted. For poor Southerners, a basket of buttered biscuits signaled good times, prosperity.

The boys in the band sing the praises of Martha White.

But by the early years of the twentieth century, the soft, red winter wheat so prized by Southern bakers for lightness and tenderness was widely available from companies like White Lily of Knoxville, Tennessee.

In the intervening years, despite the fact that biscuits were a true "quick" bread, capable of being rolled out and baked in fifteen minutes or so, enterprising Southerners conspired to shorten the time required, reduce the necessary steps.

The most important innovation was the introduction of self-rising flour, complete with a premeasured quantity of baking powder, soda, and salt. Though many companies marketed a similar product, Martha White of Nashville rose above the fray, in large part by way of sponsoring Grand Ole Opry broadcasts by a then fledgling bluegrass group known as Flatt and Scruggs. "Now you bake right with Martha White," they sang. "Goodness gracious, good and light, Martha White."

Though Flatt and Scruggs have since passed on, come Saturday night, when the Grand Ole Opry curtain rises, you can still count on hearing the Martha White jingle ringing through the hall:

For the finest biscuits ever wuz
Get Martha White Self-Rising Flour
The one all-purpose flour
Martha White Self-Rising Flour with Hot Rise

Ham with Redeye Gravy

from Benton's Smoky Mountain Hams
Serves 2 to 4

Although I offer a recipe for ham and gravy and biscuits here, please do not think this choice to be a dismissal of the Benton way with bacon and biscuits. A slice of pork belly cured by Allan, fried in a cast-iron skillet until crisp, tucked in a downy buttermilk biscuit from Sharon, is among the most platonic of eats. But such as that pales in comparison to Allan's way with ham steaks and redeye gravy. One whiff of the scents trailing from that skillet and you'll trample a vegan to get a taste.

2 slices country ham
½ cup coffee
1 tablespoon brown sugar, firmly packed

Heat a cast-iron skillet to medium. Trim the fat from the ham slices. Place the fat in the bottom of the skillet and cook for 1 minute. (If the fat is already trimmed or there isn't much, use a teaspoon of vegetable oil.) Pour ¼ cup of the coffee into the skillet. (Be careful as this will sputter.) Add brown sugar and stir until melted. Place ham slices on top of fat and cover with lid. Cook over medium heat. When steam comes out of the lid, remove lid and brown slices lightly. Remove ham to a warm plate and keep warm. Discard any remaining fat. Add the remaining ¼ cup of coffee. Increase the heat to medium-high and cook, stirring constantly. When liquid cooks down slightly, pour gravy into a bowl and serve with ham slices.

Buttermilk Biscuits

from Benton's Smoky Mountain Hams
Makes 12 biscuits

2 cups self-rising flour, preferably White Lily
1 1/4 cups buttermilk
12 pats of unsalted butter (about 6 tablespoons)

Heat the oven to 375° F.

Place the flour in a large bowl. Pour 1 cup of the buttermilk into the flour and stir to combine, making sure all the flour is moist. Continue pouring small amounts of buttermilk into the mixture until the dough follows the spoon around the bowl. (It will take most of the remaining 1/4 cup of buttermilk and the dough will be moister than your usual biscuit recipe.)

Transfer the dough to a well-floured work surface. Knead gently two to four times, working a small amount of flour into the dough so it will not be sticky to the touch. Pat the dough with fingers until dough is about a half inch thick. Using a lightly floured 2½-inch biscuit cutter, cut the dough without twisting it. Place the biscuit rounds on a baking sheet and top them with a small pat of butter. Bake until golden brown, 25 to 30 minutes. Remove to a rack to cool slightly. Serve with Ham and Redeye Gravy.

East Texas

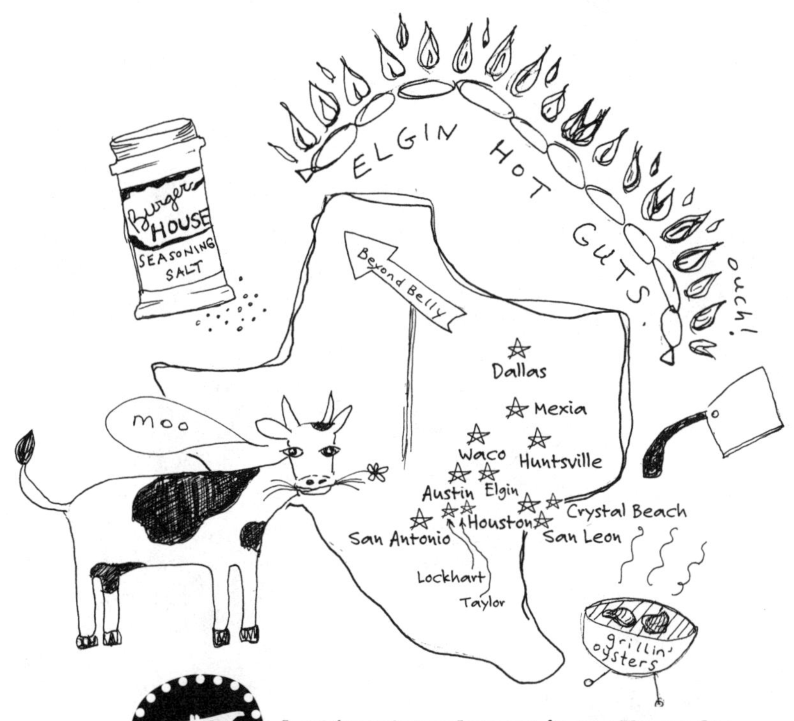

There's not much room in my Texas for vegetarians. A tub of coleslaw here. Maybe a side of side-meat-less collards there. Sugar cookies. Slices of buttermilk pie. Those sorts of things. Instead, I promise you chicken-fried steaks and double-decker burgers and hot gut sausages. Should you require confirmation of my meat tack, I suggest an audience with John Parks of Crosstown Barbecue in Elgin. His pit didn't make the cut, but his quip did. When, after a long day of eating, I ordered a quarter pound of brisket and one beef rib, he stared me down. "One rib," he stammered. "You want one rib? One rib wouldn't do nothing but make me mad."

N.B.: Readers inclined toward maps should know that this book covers all lands to the east of I-35. Left of that line, the West looms.

Austin

Chicken-Fried Steak

Chicken-fried steak is pounded beef (oftentimes round), salted and peppered and battered and fried in a manner commonly ascribed to chicken. It's almost always topped with or served alongside a puddle of creamy gravy. The etymology is queer, sure, but the resulting dish, when entrusted to a skilled cook, is a paragon of Texas cookery appropriate for breakfast (with grits), lunch (with fries), and dinner (with mashed potatoes).

I've eaten my share. I've gone *haute* at Ouisie's Table in Houston's River Oaks neighborhood, where, in addition to a battered and fried and creamed sirloin, they serve a chicken-fried steak salad with Roquefort dressing. And I've gone *vulgaire* at any number of roadside diners that promised hand-breaded meat and scratch-cooked gravy but delivered a freezer-burned shingle slicked with condensed milk. On the fringes, I once enjoyed a fine combo plate of chicken-fried quail and chicken-fried mac and cheese. And I've heard tell of chicken-fried tuna, but as of this writing I've yet to have the pleasure.

While I'm pretty sure that the idea (if not the name) behind chicken-fried steak is as old as that German veal riff, wiener schnitzel, anecdotal evidence leads me to believe that if Texans didn't invent the dish, they sure as hell perfected it. And then they embraced it as their own, pounding what was, in the day, grass-fed and pasture-raised and sinewy beef into tender steaks that took well to the batter-and-fry treatment.

I'm not alone in believing that chicken-fried steak matters more here. "As splendid and noble as barbecue and Tex-Mex are, both pale before that Great God Beef dish, chicken-fried steak," Jerry Flemmons, columnist for the *Fort Worth Star-Telegram* once wrote. "No single food better defines the Texas character; it has, in fact, become a kind of nutritive metaphor for the romanticized, prairie-hardened personality of Texans."

I learned to appreciate the nuances of CFS (as the cool kids call the object of our affection) some years back in Austin, seated at table in Threadgill's. Janis Joplin got her start singing at Threadgill's when it wasn't much more than a beer parlor. Over the course of the past couple or three decades, raconteur Eddie Wilson has guided the restaurant to fame.

The place and the steak both come with proud pedigrees, although some locals grouse that the food has slipped a notch. As far as I'm concerned, their circa 2006 CFS is all that I remember, which means that it is a little shy of fork tender and boasts a craggy crust, the fissures of which pool with a pepper-shot gravy. And, as has ever been the custom under Wilson's ownership, refills on vegetables like broccoli casserole are free.

My meal compels a beer-soaked reverie, which I indulge at Threadgill's bar before hauling clear across town to the Broken Spoke, a dance hall where CFS still takes a backseat to beer drinking and music making. Between pulls on longnecks, I fork a CFS that may well be better than the one at Threadgill's. But I'm not quite sure.

What I do know is that as the western swing music rises through the wood-floored room, I begin corraling folks and reading aloud from Flemmons' treatise. Emboldened by hitting the six-pack mark, I work the crowd with gusto. I wouldn't say that I am especially well received, but no one asks me to leave. And two people ask for a recipe.

Broken Spoke / 3201 South Lamar Boulevard / 512-442-6189
Threadgill's / 6416 North Lamar Boulevard / 512-451-5440

See pages 293–94 for Threadgill's **Country Fried Steak** recipe.

Frisco Shop

Set on the north side of Austin, this diner recalls a ranch-style house with hacienda overtones. Beige stucco walls, a red-tile roof, louvered blinds drawn to block the sun. Inside, flagstone accents, not to mention lots of Naugahyde and linoleum. All the tropes of postwar Americana are there. And so are the foods: eggs and grits for

An early Night Hawk crew, ready for a long night ahead.

breakfast; burgers for lunch; for dinner, those cottage cheese–stuffed pears that passed for salads when Eisenhower was in office, steaks, and custard pie.

Frisco Shop is the last restaurant in the Night Hawk chain, a fabled Austin institution. On Christmas Eve in 1932, Harry Akin opened the first Night Hawk downtown. He staked his claim to a clientele by promising free coffee from midnight until 6 A.M. And he built a reputation for quality based on raising his own cattle and butchering his own beef. Akin's equanimity earned him low employee turnover. His lead role in the integration of Austin restaurants won the respect of the African American community and, eventually, one term in office as mayor.

At the time of his death in 1976, Akins ran seven restaurants under the Night Hawk banner. And he operated a frozen foods division, too. Frisco Shop, which opened in 1952 and is now owned by Akin's nephew and namesake, pays homage to that past by way of a menu that brooks no calorie parsers and a staff that has adopted intransigence as a quasi-religion.

In other words, a Frisco burger still comes slathered with Russian dressing and saccharine pickle relish, then wrapped in a tight envelope of tissue paper; and a call for decorated eggs still gets you two over-easy swamped in chili with beans. As for the ladies who tread the floor and the men who work the grill, more than seven Frisco Shop employees boast forty-plus years of Night Hawk service, including the cook Junior Arnold, who began his career at the old South Congress Avenue location in 1952.

When Arnold passes—and it's likely he'll go at the grill—he'll inevitably be compared with the late and great C-Boy Parks who, while working at the Night Hawk on the Strip, across from the University of Texas campus, served as the clubhouse cook to what seemed like the entire Austin music scene.

Among the legacies of C-Boy's time in the kitchen are an off-the-menu speciality that endures at the Frisco Shop to this day: eggs blindfolded, which in the hands of C-Boy was a hybrid of poaching and frying achieved by cracking two eggs on the griddle, tossing on a couple of ice cubes, and covering the whole affair with a metal lid so that, as the ice melted, the tops of the eggs steamed while the bottoms sizzled. Such dreams as this are reason enough to drag your bones from bed on a Saturday morning.

5819 Burnet Road / 512-459-6279

Crystal Beach

Stingaree Restaurant

Barbecue crabs, adored by Gulf Coast Texans, are comparable to barbecue shrimp of New Orleans. They are misnomers. And they are bliss. To get my favorites, I drive an hour south of Houston to Galveston and take a three-mile ferry ride out to the fish-camp town of Crystal Beach on the Bolivar Peninsula.

Stingaree Restaurant, perched atop a marina within sight of the massive oil tankers that ply the shipping channel, serves both barbecue shrimp and all manner of crabs. They also dish broiled redfish. But crabs, specifically blue crabs caught in brackish waters, are the reason to make the trek.

You have a choice: barbecue crabs, fried crabs, and boiled crabs. The latter are humdrum. Ideally, you'll get barbecue crabs and convince a tablemate to get fried crabs.

Stingaree's barbecue crabs conform to the recipe developed in the 1940s by Granger's, a long-gone and much-beloved roadhouse at Sabine Pass. During the 1970s and 80s, Sartin's Seafood, which began in Beaumont but has metastasized throughout the region, perfected the technique. That means ripping the top shells off and removing the innards before rolling the crabs in cayenne-spiked barbecue spice mix (specifically any number of variations on the original Alamo Zestful Seasoning) and deep-frying them by the score.

Sartin's, which now claims three locations under ownership of various family factions, still does crabs that way. The appeal of naked crabs thrown in roiling oil and spiced with a rude seasoning mix is undeniable. And yet I dote on the comparatively more refined approach, as practiced by Stingaree's.

They call their specialty Vieno's fried crabs. The prep work is the same. But they add a couple steps. For starters, they marinate their shelled and cleaned crabs in Worcestershire sauce and other aromatics. And along with the spice mix they add a bit of breading so their fried crabs emerge from the basket with heightened texture, true substance. What's more, the spice mix has a better chance at clinging to the carapace of the crab.

Come to think of it, such refinements in preparation and such honesty in naming mean that Vieno's fried crabs are not, after all, comparable to barbecue shrimp of New Orleans. But the bliss in eating remains.

1295 Stingaree Cove / 409-684-2731

Dallas

Burger Binge

Sixty-odd miles south of Dallas, in Athens, a historical marker stands where, in the 1880s, locals say Fletcher "Old Dave" Davis first fried a beef patty and stuffed it between two slices of bread. The Athens claim is but one of many made by chamber-of-commerce types, and, like nearly all the epiphanic invention stories associated with the hamburger, it's dubious. But the marker, with its silver letters and slate background, lends a bit of gravitas to a folk food that does not get its fair share of respect.

The grand exception to the Rodney Dangerfield complex plays out daily in the diners and cafés and drive-ins of Texas or, more specifically, Dallas, where flattop burgers are relished. I'm not talking about those fern-bar behemoths that have become, for many misguided souls, the standard by which hamburgers are judged. Instead, I'm thinking of the nickel-thin to wallet-thick burgers that are cooked with care and served without pretense throughout the city.

Emblematic of the overstuffed-wallet camp is circa 1985 Wingfield's, in the south Dallas neighborhood of Oak Cliff. Set alongside a tire shop and down the street from Sugar's Unisex Beauty Supply and Salon, this white rectangle with green trim is a place of pilgrimage for cul-de-sac swells in search of an urban burger.

Walking in the door, I trip over fellow acolytes, awaiting their tissue-wrapped prizes. Slow soul grinds from a boom box. The hiss of burgers on the flattop adds a treble note. Working a galley kitchen is owner Richard Wingfield, defying the laws of juicy burger physics, cooking freshly ground and well-salted beef way past medium, stuffing crumbly hillocks of beef into double-toasted buns, smeared with mayonnaise, stacked with red onion and tomato.

Meanwhile, across town, female carhops dash about the blacktop that encircles Keller's Drive-In, champion of the nickel-thin set. By the time I arrive, the lunch rush has died down and the parking lot is mostly empty, save two old goats leaning against the tailgate of a pickup, drinking longnecks.

My beer arrives soon after I pull beneath one of the metal awnings that flank the central cookhouse. I yank the parking break on my rental and order. My burger—a number 5—arrives soon after, but not before I have the chance to drop a few quarters in the indoor-outdoor jukebox and hear David Ball sing "Thinking Problem."

Served on a metal tray hooked to my window, it's a double-decker cemented by

slices of American cheese and shellacked with a sauce that owes its inspiration to Thousand Island dressing. And as much as I like that burger, the savor pales in comparison to the pleasure of sitting in a car, in broad daylight, drinking a beer from a bottle with cocksure impunity.

Keller's Drive-In / 6537 East Northwest Highway / 214-368-1209
Wingfield's Breakfast and Burgers
2615 South Beckley Avenue / 214-943-5214

Burger House Seasoning Salt

I once was a fool for spices and condiments. Bought hickory-smoked black pepper by the quart jar. Couldn't resist a quart of homemade chowchow. Smuggled pepper vinegar home in my luggage. Never met a barbecue rub I didn't like. My kitchen cupboard looked like a Stuckey's storeroom, what with all the brightly colored labels and the kitschy packaging. Genuine Texas Beef Rib Super Swab in a glass boot bottle anyone?

Of late, though, my ardor for collecting spices and condiments has cooled. With one exception: Burger House Seasoning, a raspy mix of cumin and salt and garlic and black pepper, which holds me in such thrall that I maintain a four-bottle-a-year habit.

Jack Prometheus Koustoubardis, whose family hailed from Cephalonia, Greece, knew the stuff was good. When he mixed a batch for his Burger House in the Snider Plaza area of Dallas, he locked the door behind himself.

The present-day proprietors of the Burger House shake a goodly measure of the stuff on their burgers. And they use it on their straight-from-a-bag shoestrings, too. But I believe Burger House Seasoning Salt, now sold by the jar, deserves scratch cooking. Hand-cut fries. Hand-formed burgers. That's how I use it in my kitchen.

Burger House / 6913 Hillcrest Avenue / 214-361-0370

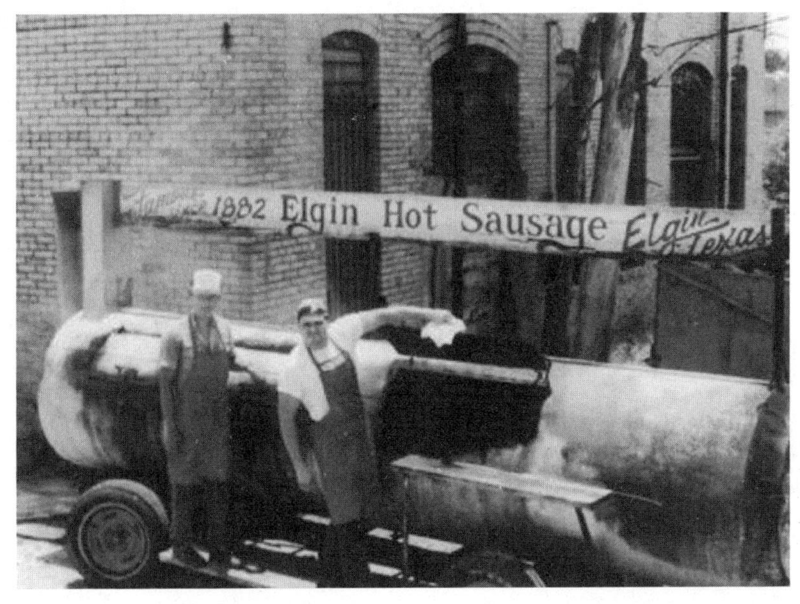

Where there's smoke, there's sausage.

Elgin

Southside Market

Texas barbecue, as we know it, was, to a certain extent, born in the state's meat markets. As my friend Robb Walsh has argued, when segregation was law, cotton pickers of African and Mexican descent patronized markets at midday, buying beef and pork and links of sausage for a takeaway lunch that conformed to whites-only dining-room dictates. Among the vestiges of that tradition is the use of pink butcher paper sheets as de facto plates—and the taste for eminently portable sausages.

The most fabled barbecue sausage in Texas is ground, stuffed, and smoked by Southside Market, a fixture in Elgin since 1882. Known as "hot guts" for their cayenne and black pepper spice and also their natural sheath, these juicy links are most commonly wrapped in a tortilla or a slice of white bread and eaten in the manner of a hot dog—or you can slice the sausage into rounds, slap a few on a saltine, cap the affair with a round of raw onion, and hit it with a glug of Southside's own hot sauce.

Bryan Bracewell and family have worked the pits here since 1968, when Bryan's grandfather, Ernest Bracewell, bought into the business. That's the year William Moon began slaughtering cows and pigs and selling meat from the back of a horse-drawn wagon.

And the Bracewells still run Southside like a market, which means that you can stop off and buy a haunch of beef or a belly of pork. More likely, though, like the cotton pickers of decades past, you will come in search of sausage, and, after taking a seat in a gymnasium of a dining room decorated with taxidermied woodland creatures, bite into a combustive all-beef link that will snap beneath your teeth and throw rivulets of greasy goodness onto the shirts of your tablemates. About that time, you'll begin casting about for a second sheet of pink butcher paper, figuring you might use it as a bib.

1212 Highway 290 / 512-285-3407

Houston

Frenchy's Chicken

Percy Creuzot opened this takeaway stand in 1969. He planned to sell spicy chaurice poor boys, like the ones he had come to know in New Orleans. Oyster loaves, too. But a used-car dealer with a lot alongside intervened.

"His name was Jesse Hearn," Creuzot, a dapper man with copper-colored glasses, born in the 1920s, says. "Told me I was a fool for selling poor boys. Told me if I wanted to pay my rent, I'd fry chicken. He was so determined; he showed me his way, mixing eggs and milk, shaking the dipped chicken in a bag of flour. It took a friend of my sister's to teach us how to spice it right, though."

At one point in the 1980s, the Creuzot family owned more than twenty branches. But a downturn in Houston's ever-volatile economy curtailed expansion plans. Today the original location and few grocery store outlets remain. As does the hot-sausage poor boy, still on the menu, still fiery. And then there's dirty rice, collard greens, seafood gumbo, and a creamy take on red beans and rice that looks so brown it might as well be purple.

All are Creole, as in Creole of Color, that mixed-race subset of Louisiana culture

oftentimes identified with New Orleans. But it's the fried chicken, fried to a relatively greaseless crisp and spiked with cayenne, on which the Creuzots stake their reputation.

Braggadocio is, in this case, defensible, for the birds that emerge from Frenchy's fryers are wondrous fusions of crust and flesh. Upon first bite, crust will fly and cayenne will burn. "But we don't go too hot," says Creuzot. "That's what we got jalapeños for; if you want heat, they'll light you up," he says, gesturing toward the pickled dirigibles that come in his three-piece box.

3919 Scott Street/ 713-748-2233

Rationalizing Tex-Mex

Seated at Loma Linda, a pink block building fitted with wrought-iron burglar bars, Robb Walsh and I lean in to examine our enchilada plates. "This is what it's all about," he says as I cut into tortilla flutes oozing with Velveeta or some Velveeta analogue. "In addition to being stuffed with processed cheese," he says, swabbing a flour tortilla through an auburn-hued puddle of sauce, "these enchiladas are topped by the most Anglicized chili gravy in the city."

I take a bite. I tell him that the viscous sauce swamping my plate resembles the goop that enveloped the Hungry-Man TV dinners of my youth. Walsh smiles and nods. I compare the gravy to the stuff WASPs ladle over mashed potatoes. Walsh keeps smiling. I sense that my mind and palate have somehow grasped a profundity, but I'm not quite sure what it is.

Back in the car, he explains his theory of Tex-Mex. If some people divine insights by reading tea leaves, I believe that Walsh can read taco-shell shrapnel. As author of *The Tex-Mex Cookbook: A History in Recipes and Photos,* he has earned the right to posture and pontificate. But at the moment, he's busy railing against writers who dismiss Tex-Mex as a bastard cuisine, a slur perpetrated against the canon of true Mexican cookery.

As we speed along the interstate that engirds Houston, Walsh says that Tex-Mex may have its roots in the interchange between Native American peoples and the colonists who first brought livestock to Texas in the late 1500s. He says that Tex-Mex is a uniquely American expression of cultural conflict and complement. And he says that chili gravy reflects an early melding of Mexican and Texan cultures. Sure, it's bland, because that's the way Anglos wanted it. Or maybe it's bland because that's the way Mexicans *thought* Anglos wanted it.

"Tex-Mex is America's oldest regional cuisine," he says, cutting his eyes my way to gauge whether I understand the import of his statement and, more important, how it is reflected in the interplay of Velveeta and chili gravy and refried beans. Don't apologize for America's regional cuisines, he argues. And while you're at it, embrace the reality of convenience foods, for we all know that true green bean casseroles require a can or two of fried onions. As a native of the Deep South, weaned on pork rinds and sandwiches of pimento cheese on Wonder bread, I know of which he speaks.

While Walsh explains his theories, we stop at three more restaurants, and I order cheese enchiladas at each. Upon counsel from my Tex-Mex swami, I request a fried egg on top and sop my tortilla into the egg-cheese-chili gravy goo that cascades over the enchiladas.

At Felix's, I even turn down the side of Spanish rice in favor of a kind of Italian-cum-Mexican chili mac, comprising limp spaghetti swaddled in chili gravy. According to Walsh, the availability of such a variant signals that we are likely at table in a time capsule, a restaurant where the offerings afford a glimpse into the primeval maw of what we now know as Tex-Mex.

At each stop, Walsh's theory of Tex-Mex as a righteously unrefined cuisine comes into sharper focus. Forkful by forkful, I come to understand that, in the combination plate of enchiladas, refried beans, and chili mac, I might glean what Walsh already knows—that after years of describing the South as a kind of gumbo, and in the face of a spiraling Hispanic population, the metaphor of the combination plate may well ring truer than any.

In an effort to be thorough, I even succumb to Walsh's offer of a meal at Mama Ninfa's, the Houston restaurant that popularized fajitas. Though I happily scarf down a platter of well-charred meat, in the end, I crave an egg-topped enchilada bursting with liquefied Velveeta, cordoned by a moat of chili gravy.

FELIX MEXICAN RESTAURANT / 904 WESTHEIMER ROAD / 713-529-3949
FIESTA LOMA LINDA / 2111 TELEPHONE ROAD / 713-924-6074
MAMA NINFA'S / 2704 NAVIGATION / 713-228-1175

Huntsville

NEW ZION MISSIONARY BAPTIST CHURCH

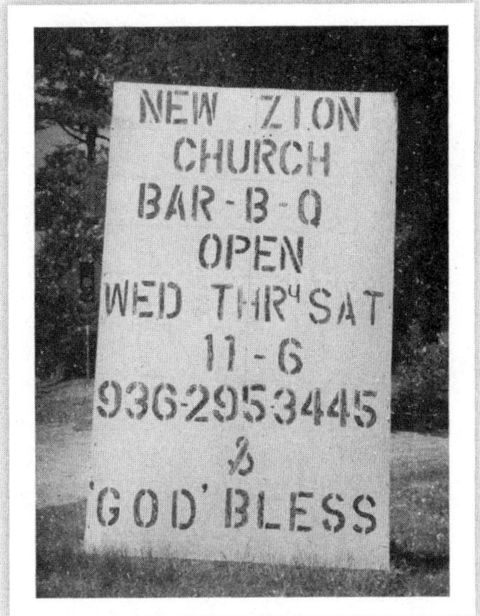

Best place in Texas for a roadside conversion.

I could compare their flame belching pits to the fiery furnaces of hell. Or I could enjoin eaters to praise the Lord and pass the brisket. I could dub a plate of their pork ribs the Holy Grail of barbecue. I could rechristen the Fellowship Hall as the Church of the Immaculate Barbecue. I could talk of holy smoke and heavenly flavor. I could belt out a few stanzas of "Amazing grace, how sweet the sauce."

But fellow culture chroniclers have been doing me one better since the early 1980s, when D. C. Ward volunteered to paint his mother's church, and his wife, Annie Mae, came along to keep him company and cook lunch. On the first day, she cooked for her husband alone and turned away the hungry and curious. But by day three she was cooking extra for anyone who stopped by. Come Sunday she was

petitioning the pastor, A. C. Harris, to cook on behalf of the church, to raise funds by way of barbecue.

To begin, Annie Mae worked a grill beneath a clutch of pecan trees. In time, the city told her she needed a facility with walls, a roof, running water. That facility, a clapboard shack fronted by two oversized barrel smokers, remains home base for the New Zion's ministry by way of meat. (Sorry, couldn't help myself.)

Here's the drill: Tread the purple AstroTurf that surrounds the pits. Present yourself at the counter. Ask for pork ribs, a side of mashed potato salad, maybe some beans. Definitely snag a slice of citrus-kissed buttermilk pie.

Take a seat at one of the tables that span the low-ceilinged room. Try your best to drown out the thirteen-incher in the corner, blaring forth with soap operas. And bite into a well-charred rib, savoring the knowledge that while most church feeds are occasional events, the parishioners of New Zion stoke their pits Wednesday through Saturday, rain or shine.

2601 Montgomery Road / 936-295-3445

Lockhart

Barbecue Dynasty

Bragging rights in Texas barbecue are oftentimes based on two things, cutlery and condiments. That's a crass distillation, but a defensible one.

It's generally accepted that barbecue joints born of the meat market tradition should at least have a history of forswearing forks, even if they now deign to offer them. Bonus points are awarded to those spots where knives were once chained to the tables to discourage stabbings—not to mention the kind of petty thievery food industry folks now dub silverware shrinkage.

As for sauce, it's a crutch; that's what the old-timers say. Meat should taste great without a swab of tomato and vinegar, which, to the purist, does nothing but mask the primal flavors instilled by the liberal use of salt and the prolonged application of smoke.

Smitty's in Lockhart was once a fork- and sauce-free zone. And it still exudes an age-old patina. Long ricks of wood flank the gravel parking lot. When you enter from the rear, flames from a post oak–fired pit lick at your ankles. And the dining room boasts faded green walls and communal tables.

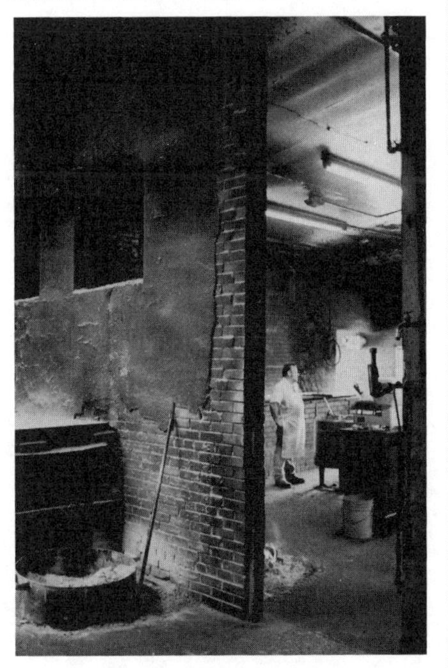

The quintessential pit.

Charles Kreuz opened the doors to what is now Smitty's in 1900. He called his grocery Kreuz Market, but meat was his forte. He sold beef tenderloins to his better customers. He ground the chuck into sausage and sold that to laborers. His style became the Texas meat market style: smoked meats served over the counter on butcher paper. No side dishes and no compromises.

A family rift in the late 1990s queered the deal. The children of Edgar "Smitty" Schmidt, whose family had bought the business from the Kreuzes in 1948, locked horns over money. By 1999 Rick Schmidt had erected a dairy barn of a building just down the road, complete with the same style pits his father had worked. Naturally, he called his place Kreuz Market.

Meanwhile, his sister, Nina Sells, put her son, John Fullilove, in charge of the old Kreuz which, if you're following the plot of this soap opera closely, you know she renamed Smitty's. The end result is a bit of bad blood and a lot of good meat.

Nowadays, Smitty's and Kreuz Market offer similar repertoires of beef and pork. A few things have changed: side dishes—like sauce, once verboten—are easier to come by. Kreuz offers sauerkraut. And the no-sauce dictates have loosened, too. Smitty's even swabs some red on its pork ribs. But much endures.

Both Smitty's and Kreuz Market smoke beef brisket and natural casing sausage that get their flavor jolt from nothing much more than smoke and salt and pepper. Both separate church and state by separating the pit room, where a worker in a white lab coat cuts and weighs your meat, from the dining room, where you retreat

with a bundle of beef brisket, pork ribs, natural casing sausage, and white bread, wrapped tight in pink butcher paper like a Cheech and Chong doobie.

And both make it damn hard to find a fork.

KREUZ MARKET / 619 NORTH COLORADO STREET / 512-398-2361
SMITTY'S MARKET / 208 SOUTH COMMERCE STREET / 512-398-9344

Mexia

GLO'S PLACE

From this roadside trailer outfitted with three folding tables and a red, white, and blue ceramic eagle, Gloria Kirven dishes burgers, fries, catfish sandwiches, and Frito pies. But her true forte is on display in a showcase by the door. Alongside the apricot, peach, and apple fried pies, above the stash of house-baked peanut butter cookies, and beneath the dozens of oatmeal cookies are plastic boxes scrawled with the legend WTS.

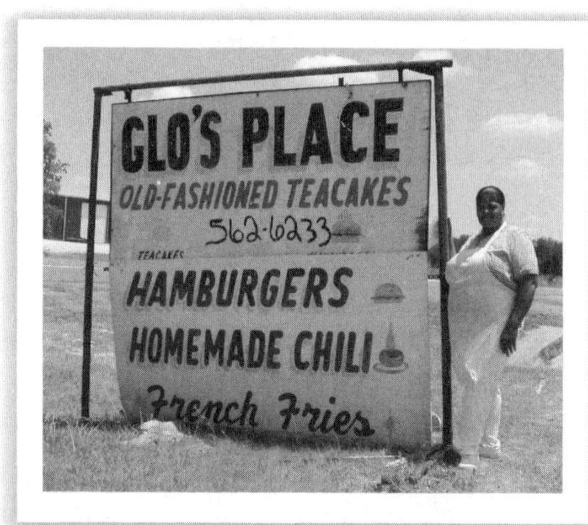

Go see Glo for your sugar fix.

Any native of Mexia will tell you those letters stand for Walk to School, as in Walk to School cookies, the sugar and butter and vanilla confections that have been on public school lunch trays here since at least the 1950s. Some believe that Lucy Eslick, who cooked for the Mexia school district for nearly forty years, got the recipe off a sugar sack. Others argue that their popularity is tagged to the availability of government butter, which, like that much maligned commodity government cheese, was foisted on school districts in need of cheap goods.

No matter, Gloria, who began peddling cookies to banks and beauty salons in the

1980s, is now the reigning queen of the WTS. Her half-a-cow butter cookies are simple mixes, plush with powdered sugar and vanilla. I'm keen on their look as well as their straightforward taste. Each bears a ridge down the center, the result of her pinching the dough when she drops the cookie on a cookie tray. And the pink ones, my favorites, get signature ridges and red food coloring, too, flourishes that Glo says local school lunchrooms have abandoned for fear of allergies but she maintains for the sake of tradition.

2293 West Highway 84 / 254-562-6233

San Antonio

Mi Tierra

It's 8:00 A.M. when I take a seat beneath a constellation of *Sputnik*-looking chandeliers and psychedelic serapes in the faux-adobe interior of Mi Tierra on Market Square. I order what has, over the course of a ramble about Texas, become my usual: cheese enchiladas in chili gravy with a fried egg on top, refried beans on the side.

A domed plastic sleeve of flour tortillas arrives fresh from the comal. I reach for a tortilla with my left hand, folding it into a kind of floury canoe. With my fork, I cut through the egg and into the enchilada, swirling cheese together with chili gravy and yolk, scooping the whole into my mouth.

This is Tex-Mex for gringos. But it's undeniably good. Come to think of it, the food and the tropes of its serving owe debts to the days of San Antonio's fabled Chili Queens, who, beginning in the 1800s, peddled their eats on the same plaza.

From makeshift stands on the square, these women of Mexican descent served street food—chili con carne, tamales, and other staples—to the demimonde who descended after dark. Of one stand that had morphed into a house restaurant, a contemporary observer wrote, "It was frequented by pimps, gamblers, and courtesans as well as the best people. The two worlds rarely had an opportunity to study each other over a bowl of chili."

Sadly, the public-health reform movement of the early twentieth century put an end to the festival of street vendors that had come to be appreciated as equal parts tourist attraction and everyman's food court. Although you could make a case for modern-day taco trucks as inheritors of the tradition, I'm more inclined to take a

seat at Mi Tierra, in business since 1941 and, in a tip of the hat to the Chili Queens, open twenty four hours a day.

218 Produce Row / 210-225-1262

San Leon

Gilhooley's

If a team of New Urbanists set out to design the perfect waterside joint according to the tenets of Gulf Coast vernacular architecture, they would be hard-pressed to find a more honest template than Gilhooley's, an end of-the-road kind of place, perched on a tongue of land that thrusts into Galveston Bay. On the drive down from Houston, I pass rag-tag RV parks, house trailers on stilts, a store called Junk and Disorderly, a boat christened *The Filthy Whore of San Leon.*

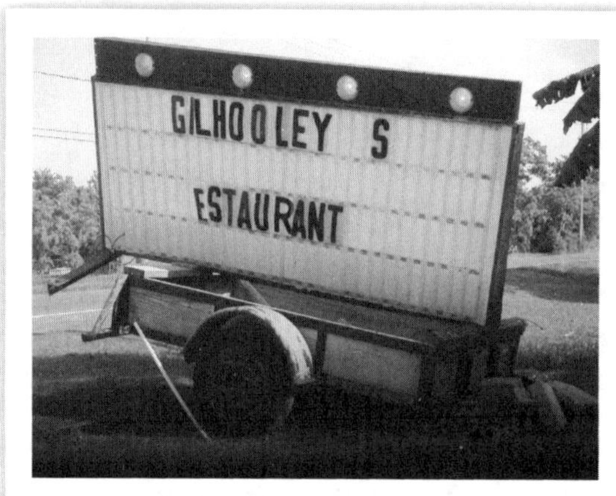

Pull in for the South's best roasted oysters.

Nowadays fishermen—some commercial, others recreational—rule this randy spit. But in the early years of the twentieth century, San Leon was sold as a planned community, a "city of gorgeous flowers and beautiful shrubbery," a "playground for untold thousands." One real estate prospectus promised "cool, delightful breezes in summer" and pledged that San Leon would soon rival Coney Island and Atlantic City. Another, and this one was key, heralded "[e]xtra large and deliciously flavored oysters in almost unlimited quantities."

Exceptional of the oysters, most of the pledges were wishful thinking at best, swindles at worst. Oysters still matter in San Leon. The best place to get a bead on how much they matter is Gilhooley's, owned and operated since 1987 by Phil Duke, and always serving local bivalves, harvested by Croatian oysterman Misho Ivic.

The place is ringed by a shell and dirt lot. There's an old boxcar at center. Inside are a U-shaped bar, low ceilings, and, along one wall, an incongruous collection of African tribal masks. Old license plates cover the truss beams in the accustomed fashion. The menu borders on encyclopedic and features a San Leon BLT, which translates on the plate as a fried bologna sandwich. (They also dish fried boudain balls, employing the preferred Texas spelling for the rice and oddments sausage, known as boudin in Louisiana.)

I order the *ur*-meal hereabouts, Oysters Gilhooley and a longneck. Back in the kitchen, they shuck a dozen, set them topless over a pecan- and oak-fueled fire, swab each with butter and Parmesan cheese, and cook until the shells shade toward black, the oysters lips curl, and the cheese burbles and spits. They arrive on a metal-lined platter that looks like it was recently liberated from a second-rate steakhouse. You will not taste—I have not tasted—a better roasted oyster. And, yes, I've been to Drago's in suburban New Orleans.

Now for the disclaimer, courtesy of longtime employee Desiree Mack: "Tell anybody who's thinking about coming that we don't allow children. None. Not even outside. I'll catch them before they set their playpen up in the courtyard. No kids, no dogs, no midgets, just like the sign says. Some of us have kids at home and we don't want them in here."

221 Ninth Street / 281-339-3813

Taylor

Taylor Café

Louis Mueller's is the Taylor joint everyone touts. The place is an institution. Before long, somebody will erect a historical marker out front. Should it close, crying and caterwauling will be heard from here to Austin. The interior, with its cathedral ceilings and government green walls gone woodsmoke brown, is a large part of the appeal. And I like the brisket, too. For those who believe barbecue is a sport with winners and losers, Louis Mueller's may well measure better than the smoked hunks of cow that emerge from the Taylor Café pits. But that's not the way I eat. And neither should you.

The Taylor Café, run by Vencil Mares, gets less love; it feels comparatively precarious. It requires your attention, your patronage. And it has lots to offer beyond mere brisket.

For starters there's bohunk sausage, a beef and pork homage to Vencil's Bohemian Czech roots, filtered through his two-year tutelage at nearby Southside Market. As for brisket, Vencil's is the sort that collapses beneath the weight of cinders and pepper, by which I mean that it's good.

The real attraction here, however, is octogenarian Vencil Mares. Take a seat at the bar, grab a can of beer—which your waitress will, at no additional charge, slide in a foam Koozie—and let him bend your ear. He'll tell you about his service in World War II, about his work as a medic in the immediate aftermath of the Normandy invasion.

If you're successful in steering the conversation away from war and toward his corner restaurant, he'll regale you with tales of its birth as a saloon in 1892. And he'll tell you about the day in 1948 when he bought the place and of how he once kept it open twenty-four hours a day, selling beer and burgers and chili and, eventually, barbecue to migratory cotton choppers. "I used to cash their checks," Vencil says. "I was their bank. And they would spend a good bit of their check with me. I was their sheriff, too. When they got in fights I was the guy who took their knives and locked them in the safe. Told them to come back for it tomorrow."

Those were also the days when segregation ruled, when the Taylor Café maintained two entrances, two bars, even two jukeboxes—one for whites, the other for blacks and Mexicans. Although the Taylor Café looks like a time warp, that policy has changed. Today, the two entrances and two bars remain intact but no one seems to care who uses which. As for the second juke, Vencil got rid of that a while back. "People kept complaining that they couldn't hear their music for somebody else's," he tells me. "So I just I mixed up all the records and told them to shut up about it. They're supposed to be here to eat and drink anyway."

101 NORTH MAIN STREET / 512-352-8475

Waco

Dr Pepper Museum and Free Enterprise Institute

It takes a certain chutzpah to sell the masses on soft drinks. Truth be told, cans of cola and their ilk contain nothing much more complex than fizzy sugar water. Marketing muscle drives the soda industry, a point proven by the worldwide love of that black fizzy sugar water known as Coca-Cola.

If you want to draw a bead on this phenomenon, there may be no better venue than the Dr Pepper Museum and Free Enterprise Institute, set in a grand Romanesque building in downtown Waco. Wander the exhibits and you'll learn that the drink that became Dr Pepper was concocted in 1885 by pharmacist Charles Alderton at Wade Morrison's Waco drugstore. According to company legend, the customary call to a soda jerk was "Shoot me a Waco." No matter, Morrison eventually named it Dr Pepper, after the father of a girl whom he had loved back east.

Such lore is interesting, but the real attractions are the exhibits that focus more generally on the soft-drink industry, which, as any thirsty soul knows, has strong roots in the South where, among many others, Coke was born in Georgia and Pepsi was birthed in North Carolina. The displays are geek troves: while I had never before seen a mechanical carbonator of twentieth-century vintage, I saw two in Waco, one that agitated the water by rocking, a second that employed a paddle.

And then there's Celery Champagne and Zu Zu Ginger Ale and Lazenby's Liquid Sunshine. I had not made their acquaintance until I made the rounds in Waco. Nor did I realize that the town also gave birth to Big Red soda, that saccharine Texas favorite, or that the place of birth was at Perfection Barber and Beauty Supply, just around the corner from Wade Morrison's drugstore. And I certainly wasn't up on all the Dr Pepper imitators until I perused a showcase full of Dr. Smooth, Dr. Cool, Dr. Terrific, Dr. Topper, Dr. Tex, and Dr. Schnee.

That just about covers the highlights of the first two floors. Typical displays for a museum of commerce. On the third floor, however, things skew strange. More to the point, things skew vaguely toward libertarian philosophies and away from the commie pinko bugbears that Eugene McCarthy once stalked.

A fleet of salesmen at the ready.

Owing to the stewardship of Foots Clements, a titan of the Dr Pepper Corporation, the third floor is home to the Free Enterprise Institute, a nonprofit organization intent on teaching grade school and middle school children the virtues of, well, free enterprise, by way of classes in soft-drink concoction and the economic theories of Adam Smith and Ludwig von Mises.

The latter commands a place of prominence, near the commemorative installation honoring inductees into the Beverage World Hall of Fame. According to a plaque heralding von Mises, "There is no third system between a market economy and socialism. Mankind has to choose between those two systems—unless chaos is considered an alternative." As for what that has to do with Dr Pepper, it seems they're breeding either economic separatists or Madison Avenue cannon fodder.

300 South Fifth Street / 254-757-1025

Country Fried Steak

from Threadgill's

Serves 8

I'm a fool for pounded and fried meats. Pork chops, venison tenderloins, or cubed beef cutlets—so long as you batter when ordered and cook until crisp, I'm a happy man. Problem is, throughout much of the South, few cooks now batter to order. Texas is the exception, where chicken-fried steak is a sacrament. This recipe, adapted from Eddie Wilson's *Threadgill's: The Cookbook*, uses a nontraditional reverse dip, resulting in a frilly crust.

Country Fried Steak

2 large eggs
2 cups whole milk, room temperature
3 cups all-purpose flour
½ teaspoon salt
½ teaspoon freshly ground black pepper
½ teaspoon hot paprika
½ teaspoon garlic powder
2 cups canola oil, for frying
8 6-ounce tenderized beef cutlets (also known as cube steak), room temperature

Skillet Gravy

Oil left from the skillet
2 to 3 tablespoons all-purpose flour
2 cups whole milk, room temperature
1 teaspoon Tabasco sauce, or to taste
2 teaspoons freshly ground black pepper
Salt

To prepare the steak, whisk the eggs and milk together in a bowl and set aside. Combine the flour, salt, pepper, paprika, and garlic powder in another bowl and set aside.

Heat the oil in a cast-iron skillet or Dutch oven over medium-high heat until an instant read thermometer registers 350° F. Dip a cutlet into the egg wash, then in the seasoned flour. Return to the egg wash for a quick dip, then immediately to heated oil in the skillet. (Be careful: the oil will pop, spit, and hiss.) Repeat without crowding the skillet. Cook until brown, 3 to 5 minutes. Using an offset spatula, turn and cook an additional 3 minutes. Remove to a plate lined with paper towels and keep warm. Repeat with remaining ingredients. Reserve leftover oil from the skillet for the gravy.

To make the gravy, remove the skillet from the heat and pour off the cooking oil, leaving the brown bits and cracklings, until 2 to 3 tablespoons of oil remain in the skillet. Return the skillet to medium heat. Sprinkle the flour into the oil, stirring as you go until you have a golden roux. Cook until smooth, about 2 minutes. Add milk and stir until smooth. Add the Tabasco and pepper. Season to taste with salt. (Gravy making is not an exact science. It's supposed to be thick, but if you think it's too thick, add more liquid until you're satisfied.) Serve immediately with Country Fried Steak.

VIRGINIA

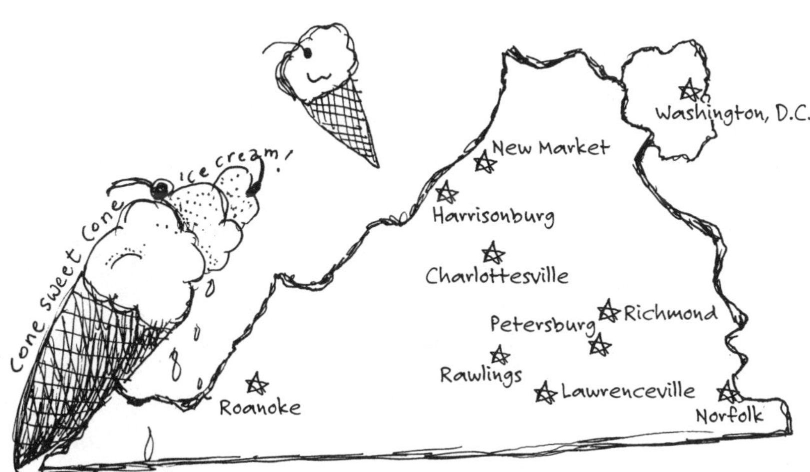

If I had my way, the welcome sign at the state border would read, "Welcome to the Old Dominion, seat of democracy, birthplace of presidents, and home of the perfect cup of peanut soup." The latter, of course, is a reference to the creamy potage popularized by the Hotel Roanoke and now served by New Market's finest, the Southern Kitchen. Follow that with a spot of ice cream from Doumar's of Norfolk—one of the claimants as originator of the modern ice-cream cone—and you have a meal worth traversing the state for. Still hungry? Well, head on up to Ben's Chili Bowl in Washington, D.C., for a half-smoked sausage blanketed in chili and a talk with present-day proprietor, Nizam Ali, who will regale you with tales of the days when the Civil Rights Movement was in full swing and his family restaurant was the meeting place for student activists and politicos alike.

Charlottesville

White Spot

You had best learn the lingo before you go because everybody else at this college dive speaks in the cryptic language of the regular. A "Gusburger" is a hamburger topped with an egg fried hard and smeared with any number of condiments. (It probably owes its inspiration to the Western burger made famous by the Texas Tavern down in Roanoke.) A "Motorburger" is a double Gus with ham. "One Hell of a Mess" is just that: patty sausage, fried eggs, hash browns, and toast, all drenched in gravy. In essence it's a slop bucket on a plate. A "Grill With" is two Duchess-brand cake donuts, heated on the griddle and served with a scoop of vanilla ice cream. "It sounds nasty but it really is good," says the counterman. "The grease from the burgers gives the donuts a nice flavor." As for why the place is called the White Spot, no one seems to know, save a greasy kid with distillery breath and the countenance of a suck-egg dog. "There used to be a barber shop here," he tells me. "It was an old one-stooler, and when they moved it out to make way for this place, the floor was so dirty that the only white spot was where the base of the chair had attached to the floor."

On Friday and Saturday nights, a seat on one of the White Spot's eleven orange vinyl-capped stools is a hard-won prize for besotted college students in search of the holy grail of grease. Like the late, lamented Blanche's in Athens, Georgia, where, if you asked nicely, the wizened proprietress would whip up a gamy goat-meat omelet, the White Spot is an integral part of the college experience, cherished by those lucky few able to spend a good five years or so squandering their daddy's money while earning their undergraduate degree.

1407 University Avenue / 434-295-9899

Harrisonburg

Kline's Dairy Bar

Though the counter help can be sweet as sugar, and the custard tastes like the next best thing to homemade, the real stars of the show at this pink-and-blue-tile confection of a building are the two cast-aluminum Electro Freeze machines that sit behind the counter—dull, silvery cylinders with a vaguely Deco look—churning the custard to a soft, luxurious thickness.

"They say Miz Bess Kline bought those machines used back in 1943," says the fresh-faced college coed as she flips open an adjacent freezer lid to reveal a shallow trough filled with whorls of creamy blueberry custard studded with shards of bright blue fruit. "Regular ice cream is full of air, but not the kind we make. It's real high in butterfat, too; something like 10 percent or more." I snag a double-dip cone, and trailing drops of sweet cream retreat to the asphalt parking lot where, between licks, I drip a pattern worthy of Pollock on the pavement.

58 East Wolfe Street / 540-434-6980

Lawrenceville

Brunswick Stewmasters

There's an ongoing debate between Georgians and Virginians as to where Brunswick stew originated. The city of Brunswick along the Atlantic coast, say Georgians. The county of Brunswick, in the heart of the Southside, say Virginians. In support of their claim Georgians trot out a cast-iron cauldron in which the first batch of the fabled game stew was cooked, while Virginians tell the story of Creed Haskins, who in concert with his cook, Jimmy Matthews, concocted the first such stew back in 1828. Truth be told, both stories are apocryphal, for at its essence, Brunswick stew is a huntsman's dish, thick with squirrels and other sharpshooter prizes. Simply put, such a dish probably wasn't invented by any one person or persons but owes its origins to the ages.

I'm a Georgian by birth, reared on Brunswick stew. And at the risk of being banned from my native state, I'll have to admit that if Virginia didn't invent the stuff, they have most assuredly perfected it. When done well, Virginia Brunswick stew is a pale umber in color, studded with pegs of corn and pillows of butter beans, rich with strands of tender, dark chicken, suffused with tomatoes and potato, spiked with a bit of pepper, gilded with a healthy dollop of butter. Stirred to a froth with a special paddle, the stew has a light, almost airy consistency. "That stuff they make in Georgia isn't Brunswick stew," says stewmaster John Clary. "That's chili. Or maybe it's soup, but it's definitely not Brunswick stew. At least in Kentucky they've got enough sense to call the stuff they make burgoo."

On the day I meet up with John in Chase City, Virginia, he has been working with his crew since 3:30 in the morning, peeling potatoes and onions, boiling boneless chicken thighs, and stirring the pot, always and forever stirring. Stewmasters like John are known by name throughout Southside Virginia. Like a DJ at a hip dance club, or a chef at a white-tablecloth restaurant, they are celebrities of a sort. And people seek them out, buying quarts of stew by the dozen. "We've already got close to seventy-five gallons presold," John tells me. Most weekends during the fall, winter, and early spring, John cooks stew with his friends, raising funds for the local fire department or church, kindergarten or high school marching band. "We cook for causes," says John. "It's our sort of public service."

After what seems like an interminable wait, I put down my notepad and pen and pick up a spoon. John instructs one of the rookies to "dip me up a bowl." The stew is perfection, a creamy blend of chicken and vegetables with a top note of pepper and pork, so light it's almost soufflé-like. Forgive me, Georgia.

To find out where and when John is cooking next, call him at 434-848-2222. "We usually don't stray too far from home," says the Lawrenceville, Virginia, resident.

New Market

Southern Kitchen

The peanut soup served at this trim little diner—replete with boomerang-print linoleum tabletops and a beige Permastone exterior—may well be the best I've ever tasted: pale blond, delicate, flecked with sweet onion, topped with crushed nuts, at once creamy and just a tad grainy. After sampling sorry, goopy versions that taste like condensed Campbell's cream of chicken soup mixed with a dab of Jiff, it's a revelation.

That such a soup would show up on a Virginia menu should come as no surprise. Virginians are a peanut-mad people. But what's this stellar bisque doing in the Shenandoah Valley? Aren't all the peanuts grown down in Southside Virginia? "Well, yes, that's true," says Eddie Newland, whose mother and father opened the Southern Kitchen back around 1957. "But Mama just had a great peanut soup recipe, so she started serving it."

Judging by the contented smiles of the locals who pack the green vinyl booths morning, noon, and night, Mrs. Newland had some great recipes for more than just soup: fried chicken, crusty and savory, served on a heavy white platter ringed with magnolia blossoms; redbrick country ham with a salty bite; startlingly sweet stewed tomatoes served atop a base of saltine crackers; matchbox-sized biscuits, light and airy and buttery; electric-yellow coconut cream pie, crowned with high-flying meringue.

"What's the secret to your success?" I ask Eddie. His answer echoes an old Southern refrain: "We've had good help in the kitchen all along."

9576 South Congress Street / 540-740-3514

Norfolk

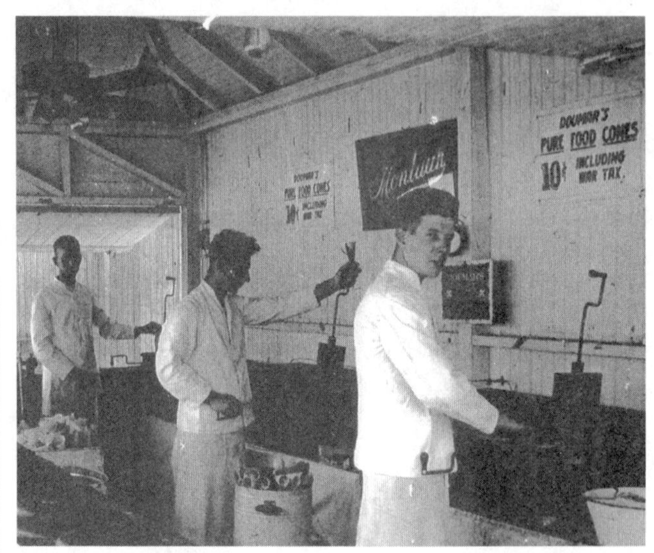

Working the waffle irons at Doumar's in Ocean View Park.

Doumar's

If you're lucky enough to make it to Al Doumar's drive-in between the hours of, say, 2:00 and 4:00 in the afternoon, you'll spot the old man at work, a quiver of straws in his shirt pocket, a bright bow tie fixed around his neck. Stationed at the front window, a captain at the prow of the family ship, he works a series of four cast-iron, gas-fired waffle irons that resemble a combination of medieval forge and pinball machine. He's making ice-cream cones—toasting buckwheat-colored batter to a golden hue, peeling the pliable square from the waffle iron, shaping it into a cone on a wooden mandrel, and setting the sweet treat into a rack to await the next scoop of vanilla, chocolate, or black walnut. Al's movements are blessed with economy, touched with grace. He makes cones just the way his uncle before him did, and if you've got a spare ten minutes, he'll tell you how it all came to be. His story of ethnicity and entrepreneurship is part and parcel of the Southern experience.

"Abe Doumar, my uncle, immigrated here from Damascus, Syria," says Al. "One day while working at the 1904 World's Fair in St. Louis, he bought a waffle and thought to roll it into a cone, adding a scoop of ice cream on top. The ice-cream cone! In a short time, he was in business for himself. By 1905 he had set up a stand on Coney Island. He started traveling to all the state fairs and expositions. He'd team up with an ice-cream maker, erect a stand out of two-by-fours, and set to work selling ice-cream cones. He worked fairs from New York down to Florida before finally settling here in Norfolk at Ocean View Park back when it was the greatest resort south of Atlantic City."

Today's version of Doumar's seems far removed from its Victorian birth. Seated at one of the orange leatherette-capped stools, gazing out at the 1950s-era circus big-top sign, you will not be surprised to learn that carhops still work the parking lot. Did I mention that the cheeseburgers are great, too? Smashed flat, slathered with sweet relish, mustard, and onions, before being wrapped in thin wax paper, they rival the vanilla-perfumed waffle cones in appeal. Oh, and don't forget a limeade to wash it all down.

1919 Monticello Avenue / 757-627-4163

Petersburg

Dixie Restaurant

From outside, the Dixie, with its weary gray façade and hand-lettered sign, looks like a thousand other small-town greasy spoons. Inside the narrow dining room, five stools with cracked green leatherette seats face the counter and fifteen-odd booths covered in the same institutional fabric hug the walls. A pressed-tin ceiling painted a dull beige looms overhead.

Aged locals dote on their Tuesday lunch special, chicken and dumplings, or Thursday's chicken livers on toast. Teens clamor for Dixie dogs, the aesthetes among them ordering their dogs upside down, with the mustard, onions, and chili cradled in the bun beneath the wiener.

But take a gander at the breakfast menu, and you'll know there's something special afoot. The menu promises that eggs are scrambled, not with a slice of processed cheese goo, but with sharp cheddar. City ham, country ham, bacon, sausage, or

brains, yes brains, are available for the asking. And then there are the fish offerings: herring roe, salt mackerel, salt herring, or trout—vestiges of the time when the Dixie-fed warehouse workers were involved in the coastal fish trade.

Taking a cue from my waitress, I order mackerel fried "hard" with a side of applesauce and a few slices of tomato. It's a trencherman's breakfast, rudely salted and oddly satisfying, tasting of brawn and brine and life on the docks circa 1890. Picking my way through the bones for the sweet meat, I crunch into the tail, shattering it like a piscine pork rind. A spoonful of applesauce, a crescent of tomato, and a few swigs of coffee follow, and soon I'm on my way.

250 North Sycamore Street / 804-732-5761

Rawlings

Nottoway Restaurant

The construction of the interstate highway system in the 1960s and 1970s sounded a death knell for many small Southern cafés and rib huts, chicken shacks and dairy bars. Highway 61 and Route 66, the Lincoln Highway and the Dixie Highway—if not gone, they were all but forgotten. Westbound tourists no longer threaded their way through downtown Memphis traffic along Highway 70, stopping off at Leonard's for a brown pig sandwich. Southbound Atlanta travelers no longer wound past the Big Chicken on Highway 41, pulling over for dinner before swooping down into the city.

Many cafés closed their doors, selling off their businesses lock, stockpot, and beer barrel. A precious few stayed on to fight. Nottoway Restaurant was one of those few.

Nottoway flourished back when Highway 1 was the primary southbound artery for snowbirds, intent on wintering in Florida. At first, in the 1930s, it was just a little filling station. By the 1940s the Harrison family added a lunchroom. By the 1950s a twelve-room motel was built—all facing on Highway 1, all dependent upon the daily flow of traffic and dollars. Tourists and locals alike flocked to the Nottoway for salt-cured country ham and skillet-fried chicken, flaky scratch biscuits and billowy yeast rolls.

But when I-85 came through, that all changed. "It looked bad at first," says Sandra

Harrison, daughter-in-law of Nottoway founders Mr. and Mrs. L. C. Harrison. "We were afraid the interstate would just pass us by. But we were lucky. Governor Albertis Harrison was our cousin, and he lobbied to get us an interchange. He's dead now so I guess it's okay to tell the tale," she says to me with a laugh. "So we turned everything around so that we drew traffic from the exit rather than just old Highway 1. It came out all right. My children kind of grew up with that interstate; my son Chip learned to ride his tricycle on a stretch of that pavement before it opened back in '67."

Today, the Nottoway has expanded into a compound of sorts with a comfortable but dowdy restaurant, a fifty-five-room motel, a convenience store, and a gas station. And the food? One taste of a ham roll—a coarse slice of salty ham enveloped by a light, slightly sour yeast roll—and you'll be singing the praises of the late governor.

20316 Boydton Plank Road / I-85, Exit 39 / 804-478-7875

Richmond

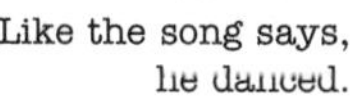
Like the song says, he danced.

Thanks to the eponymous song by Jerry Jeff Walker, we all know that Mr. Bojangles danced. A native of Richmond born in 1878, Bill Robinson became the first black solo act in white vaudeville, earning as much as $6,500 a week. By the 1930s, he was starring alongside Shirley Temple in a series of four films including *The Little Colonel* and *The Littlest Rebel.* Upon his death in 1949, 500,000 people lined the streets of New York to pay homage as his funeral procession passed. In 1973 a statue of Robinson was erected in Jackson Ward, Richmond's storied black neighborhood.

So how did this toast of stage and screen get his big break? Ask around Richmond and you're likely to hear this story: In his youth

Robinson supplemented his dancing income by signing on for a variety of odd jobs, including an occasional stint as a waiter, oftentimes at the famed Jefferson Hotel. One evening, as the story goes, he was serving a distinguished gentleman resplendent in a white suit. Nervous, excited, or just plain careless, Robinson spilled oyster soup down the man's shirtfront. "Think nothing of it," said the man. "It could happen to anybody." Gratified that the man didn't throw a hissy fit, Robinson danced a soft-shoe routine in appreciation. Turns out the white-suited man was a promoter, Marty Forkins, who knew talent when he saw it. In short time, Forkins sponsored Robinson's initial debut in New York, and the rest is history.

In his youth Robinson supplemented his dancing income by signing on for a variety of odd jobs, including an occasional stint as a waiter, oftentimes at the famed Jefferson Hotel.

An apocryphal story? Maybe, but it fits the pattern of how many white Southerners have often addressed black waiters, as equal parts servant, savant, and entertainer. Dance, smile, sing, and shuffle, and you might just get *your* break. At Lusco's Restaurant in Greenwood, Mississippi, old line patrons still talk of waiter Booker Wright, who would recite the menu in a singsong fashion to the delight of all, and take a twelve-person order without benefit of pad or paper. In Smyrna, Georgia, folks reminisce about how the kerchiefed mammies at Aunt Fanny's Cabin would belt out a gospel number between courses, filling tea glasses as they went. And today, the House of Blues in New Orleans packs 'em in as fresh-faced black kids praise Jesus and pass the collards.

Sally Bell's Kitchen

In all my born days, I had never eaten a sandwich that tasted as good as the white-bread-encased chicken salad and pimento cheese treats my aunt Ruth Barrett made. Trimmed of their crust, lavished with a thick smear of Duke's mayonnaise and then double wrapped—first in wax paper bound with masking tape, and then in a thick blanket of aluminum foil—for me, they were the ultimate evocation of care and comfort, a bland yet beatific blessing bestowed by my mother's only sister, my surrogate grandmother.

I've still never eaten a better sandwich, but on a recent visit to Sally Bell's Kitchen, a Richmond institution since 1924, I tasted treats that were made with the same care. A case in point: deviled eggs. The ladies at Sally Bell's do it by the book, boiling the egg whites to a springy turn; mashing the yolks with a bit of mustard, a smidgen of relish, and a dusting of paprika. For over sixty years Estelle Curtis made more than 300 of the little jewels each day, wrapping each in its own pouch of wax paper. Nowadays that task falls to her daughter, Dazaire Thompson, but little else has changed at this vibrant bakery and sandwich shop.

Step up to the counter and order a boxed lunch: chicken salad, cream cheese and nut, egg salad, pimento cheese, corned beef spread, or a number of other offerings, served on thin, sliced white bread, swaddled in a white pasteboard box alongside a dainty paper cup of creamy potato salad studded with flecks of celery. You also get a deviled egg half, a sharp cheese wafer crowned with a pecan, and a cupcake in . . . gasp . . . your choice of flavors, including caramel, strawberry, orange, lemon, and, my favorite, pineapple, the latter tinted an inexplicably bright shade of lime green. After you make your choices, the nice ladies will wrap the box in twine and fix it with a bow. I can't imagine even MeMa assembling a lunch with more care.

708 West Grace Street / 804-644-2838

Limeade

Richmond claims limeade as its semiofficial beverage, much like Auburn, Alabama, claims lemonade as its civic drink.

In Auburn, the undisputed vendor of choice is Toomer's Corner, site of an old pharmacy that in its heyday served fresh-squeezed lemonade from a marbletop soda fountain. Although Toomer's still sells lemonade, it's now better known for being the corner where Tiger football fans celebrate football victories by draping the neighborhood trees in toilet paper bunting. (Among those fans inclined toward Lynchburg lemonades, many find the pale yellow liquid peddled by Toomer's an ideal mixer.)

In Richmond a love of limeade does not come draped in bunting. But perhaps it should. Sherbet green and ice white would be the color scheme of choice. In Richmond limeade knows no bounds. Over at Phil's Continental Lounge on Grove Avenue, they even sling a grown-up's version, spiked with vodka.

Traditionalists can get their fix at the Mechanicsville Drug Store. Or the Westbury Pharmacy. And that makes good sense, because the style of limeade served in Richmond—fresh-squeezed lime juice, sugar, and fizzy water—probably owes its popularity to the legions of kids with soda guns who once worked the counters in long-shuttered Richmond drugstores.

Nowadays, origin points to the contrary, barbecue stands are the most heralded limeade spots. Bill's Barbecue, in business since 1930 and now boasting a half-dozen or so locations, has its advocates. So does Dunn's Bar-B-Que, smoking pigs since 1935. To be frank, I've never been as keen on their minced barbecue sandwiches. But their limeades—well, that's another matter. No other drink refreshes quite as well, in my humble opinion, and recalling lesser limeades of my childhood past, I'm thinking it's the fizzy water that makes the difference.

BILL'S BARBECUE / 927 MYERS STREET / 804-358-7763

Roanoke

ROANOKE CITY MARKET

There was a time not too long past when come Saturday morning you could stroll down to the courthouse square of most any Southern town and buy a basket of squash, a mess of greens, or a tray of tomatoes from one of the farmers who had made the drive in from the country before dawn to sell homegrown produce from the gate of their old pickup, or stacked high on a flimsy table cobbled together from scrap two-by-fours.

Few are the cities that allow such entrepreneurial activity these days. Sure, there are a few storied city markets like Montgomery Alabama's Curb Market and Atlanta Georgia's Municipal Market, but they are indoor gatherings. Roanoke's City Market is still, for the most part, a fair weather, outdoor affair. And since 1882 when twenty-five hucksters obtained their vending licenses, folks have been peddling the bounty of the land in the very heart of the city along narrow streets framed by redbrick buildings. On my last visit, summer was giving way to fall, and the stalls were piled high with copper-colored local chestnuts, Stayman apples, Seckel pears, blushing yellow Rambo apples, flats of Bent Mountain tomatoes and wood slat baskets filled to overflowing with loose leaves of dusky mustard, kale, and rape greens.

MARKET SQUARE, DOWNTOWN

TEXAS TAVERN

A remnant of the days when White Castle, Royal Castle, White Tower, and Krystal franchises were spreading across the South promising sanitary conditions, consistent quality burgers, and low, low prices, the Texas Tavern is the last in a small chain of restaurants. (In nearby Lynchburg, there's a Texas Inn that began life as a Texas Tavern and serves similar food, but it's a rude place, grimy and greasy, not worthy of its kin.)

The Texas Tavern is a tiny place, a wedge of white brick retro Americana trimmed in red, flanked by high-rise bank buildings. Out front, a red neon arrow arcs downward, blinking "Eat, Eat, Eat." Inside, the walls are covered in a sort of white laminate tile. Ten stools capped with red vinyl seats face a dimpled, dull metal counter made from Monel, a once popular blend of aluminum and stainless steel. "We don't cash checks or play with bumblebees" says the tattered sign posted on the back wall. It's *that* kind of place.

A temple of greasy goodness, open twenty-four hours a day, seven days a week.

At the suggestion of Matt Bullington, whose grandfather, Nick Bullington, opened the place back in 1930, I order a "Cheesy Western" and a "Chili With." A good fifteen seconds later grillman Dan Siler, a veteran of more than forty years at the Texas, plops my order down: a cheeseburger topped with a thin egg omelet, cradled in a bun

slathered with a healthy portion of piquant, mustardy pickle relish. On the side is a bowl of somewhat soupy chili, with a thin skein of chopped onions floating on top.

I attack my "Cheesy Western," and Matt fills me in on Texas Tavern history: "My grandfather was an advance man for Ringling Brothers Circus. He traveled the world, even owning his own circus in South America. While he was in San Antonio, Texas, he picked up the chili recipe and the name, figuring that he could sell anything Texas to anybody."

I say that sounds about right to me and tell him of the stories I've heard of the fabled chili queens of San Antonio, said to sell their spicy meat stews on the streets of the old city. Matt, a self-described student of Texas Tavern lore, ponders that for a moment and turns to greet a customer, shouting out his regular order to Dan before the man even gets settled. "Matt's got a mind like an elephant," says the new arrival, a blue-suited patrician, his face creased by a fatherly smile.

114 Church Avenue SW / 540-342-4825

Washington, D.C.

Never mind what John F. Kennedy said about Washington being a city of Northern manners and Southern efficiency. There are good Southern-fried eats—and good stories—to be found among the white marble monotony.

All Saints Cafeteria

Rising like a gilded palace above the mean streets of northwestern D.C., the United House of Prayer for All People of the Church on the Rock of the Apostolic Faith has been at the corner of Sixth and M Streets since the 1930s. This is no somber brick Baptist church. Almost two blocks long, the building is a riot of whimsy and grandeur. A gold dome crowns the sanctuary. Above the door to the church offices, a gold-trimmed black angel arcs heavenward. And monstrous concrete lions frame the entrance to the cafeteria and baptismal pool.

Founded in the 1920s by the late C. M. "Daddy" Grace, a flamboyant, charismatic spiritual leader given to wearing purple suits and parading pasha-style among throngs of rose petal–tossing supplicants, the church is one of more than 100 congregations scattered throughout the country that relies on a literal interpretation of Psalm 150: "Praise ye the Lord. Praise Him with the sound of the trumpet. Praise Him with psaltery and harp. Praise Him with timbrel and dance. Praise Him with stringed instruments and organs. Praise ye the Lord."

Accordingly, services at the church are raucous, extemporaneous, indeed downright soulful. And as you might expect, so is the food served at church cafeterias. Before Daddy Grace was called to the altar, he earned a living as a short-order cook on the Southern Railroad, an experience that may well have inspired him to build a restaurant in each of the denomination's churches.

At the M Street location, there are actually two cafeterias. One, a little warren of a space facing Sixth Street, has been long presided over by sixty-something-year-old Paul Short, who started wiping tables there when he wasn't much more than ten. The second, a larger and grander space, known as Saints Paradise Cafeteria, is a subterranean solarium of sorts, a bright banquet room lit by row upon row of skylights. Come lunch time, construction workers and politicos alike jockey for position in line, fearful that, as one man told me, "the church ladies will run smack out of fried pork chops."

By the time I get to the steam table, there are still plenty of pork chops to be had, not to mention fresh collard greens swimming in potlikker, and eggy macaroni and cheese capped with a sharp and crisp mantle of cheddar. Lurid, lipstick-bright slices of red velvet cake are piled high atop the sneeze guard.

Behind the counter almost all the workers are women, middle-aged for the most part, smiling, church mothers of the old school. In some congregations they are known as kitchen mechanics, ladies who in times of need are called on to cook casseroles and fry chicken to sustain the bereaved or raise funds to repair the church sanctuary.

I ask the lady who hands me a tall tumbler of iced tea why she chose to work at the church cafeteria. "This isn't a job, honey," she tells me. "I come in here and cook because I want to, just like my momma did. My work here is like a tithe. And the church gives us a little donation back for our time. But you know, working here, we praise the Lord every day, with every pan of cornbread, every mess of collards."

601 M Street NW / 202-789-2289

Chitlin Market (and Trailer)

Shauna Anderson wants to be your chitlin vendor of choice. "Selling chitlins is all about trust," she tells me when I visit the suburban Cape Cod home she has transformed into a combination restaurant and commissary for chitlin deliveries. "Chitlins are very personal. A good cook knows that clean chitlins are where it all starts," she says of the laborious process of scouring pig intestines, a skill she learned from her grandmother.

Anderson opened her chitlin business in 1995. At the time, she was working as an accountant. Her idea was simple. Cleaned chitlins were hard to come by. And tax season only lasted a few months. She would clean chitlins during her downtime. It was an idea whose time had evidently come, for consumers, wary of the low-rent white buckets of chitlins available at traditional groceries, bought every hog intestine that Anderson and her compatriots could clean.

The following ten years were a blur. One week, producers from the *Oprah Winfrey Show* would call. Next, it's poet Nikki Giovanni on the line, placing her regular order, a ten-pound bucket. By 2003 she's taking the stage at the Smithsonian's Anacostia Museum, talking about the history of African American entrepreneurship.

Over time, what began as a seat-of-the-pants operation morphed into a delivery service with a kitchen trailer that wends its way through Washington, D.C., dishing chitlins, stewed in her trademark vinegary sauce, as well as potato salad and cake-like cornbread. Internet orders for ten-pound buckets continue to spiral upward.

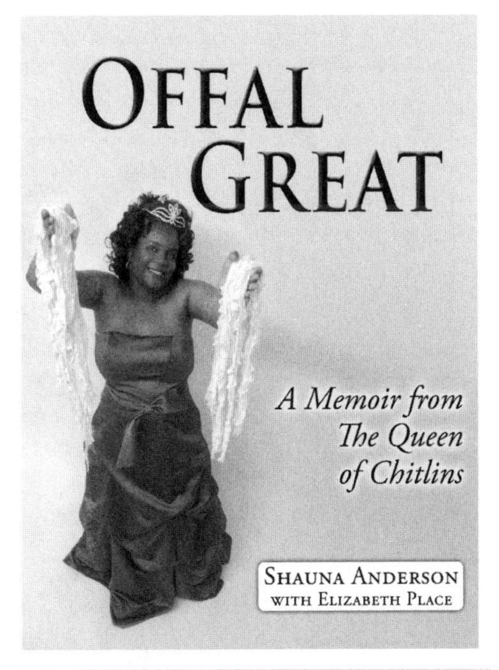

No, those are not feather boas.

More recently Anderson has written a memoir, *Offal Great*. And she has adapted that memoir for the screen, sketching scenes of the days when Anderson, still in her crib, would watch her mother, a performer of some note, sing at Chitlin Circuit clubs. And then, of course, there's her Gourmet Chitlin Seasoning Blend which, if Anderson has her way, will soon be available nationwide. The side label of this brownish vinaigrette-like stuff says that it can also be used with "pigs feet, hog maws and other uncured pork products." And on the front, beneath a whimsical portrait of Anderson, is her slogan, "It takes good eyes to really clean chitlins."

5711 AGER ROAD / HYATTSVILLE, MARYLAND
(WITH CHITLIN WAGON DELIVERIES TO METROPOLITAN D.C.) / 866-436-9381

FLORIDA AVENUE GRILL

The Florida Avenue Grill is the café of choice for homesick Southerners, the early morning haunt of legions of cab drivers, a safe haven in the ever tumultuous D.C. political scene.

In business since 1944, it's a narrow little joint with faux fieldstone siding and a long twenty-odd-seat counter that snakes its way backward from the front door. The

walls are plastered with framed black and white celebrity glossies—the Four Tops, the Fifth Dimension—and politicians—Supreme Court justice Clarence Thomas, former surgeon general Jocelyn Elders—waxing nostalgic about Florida Avenue's pork chops and scrapple, fried apples and stewed cabbage. But the really important documents are those displayed by the front door, certificates of service signed with a flourish by manager Lacey Wilson, son of founders Carl and Esther Wilson: Ophelia Jones, twenty-five years; George Taylor, fifteen years; Viola Pointdexter, twenty-five years, among others.

I order pork chops and scrambled eggs with a side of fried apples. When the waitress places my plate before me on the counter, an elderly gentleman seated two stools over leans my way. "Those pork chops are the best you'll ever taste," he offers. "And you know why? Because they taste like they did down south before everybody lit out for the cities. Nothing ever changes around here. Not the owners, not the food. Hell, the cook is damn near fossilized, he's been here so long." I nod in agreement, turn my attention back to my plate, and set fork to chop.

1100 Florida Avenue NW / 202-265-1586

Ben's Chili Bowl

On April 4, 1968, James Earl Ray assassinated Martin Luther King Jr. in Memphis, Tennessee. That night riots swept the country as black citizens, exhausted and embittered by a long and fitful struggle for equality, unleashed decades of anger. Scores of businesses and homes were wrecked and robbed, looted and burned. Some of the worst damage was done in D.C. along the U Street corridor, known in its halcyon days as the Black Broadway.

One of the few businesses that survived unscathed was Ben's Chili Bowl, a neighborhood fixture since 1958. "My dad spray-painted 'Soul Brother' on the front windows that night, so they would know it was black-owned and not burn the place," Nizam Ali, son of restaurant founder Ben Ali, recalls. "And even then he spent the night inside with a rifle to make sure."

In the days following the riots, Ben's Chili Bowl further cemented its role as a U Street gathering spot, when Student Nonviolent Coordinating Committee president Stokely Carmichael—whose office was just across the street—convinced police to allow "the Bowl" to stay open past curfew time.

Today, Ben's Chili Bowl still matters. And folks still clamor for their tasty half-smoked sausages, cradled in a steamed bun and smothered in a blanket of cumin-spiked chili.

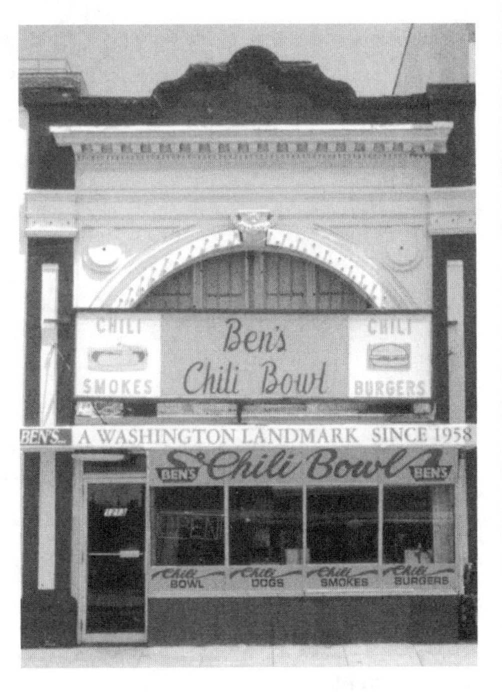

Great chili dogs and a slice of the Civil Rights Movement history.

On a recent fall afternoon, the place is hopping. The jukebox booms forth the sounds of Parliament Funkadelic. Row after row of fat, red weenies sizzle on the front grill. A line of hungry eaters bucks for position at the boomerang-shaped counter, hoping to claim a seat at one of the oh-so-1950s stools capped with sparkly red vinyl. And Nazim works the crowd, greeting old friends, refilling tumblers of iced tea, ladling chili on dogs, swabbing down tables. I finish my dog and lick the last bit of grease from my fingers before asking, "So what does the future hold for the Bowl?"

"I went to law school," Nazim says by way of explanation. "Passed the bar, too. But I asked myself, 'Why would I want to be just one of a million other lawyers in D.C., when I can work here, keeping my parents' dream alive, keeping this place's history alive?'"

1213 U Street NW / 202-667-0909

Peanut Soup

an homage to the Hotel Roanoke

Serves 6 to 8

Peanut soup was au courant in the mid-1970s when a farmer from Plains, Georgia, took the oath of office as president of the United States. Truth be told, everything peanut was popular back then, a fine example being the restaurant in Fond du Lac, Wisconsin, which, soon after the election, introduced a Jimmy Carter cocktail made with crème de cacao, bourbon, and a teaspoon of creamy peanut butter. Nowadays, peanut soup is harder to come by, but for reasons that remain unclear to me, Virginia seems to be the last redoubt. This recipe, adapted from the Hotel Roanoke, was a bit easier to cadge than the one from the Southern Kitchen in New Market, but it's in the same spirit. And one more thing: the celery is essential here, adding a bright vegetal note to a rich soup.

½ cup (1 stick) unsalted butter
2 celery ribs, finely chopped
1 small onion, finely chopped
3 tablespoons all purpose flour
8 cups (2 quarts) homemade chicken stock or low-sodium chicken broth
2¼ cups creamy peanut butter
1 tablespoon freshly squeezed lemon juice
1 teaspoon salt
¼ teaspoon celery salt
½ cup ground peanuts, for serving

Heat the butter in a saucepan over medium heat. Add the celery and onion. Cook until the onion is translucent, 3 to 5 minutes. Add the flour and stir to combine. Stir in chicken stock and bring to a boil. Reduce the heat to low and simmer for flavors to combine, 30 minutes.

Remove from heat and strain into a second saucepan. Whisk in peanut butter, lemon juice, salt, and celery salt until smooth and well combined. Taste and adjust for seasoning with salt. Sprinkle ground peanuts on top before serving.

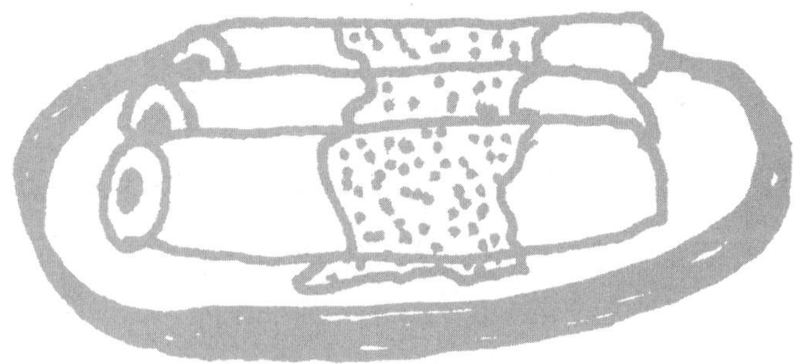

Thanks Y'all

My debts are many.

In New Orleans, Anne and Matt Konigsmark, Lolis Elie, Sara Roahen, Brooks Hamaker, Pableaux Johnson, and Brett Anderson set me on the right path. Missy Ketchum showed me Jacksonville. Bud Kennedy plotted East Texas. Robb Walsh was my go-to guy in Houston and environs. Rod Davis drove me about Dallas. Jeff Siegel steered me clear of bad pizza. Missy Ming Smith dug around Huntsville. Alecya Galleway shared her history of San León. Rhonda Reeves and Georgeanna Milam made sense of Lexington. Ronni Lundy and Sarah Fritschner and Marty Rosen opened a Pandora's box of good eats in Louisville. John Fleer introduced me to Tennessee ham man Allan Benton. In Richmond, Julia-Carr Baylor opened up the world of limeade. Matt McMillen offered a tub of cleaned chitlins. Jamie Estes wrangled sandwiches.

Charleston came courtesy of the Lee Brothers. Susan Puckett served up Carver's in Atlanta. Leslie Kelly revealed gems in Memphis. Thomas Williams and Mary Beth Lasseter scouted Nashville. Carol Puckett, Martha Foose, Luther Brown, and LeAnne Gault dished the Delta. Malcolm White sketched the Mississippi Gulf Coast and Jackson. David Holloway and Ern Laird tempted me with Mobile. Ken Ford, Jim Shirley, and Carl Wernicke dished Pensacola. Ashley Stiff, Mark Hinson, and Diane Roberts laid out Tallahassee. Joyce Wilson and Lynn Nesmith showcased the Panhandle. Jimmy Connor of Gainesville spun the dial in Florida. Staff at the Florida Collection of the Jacksonville Public Library were kind and forthcoming. Charles Tingby at the St. Augustine Historical Society pulled files and spun tales.

Great support was provided by my colleagues Ann Abadie, Charles Reagan

Wilson, Sarah Dixon Pegues, and Mary Hartwell Howorth of the Center for the Study of Southern Culture at the University of Mississippi. Under the same roof, at the Southern Foodways Alliance, Mary Beth Lasseter, Amy Evans, and Melissa Hall kept me out of the ditches. Over at the Center for Documentary Projects, also at Ole Miss, Andy Harper and Joe York ate their fill and reported their findings.

In addition to receiving recommendations from friends and colleagues, I consulted a plethora of written sources. My favorite books were Don O'Briant's *Backroad Buffets and Country Cafes*; Greg Johnson and Vince Staten's *Real Barbecue*; *Smokestack Lightning* by Lolis Eric Elie; *Hungry Herman's Eating Out in Alabama* by some guy named Herman; the *Cajun Country Guide* by Macon Fry and Julie Posner; *The Place Setting* by Fred Sauceman; *North Carolina Barbecue* by Bob Garner; *Barbecue, Lexington Style* by Johnny Stogner; *Legends of Texas Barbecue* by Robb Walsh; and, of course, *Southern Food* by John Egerton.

Periodicals, especially *Louisiana Cultural Vistas*, *Mississippi Folklife*, and *Alabama Heritage*, were a boon. In writing about watercress, the fall 2002 edition of the latter was essential. Online resources consulted include www.southernfoodways.com, www.hollyeats.com, www.seriouseats.com, www.roadfood.com, www.egullet.org, and www.dixiedining.com.

For photographic contributions above and beyond the call of duty, I thank Cassie Drennon, Pableaux Johnson, and Amy Evans. Amy's photos are scattered everywhere. Al Clayton and Bill Ferris shared their best. Cassie shot the Jesus produce one. Pableaux captured Texas and Louisiana. Thanks to Larry Smith at ETSU for the Snappy Lunch photo. David Gelin of Atlanta was very generous with his images. Look for his book, *Barbecue Joints: And the Good Folks Who Own Them* in stores soon. The photograph of Georgia Gilmore comes from *There by the Grace of God: The Autobiography of the Reverend Solomon S. Seay* and is published courtesy of the Solomon S. Seay Sr. family. And throughout the book are photographs supplied by the people and restaurants I profile.

Virginia Willis, with whom I also worked on the series "Saving Southern Food," published in the *Atlanta Journal-Constitution*, was a marvel of a recipe tester. And Georgeanna Milam, who, by the time you read this will be a graduate of the Southern Studies master's program at Ole Miss, did fact-checking work.

For her friendship in the face of adversity, I thank Judy Long. For her undeniable skills as an editor, and for her patience and friendship, I thank Kathy Pories. For shepherding this thing into print, and for always having my back, I appreciate the good work of my agent David Black and his colleague Dave Larabell.

Thanks also to my mentors in the food world, John Egerton, Jessica Harris, and John Martin Taylor.

Last, and by no means least, I thank my wife, Blair, and my son, Jess, who endured my absences and did their best to embrace the taste of my latest obsession.

Note: Some of this writing first appeared (in different form) in the *Atlanta Journal-Constitution* as well as the magazines *Delta*, *Gourmet*, *Oxford American*, *Saveur*, *Sweet Tea Journal*, and *U.S. Airways*.

Photograph Credits

Many of the photographs in *Southern Belly* were loaned by the people and places profiled herein. Thank you all. Bear in mind that, in keeping with the historical tone of the book, many of the photographs depict a time twenty, fifty, even seventy years past.

Pg. vii: Dedication, courtesy of Vanishing Georgia Collection, Georgia Department of Archives & History.
Pg. ix: Today's Menu, courtesy of Cassie Drennon, photographer.
Pg. xi: Menu Board, photograph by the author.

Alabama

Pg. 2: Bob's Hickory Bar-B-Q, courtesy of Van Sykes. Bob Sykes, photographer.
Pg. 9: Big Bob Gibson's Bar-B-Que, courtesy of Don McLemore.
Pg. 12: Eugene Walter, courtesy of Curt Richter, photographer.
Pg. 15: Wintzell's Oyster House, courtesy of Wendell Quimby.
Pg. 17: Georgia Gilmore, from *There by the Grace of God: The Autobiography of Reverend Solomon S. Seay*, published courtesy of the Solomon S. Seay Sr. family.
Pg. 25: Archibald's, courtesy of Ginger Ann Brook, photographer.
Pg. 29: Car Lot Bar-B-Que, photograph by the author.

Arkansas

Pg. 24: Lawrence Craig, photograph by the author.
Pg. 36: Mary's Family Pie Shop, photograph by the author.
Pg. 39: Bullock's Café, photograph by the author.
Pg. 41: Tamale cart, courtesy of Amy Evans, photographer, www.amycevans.com.

Florida

Pg. 52: 13 Mile, photograph by the author.
Pg. 56: Cover of the 1942 edition of *Cross Creek*, Charles Scribner's Sons.
Pg. 58: Louis' Lunch, photograph by the author.
Pg. 60: The Sheik, photograph by the author.
Pg. 62: Ted Peters Famous Smoked Fish, photograph by the author.
Pg. 65: Fish sign, photograph by the author.
Pg. 69: Fried chicken, courtesy of Amy Evans, photographer, www.amycevans.com.

Georgia

Pg. 78: Chitterling sign, photograph by the author.
Pg. 80: Deacon Burton, courtesy of Lenn Storey.
Pg. 83: The Varsity, courtesy of the Varsity.
Pg. 84: Flossie Mae, courtesy of the Varsity.
Pg. 85: Lester Maddox, Cover of a record made from live recording of July 10, 1964, news conference.
Pg. 87: Mary Mac's, courtesy of Mary Mac's.
Pg. 89: Old Clinton Bar-B-Q, photograph by the author.
Pg. 94 and 95: Nu-Way Weiners, courtesy of Spyros Dermatas.
Pg. 97: Mrs. Wilkes', courtesy of the Wilkes family.

Kentucky

Pg. 107: Duncan Hines and admirer, photograph courtesy of the family of Duncan Hines.
Pg. 111: Hams, courtesy of Amy Evans, photographer, www.amycevans.com.
Pg. 115: The Brown Hotel, courtesy of the Brown Hotel, photograph by John Nation.
Pg. 118: Flabby's, photograph by the author.
Pg. 122: Moonlite Bar-B-Que Inn, courtesy of the Bosley family.

Louisiana

Pg. 128: Oysters, courtesy of Pableaux Johnson, photographer, www.bayoudog.com.
Pg. 133: Hot Boudin, courtesy of Pableaux Johnson, photographer, www.bayoudog.com.
Pg. 134: Johnson's Grocery, courtesy of the Johnson family.
Pg. 138: Antoine's Kitchen, courtesy of the New Orleans Public Library.

Pg. 140: Po Boys sign, courtesy of Pableaux Johnson, photographer, www.bayoudog.com.
Pg. 142: Hansen's, courtesy of Pableaux Johnson, photographer, www.bayoudog.com.
Pg. 143: Leidenheimer's, courtesy of Sandy Whann of Leidenheimer's.
Pg. 145: Parkway Tavern, courtesy of Pableaux Johnson, photographer, www.bayoudog.com.
Pg. 148: Rocky and Carlo's, photograph by the author.
Pg. 150: Casamento's, photograph by the author.
Pg. 156: Willie Mae's, courtesy of the Seaton family.
Pg. 158: Herby K's, courtesy of Janet Bean.
Pg. 159: Jim's Kountry Pies, photograph by the author.

Mississippi

Pg. 168 and 169: Hot Tamales in the Land of the Blues, photographs by the author.
Pg. 172: Joe Pope, White Front Café, courtesy of Amy Evans, photographer, www.amycevans.com.
Pg. 175: Doe's Eat Place, courtesy of Gary Saunders and dixiedining.com.
Pg. 177: Lusco's, courtesy of Amy Evans, photographer, www.amycevans.com.
Pg. 179: Leatha Jackson of Leatha's, photograph by the author.
Pg. 187: Taylor Grocery, courtesy of Jessica Perkins, Hayden Perkins, photographer.

North Carolina

Pg. 193: Barbecue, Skylight Inn, courtesy of David Gelin, photographer. From his forthcoming book, *Barbecue Joints: And the Good People Who Own Them.*
Pg. 200: A Civil Rights Movement March, courtesy of North Carolina Collection, University of North Carolina Library at Chapel Hill.
Pg. 205: Lexington Barbecue, courtesy of David Gelin, photographer. From his forthcoming book, *Barbecue Joints: And the Good People Who Own Them.*
Pg. 208: Snappy Lunch, photograph by Larry Smith, East Tennessee State University. See his work in Fred Sauceman's *The Place Setting: Timeless Tastes of the Mountain South, from Bright Hope to Frog Level.*
Pg. 212: Short Sugar's, courtesy of David Gelin, photographer. From his forthcoming book, *Barbecue Joints: And the Good People Who Own Them.*
Pg. 215: Texas Pete Hot Sauce, courtesy of Ann Garner Riddle.

South Carolina

Pg. 221: Bowen's, courtesy of Al Clayton, photographer, author of a number of books, including *Still Hungry in America.*

Pg. 222: Jestine Matthews, courtesy of Dana Berlin Strange.

Pg. 229: Cromer's P-Nuts, photograph by the author.

Pg. 231: Maurice Bessinger, courtesy of Maurice's Gourmet Barbeque.

Pg. 232: Roadside Produce Sign, courtesy of Cassie Drennon, photographer.

Pg. 233: Eugenia Duke, courtesy of C. F. Sauer Company.

Pg. 236: Sweatman's Bar-b-que, photograph by the author.

Pg. 240: Beacon Drive-In, courtesy of the Beacon Drive-In.

Tennessee

Pg. 244: Krystal, courtesy of the Krystal Company.

Pg. 248: Dr. Enuf, courtesy of Creative Energy.

Pg. 251: Miss Mary Bobo's Boarding House, courtesy of Lynne Tolley.

Pg. 253: Gus's World Famous Fried Chicken, photograph by the author.

Pg. 255: Piggly Wiggly, courtesy of the Pink Palace Museum.

Pg. 258: Payne's, photograph by the author.

Pg. 264: Mayo's-Mahalia Jackson, photograph by the author.

Pg. 267: Flatt & Scruggs, courtesy of the Martha White Company.

Texas

Pg. 274: The Night Hawk, courtesy of the Austin History Center, Austin Public Library.

Pg. 279: Elgin Hot Sausage, courtesy the Bracewell family.

Pg. 283: New Zion Church sign, photograph by the author.

Pg. 285: Barbecue pit, courtesy of Carol Roesch, photographer.

Pg.286: Glo's Place, photograph by the author.

Pg. 288: Gilhooley's, photograph by the author.

Pg. 292: Dr Pepper trucks, courtesy of the Dr Pepper Museum and Free Enterprise Institute.

Virginia

Pg. 300: Doumar's, courtesy of Albert Doumar.

Pg. 303: Bill "Bojanglas" Robinson, photograph by Carl Van Vechten. Courtesy of the Carl Van Vechten Photographs Collection, Library of Congress.

Pg. 307: Texas Tavern, courtesy of Jim Bullington.
Pg. 311: Cover of the book *Offal Great: A Memoir from the Queen of Chitlins,* from First Place Publishing Company.
Pg. 313: Ben's Chili Bowl, courtesy of Nizam Ali.

Pg. 315: Road sign, photograph by William R. Ferris. Courtesy of the Ferris Collection, Southern Folklife Collection, Wilson Library, University of North Carolina at Chapel Hill.

Places

All Saints Cafeteria 309
601 M Street NW
Washington, DC
202-289-1916

Anson Mills 225
Charleston, SC
803-467-4122

Ann's Wagon Wheel 195
169 Highway 111
Beulaville, NC
910-298-4272

Archibald's Bar B Que 25
1211 Martin Luther King Jr. Boulevard
Northport, AL
205-345-6861

Arnold's Country Kitchen 262
605 Eighth Avenue South
Nashville, TN
615-256-4455

The Bar-B-Que Shop 259
1782 Madison Avenue
Memphis, TN
901-272-1277

Bayley's 22
10805 Dauphin Island Parkway
Theodore, AL
251-973-1572

Beach Road Chicken Dinners 59
4132 Atlantic Boulevard
Jacksonville, FL
904-398-7980

Beacon Drive-In 239
255 John B. White Sr. Boulevard
Spartanburg, SC
864-585-9387

Beacon Light Tea Room 263
6276 Highway 100
Lyles, TN
931-670-3880

Bean Barn 246
515 East Church Street
Greeneville, TN
423-638-8329

Beaumont Inn 113
638 Beaumont Inn Drive
Harrodsburg, KY
859-734-3381

Ben's Chili Bowl 312
1213 U Street NW
Washington, DC
202-667-0909

Benton's Smoky Mountain Hams 252
2603 Highway 411
Madisonville, TN
423-442-5003

B. E. Scott's Barbecue 249
10880 Highway 412 West
Lexington, TN
731-968-0420

Best Stop 134
619 Highway 93 North
Scott, LA
337-233-5805

Big Apple Inn 180
509 North Farish Street
Jackson, MS
601-354-9371

Big Bob Gibson's Bar-B-Que 9
1715 Sixth Avenue SE
Decatur, AL
256-350-6969

Big Jim's 171
1700 State Street
Clarksdale, MS
662-645-5600

Bill's Barbecue 306
927 Myers Street
Richmond, VA
804-358-7763

Bill's Hamburgers 164
310 North Main Street
Amory, MS
662-256-2085

Black's Oyster Bar 129
319 Pere Megret Street
Abbeville, LA
337-893-4266

Blenheim Ginger Ale 238
Highway 301 North & Interstate 95
South of the Border, SC
843-774-0322

Bob Sykes Bar-B-Q 2
1724 Ninth Avenue
Bessemer, AL
205-426-1400

Bowen's Island Restaurant 221
1870 Bowen's Island Road
Charleston, SC
843-795-2757

Bozo's 141
3117 Twenty-first Street
Metairie, LA
504-831-8666

Bradley's Country Store 68
10655 Centerville Road
Tallahassee, FL
904-829-6974

Bright Star 4
304 Nineteenth Street
Bessemer, AL
205-426-1861

Broken Spoke 273
3201 South Lamar Boulevard
Austin, TX
512-442-6189

Brown Hotel 115
335 West Broadway
Louisville, KY
502-583-1234

Bullock's Café 39
201 Missouri Street
Helena, AR
870-338-1183

Bully's Soul Food 181
3118 Livingston Road
Jackson, MS
601-362-0484

Burger House 278
6913 Hillcrest Avenue
Dallas, TX
214-361-0370

Calvary Waffle Shop 256
102 North Second Street
Memphis, TN
901-525-3036

Car Lot Bar-B-Que 28
235 Bankhead Highway
Winfield, AL
205-487-2281

Carolina Plantation Rice 225
Charleston, SC
843-395-8058

Carver's Country Kitchen 77
1118 West Marietta Street
Atlanta, GA
404-794-4410

Casamento's 149
4330 Magazine Street
New Orleans, LA
540-895-9761

Central Grocery 146
923 Decatur Street
New Orleans, LA
504-523-1620

Chamoun's Rest Haven 166
419 North Street
Clarksdale, MS
601-624-8601

Chet's Seafood 66
3708 Navy Boulevard
Pensacola, FL
850-456-0165

Chitlin Market 310
5711 Ager Road
Hyattsville, MD
866-436-9381

Chris' Hot Dogs 18
138 Dexter Avenue
Montgomery, AL
334-265-6850

Chuck's Bar-B-Que 21
905 Short Avenue
Opelika, AL
334-749-4043

Clear Run Farms 203
Highway 421 and 41
Harrels, NC
910-532-4470

Clemson Ag Sales Center 227
118 Newman Hall
Clemson, SC
864-656-3242

Coffee Cup 63
914 South Clarkson Street
Charlotte, NC
704-375-8855

Coffee Club 196
520 East Cervantes Street
Pensacola, FL
850-432-7060

Corner Pool & Lunch 109
500 Court House Square
Burkesville, KY
502-864-5977

Cozy Corner 259
745 North Parkway
Memphis, TN
901-527-9158

Craig's Barbecue 35
Highway 70 West
De Valls Bluff, AR
870-998-2616

Crechale's 182
3107 Highway 80 West
Jackson, MS
601-355-1840

Cromer's P-Nuts 229
1241 Assembly Street
Columbia, SC
803-779-2290

Deposito's 96
187 Macceo Drive
Savannah, GA
912-897-9963

Dinglewood Pharmacy 91
1939 Wynnton Road
Columbus, GA
706-322-0616

Dinner Bell 185
229 Fifth Avenue
McComb, MS
601-684-4833

Dixie Restaurant 301
250 North Sycamore Street
Petersburg, VA
804-732-5761

Doe's Eat Place 175
502 Nelson Street
Greenville, MS
662-334-3315

Doug Freeman 110
605 New Hope Road
Cadiz, KY
270-522-8900

Doumar's 300
1919 Monticello Avenue
Norfolk, VA
757-627-4163

Drago's 141
3232 North Arnoult Road
Metairie, LA
504-888-9254

Dreamland 24
5535 Fifteenth Avenue East
Tuscaloosa, AL
205-758-8135

Dr Pepper Museum and Free Enterprise Institute 291
300 South Fifth Street
Waco, TX
254-757-1025

Dupuy's Oyster House 129
108 South Main Street
Abbeville, LA
337-893-2336

Ed and Kay's 33
15228 Interstate 30 (Sevier Street Exit)
Benton, AR
501-315-3663

Eddie's 228
1301 Assembly Street
Columbia, SC
803-779-6222

Farmer's Market Restaurant 209
1240 Farmer's Market Drive
Raleigh, NC
919-833-7973

Felix Mexican Restaurant 283
904 Westheimer Road
Houston, TX
713-529-3949

Fiesta Loma Linda 283
2111 Telephone Road
Houston, TX
713-924-6074

Flabby's Schnitzelburg 117
1101 Lydia Street
Louisville, KY
502-637-9136

Florida Avenue Grill 311
1100 Florida Avenue NW
Washington, DC
202-265-1586

Frenchy's Chicken 280
3919 Scott Street
Houston, TX
713-748-2233

Fresh Air 91
1164 Highway 42
Flovilla, GA
770-775-3182

Frisco Shop 273
5819 Burnet Road
Austin, TX
512-459-6279

Fuller's 207
3201 North Roberts Avenue
Lumberton, NC
910-738-8694

Gilhooley's 288
221 Ninth Street
San Leon, TX
281-339-3813

Glo's Place 286
2293 West Highway 84
Mexia, TX
254-562-6233

Guiding Star 130
4404 Highway 90 West
New Iberia, LA
337-365-9113

Gus's World Famous Fried Chicken 253
212 Highway 70
Mason, TN
901-294-2028

H&H Café 93
807 Forsyth Street
Macon, GA
912-742-9810

Hall's on the River 124
1225 Boonesboro Road
Winchester, KY
859-527-6620

Hansen's Sno Bliz 141
4801 Tchoupitoulas Street
New Orleans, LA
504-891-9788

Harold's Barbecue 79
171 McDonough Boulevard SE
Atlanta, GA
404-627-9268

Herby K's 157
1833 Pierre Avenue
Shreveport, LA
318-424-2724

Herman's Rib House 37
2901 College Avenue
Fayetteville, AR
501-442-9671

Hick's Tamales 170
305 South State Street
Clarksdale, MS
662-624-9887

Honey's Restaurant & Billiards 246
109 East Market Street
Fayetteville, TN
931-433-1181

Hotel Talisi 21
14 Sistrunk Street
Tallassee, AL
334-283-2769

Indian Pass Raw Bar 54
Highway 30-A and Indian Pass Road
Apalachicola, FL
850-227-1670

Jerry's Drive-In 66
2815 East Cervantes Street
Pensacola, FL
850-433-9910

Jestine's Kitchen 222
251 Meeting Street
Charleston, SC
843-722-7224

Jim's Kountry Pies 159
3606 Romero Road-Coteau
Youngsville, LA
337-365-7465

John Gorrie Museum and State Park 54
46 Sixth Street
Apalachicola, FL
850-653-9347

Johnson's Grocery 134
700 East Maple Avenue
Eunice, LA
337-457-9314

Judy's Castle 108
1302 Highway 31
Bowling Green, KY
270-842-8736

Keller's Drive-In 278
6537 East Northeast Highway
Dallas, TX
214-368-1209

Kim's Pork Rinds 167
417 Third Street
Clarksdale, MS
662-627-2389

Kline's Dairy Bar 297
58 East Wolfe Street
Harrisonburg, VA
540-434-6980

Kreuz Market 286
619 North Colorado Street
Lockhart, TX
512-398-2361

Leatha's 179
6374 Highway 98
Hattiesburg, MS
601-271-6003

Leo and Susie's Green Top Café 10
7530 Highway 78
Dora, AL
205-648-9838

Lexington Barbecue 204
10 Highway 29 & 70 South
Lexington, NC
336-249-9814

Li'l Dizzy's 153
1500 Esplanade Avenue
New Orleans, LA
504-569-8897

Lindsey's 44
203 East Fourteenth Street
Little Rock, AR
501-374-5901

Liuzza's 146
3636 Bienville Street
New Orleans, LA
504-482-9120

Louis' Lunch 58
436 SE Second Street
Gainesville, FL
352-372-9294

Loveless Café and Motel 263
Highway 100 and the Natchez Trace
Nashville, TN
615-646-9700

Lusco's 176
722 Carrollton Street
Greenwood, MS
662-453-5365

Mama Ninfa's 283
2704 Navigation
Houston, TX
713-228-1175

Marina Oyster Barn 66
505 Bayou Boulevard
Pensacola, FL
850-433-0511

Marjorie Kinnan Rawlings Historic State Park 56
18700 Country Road 325
Cross Creek, Fl
325-466-3672

Martha Lou's Kitchen 223
1068 Morrison Drive
Charleston, SC
843-577-9583

Martin's 19
1796 Carter Hill Road
Montgomery, AL
334-265-1767

Mary Mac's Tea Room 86
224 Ponce de León Avenue
Atlanta, GA
404-876-1800

Mary's Family Pie Shop 36
Highway 70 West
De Valls Bluff, AR
870-998-2279

Mary Maestri's 46
956 Highway 412 East
Tontitown, AR
479-361-2536

Maurice Bessinger's Piggie Park 230
4411 Devine Street
Columbia, SC
803-782-9547

Mayflower Café 183
123 West Capitol Street
Jackson, MS
601-355-4122

Mayo's-Mahalia Jackson Fried Pies and Chicken 264
2618 Buchanan Street
Nashville, TN
615-742-1899

Mazzoni's 119
2804 Taylorsville Road
Lousiville, KY
502-451-4436

McClard's 41
505 Albert Pike Road
Hot Springs, AR
501-624-9586

Mecca 211
13 East Martin Street
Raleigh, NC
919-832-5714

Midway B-B-Q 220
811 Main Street
Buffalo, SC
864-427-4047

Miss Mary Bobo's Boarding House 250
295 Main Street
Lynchburg, TN
931-759-7394

Mi Tierra 287
218 Produce Row
San Antonio, TX
210-225-1262

Mom & Nikki's 99
714 Martin Luther King Jr. Boulevard
Savannah, GA
912-233-7636

Montgomery Curb Market 20
1004 Madison Avenue
Montgomery, AL
334-263-6445

Moonlite Bar-B-Que Inn 121
2840 West Parish Avenue
Owesboro, KY
270-684-8143

Mrs. Wilkes' 97
107 West Jones Street
Savannah, GA
912-232-5997

The Napoleon House 146
500 Chartres Street
New Orleans, LA
504-524-9752

New Orleans Style Seafood Poboys 165
10271 D'Iberville Boulevard
D'Iberville, MS
228-392-8683

Newsome's Country Hams 112
208 East Main Street
Princeton, KY
270-365-2482

New Zion Missionary Baptist Church 283
2601 Montgomery Road
Huntsville, TX
936-295-3445

Niki's West 5
233 Finley Avenue
Birmingham, AL
205-252-5751

Nottoway Restaurant 302
20316 Boydton Plank Road (I-85, Exit 39)
Rawlings, VA
804-478-7875

Nu-Way Weiners 94
430 Cotton Avenue
Macon, GA
478-743-1368

Old Clinton Bar-B-Q 89
Highway 129
Clinton, GA
478-986-3225

Oscar's Hot Tamales (now Hick's) 170
305 South State Street
Clarksdale, MS
662-624-9887

O'Steen's Restaurant 66
205 Anastasia Boulevard
St. Augustine, FL
904-829-6974

Papa Joe's Oyster Bar 54
301-B Market Street
Apalachicola, FL
850-653-1189

Parasol's 144
2533 Constance Street
New Orleans, LA
504-899-2054

Parkway Tavern 145
538 Hagan Drive
New Orleans, LA
504-482-3047

Pascal's Manale 147
1838 Napoleon Avenue
New Orleans, LA
504-895-4877

Pasquale's Tamales 40
Helena, AR
877-572-0500

Paul's Barbecue 92
Highway 78, Downtown Lexington
Lexington, GA
706-743-8254

Payne's 257
1762 Lamar Avenue
Memphis, TN
901-272-1523

Peggy's 186
512 Bay Street
Philadelphia, MS
601-656-3478

The Pitmaster 214
6228 Ward Boulevard
Wilson, NC
252-237-8645

Price's Chicken Coop 197
1614 Camden Road
Charlotte, NC
704-333-9866

Prince's Hot Chicken Shack 265
123 Ewing Drive
Nashville, TN
615-226-9442

Richard's Seafood Patio 130
1516 South Henry Street
Abbeville, LA
337-893-1693

Roanoke City Market 306
Market Square, Downtown
Roanoke, VA

Rocky and Carlo's 148
613 West St. Bernard Highway
Chalmette, LA
504-279-8323

R. O.'s Bar-B-Cue 198
1318 West Gaston Avenue
Gastonia, NC
704-866-8143

Ruby's Café 135
221 West Walnut Avenue
Eunice, LA
337-550-7665

Sally Bell's Kitchen 304
708 West Grace Street
Richmond, VA
804-644-2838

Sanders' Peach Shed 232
Highway 321
Filbert, SC
803-684-6062

Shadden's Grocery 44
19771 Highway 49
Marvell, AR
870-829-2255

Shealy's Bar-B-Que House 237
340 East Columbia Avenue
Leesville, SC
803-532-8135

Shingles Chicken Shack 69
905 Miles Street
Tallahassee, FL
850-681-2626

Short Sugar's Drive-In 212
1328 South Scales Street
Reidsville, NC
336-342-7487

Silver Moon Café 131
206 West Chimes Street
Baton Rouge, LA
225-387-3345

Sims' Bar-B-Que 43
716 West Thirty-Third Street
Little Rock, AR
501-372-6868

Skylight Inn 193
1501 South Lee Street
Ayden, NC
252-746-4113

Smitty's Market 286
208 South Commerce Street
Lockhart, TX
512-398-9344

Snappy Lunch 208
125 North Main Street
Mt. Airy, NC
336-786-4931

Solly's Hot Tamales 172
1921 Washington Street
Vicksburg, MS
601-636-2020

Son's Place 81
100 Hurt Street
Atlanta, GA
404-581-0530

Southern Kitchen 299
9576 South Congress Street
New Market, VA
540-740-3514

Southside Market 279
1212 Highway 290
Elgin, TX
512-285-3407

Spalding's Bakery 114
780 Winchester Drive
Lexington, KY
859-252-3737

Specialty Foods South 225
Charleston, SC
843-766-2580

Speed's Kitchen 100
Shellman Bluff, GA
912-832-4763

Starnes' Barbecue 123
1008 Joe Clifton Drive
Paducah, KY
270-444-9555

Stingaree Restaurant 276
1295 Stingare Cove
Crystal Beach, TX
409-684-2731

Suburban Social Club 120
3901 South Third Street
Louisville, KY
502-368-3161

Sweatman's Bar-b-que 236
Highway 453
Holly Hill, SC

Sweet Auburn Bread Company 79
234 Auburn Avenue NE
Atlanta, GA
404-221-1157

Sweet Auburn Curb Market 78
209 Edgewood Avenue
Atlanta, GA
404-659-1665

Swett's Dinette 265
2725 Clifton Avenue
Nashville, TN
615-329-4418

Taylor Café 289
101 North Main Street
Taylor, TX
512-352-8475

Taylor Grocery 187
Highway 338
Taylor, MS
662-236-1716

Ted Peters Famous Smoked Fish 62
1350 South Pasadena Avenue
Pasadena Beach, FL
727-381-7931

Tee Eva's 155
4430 Magazine Street
New Orleans, LA
504-899-8350

Texas Tavern 307
114 Church Avenue SW
Roanoke, VA
540-342-4825

Threadgill's 273
6416 North Lamar Boulevard
Austin, TX
512-451-5440

Tony the Peanut Man 226
On the Streets of Charleston
Charleston, SC'
843-343-6362

Uncle Bill's Creole Filé 132
Baton Rouge, LA
225-388-0893

Vandy's 101
22 West Vine Street
Statesboro, GA
912-764-2444

The Varsity 82
61 North Avenue
Atlanta, GA
404-881-1706

Venesian Inn 47
582 Hwy 412 West
Tontitown, AR
479-361-2562

Walls Bar-B-Que 99
515 East York Lane
Savannah, GA
912-232-9754

War Eagle Mill 47
Off Highway 12
War Eagle, AR
479-789-5343

Waysider 26
1512 Greensboro Avenue
Tuscaloosa, AL
205-345-8239

Weaver D's 76
1016 Broad Street
Athens, GA
706-353-7797

White Front Café 172
902 Main Street
Rosedale, MS
662-759-3842

White Spot 296
1407 University Avenue
Charlottesville, VA
434-295-9899

White Trolley 174
1215 Highway 72 East
Corinth, MS
662-287-4593

Whiteway Deli 60
1510 King Street
Jacksonville, FL
904-398-0355

Wilber's 199
Highway 70
Goldsboro, NC
919-778-5218

Willie Mae's Scotch House 156
2401 St. Ann Street
New Orleans, LA
504-822-9503

Wilson's Soul Food 76
351 North Hall Street
Athens, GA
706-353-7289

Wingfield's Breakfast and Burgers 278
2615 South Beckley Avenue
Dallas, TX
214-943-5214

Wintzell's Oyster House 15
605 Dauphin Street
Mobile, AL
251-432-4605

Woolworth's Lunch Counter 200
132 South Elm Street
Greensboro, NC
336-274-9199

The Yearling 57
14531 Country Road 325
Cross Creek, FL
352-466-3999